1295

WIMBLEDON PUBLISHING COMPANY'S

LIBRARY OF QUALITY IN EDUCATION

MATHEMATICS II

By

Serena Alexand

Colet Court and St Paul's Sch

Wimbledon Publishing Company

ISBN 1 898855 04 8

Dedicated to the Very Highest Quality in Education

MATHEMATICS II
KEY STAGE 4

LIBRARY OF QUALITY IN EDUCATION
General Editor: K.S.Sood
B.Sc, M.Phil, ARCS

First Published in Great Britain in 1997 by
WIMBLEDON PUBLISHING COMPANY LIMITED
P.O.BOX 9779 London SW19 7ZG. Fax: 0181 944 0825

ISBN 1 898855 04 8

Produced in Great Britain
Typesetting by GTI Typesetters, London
Cover Design by Malvinder S Soor, P.M.Graphics

SERENA ALEXANDER

Serena Alexander has had a keen interested in mathematics from her early days. Born in 1954, she attended Godolphin and Latymer School in Hammersmith, London. By the age of 13, she had worked her way through Martin Gardner and Edward du Bono. She took an early interest in education, but this was not encouraged by her teachers. She went on to read Architecture at Bristol. After graduating, she moved to the City, trading commodities and progressed into becoming a Company Secretary of a PR firm.

By 1987, with two small children to look after and educate, she moved back into education, taking a PGCE in mathematics. There she found that mathematics education had changed a lot since her own school days with far grreater emphasis on her own love of investigative problem solving and practical mathematics.

Serena has taught in both the maintained and the private sector and now teaches at St Paul's Preparatory School (Colet Court) and St Paul's School for Boys. She has also developed computer software for school administration.

Serena has strong outdoor interests in out of school hours (time permitting!). Her main sporting passion is yachting. She was a Race Officer for two of Admiral's Cup Series.

LIBRARY OF QUALITY IN EDUCATION

The basic premise of the Quality in Education series is to make available to teachers, pupils and their parents excellent resource material for the ultimate benefit of the pupils. The resource material in these books can be used to navigate the child to work from the average level to the out-standing level. The books are full of material which provide challenging exercises and enable the pupils to achieve 'horizontal' proficiency in learn-ing, i.e. proficiency based on the level of knowledge that a pupil is ex-pected to have, but extending the application of the knowledge to more challenging situations.

General Editor
January 1997

Mathematics 11-14
Volume 2

Introduction

The second Book in the series covers all of National Curriculum Mathematics at levels 7 and 8. Where necessary topics are introduced at an earlier level to revise the basic principles before moving on to the higher levels. The topics are usually introduced using everyday examples, but at the more abstract levels of Algebra and Geometry this is not always possible.

This book is intended for Year 8 or Year 9 pupils. It should be suitable for Year 9 pupils in the 11-16 schools and for the 13-18 schools which have an intake of Year 9 pupils, particularly those who have taken the Common Entrance with or without the optional Paper 3.

The first part of the book complete the syllabus for pupils taking Paper 3 at Common Entrance. As some of the topics required for Paper 2 are set at level 7 then those topics covered in Book 1 are repeated in this section to give flexibility of teaching.

The second part of the book completes the syllabus for levels 7 and 8. Some of these topics are on the various Scholarship papers and others may be of interest to non Scholarship classes to extend their knowledge and to give further practice if appropriate. Some of the topics introduced in the first part of the book, for example simultaneous equations, appear again in the second , but with harder problems. This may be of assistance to schools with an intake at Year 9, that need to revise and extend pupil knowledge.

This book takes the view that is implied in the Attainment Target 1 of the National Curriculum, that pupils should be able to apply their mathematics to more complicated problems as they work through different levels, even if such problems are not specifically mentioned.

The higher levels of the National Curriculum require the use of a calculator to solve problems. This book expects students to use a calculator unless non calculator methods are specified. Instructions on the use of a normal scientific calculator are given, but it must be noted that calculators do vary in their exact use and that each pupil should be careful to keep, and to refer to, the instructions. Good practice when using calculators is referred to throughout the book, with examples showing the recording of calculations.

The revision exercises in this book are different from those in Book One. They contain fewer but longer questions, similar to those found on GCSE papers, Key Stage 3 tests and Paper 3 of Common Entrance.

The chapters are interspersed with various activities, practical tasks, investigations and puzzles. Some of these are on the curriculum but non-examinable, and others are there to extend pupils' interests and awareness of mathematics.

Contents

Contents

CHAPTER 1

Working With Numbers

Introduction

When working with numbers at the higher levels it is important that the correct vocabulary is used and understood. Over the years you should have become used to hearing and using several words to describe numbers.

Natural Numbers

Natural numbers are the first numbers that you learnt to count: 1, 2, 3, 4, etc. They can be added, subtracted, multiplied and divided. Although you can, and frequently should, use a calculator, you can save a great deal of time if you can do simple arithmetic in your head. Try this first exercise, just write down the answer only to each question. It should not take you more than 15 minutes!

Exercise 1A

Number your page from 1 to 60 before you start. Take the time as you start and see how long it takes you to complete the exercise, write down answers only.

1. 7×5
2. 8×9
3. $36 + 12$
4. $42 \div 7$
5. $32 - 11$
6. $14 + 7$
7. 3×8

8. $24 + 74$
9. $36 \div 9$
10. $38 - 17$
11. $18 + 22$
12. 7×9
13. $72 \div 12$
14. $68 - 43$

15. 5×7
16. $39 - 23$
17. $11 + 35$
18. $24 \div 8$
19. 8×7
20. $29 + 11$

21. 25×3
22. $32 + 9$
23. $125 \div 5$
24. $42 - 6$
25. 13×3
26. $19 + 24$
27. $33 - 17$

28. $72 \div 3$
29. $180 - 56$
30. 90×3
31. $127 + 53$
32. $144 \div 8$
33. $35 - 19$
34. $47 + 39$

35. 45×7
36. $72 \div 36$
37. $27 + 28$
38. $200 - 137$
39. 35×6
40. $39 + 47$

41. $225 - 180$
42. $225 \div 45$
43. $225 \div 15$
44. 19×6
45. 19×9
46. $200 - 79$
47. 99×2

48. 99×8
49. $128 + 52$
50. $207 + 153$
51. $305 - 125$
52. $288 \div 12$
53. 13×13
54. 15×15

55. 75×3
56. 25×9
57. 125×4
58. 20×500
59. $3600 \div 90$
60. $100\,000 \div 80$

Long Multiplication And Long Division

The questions above could be solved using simple arithmetic. When this becomes too difficult long multiplication and long division have to be used. Many people want to simply use a calculator, but there are always occasions when a calculator is not at hand, and "pencil and paper" methods have to be used. For long multiplication we break the smaller number into a multiple of ten and a unit.

For example: 23 becomes 20 + 3,

then we can write 125×23 as $125 \times (3 + 20)$:

Example:	
125×23	$\begin{array}{r} 125 \\ \times\ 23 \\ \hline 375 \\ 2500 \\ \hline 2875 \end{array}$ $\begin{array}{l} (\times 3) \\ (\times 20) \end{array}$ $125 \times 23 = 2875$

Long division is done in the same way as short division, but all the working out is shown so that the remainders can be calculated clearly and accurately.

Example:	(You check if necessary by multiplying over here)
$1495 \div 23$	$\begin{array}{r} 6\,5 \\ 23{\overline{)\,1\,4\,9\,5}} \\ 1\,3\,8 \\ \hline 1\,1\,5 \\ 1\,1\,5 \\ \hline \ldots \end{array}$ $\begin{array}{l} (\div) \\ (\times) \\ (-\,\&\downarrow,\div) \\ (\times) \\ (-) \end{array}$ $\begin{array}{cc} 23 & 23 \\ \times 6 & \times 5 \\ \hline 138 & 115 \end{array}$

Exercise 1B

Calculate the following showing all working clearly:

1. 27×36	**8.** 713×43	**15.** $1247 \div 29$
2. 47×29	**9.** 867×31	**16.** $1161 \div 43$
3. 89×47	**10.** 926×63	**17.** $608 \div 32$
4. 68×91	**11.** $391 \div 17$	**18.** $1363 \div 47$
5. 124×72	**12.** $989 \div 23$	**19.** $1224 \div 72$
6. 213×69	**13.** $703 \div 19$	**20.** $999 \div 37$
7. 318×42	**14.** $1302 \div 31$	

Exercise 1C

Answer the questions below, showing all your working clearly:

1. There are 365 days in a year and 24 hours in a day. How many hours are there in a year?

2. How many minutes are there in a year? How many seconds are there in a year?

3. In the imperial system of weight there are 16 ounces in a pound and 14 pounds in a stone. How many ounces are there in 7 stone?

4. The Americans talk about their weight in terms of pounds only. If my friend weighs 118 pounds what is this in stones and pounds?

5. "Julius Caesar said with a smile
There are one, seven, six, 'oh' yards in a mile."
How many yards are there in twenty five miles?

6. What is 8,000 yards in miles and yards?

7. A fast food shop sells on average 176 hamburgers each hour. How many hamburgers does the shop sell in a seventeen hour day?

8. There are 22 pupils in my class and we all have milk at break. Milk comes in cartons containing one third of a pint. If a school term lasts 12 weeks and there are five days in each week how many pints of milk does my class drink during that term?

9. Rough books come in cartons of 500. How many classes of 22 does one carton supply if every pupil needs one rough book?

10. My teacher is photocopying our Maths exam. The exam is on four sheets of paper, and there are 92 pupils taking the exam.
a) How many sheets of paper is that?
b) The photocopier copies 24 sheets in a minute. How long does it take my teacher to photocopy the exam?

11. I earn £6 an hour, I work 8 hours a day, five days a week and there are 52 weeks in the year. How much do I earn in a year?

12. From my earnings I save £25 a week towards a holiday. If the holiday cost is £672 for how many weeks must I save?

Integers

A whole number is an <u>integer</u>, and so natural numbers are all integers. Integers, however, also include 0 or zero, and negative numbers such as –3, –2, –1.

Fractions

Any number that is not a whole number, or an integer includes a "bit" of a whole number, or a fraction. **Proper fractions** are fractions that are less than one, such as $\frac{1}{2}$, $\frac{3}{4}$ and $\frac{27}{33}$. **Improper fractions** are fractions greater than one, such as $\frac{3}{2}$, $\frac{7}{4}$ and $\frac{127}{33}$.

Decimal fractions are fractions written in decimal form, such as 1.25, – 3.72 and 14.67. These are usually called just "decimals". **Recurring decimals** are decimals whose numbers after the decimal point recur in a regular pattern such as 1.333 333 333 ... and 0.181 181 181 181 ...

Negative numbers form the set of natural numbers that are less than zero. Negative numbers can be added, subtracted, multiplied and divided in a similar fashion to natural numbers. There are some differences when using negative numbers, as $4 - 4 = 0$ but $4 - (-4) = 8$, and it can help to draw the number line to think about what is happening:

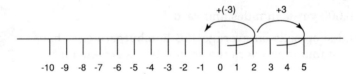

While	$2 + 3 = 5,$	but $(-2) + 3 = 1$	and	$2 + (-3) = 2 - 3 = -1$
similarly	$5 - 3 = 2,$	but $3 - 5 = -2$	and	$5 - (-3) \qquad = 5 + 3$
= 8				
	$2 \times 3 = 6$	but $2 \times -3 = -6$	and	$(-2) \times (-3) = 6$
	$6 \div 3 = 2$	but $6 \div (-3) = -2$	and	$(-6) \div (-3) = 2$

Exercise 1D

Calculate these. Write down the question, any working out, and the answer:

> For example:
>
> $$-3 - (-7) = -3 + 7$$
> $$= 4$$

1. $-3-4$	**11.** $3 \times (-4)$	**21.** $4-9$
2. $5-8$	**12.** $12-(-5)$	**22.** $7-3$
3. $3+(-6)$	**13.** $14-8$	**23.** $4 \times (-3)$
4. $(-4) \times (-4)$	**14.** $-4-8$	**24.** $12 \div (-6)$
5. $3 \times (-3)$	**15.** $-4-(-8)$	**25.** $5+(-6)$
6. $-8+5$	**16.** $5 \times (-2)$	**26.** $(-5)+(-2)$
7. $-13-9$	**17.** $16 \div (-4)$	**27.** $8-3$
8. $(-3) \times 7$	**18.** $7-(-5)$	**28.** $-8 \times (-2)$
9. $12 \div (-3)$	**19.** $-25 \div 5$	**29.** $-24 \div 8$
10. $(-24) \div (-8)$	**20.** $(-5) \times (-5$	**30.** $100 \div (-10)$

Factors And Multiples

Any natural number can be written as the multiple of other numbers. The simplest number, 1, can be written as 1×1, but other numbers can be written using at least two different numbers:

$$24 = 1 \times 24, \text{ or } 2 \times 12, \text{ or } 3 \times 8 \text{ or } 4 \times 6$$

We say that 1, 2, 3, 4, 6, 8, 12, and 24 are all **factors** of 24, and that 24 is a **multiple** of 1, 2, 3, 4, 6, 8, 12, and 24.

If we had to write the multiples of 5 that were less than 30 we would write:

$$5, 10, 15, 20, 25,$$

Prime Numbers

A prime number is a number whose only factors are itself and one. The set of prime numbers starts :   2, 3, 5, 7, 11, 13, 17, 23, 29 ...
(N.B. 'One' only has '1' as a factor and is not counted - it is a very special number with other properties than mean that it cannot be prime)

Prime Factors

A number can be broken down into factors that are prime numbers by successive division.

For example:

To find the prime factors of 210:

$$\begin{array}{r} 2)\overline{210} \\ 3)\overline{105} \\ 5)\overline{35} \\ 7)\overline{7} \\ 1 \end{array}$$

$$210 = 2 \times 3 \times 5 \times 7$$

Product

A product is the result of a multiplication. When 210 is written:

$$210 = 2 \times 3 \times 5 \times 7$$

it is written as the **product of its prime factors.** If you are asked for **the product of 5 and 6** the answer is 30.

Exercise 1E

1. Which of these numbers are prime numbers?
    5, 17, 25, 27, 32, 37, 48

2. Which of these are factors of 36?
    1, 2, 3, 4, 5, 6, 7, 9, 10, 36, 72, 360

3. Which of these are multiples of 12?
    1, 2, 3, 4, 5, 6, 8, 12, 24, 36

4. Which of these are prime factors of 42?
    1, 2, 3, 6, 7, 14, 21, 42

5. Which of these are prime factors of 20?
    1, 2, 4, 5, 10, 20

6. Which of these are prime factors of 17?
    1, 2, 5, 17, 34

7. a) What is the product of 12 and 7 ?
    b) What is the sum of 13 and 3 ?
    c) What is the product of 6 and 7?

8. Continue the given list of prime numbers as far as 50.

9. List all the factors of
    a) 65   b) 101   c) 19   d) 72

10. Write the following numbers as a product of their prime factors:
    a) 504   b) 136   c) 1000   d) 945

11. a) List all the factors of 24 and all the factors of 42.
    b) Which factors do they have in common?
    c) Which is the highest?

This is known as the Highest Common Factor or H.C.F. of 24 and 42.

12. Find the Highest Common Factor of the following pairs of numbers:
    a) 8 and 10   b) 20 and 30   c) 100 and 360

13. List the first 10 multiples of 4.

14. List the first 10 multiples of 6.

15. List the first 10 multiples of 10.

16. Look at the lists that you have made in questions 13, 14 and 15. What is the lowest number that is a multiple of
    a) 4 and 6   b) 4 and 10   c) 6 and 10.

These numbers are called **Lowest Common Multiples**, or **L.C.M.** of each pair of numbers.

17. Find the Lowest Common Multiples of the following pairs of numbers:
    a) 8 and 10   b) 20 and 30   c) 100 and 360

In the above examples H.C.F. and L.C.M. were quite easy to find by the inspection of the various factors and multiples. For larger numbers this is not always as simple. Consider the question:

What is the Highest Common Factor of 210 and 375?

To solve this each number must be broken down into its prime factors:

For example:
  What is the H.C.F. of 210 and 375?
  Common Factors are 3 and 5, and so the H.C.F. = 3 × 5 =15

$$
\begin{array}{r}
2\,)\,\underline{210} \\
3\,)\,\underline{105} \\
5\,)\,\underline{\ \ 35} \\
7\,)\,\underline{\ \ \ 7} \\
1
\end{array}
\qquad
\begin{array}{r}
3\,)\,\underline{375} \\
5\,)\,\underline{125} \\
5\,)\,\underline{\ \ 25} \\
5\,)\,\underline{\ \ \ 5} \\
1
\end{array}
$$

---

18. Using your answers to question 10 find the H.C.F. of the following pairs of numbers:
   a) 504 and 945   b) 136 and 504
   c) 945 and 1000   d) 136 and 945

19. Find the H.C.F. of 330 and 175

20. Find the H.C.F. of 132 and 165

21. Find the H.C.F. of 812 and 638

Suppose we had been asked to find the Lowest Common Multiple of 210 and 375. That is not a simple matter of looking at the first few multiples. We need to look at the prime factors again.

For example:
  Find the Lowest Common Multiple of 210 and 375.
  $$210 = 2 \times 3 \times 5 \times 7 \qquad 375 = 3 \times 5^3$$
  L.C.M. $= 2 \times 3 \times 5 \times 5 \times 5 \times 7$
           $= 5250$
  The Lowest Common Multiple must be the smallest product that <u>*contains*</u> ***ALL*** *the factors of **EACH** number.*

---

22. Using your answers to question 10 find the L.C.M. of the following pairs of numbers: (use your calculator)
   a) 504 and 945   c) 136 and 504
   b) 945 and 1000   d) 136 and 945

23. Find the L.C.M. of 330 and 175

24. Find the L.C.M. of 132 and 165

25. Find the L.C.M. of 812 and 638

Using A Calculator

From now until your GCSE examination you will need a Scientific Calculator. If you do not have one already then you should ask your mathematics teacher for help in deciding which is best for you. If that is not possible then go to a shop with a large selection of calculators and ask their advice. Make sure that you stress that you want a Scientific Calculator suitable for GCSE examinations not for A levels. Some calculators do so much that they are expensive and complicated to use. Your calculator needs to have **bracket functions, fraction buttons, trigonometric** and **index functions**.

Keep your calculator manual - file it in your Maths file!

Modern calculators are changing all the time, you cannot expect your teacher to know exactly how each calculator functions and where all the necessary buttons are. You will need to refer to the manual when you are exploring some new areas of mathematics. Your calculator will look something like this:

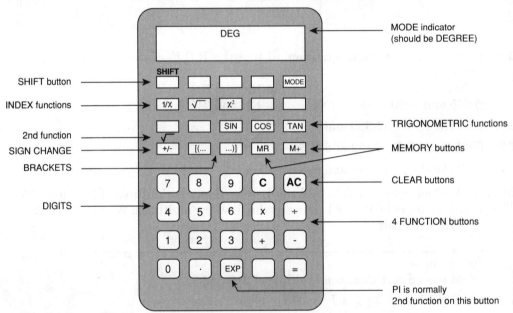

Exercise 1F

Follow these simple steps to get to know your calculator.
If you are stuck consult the manual, if you are *still* stuck ask your teacher. Use worksheet 1/1 with this exercise.

1.   Turn your calculator ON. Now turn it OFF, now turn it ON again.

2.   Calculate $45 + 16$. Write down the answer.

3.   Calculate $34\,537 - 12\,529$. Write down the answer.

4.   Calculate $4 \div 99$. Write down the answer.

5.   Calculate $45\,234 \times 416$. Write down the answer.

You have now used the basic four functions with simple calculations. Now you need to know more about your calculator.

The Mode

The only mode you need to know about is normal, or computational. You will need to refer to your manual. For slightly older models pressing the mode button and then 0 leaves you in the correct mode. For newer models press the mode button and then the number under COMP. If you are in the correct mode the only **LETTERS** on the display will be **DEG**. If this is not the case ask your teacher. If you ever get peculiar answers to your calculations then you are probably in the wrong mode!

Negative Numbers

First let us see how to calculate with negative numbers.

Look for this button: $\boxed{+/-}$. This is the plus/ minus button that reverses the sign of any figure.

6.   Enter 45, now press the +/– button. Your number becomes –45.
      Now add 16. What is your answer? Compare this to your answer to question 1.

7.   Rework Exercise 1D using your calculator. Check that your answers agree with the answers that you worked out before.

Brackets

A Scientific Calculator has an inbuilt bracket function which you need to be aware of. It will always multiply and divide before it adds and subtracts. If you want to do the sum 4 + 5 × 7 you might expect the answer 63, but what does your calculator give you? 39! The calculator has calculated 5 × 7 and then added 4. To make the sum work in the same order of operations as is written you must write the calculation using brackets: (4 + 5) × 7.

Find this button $\boxed{[(...}$ which is the 'open brackets' button and press this before

entering 4 + 5, then press the 'close brackets' button: $\boxed{...)]}$ before entering × 7. This time you should obtain the answer 63.

8.   a) (3 + 6) × 5   b) 9 × (2 + 4)   c) (5 + 6) + (3 × 5)
      d) (5 – 7) × 5   e) 20 ÷ (6 + 4)   f) (20 ÷ 5) ÷ (5 × 4)

With more complicated calculations you may need to nest brackets within brackets.
For example : 2 × (3 × (4 + 7) + 5) would need the sequence of keys:

$$\boxed{2}\;\boxed{\times}\;\boxed{[(...}\;\boxed{3}\;\boxed{\times}\;\boxed{[(...}\;\boxed{4}\;\boxed{+}\;\boxed{7}\;\boxed{...)]}\;\boxed{+}\;\boxed{5}\;\boxed{...)]}\;\boxed{=}$$

to get the answer 76.

9.   a) 4 × (5 × (3 × 6) + 5)   b) 9 × (2 + (24 ÷ 4) + 1)
      c) 2 × {(5 + 6) + (3 × 5)}   d) 20 ÷ {(15 ÷ 5) + 2}

Second Functions

Second functions are the functions written above the actual function button. Typically the index functions are second functions and we will look at these in more detail in Chapter 3. Some memory buttons are also second functions.

Using the Memory

For complicated calculations you need an accurate answer and obtain this by using the calculator's memory. To enter a function in the memory you press the M+ button; to delete it press M–, to recall the number in the memory press MR. Finally to clear the memory press MC or MCl. Some of these may be second functions. There may be other Memory buttons which your manual will tell you about.

The questions below may either be done using the memory or using brackets. Try doing them both ways and make sure that you get the same answer both times. If answers are not whole numbers write down the full display on your calculator.

For example suppose you have the calculation: $\dfrac{25}{7} - \dfrac{13}{5}$

Using brackets this can be rewritten as $(25 \div 7) - (13 \div 5)$

or using the memory: Check memory is clear (no M on display)

                        calculate $25 \div 7$ and press M+

                        then calculate $13 \div 5$ and press M–

                        MR will give you the answer : 0.9714285

                        Remember to clear the memory.

10. $\dfrac{100}{12} + \dfrac{98}{6}$

11. $(312 \div 25) - (17 \times 16)$

12. $\dfrac{312 + 251}{23 \times 45}$

13. $\dfrac{158 + 753}{214 - 196}$

14. $\dfrac{311}{204 \times 146}$

15. $\dfrac{451 \times 5}{263 \times 37}$

16. $\dfrac{312}{23} - \dfrac{420}{81}$

17. $\dfrac{31 \times 26}{81 - 62}$

Simple Index Functions

18. Find these squares: 3^2, 17^2, 21^2, 144^2

19. Find these square roots: $\sqrt{64}$, $\sqrt{361}$, $\sqrt{676}$, $\sqrt{64516}$.

20. Calculate $\dfrac{1}{8}$ (Use the reciprocal button that is $\dfrac{1}{x}$, it may be a second function) Now push the reciprocal button again, then again and again. What do you notice? Try this with some other numbers.

Writing Answers

For some questions working out has to be done in stages. When you are using a calculator it is important that each stage of working out is clearly shown. Although the calculator will **calculate** correctly - it will calculate only what **you** put in. Therefore if you put in the wrong sequence of key presses you will get the wrong answer!

Exercise 1G: Use Worksheet 1/2 for question 10.

1.   Write out your 17 times table. To do this put 17 in the memory, (17 M+) and then $2 \times MR =$, $3 \times MR =$ etc.

$$1 \times 17 = 17$$
$$2 \times 17 = 34$$
$$3 \times 17 = ...$$
$$4 \times 17 = ...$$

2.   The number 66 can be made by adding 4 consecutive numbers. What are they?

3.   The number 1716 is the result of multiplying 3 consecutive numbers, what are they?

4.   Without doing the calculations what size of answer would you expect to the following sums, choose A, B or C:

   (i) 98×48 (ii) $72\,954 \div 24$ (iii) $11\,532 - 7\,312 + 534 - 1826$
   A: About 5000   A: about 300   A: Between 10 000 and 12 000
   B: About 4000   B: about 3000   B: Between 2 000 and 4000
   C: About 2000   C: about 4000   C: Between 1000 and 2000

   Now work them out and see which estimates were correct.

5.   It is easy to press the wrong button. You need to check that the answer is about the right size and starts or ends in the correct digit. In the four sums below state how you know that the answer must be wrong:

$$321 \times 3 = 1926$$
$$1234 - 692 = 1926$$
$$80892 \div 24 = 1926$$
$$241 \times 9 = 1926$$

6.   The most common mistake to make is to press an adjacent key (for example 4 instead of 1) or to switch round two digits (for example press 21 instead of 12). Can you find which mistake was made in each of the four calculations above?

7.   Using the memory efficiently can save you a lot of time. Here is a number pattern to investigate. The pattern uses the same calculation in every line. If you store the answer to that calculation in your memory (M+) and then recall it (MR) to use it again you will save time:

$$137 \times 1 \times 73 =$$
$$137 \times 2 \times 73 =$$
$$137 \times 3 \times 73 =$$
$$137 \times 4 \times 73 =$$

   How far can you continue the pattern until the pattern in the answer changes? Predict your answer and then test it.

8.   Here is a similar pattern, investigate this one:
$$143 \times 1 \times 7 =$$
$$143 \times 2 \times 7 =$$
$$143 \times 3 \times 7 =$$
$$143 \times 4 \times 7 =$$
How far can you continue this pattern until the pattern in the answer changes? Predict your answer and then test it.

9.   Consider this calculation: $\dfrac{515+139}{342-124}$

There are two ways of solving this on your calculator:
a) Use the memory function: Subtract the bottom two digits, store the answer in the memory. Add the top digits together and then divide by the number in the memory.
b) Use the brackets function by calculating the sum as $(515 + 139) \div (342 - 124)$
Did you get the same answer both times?

10.   Captain H2O has a challenge! He has to visit the space stations on Worksheet 1/2. If he goes to them in the correct order then he has completed the challenge successfully. If he does not, then he fries! His orders are in the form of mathematical calculations. Starting from Earth he has to calculate the correct answer which will tell him where to go next. Can you help him complete the challenge? (You need to read the numbers for your answers as letters.)

Most calculators have a **constant function**. This repeats a function over and over again every time you press the = sign.

Try entering 17 then + and + again, now push = again and again. You should have the 17 times table that you worked out in question 1.

11.   **The Famous Chess Board Problem**

A Philosopher helped his Ruler in a time of great difficulty and was offered anything he wanted as a reward. The philosopher said he simply wanted 1 grain of rice on the 1st square of a chessboard, two grains on the second, four on the third, eight on the fourth and so on, doubling each time. The Ruler laughed and was pleased that he did not have to pay out lots of money. Use the constant function ($\times$ 2) to work out how many grains of rice were on the 20th square, and why the Ruler soon stopped laughing!

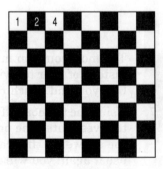

12.   If you had a piece of paper 0.15 mm thick and folded it in half 50 times how high would it be? Now try it and see if you are correct!

Extension Exercise 1

Let us take a closer look at the reciprocal button and see how it can help us solve problems.

1. Look at the sum $\dfrac{1}{3^2+4^2}$. Work this out first using either the memory or brackets function of your calculator.

    Now try just working out the bottom line. You should get the answer 25. Now press the reciprocal button (1/x) and this answer should be the same as your original.

    Your working for the above should look:

    Either $\dfrac{1}{3^2+4^2} = 1 \div 25$ or $\dfrac{1}{3^2+4^2} = \dfrac{1}{25}$
    $= 0.04$ $= 0.04$

As your calculations become more complicated it is a good idea to write down all stages. Record any answers that your calculator gives you in case you need to use them again.

2. Try calculating these in two ways, one of which should be with the reciprocal button.

    a) $\dfrac{1}{5 \div 25}$ b) $\dfrac{1}{0.2 \times 0.4}$ c) $\dfrac{1}{0.1 - 0.06}$

3. For a sum such as $\dfrac{5^2}{3^2+4^2}$ you should find the bottom line first, 3^2+4^2 then find its reciprocal $\dfrac{1}{3^2+4^2}$ and then multiply by the top. What is the answer?

4. Try calculating these with the reciprocal button.

    a) $\dfrac{5}{5 \div 25}$ b) $\dfrac{8}{0.2 \times 0.4}$ c) $\dfrac{4}{0.1 - 0.06}$

5. Sometimes we need to find the reciprocal of a reciprocal like this: $\dfrac{1}{\frac{1}{4}}$. Try this for other numbers.

6. What is special about the reciprocals of 11, and multiples of 11?

7. The Ancient Egyptians found reciprocals very useful because they could only write **unit** fractions such as $\dfrac{1}{5}$ and not **multiple** fractions such as $\dfrac{3}{5}$. $\dfrac{3}{5}$ had to be written as the sum of **unit** fractions. Can you find which 3 different unit fractions add up to $\dfrac{3}{5}$.

8. Slopes can be given as a fraction, so a slope of $\frac{1}{10}$ means

    a slope of 1 in 10.

    From a papyrus written in about 1650BC we are told that the slope of one
    pyramid is $\frac{1}{2} + \frac{1}{5} + \frac{1}{50}$. What is the value of this?

9. Try this reciprocal series:$1, \quad \dfrac{1}{1+1}, \quad \dfrac{1}{1+\dfrac{1}{1+1}}, \quad \dfrac{1}{1+\dfrac{1}{1+\dfrac{1}{1+1}}} \quad ....$

    Try continuing the series. Write down your answer each time to 3 significant
    figures. Stop when you get the same answer every time, what is the answer?

10. As speed increases then the time taken to travel the same distance or to do the
    same action decreases.
    If I am filling a tank with a pipe that will fill the whole tank in 10 minutes then
    after 1 minute the tank is $\frac{1}{10}$ th full.
    a) If I use a different pipe to fill the tank, one that would fill the tank in 5
    minutes, how full will the tank be after one minute?
    b) If I turn on both pipes how full will the tank be after (i) one minute? (ii) two
    minutes?
    c) How long does it take to fill the tank?
    d) If the first tap fills the tank in x minutes and the second in y minutes can you
    write an expression in x and y to give the time it takes to fill the tank?

11. An intergalactic traveller is trapped in an ancient water torture tank. The evil
    alien switches on two taps. One fills the tank on its own in 9 minutes, and the
    other fills the tank on its own in 6 minutes. It takes the intergalactic traveller 3
    minutes and 30 seconds to inflate his oxygen mask. Is he in time or does he
    drown first?

Summary Exercise 1

Answer the questions 1-10 mentally.

1. $52 + 33$
2. $65 - 41$
3. 12×8
4. $144 \div 12$
5. $134 + 59$

6. $124 - 38$
7. 108×4
8. $116 \div 4$
9. 148×3
10. $138 \div 6$

11. Answer these without a calculator. Write down the question and any necessary working:

   a) $-7 + (-4)$
   b) $4 - (-7)$
   c) $(-3) \times (-4)$
   d) $14 \div (-2)$
   e) $-4 + 12$

   f) $3 + (-8)$
   g) $15 \times (-5)$
   h) $6 - 9$
   i) $-3 + (-9)$
   j) $(-18) \div (-6)$

12. Which of these numbers are prime numbers?
   1, 4, 5, 9, 13, 24, 31, 99.

13. Write down all the factors of 28.

14. Which of these are multiples of 6?

15. What is the **H.C.F** of   a) 16 and 24 b) 252 and 714

16. What is the **L.C.M** of   a) 8 and 10   b) 168 and 462

Write down your working-out clearly for the next three questions 12-15. Do not use a calculator.

17. On an intergalactic expedition I have packed 25 space pods weighing 12kg each, 38 space suits weighing 28kg each and 9 extra-terrestrial repellent missiles weighing 135kg each. Have I packed more than the 2500kg limit?

18. The weight of one astronaut plus his kit is 84kg. The total weight allowance on the space station is 4000kg. If there are 23 astronauts how much weight allowance is there left?

19. One quarter of the total weight allowance is for food. Each astronaut is allowed 1kg of food per day. How many days can the astronauts survive on their food allowance?

You may use a calculator for the remaining questions.

20. $\dfrac{319}{29} - \dfrac{420}{19}$

21. $\dfrac{35 - 17}{25 + 47}$

22. $\{2(74 - 26) - 3(25 + 17)\}$

23. $2 \times (5 \times (6 + 17) - 4)$

24. $\dfrac{214 + 672}{32 \times 45}$

25. $\dfrac{1412 - 987}{612 - 284}$

Activity 1 - Calculator Puzzles And Games

Guess The Number

Ask a friend to think of a number between 10 and 91. Tell him to write it down. Then using a calculator tell him to:

Double it	[X] [2]
Add 6	[+] [6]
Divide by 2	[÷] [2]
Add 2	[+] [2]
Multiply by 8	[X] [8]
Subtract 40	[−] [4] [0]

Now you ask them the result. On your calculator enter the result, and divide by 8. You should now have the original number.

Down To Zero

Find the Random Number Button on your calculator (usually a second function marked RAN). If this is a three figure decimal, multiply by 100 to make a three figure digit. Now see how many stages it takes you to reach zero. At each stage you can add, subtract, multiply or divide by a single digit number.

Example:

Try a race with a friend, you will have to record every stage of your calculations!

	4.71
[X] [1] [0] [0] [=]	471
[÷] [3] [=]	157
[−] [4] [=]	153
[÷] [9] [=]	17
[−] [9] [=]	8
[−] [8] [=]	0

Countdown

Make 10 cards each with one of the numbers: 100, 75, 50, 25, 9, 8, 7, 6, 5, 4, 3, 2, 1. Pick six of them, either at random or one from the first four, and five from the rest.

Use the calculator to give you a 3 figure random number. Now can you make that number from your six numbers on the cards by adding, subtracting, multiplying or dividing as necessary? Can you beat the rest of the class.

Finding Remainders

Your teacher has asked you what the remainder is when you divide 1760 by 19. As you are not very good at long division you secretly use your calculator. But you get the answer 92.631579 which is not much help.

Here is what you do:

Subtract the whole number answer	$(- 92 =)$
Multiply the decimal remainder by the divisor	$(\times \ 19)$
You get the remainder!	(12)

Try this for some other long divisions. You should nearly always end up with a whole number answer (or you could check with long division of course!)

Calculating Easter

As you know Easter falls on a different date every year. It may seem to be chosen randomly, but it is actually based on the phases of the Moon. The Sun, Earth and Moon line up once every 19 years. The intervening years are called the Phases of the Moon.

To find which phase the moon is in: **Divide the Year by 19**
Let the answer be A and the whole number remainder be B

Find the century the year is in: **Divide the Year by 100**
Let the answer be C and the whole number remainder be D

Check for the leap years: **Divide C by 4**
Let the answer be E and the whole number remainder be F
                    Calculate $(C + 8) \div 25$
Let the answer be G and ignore the remainder
                    Calculate $(C + 1 - G) \div 3$
Let the answer be H and ignore the remainder
                    Calculate $(19 \times B) + (C + 15) - (E + H)$
Let the answer be J   **Calculate $J \div 30$**
Ignore the answer but let the whole number remainder be K
                    Calculate $D \div 4$
Ignore the answer but let the whole number remainder be M
                    Calculate $(2 \times F) + (2 \times L) + 32 - (K + M)$
Let the answer be N   **Calculate $N \div 7$**
Ignore the answer but let the whole number remainder be P
                    Calculate $B + (11 \times K) + (22 \times P)$
Let the answer be Q   **Calculate $Q \div 451$**
Let the answer be R and ignore the whole number remainder
                    Calculate $(K + P + 114) - (7 \times R)$
Let the answer be S   **Calculate $S \div 31$**
Let the answer be X and the whole number remainder be Y

X is the month of the day and Y is the day!   (wheew!)

Chapter 2

Fractions And Decimals

The first four exercises and the Foreign Exchange exercise are a consolidation of the first five exercises in Book 1 Chapter 11

In the last chapter we were only concerned with calculating with whole numbers. However division problems often give rise to remainders and we need to be able to deal with these. Also our system of measurement - the metric system- is based on decimals and we must be able to calculate with fractions and with decimal fractions (which we will call decimals).

Multiplying With Decimals

Consider the problem: Find the area of a rectangle 50cm by 30cm.
The answer is 1500cm, but suppose the question had asked for the answer to be given in square metres.

We change the units to metres first :

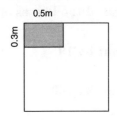

$$\text{Area} = 0.3 \times 0.5$$
$$= 0.15 \ \text{m}^2$$

The area is 0.15 square metres,
or 15 hundredths of the whole square meter.

If we multiply a positive number by a number less than one we get a smaller answer.
If we multiply tenths by tenths we will get hundredths,
If we multiply tenths by hundredths we get thousandths etc.

Another way of thinking about this is to look at the numbers after the decimal point. In our example we had

$\text{Area} = 0.3 \times 0.5$ two numbers , in total, after the decimal points
$\quad\quad\quad = 0.15 \ \text{m}^2$ *two numbers after the decimal point in the answer*

Exercise 2 A
Find the answers to these multiplication sums:

> Example: a) $0.25 \times 5 \ = 1.25$
> b) $0.35 \times 0.3 = 0.105$
> c) $1.5 \times 1.2 \ = 1.80$
> $\quad\quad\quad\quad\quad = 1.8$

1. 0.3×0.6
2. 0.3×0.06
3. 0.03×0.006
4. 0.06×3
5. 0.7×0.2
6. 0.12×0.4
7. 0.42×0.3
8. 0.24×3
9. 0.11×5
10. 1.2×0.4
11. 1.3×1.2
12. 3.2×0.4
13. 4.5×2
14. 0.5×0.4
15. 1.5×6
16. 6.3×5
17. 8.1×0.12
18. 1.02×0.07
19. 0.002×0.4
20. 0.103×0.3
21. 1.2×0.06
22. 4.2×0.7
23. 10.2×0.5
24. 12.2×3.4
25. 45.2×4.2
26. 2.14×0.5
27. 3.12×0.14

Dividing Decimals

Dividing into a decimal follows the same principles as normal division:

As $14 \div 2 = 7$
So $1.4 \div 2 = 0.7$

For more complicated problems we may need to write out the sum, so it is important that the decimal points stay above each other in the division.

$$5 \overline{) 19.5} = 3.9$$

Unlike normal division the first one or more 0's can be important, as they tell us where the decimal place is:

$1.95 \div 5$ $5\overline{)1.95} = 0.39$ $1.038 \div 12$ $12\overline{)1.038} = 0.086$

Exercise 2B

1. $1.5 \div 3$
2. $0.27 \div 9$
3. $0.35 \div 5$
4. $1.2 \div 4$
5. $1.44 \div 12$
6. $0.036 \div 6$
7. $6.4 \div 8$
8. $4.5 \div 9$
9. $0.72 \div 12$
10. $0.066 \div 11$
11. $2.8 \div 7$
12. $4.2 \div 7$
13. $0.018 \div 2$
14. $1.32 \div 11$
15. $0.108 \div 12$

Sometimes extra noughts have to be added after the last digit:

Example : $1.5 \div 8 = 8\overline{)1.5^70^60^40} = 0.1875$

16. $1.5 \div 2$
17. $0.7 \div 4$
18. $0.03 \div 6$
19. $0.6 \div 12$
20. $1.05 \div 4$
21. $2.01 \div 12$
22. $0.21 \div 6$
23. $1.08 \div 12$
24. $0.72 \div 5$
25. $0.0027 \div 18$
26. $1.03 \div 8$
27. $12.1 \div 16$
28. $4.5 \div 8$
29. $0.405 \div 18$
30. $0.31 \div 4$

Division By Decimals

How many halves are there in 4, i.e. what is $4 \div 0.5$?

We know the answer is 8, and we know that $40 \div 5$ is 8

When the question is more complicated: e.g. $40 \div 0.005$ it is very difficult to work out exactly where the decimal point goes in the answer. Is it 80, 800, 8000 or 80 000 ?

As dividing by a decimal is difficult we try to avoid doing it.

If we write $40 \div 0.005 = \dfrac{40}{0.005}$

we can multiply 0.005 by 1000 to eliminate the decimal point, we must also then multiply the 40 by 1000, and so our calculation becomes:

$$
\begin{aligned}
\text{Example:} \qquad 40 \div 0.005 &= \frac{40}{0.005} \times \frac{1000}{1000} \\[2mm]
&= \frac{40000}{5} \\[2mm]
&= 8000
\end{aligned}
$$

In the example the original calculation has been multiplied by $\frac{1000}{1000}$. $\frac{1000}{1000}$ equals 1 (one). You know that multiplying by one does not change anything. Therefore, you can multiply by $\frac{10}{10}$, $\frac{100}{100}$ or $\frac{1000}{1000}$ without changing the meaning of the calculation.

Exercise 2C

Do the first twelve in your head but check by multiplication that your decimal point is in the right place:

> Example: $4 \div 0.2 = 20$ *(check $0.2 \times 20 = 4$)*

1. $8 \div 0.2$	**5.** $24 \div 0.06$	**9.** $210 \div 0.3$
2. $16 \div 0.4$	**6.** $32 \div 0.8$	**10.** $180 \div 0.006$
3. $12 \div 0.3$	**7.** $24 \div 0.3$	**11.** $150 \div 0.5$
4. $36 \div 0.12$	**8.** $14 \div 0.07$	**12.** $90 \div 0.5$

You need to write the working out in full for the following:

13. $1.05 \div 0.6$	**19.** $4.5 \div 0.005$	**25.** $3.12 \div 0.006$
14. $2.4 \div 0.03$	**20.** $3.6 \div 0.9$	**26.** $7.02 \div 0.9$
15. $3.2 \div 0.8$	**21.** $480 \div 0.6$	**27.** $3.51 \div 0.03$
16. $0.64 \div 0.008$	**22.** $120 \div 0.6$	**28.** $27.6 \div 0.06$
17. $2.8 \div 0.007$	**23.** $20.4 \div 0.8$	**29.** $3.01 \div 0.007$
18. $0.63 \div 0.09$	**24.** $1.08 \div 0.004$	**30.** $41.1 \div 0.003$

Exercise 2D - Area Problems

When you multiply a number by another number greater than one, the answer is more than the original number (e.g. $8 \times 2 = 16$). When a number is multiplied by another number less than one, the answer is less than the original number (e.g. $8 \times 0.2 = 1.6$).

Example: Find the area of this rectangle:

$$\text{Area} = \text{base} \times \text{height}$$
$$= 2.4 \times 0.2$$
$$= 0.48\text{m}^2$$

0.2m

2.4m

---

1. A rectangle 0.2m by 5m has an area of one square metre. What other rectangles have an area of exactly one square metre? Can you find five?

2. Can you find five rectangles with an area of 2m^2?

3. A rectangle with an area of 4m^2 has one side of 0.5m. What is the length of the other side?

4. A rectangle with an area of 4cm^2 has one side of 20cm. What is the length of the other side?

5. A square has an area of 0.09m^2. What are the lengths of its sides?

For questions 6-10 you will need Worksheets 2/1 and 2/2. Use a calculator to check your answers.

6. Find the areas of the rectangles on the worksheet.

7. Find the area of the triangles on the worksheet.

8. The area and one side of the rectangles are given. Find the missing sides.

9. Find the height of this triangle.

10. The area and the base of the triangles are given. Find the corresponding height of each triangle.

Estimating

There are times when an exact answer to a problem is not needed. If I have to cut a one metre plank into 3 equal pieces the exact answer is 0.333333...m. As it is impossible to cut a plank with great accuracy the answer is only needed to a sensible number of decimal places. In this example the answer to the nearest millimetre would be sensible, and so the answer is 0.333m.

Exercise 2E   (for discussion)

Use your calculator to work out the solutions to each of these problems and give your answer to a sensible degree of accuracy.

1. A length of ribbon 2 metres long is cut into 9 equal lengths. How long is each length?

2. A class of 25 is divided into 3 groups for a class outing. How many are in each group?

3. I have a jug of 2.4 litres of squash to be divided between 18 boys. How much does each boy get?

4. A commercial traveller drives for 400 miles each day. How many days will it take him to travel round his distribution network of 3500 miles?

5. Revise your answer to question 4 as the commercial traveller has a "working week" of 5 days, i.e. he has to stay in a hotel for 2 days a week.

6. A delivery of 100kg of builders' sand is divided between 12 houses. How much sand is delivered to each house?

7. If there are 39.375 inches to a metre, and 12 inches in a foot, how many metres are there in 10 feet?

8. When I leave the top off a bottle of cleaning fluid about 8% evaporates in one hour. I started with 240ml. How much is left an hour later?

9. The population of the country of Geramania has increased by 7% over the last decade. If the population was 1.5 million 10 years ago what is it now?

10. The local electrical shop is advertising 15% off everything in the sale. If a personal CD player cost £79 before the sale what will it cost now?

Degree Of Accuracy

When an answer is given that is not exact it is necessary to qualify how accurate your answer is. The methods that are most commonly used to do this are using significant figures or decimal places. In some cases the answer is to the nearest whole number or to the nearest 100, 1000 and so on.

Decimal Places And Significant Figures - Revision

Decimal Places.

The 1st decimal place is the first number after the decimal point,
the 2nd decimal place is the 2nd number after the decimal point etc.

Significant Figures

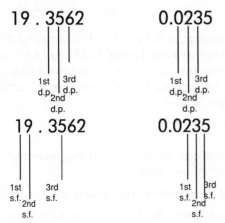

The 1st significant number is the first non - zero figure.

The 2nd significant figure is the next figure, whatever its value, the third is next and so on.

When rounding off to a number of decimal places or significant figures consider the **next** figure, only, to the one required. If that is 5 or more then round up:

19.3562 = 19.4 (to 1 d.p.)	19.3562 = 20 (to 1 s.f.)
19.3562 = 19.36 (to 2 d.p.)	19.3562 = 19 (to 2 s.f.)
19.3562 = 19.356 (to 3 d.p.)	19.3562 = 19.4 (to 3 s.f.)
	19.3562 = 19.36 (to 4 s.f.)

0.0235 = 0 (to 1 d.p.)	0.0235 = 0.02(to 1 s.f.)
0.0235 = 0.24 (to 3 d.p.)	0.0235 = 0.024(to 2 s.f.)
0.0235 = 0.0235(to 3 s.f.)	

Exercise 2G

Write these numbers to the decimal places or significant figures specified:

1. Write 516.1528 to:
   a) 1 s.f.   b) 1 d.p.   c) 3 s.f.   d) 3 d.p.

2. Write 0.13652 to:
   a) 2 s.f.   b) 2 d.p.   c) 4 s.f.   d) 4 d.p.

3. Write 9.3568 to:
   a) 1 s.f.   b) 1 d.p.   c) 3 s.f.   d) 3 d.p.

4. Write 0.83275 to:
   a) 1 s.f.   b) 1 d.p.   c) 4 s.f.   d) 4 d.p.

5. Write 1.9999 to:
   a) 1 s.f.   b) 1 d.p.   c) 3 s.f.   d) 3 d.p.

6. Write 10.90909 to:
   a) 2 s.f.   b) 1 d.p.   c) 4 s.f.   d) 3 d.p.

Using Your Calculator

When you are using your calculator it is very easy to miss out a "0" or the decimal point, and therefore it is good practice to **estimate** the expected answer first. When you then do your calculation on the calculator you should then be able to spot any error immediately.

The easiest way to estimate is to write each figure to one significant figure and then work out the answer. Give your answer to one significant figure.

For example: a) $0.48 \times 3212 \approx 0.5 \div 3000$
$$\approx 1500$$
$$\approx 2000$$
on the calculator $0.48 \times 3212 = 1541$

b) $\dfrac{34.12}{621 \times 0.048} \approx \dfrac{30}{600 \times 0.05}$
$$\approx \dfrac{30}{30}$$
$$= 1$$

on the calculator $\dfrac{34.12}{642 \times 0.048} = 1.1446...$

In the second example it was important that the calculator keys were pressed in the correct sequence: $34.12 \div 621 \div 0.048 =$ or $34.12 \div (621 \times 0.048) =$

It is very easy to make a simple error using a calculator!

REMEMBER
The calculator will only give the correct answer if you enter the correct calculation.

Exercise 2G

Estimate the answer to these, showing your working clearly, and give your answer to one significant figure. Then calculate the exact answer using your calculator.

1. 925×0.00521

2. $348 \div 0.056$

3. 0.053×0.9873

4. $0.836 \div 38$

5. $\dfrac{291}{0.721 \times 0.683}$

6. $\dfrac{38.3 \times 5.42}{0.0572}$

7. $\dfrac{3.450 \times 24.98}{0.721 \times 382}$

8. $\dfrac{9.34}{0.251} + \dfrac{361}{0.732}$

9. $\dfrac{0.0053}{0.921} - \dfrac{16.8}{59132}$

10. $\dfrac{34.12 \times 0.671}{0.045} + \dfrac{0.0124}{0.681 \times 37.3}$

11. $\dfrac{21.7 \times 3.8}{0.47 \times 0.51} - \dfrac{0.69 \times 312}{0.71 \times 381}$

12. $\dfrac{0.31 \times 481}{38} \div \dfrac{491}{0.68 \times 415}$

FOREIGN EXCHANGE

Foreign exchange rates are given to the nearest penny, the nearest cent, the nearest franc, etc. In other words they are given to two decimal places.

If there are 9.0 French Francs to the £ (pound sterling) then:

$$£1 = 9.0 \text{ FF}$$
$$1 \text{ FF} = £1 \div 9.0$$
$$= £0.11$$

$$£100 = 900 \text{ FF}$$
$$\text{FF}100 = £100 \div 9.0$$
$$= £11.11$$

Exercise 2H

Calculate the following using the exchange rates below and give your answers to two decimal places. Remember English currency is known as 'Pounds Sterling', or just 'Sterling (N.B. The values of currency are only approximate. Remember that the values change every second!:

> £1 = US$1.64 (United States Dollars)
> £1 = FF10.2 (French Francs)
> £1 = DM3.04 (German Deutsche Marks)
> £1 = SFr2.79 (Swiss Francs)
> £1 = HK$11.68 (Hong Kong Dollars)
> £1 = Y175 (Japanese Yens)

1. What is the value in Pounds Sterling of
    a) US$100   b) FF100   c) DM100
    d) Yen100   e) Sfr100

2. I have a £50 note and the foreign exchange clerk changes my money into French Francs, but the smallest note he has is a 10 franc note. How many French Francs do I get and how much change do I have in sterling?

3. I start with £100, I spend FF250 in France before crossing over the border to Switzerland. If I change my remaining money into Swiss Francs how much money do I now have?

4. I went to Hong Kong with £200, which I changed into HK$. I did a lot of shopping because you can buy so many bargains. Before I came home I changed what was left of my money back into sterling. I had £20. How many HK$ did I spend?

5. My American cousin came over here with a $100 bill. He changed it to sterling, went to lots of museums and galleries, and then changed what was left of his money back into US$. He had $15 left. How much did he in spend in England?

6. A skiing holiday cost £350, but I have to add the cost of hiring skis which is FF125, ski lessons which are FF825 and my ski pass which is FF750. What is the total cost of my holiday in sterling?

Summary Exercise 2

1. a) 0.3×0.4 b) 0.5×0.06 c) 1.2×0.03 d) 0.05×0.4

2. a) $20 \div 0.4$ b) $3 \div 0.6$ c) $32 \div 0.8$ d) $2.4 \div 0.04$

3. Find five rectangles with an area of 1.5m^2

4. Find the area of these triangles:

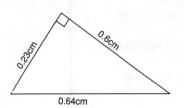
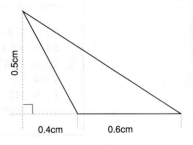

5. Give these numbers to (i) 2 d.p. (ii) 3 d.p.
        a) 4.254 9   b) 12.045 83   c) 4.009 99

6. Give these numbers to (i) 2 s.f. (ii) 3 s.f.
        a) 143 342   b) 0.045 673   c) 49 999

7. Estimate your answers to these, showing your working clearly.
        Give your answers to one significant figure.
        a) $\dfrac{34.8 + 51.2}{0.49 \times 39.9}$ b) $\dfrac{312.3 \times 0.789}{41.3 \times 0.052}$

8. Zib the spaceman buys 3.2 obs of Guff at \$0.8 per ob, 6.4 obs of Goff at \$1.2 per ob and 0.7 obs of Gaff at \$0.6 per ob. How many dollars does he spend? If there are \$4.5 to the £ what is this in pounds?

9. There are now 7.8 French Francs to the pound. I have to take enough French Francs with me when I go skiing to pay for my ski-hire, ski-pass and lessons. This is the information in the brochure:

> Ski - Hire   FF950
> Ski-pass   FF1150
> Lessons   FF1000

a) How many pounds should I change into French Francs to cover this?
b) Last year the rate of exchange was 8.7 French Francs to the pound, but the costs in French Francs were the same. How many more pounds do I need to cover my expenses this year than I did last year?

Activity 2 - The National Elf Problem.

You might not know this but there is a national shortage of Elves. Santa is having a real problem. His recruitment drive is not bringing them in. Why can he not recruit more elves?

Santa and Rudolph decide to go on an Elf Drive and find out how many Elves there actually are. Here is the result of their first survey of a typical elf residential area:

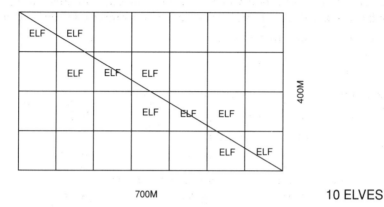

700M   10 ELVES

Now Elves are peculiar people and they like being near one or two other elves but not too close to too many. Santa and Rudolph discovered that if you find a rectangle of land with no humans in then the Elves divide that land into a grid of 100m squares. They then lay an Elf Communication Line in a diagonal from the top left to the bottom right of the rectangle, and an Elf lives in every square that the communication line crosses.

Here is a smaller Elf gathering:

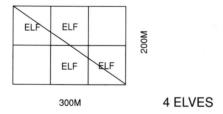

300M   4 ELVES

How many Elves live in a rectangle:
    a) 200m by 200m ?
    b) 300m by 400m ?
Investigate the problem further and find how many Elves live in a rectangle:
    c) 800m by 900m
    d) 100x metres by 100y metres.

Chapter 3

Fractions

This chapter is a condensed version of chapters 5 and 12 from Book 1 and provides a review of all fraction arithmetic.

You should be familiar with equivalent fractions, mixed numbers, cancelling down, converting fractions to decimals and percentages and simple addition and subtraction.

Try this first exercise just to revise these:

Exercise 3A

1. Replace the * to make these fractions equivalent:

    a) $\dfrac{3}{4} = \dfrac{*}{12}$ b) $\dfrac{2}{5} = \dfrac{12}{*}$ c) $\dfrac{4}{9} = \dfrac{*}{180}$ d) $\dfrac{5}{6} = \dfrac{125}{*}$

2. Write these improper fractions as mixed numbers:

    a) $\dfrac{25}{3}$ b) $\dfrac{12}{5}$ c) $\dfrac{72}{7}$ d) $\dfrac{126}{9}$

3. Write these mixed numbers as improper fractions:

    a) $3\frac{1}{4}$ b) $5\frac{2}{5}$ c) $8\frac{5}{7}$ d) $12\frac{9}{11}$

4. Cancel these fractions down to their lowest terms:

    a) $\dfrac{25}{40}$ b) $\dfrac{24}{126}$ c) $\dfrac{34}{136}$ d) $\dfrac{32}{132}$

5. Write each of these percentages as (i) a decimal and (ii) a fraction (in its lowest terms):

    a) 25 %   b) 33%   c) 84%   d) $66\frac{2}{3}$

6. Write these decimals as (i) fractions and (ii) percentages:

    a) 0.2   b) 0.35   c) 0.64   d) 3.24

7. Write these fractions as (i) decimals and (ii) percentages:

    a) $\dfrac{3}{4}$ b) $\dfrac{5}{8}$ c) $\dfrac{7}{12}$ d) $\dfrac{36}{5}$

8. Write:
    a) 12 minutes as a fraction of an hour.
    b) 300g as a fraction of a kilogram.
    c) 35p as a fraction of £2.00
    d) 30cm as a percentage of 4 metres.
    e) 450ml as a percentage of 5 litres.
    f) 1.25km as a percentage of 10km.

Adding Fractions

It is possible to compare fractions with different denominators, and it is also possible to add them directly, but only when they have the same denominator.

If we are asked $\dfrac{3}{10} + \dfrac{7}{12}$

we cannot directly add tenths to twelfths.

We have to write both fractions as their equivalent fractions, but with a **lowest common denominator** to keep the numbers as small as possible.

Now the lowest common multiple of 10 and 12 is 60, and

$$\frac{3}{10} = \frac{3 \times 6}{10 \times 6} = \frac{18}{60} \quad \text{and} \quad \frac{5}{12} = \frac{5 \times 5}{12 \times 5} = \frac{25}{60}$$

and so we write the fraction addition like this:

$$\frac{3}{10} + \frac{5}{12} = \frac{18 + 25}{60}$$
$$= \frac{43}{60}$$

Exercise 3B

Add these fractions, remember to put the answer in its simplest form. If the answer is an improper fraction e.g. $\frac{13}{12}$ **write it as a mixed number:** $1\frac{1}{12}$

1. $\dfrac{2}{5} + \dfrac{1}{4}$

2. $\dfrac{1}{7} + \dfrac{3}{5}$

3. $\dfrac{2}{3} + \dfrac{1}{5}$

4. $\dfrac{5}{12} + \dfrac{3}{8}$

5. $\dfrac{2}{15} + \dfrac{4}{9}$

6. $\dfrac{5}{6} + \dfrac{3}{4}$

7. $\dfrac{5}{6} + \dfrac{3}{4}$

8. $\dfrac{5}{6} + \dfrac{3}{10}$

Addition With Mixed Numbers

Example:

$$3\tfrac{1}{8} + 2\tfrac{11}{12} = 5\tfrac{3+22}{24}$$
$$= 5\tfrac{25}{24}$$
$$= 6\tfrac{1}{24}$$

9. $1\frac{1}{5} + 3\frac{2}{3}$

10. $2\frac{1}{7} + 3\frac{3}{5}$

11. $1\frac{2}{5} + 4\frac{1}{8}$

12. $5\frac{3}{8} + 3\frac{1}{16}$

13. $2\frac{4}{5} + 2\frac{2}{15}$

14. $6\frac{5}{12} + 3\frac{5}{8}$

15. $1\frac{1}{6} + 3\frac{3}{10}$

16. $4\frac{5}{6} + 2\frac{3}{4}$

17. $5\frac{1}{12} + 3\frac{2}{3}$

18. $7\frac{2}{9} + 2\frac{2}{15}$

19. $3\frac{5}{8} + 3\frac{3}{10}$

20. $6\frac{13}{15} + 4\frac{11}{12}$

Subtraction

Subtraction of fractions follows the same first steps as addition. Find the lowest common denominator, find the equivalent fractions and then subtract:

Exercise 3C

> Example: a) $\frac{3}{5} - \frac{1}{3} = \frac{9-5}{15}$ b) $3\frac{3}{7} - 1\frac{1}{4} = 2\frac{12-7}{28}$
>
> $= \frac{4}{15}$ $= 2\frac{5}{28}$

1. $\frac{4}{5} - \frac{2}{3}$

2. $\frac{2}{3} - \frac{1}{4}$

3. $\frac{5}{8} - \frac{1}{6}$

4. $3\frac{4}{7} - 1\frac{2}{5}$

5. $5\frac{2}{3} - 2\frac{2}{7}$

6. $\frac{7}{8} - \frac{5}{6}$

7. $4\frac{4}{5} - 1\frac{1}{3}$

8. $\frac{5}{12} - \frac{1}{4}$

9. $6\frac{2}{5} - 3\frac{2}{9}$

10. $5\frac{4}{9} - 1\frac{1}{3}$

11. $3\frac{4}{7} - 2\frac{1}{3}$

12. $1\frac{2}{5} - 1\frac{1}{3}$

As in any other subtraction there will be times when the first subtraction is not possible (5 - 9); as usual you must then **borrow** from the next number on the left. Remember that you are not borrowing ten units - you will be borrowing 8 eighths, 12 twelfths, 16 sixteenths or whatever:

> Example:
>
> $3\frac{1}{3} - 1\frac{3}{4} \quad = 2\frac{4-9}{12}$ (4 minus 9 will not go, we borrow one unit)
>
> $= 1\frac{16-9}{12}$ (one unit $= \frac{12}{12}$ and 12 + 4 = 16)
>
> $= 1\frac{7}{12}$

13. $\frac{3}{5} - \frac{1}{3}$

14. $4\frac{1}{4} - 1\frac{2}{3}$

15. $\frac{7}{8} - \frac{2}{3}$

16. $2\frac{1}{6} - \frac{5}{8}$

17. $3\frac{1}{6} - 1\frac{2}{9}$

18. $2\frac{2}{7} - 1\frac{2}{5}$

19. $\frac{5}{8} - \frac{3}{16}$

20. $5\frac{1}{6} - 2\frac{3}{4}$

21. $2\frac{2}{5} - 1\frac{2}{3}$

22. $4\frac{3}{8} - 1\frac{2}{5}$

23. $1\frac{1}{5} - \frac{2}{3}$

24. $3\frac{3}{4} - 1\frac{7}{8}$

A Fraction Of An Amount

'Half an hour' is thirty minutes. We divide sixty minutes by 2.

'Half a metre' is 50 cm. We divide 100 cm by 2.

'Three quarters of an hour' is forty five minutes because 60 minutes is divided by four, and then multiplied by three.

Exercise 3D

Example: Find $\frac{1}{5}$ of 25.

$$\frac{1}{5} \text{ of } 25 = 25 \div 5$$
$$= 5$$

Find $\frac{3}{4}$ of 1m. Give the answer in cm.

$$\frac{3}{4} \text{ of } 1\text{m} = 1000 \div 4 \times 3$$
$$= 250 \times 3$$
$$= 750 \text{ cm}$$

1. Find $\frac{1}{4}$ of 16.

2. Find $\frac{1}{7}$ of 35.

3. Find $\frac{1}{8}$ of 104.

4. Find $\frac{1}{9}$ of 126.

5. Find $\frac{1}{4}$ of 81.

6. Find $\frac{1}{8}$ of 74.

7. Find $\frac{3}{4}$ of 48.

8. Find $\frac{2}{3}$ of 72.

9. Find $\frac{3}{5}$ of 1 m. Give the answer in cm.

10. Find $\frac{2}{3}$ of 1 hour. Give the answer in minutes.

11. Find $\frac{3}{4}$ of 1 kg. Give the answer in grams.

12. Find $\frac{5}{8}$ of 3 km. Give the answer in km and m.

13. Find $\frac{5}{6}$ of 3 hours. Give the answer in hours and minutes.

14. Find $\frac{4}{5}$ of 6 m. Give the answer in mm.

15. Find $\frac{5}{12}$ of a minute. Give the answer in seconds.

For more complicated fractions of an amount we may need to write down the calculation. Remember that 'of' can be written as '×'. (The I in BIDMAS stands for "Index").

Consider: What is $\frac{2}{5}$ of 240?

$$\frac{2}{5} \text{ of } 240 = \frac{2}{5} \times 240$$

These calculations are simplest if both terms are fractions,

and so we can write the 240 as $\frac{240}{1}$. The sum becomes $\frac{2}{5} \times \frac{240}{1}$, we can cancel this down in the same way that we cancel down equivalent fractions, by dividing top and bottom by the same common factor:

For example: Find $\frac{7}{9}$ of 135

$\frac{7}{9}$ of 135 $= \frac{7}{9} \times \frac{135}{1}$

$= 7 \times 15$

$= 105$

16. Find $\frac{5}{14}$ of 364.

17. Find $\frac{3}{7}$ of 420.

18. Find $\frac{5}{16}$ of 240.

19. Find $\frac{3}{26}$ of 130.

20. Find $\frac{4}{25}$ of 125.

21. Find $\frac{5}{9}$ of 493

22. Find $\frac{9}{40}$ of 520

23. Find $\frac{7}{18}$ of 126.

24. Find $\frac{5}{24}$ of 312.

25. Find $\frac{9}{16}$ of 712.

Multiplying Fractions

In the above examples we multiplied a whole number by a fraction. We use the same principle when we have to multiply a fraction by a fraction.

Example:

$$\frac{2}{7} \times \frac{21}{26} = \frac{\cancel{42}^{6}}{\cancel{182}_{26}}$$

multiply the top numbers together
multiply the bottom numbers together
and divide by common factor: 7

$$= \frac{\cancel{6}^{3}}{\cancel{26}_{13}}$$

are there any more common factors? Yes 2.

$$= \frac{3}{13}$$

In this example there was quite a complicated multiplication: 7 × 26.
There is no reason why we cannot divide by the factors **before** the multiplication.
This then gives much easier products:

Example:

$$\frac{2}{7} \times \frac{21}{26} = \frac{\cancel{2}^{1}}{\cancel{7}_{1}} \times \frac{\cancel{21}^{3}}{\cancel{26}_{13}}$$

divide by common factors : 2 and 7.

$$= \frac{3}{13}$$

Exercise 3E

1. $\dfrac{2}{3} \times \dfrac{9}{10}$

2. $\dfrac{4}{5} \times \dfrac{15}{16}$

3. $\dfrac{9}{14} \times \dfrac{7}{12}$

4. $\dfrac{4}{9} \times \dfrac{3}{4}$

5. $\dfrac{8}{9} \times \dfrac{3}{10}$

6. $\dfrac{5}{8} \times \dfrac{16}{25}$

7. $\dfrac{6}{7} \times \dfrac{4}{9}$

8. $\dfrac{2}{9} \times \dfrac{3}{8}$

9. $\dfrac{7}{10} \times \dfrac{5}{14}$

10. $\dfrac{6}{7} \times \dfrac{2}{9}$

11. $\dfrac{2}{3} \times \dfrac{4}{5}$

12. $\dfrac{20}{21} \times \dfrac{8}{9}$

We can use the same principle with three or more fractions multiplied together:

For example:
$$\frac{4}{5} \times \frac{10}{21} \times \frac{7}{8} = \frac{4^1}{5} \times \frac{\cancel{10}^2}{\cancel{21}_3} \times \frac{7^1}{8_2}$$
$$= \frac{1 \times 2^1 \times 1}{1 \times 3 \times 2_1}$$
$$= \frac{1}{3}$$

13. $\dfrac{2}{3} \times \dfrac{6}{7} \times \dfrac{14}{15}$

14. $\dfrac{4}{5} \times \dfrac{15}{16} \times \dfrac{2}{3}$

15. $\dfrac{8}{9} \times \dfrac{6}{7} \times \dfrac{21}{22}$

16. $\dfrac{5}{6} \times \dfrac{4}{7} \times \dfrac{14}{15}$

17. $\dfrac{7}{9} \times \dfrac{6}{15} \times \dfrac{3}{14}$

18. $\dfrac{2}{9} \times \dfrac{6}{11} \times \dfrac{4}{5}$

19. $\dfrac{2}{7} \times \dfrac{5}{6} \times \dfrac{7}{8} \times \dfrac{4}{5}$

20. $\dfrac{3}{14} \times \dfrac{4}{5} \times \dfrac{7}{18} \times \dfrac{10}{13}$

21. $\dfrac{10}{11} \times \dfrac{2}{5} \times \dfrac{22}{25} \times \dfrac{5}{8}$

22. $\dfrac{2}{3} \times \dfrac{4}{15} \times \dfrac{5}{8} \times \dfrac{3}{16} \times \dfrac{2}{9}$

23. $\dfrac{1}{2} \times \dfrac{2}{3} \times \dfrac{3}{4} \times \dfrac{4}{5} \times \dfrac{5}{6} \times \dfrac{6}{7}$

24. $\dfrac{1}{2} \times \dfrac{3}{4} \times \dfrac{5}{6} \times \dfrac{7}{8} \times \dfrac{9}{10} \times \dfrac{11}{12}$

These multiplication sums have all been with fractions less than one. The answer to these has also been less than one, but we often need to multiply numbers greater than one, or mixed numbers. To do this we simply change the mixed numbers into improper fractions and then cancel and multiply as before.

Exercise 3F

Example: $1\frac{2}{3} \times 2\frac{2}{5} = \frac{5^1}{3^1} \times \frac{12^4}{5^1}$

$$= \frac{4}{1}$$

$$= 4$$

1.	$1\frac{1}{4} \times \frac{2}{5}$	**7.**	$4\frac{2}{7} \times \frac{7}{10}$	**13.**	$1\frac{1}{4} \times 2\frac{2}{3} \times 1\frac{2}{5}$
2.	$\frac{1}{4} \times 2\frac{2}{5}$	**8.**	$3\frac{1}{7} \times \frac{11}{7}$	**14.**	$2\frac{1}{2} \times 3\frac{1}{3} \times 1\frac{1}{4}$
3.	$\frac{2}{3} \times 1\frac{1}{5}$	**9.**	$\frac{4}{5} \times 4\frac{2}{7}$	**15.**	$4\frac{2}{3} \times 3\frac{1}{7} \times 1\frac{1}{11}$
4.	$3\frac{1}{3} \times \frac{3}{5}$	**10.**	$5\frac{4}{5} \times \frac{5}{8}$	**16.**	$1\frac{1}{2} \times 3\frac{4}{5} \times \frac{2}{3} \times 1\frac{1}{4} \times 5\frac{1}{7} \times \frac{7}{8}$
5.	$\frac{7}{8} \times 2\frac{2}{7}$	**11.**	$1\frac{1}{4} \times 2\frac{2}{5}$	**17.**	$1\frac{1}{2} \times 1\frac{1}{3} \times 1\frac{1}{4} \times 1\frac{1}{5} \times 1\frac{1}{6} \times 1\frac{1}{7}$
6.	$\frac{3}{4} \times 2\frac{1}{6}$	**12.**	$1\frac{1}{5} \times 2\frac{1}{2}$	**18.**	$\frac{1}{2} \times 1\frac{2}{3} \times 2\frac{3}{4} \times 3\frac{4}{5} \times 4\frac{5}{6}$

Dividing With Fractions

When we write $4 \times \frac{1}{2}$ we get the answer 2 because four halves are two.
This sum could also be $4 \div 2 = 2$

or $\frac{4}{2} = 2$

or $\frac{1}{2}$ of 4 is 2
or we could use decimals: $4 \times 0.5 = 2$
or even :   50% of 4 is 2.

All the above sums mean the same. There are just several different ways of saying
the same thing.

Exercise 3G
Write these in as many different ways as you can:

1.	$\frac{1}{4}$ of 8	**5.**	$6 \times \frac{2}{3}$	**8.**	25 % of 12
2.	$6 \div 2$	**6.**	$10 \div 3$	**9.**	$\frac{5}{4}$
3.	$10 \times \frac{3}{5}$	**7.**	$\frac{1}{8}$ of 16	**10.**	0.3×3
4.	$9 \div 4$				

We can see that $\div 2$ is the same as $\times \frac{1}{2}$, similarly $\div \frac{1}{2}$ is the same as $\times 2$. In other words the $\div$ sign changes to $\times$ and the fraction is turned upside down.

This works for all fractions, so $\div \frac{3}{4}$ is the same as $\times \frac{4}{3}$.

Example: $\quad 4 \div \frac{4}{5} = \frac{4^1}{1} \times \frac{5}{4^1} \qquad\qquad \frac{2}{3} \div \frac{4}{5} = \frac{2^1}{3} \times \frac{5}{4^2}$

$$= 5 \qquad\qquad\qquad\qquad\qquad = \frac{5}{6}$$

Do these divisions. If your answer is an improper fraction you should turn it into a mixed number.

11. $\dfrac{3}{5} \div \dfrac{6}{7}$ 15. $\dfrac{7}{12} \div \dfrac{5}{9}$ 19. $\dfrac{4}{5} \div \dfrac{8}{9}$

12. $\dfrac{3}{4} \div \dfrac{7}{8}$ 16. $\dfrac{9}{10} \div \dfrac{3}{5}$ 20. $\dfrac{5}{6} \div \dfrac{5}{9}$

13. $\dfrac{2}{3} \div \dfrac{8}{9}$ 17. $\dfrac{11}{12} \div \dfrac{9}{10}$ 21. $\dfrac{2}{3} \div \dfrac{4}{9}$

14. $\dfrac{8}{9} \div \dfrac{2}{3}$ 18. $\dfrac{5}{9} \div \dfrac{10}{21}$ 22. $\dfrac{4}{5} \div \dfrac{7}{10}$

Example $\qquad\qquad \frac{2}{3} \div 2\frac{1}{6} = \frac{5}{3} \div \frac{13}{6}$

$$= \frac{5}{3^1} \times \frac{6^2}{13}$$

$$= \frac{10}{13}$$

---

23. $2\dfrac{1}{4} \div \dfrac{3}{8}$ 29. $2\dfrac{2}{3} \div \dfrac{1}{9}$ 35. $4\dfrac{2}{5} \div 1\dfrac{7}{15}$

24. $3\dfrac{2}{3} \div 4$ 30. $2\dfrac{1}{4} \div 1\dfrac{7}{8}$ 36. $3\dfrac{2}{3} \div 1\dfrac{2}{9}$

25. $4\dfrac{1}{5} \div 2$ 31. $2\dfrac{4}{5} \div 1\dfrac{7}{10}$ 37. $4\dfrac{1}{5} \div 1\dfrac{2}{5}$

26. $5\dfrac{3}{4} \div 3$ 32. $2\dfrac{2}{3} \div 1\dfrac{1}{9}$ 38. $5\dfrac{3}{4} \div 1\dfrac{7}{8}$

27. $4\dfrac{2}{5} \div 3\dfrac{2}{3}$ 35. $3\dfrac{3}{4} \div 1\dfrac{3}{7}$ 39. $4\dfrac{1}{6} \div 1\dfrac{7}{8}$

28. $2\dfrac{2}{5} \div 2\dfrac{4}{15}$ 34. $4\dfrac{2}{7} \div 1\dfrac{1}{9}$ 40. $1\dfrac{3}{5} \div 2\dfrac{3}{4}$

Extension Exercise 3

Fractions on the calculator.

Look for the fraction button on your calculator.
It usually looks like this : $\boxed{a^{\,b}\!/_{c}}$

To enter a mixed number, for example $1\frac{2}{5}$, you press the sequence:

$$\boxed{1}\;\boxed{a^{\,b}\!/_{c}}\;\boxed{2}\;\boxed{a^{\,b}\!/_{c}}\;\boxed{5}$$

and the display reads:

$$\boxed{\qquad\qquad\qquad\qquad 1\;\lrcorner\;2\;\lrcorner\;5\qquad}$$

now try adding $1\frac{2}{5}$, again, you should get the answer $1\frac{4}{5}$.

Try calculating the first few adding, subtracting, multiplying and dividing questions in the earlier exercises. When you are happy with those try doing these questions with your calculator:

Remember that you may need to use the memory and brackets facilities.

1. $2\frac{5}{6} - \frac{8}{15}$

2. $\dfrac{\frac{2}{3} - \frac{4}{7}}{\frac{2}{15}}$

3. $3\frac{3}{4} - \frac{13}{18}$

4. $\dfrac{\frac{3}{4} + \frac{3}{7}}{\frac{5}{18}}$

5. $\dfrac{3\frac{1}{3} - 1\frac{4}{9}}{\frac{8}{9}}$

6. $\dfrac{1\frac{4}{7} - \frac{7}{10}}{\frac{3}{14}}$

7. $\dfrac{1\frac{2}{9} + 1\frac{5}{6}}{1\frac{2}{9}}$

8. $\dfrac{3\frac{3}{5}}{1\frac{2}{7}} - \dfrac{2\frac{1}{4}}{1\frac{1}{5}}$

9. $\dfrac{4\frac{4}{15} - 2\frac{5}{12}}{4\frac{5}{6} - 2\frac{7}{8}}$

10. $\dfrac{1\frac{3}{5} + 2\frac{5}{7}}{3\frac{2}{7} - 1\frac{7}{10}}$

11. $1 - \frac{1}{4}\left(1 - \frac{1}{4}\left(1 - \frac{1}{4}\right)\right)$

12. $1 - \frac{1}{4}\left(1 - \frac{1}{3}\left(1 - \frac{1}{5}\right)\right)$

13. $\dfrac{1 + \frac{1}{4}\left(1 + \frac{1}{2}\left(1 - \frac{3}{4}\right)\right)}{1 - \frac{3}{4}\left(1 - \frac{1}{4}\left(1 + \frac{3}{4}\right)\right)}$

Now try these decimal calculations using your calculator:

14. $\dfrac{2.4(3.84 + 5.63)}{3.46 - 1.87}$

15. $\dfrac{3.1(6.72 - 4.72) + 2.6(3.29 - 1.91)}{6.3(3.46 - 2.97)}$

16. $\dfrac{6.7(13.67 + 9.72) - 2.8(6.31 + 3.74)}{1.9(2.36 + 7.21) - 1.3(3.58 + 1.86)}$

17. $\dfrac{0.3(34.65 - 25.87) + 0.2(1.34 + 33.56)}{11.2(0.98 + 0.56) - 13.1(0.78 - 0.59)}$

18. The teacher set the class to work out the series:

$$\frac{1}{1} + \frac{1}{2} + \frac{1}{3} + \frac{1}{4} + \frac{1}{5}\dots$$

stopping when the sum exceeds $2\frac{1}{2}$. What will the final answer be, as a fraction? Molesworth was not paying attention, as usual, and the series he was summing was:

$$\frac{1}{1} + \frac{1}{2} + \frac{1}{4} + \frac{1}{8} + \dots$$

what was Molesworth's final answer?

19. Calculate the answer to these fraction multiplications without using a calulator:

(i) $\quad \frac{1}{2} \times \frac{2}{3} \times \frac{3}{4} \times \frac{4}{5} \times \frac{5}{6}$

(ii) $\quad (1 - \frac{1}{2})(1 - \frac{1}{3})(1 - \frac{1}{4})(1 - \frac{1}{5})(1 - \frac{1}{6})$

(iii) $\quad (1 + \frac{1}{2})(1 + \frac{1}{3})(1 + \frac{1}{4})(1 + \frac{1}{5})(1 + \frac{1}{6})$

(iv) $\quad (1 - \frac{1}{4})(1 - \frac{1}{9})(1 - \frac{1}{16})(1 - \frac{1}{25})(1 - \frac{1}{36})$

20. Question 19 involved multiplying together the first five terms of a definite pattern. Can you predict the answer if the first ten terms of each pattern were multiplied together? Check your answer.

21. Calculate the answer to these without using a calculator:

a) $\quad \frac{1}{2} \div \frac{3}{4}$

b) $\quad ((\frac{1}{2} \div \frac{3}{4}) \div \frac{5}{6})$

c) $\quad ((\frac{1}{2} \div \frac{3}{4}) \div \frac{5}{6}) \div \frac{7}{8}$

d) Continue the series for a few more terms.

Summary Exercise 3

Do not use a calculator for this exercise

1. Write these decimals as (i) fractions and (ii) percentages:

    a) 0. 24   b) 1.35   c) 0.125

2. Write these fractions as (i) decimals and (ii) percentages:

    a) $\dfrac{3}{5}$ b) $\dfrac{2}{3}$ c) $1\dfrac{17}{20}$

3. a) $\dfrac{3}{4} + \dfrac{5}{6}$ b) $2\dfrac{3}{5} + 3\dfrac{5}{7}$ c) $4\dfrac{2}{3} + 3\dfrac{4}{5}$ d) $2\dfrac{2}{7} + \dfrac{3}{4}$

4. a) $\dfrac{5}{8} - \dfrac{2}{5}$.   b) $4\dfrac{2}{3} - 2\dfrac{5}{8}$ c) $4\dfrac{2}{3} - 2\dfrac{1}{5}$ d) $2\dfrac{1}{7} - 1\dfrac{3}{4}$

5. Find $\dfrac{2}{7}$ of 413.

6. Find $\dfrac{3}{8}$ of 3 kg. Give your answer in grams.

7. Which of these is the odd one out:

    a) $\dfrac{1}{4}$ of 25   b) $25 \div 4$ c) $\dfrac{25}{4}$ d) $4 \div 25$

8. a) $\dfrac{2}{5} \times \dfrac{15}{16}$ b) $\dfrac{15}{16} \times \dfrac{7}{20} \times \dfrac{8}{21}$

9. a) $\dfrac{3}{4} \times \dfrac{2}{7}$ b) $7\dfrac{2}{3} \times 2\dfrac{5}{8}$ c) $2\dfrac{1}{3} \times 1\dfrac{2}{7}$

10. a) $\dfrac{2}{15} \div \dfrac{4}{5}$ b) $2\dfrac{5}{8} \div 1\dfrac{3}{4}$ c) $7\dfrac{1}{5} \div 3\dfrac{9}{10}$

11. a) $\dfrac{1\frac{3}{4} + 3\frac{1}{5}}{4\frac{1}{8} - 2\frac{1}{5}}$

12. a) $\left(1 - \dfrac{1}{50}\right) \times \left(1 - \dfrac{1}{49}\right) \times \left(1 - \dfrac{1}{48}\right)$

    b) What happens if you extend the multiplication pattern in question 12 a) until $\left(1 - \dfrac{1}{2}\right)$.

Activity 3 - Fraction, Decimal and Percentage Dominoes

Fraction, Decimal and Percentage Dominoes

On worksheet 3/1 you will find a set of dominoes. Cut these out and play dominoes.

The Traditional Game.

For up to four players

Turn all the pieces upside down and shuffle them around the table. Each player takes one domino each in turn until all players have seven.

The player with the highest double starts (in this game the player with the double half, if no one has the double half then it is found from the remaining pieces and placed on the table. The player who picked up the last piece then starts)

He places the double on the table and the other players have to add a matching domino to the first. This could look like this:

$\frac{1}{2}$	$\frac{1}{2}$	0.5	20%

The next player has to match a domino up to one of the ends of the chain. This could look like this:

$\frac{1}{2}$	$\frac{1}{2}$	0.5	20%	$\frac{1}{5}$	0.7

The next player then adds on to the end of the chain. If the chain is getting too long then it can bend like this:

$\frac{1}{2}$	$\frac{1}{2}$	0.5	20%	$\frac{1}{5}$	0.7	

If a player cannot go he "passes" and forfeits his turn. The winner is the first player to put down all his pieces, and he score is the sum of all the numbers on the remaining players dominoes.

The Puzzle

The dominoes on the worksheet can be placed in a continuous rectangle with no pieces left out. All touching squares must be equal in value. Can you make this rectangle?

Chapter 4

Indices

When we worked out the prime factors of 375 we wrote the numbers $5 \times 5 \times 5$ as 5^3.
The little number 3 is known as the index number and tells us how many 5÷s are
multiplied together.

$5 \times 5 \times 5 \times 5 \times 5 = 5^5 = 3125$ (5^5 can be read as five to the power '5')
$5 \times 5 \times 5 \times 5 = 5^4 = 625$ (5^4 can be read as 'five to the power 4')
$5 \times 5 \times 5 = 5^3 = 125$ (5^3 can be read as 'five cubed')
$5 \times 5 = 5^2 = 25$ (5^2 can be read as 'five squared')
$5 = 5$ or 5^1

Exercise 4A

Use a calculator when necessary with this exercise.

> Examples:
> Write $5 \times 5 \times 5$ in index form
> $$5 \times 5 \times 5 = 5^3$$
> Work out the answer to 5^3
> $$5^3 = 125$$
> Write 125 in index form
> $$125 = 5 \times 5 \times 5$$
> $$= 5^3$$

1. Write these numbers in index form:
a) $2 \times 2 \times 2$ c) 9×9 e) $3 \times 3 \times 3$
b) 8×8 d) $2 \times 2 \times 2 \times 2 \times 2$ f) $4 \times 4 \times 4$

2. Work out the actual numbers in question 1.

3. Write these numbers in index form:
a) 9   c) 16   e) 49   g) 144
b) 243   d) 343   f) 1331   h) 169

Consider what happens when we multiply and divide indices:
$$5^3 \times 5^2 = 5 \times 5 \times 5 \times 5 \times 5$$
$$= 5^5 \qquad \textit{N.B. } 3 + 2 = 5 \textit{ i.e ADD the indices}$$
$$5^4 \div 5^2 = 5 \times 5 \times 5 \times 5 \div 5 \times 5$$
$$= \frac{5 \times 5 \times 5 \times 5}{5 \times 5}$$
$$= 5 \times 5$$
$$= 5^2 \qquad \textit{N.B. } 4 - 2 = 2 \textit{ i.e. SUBTRACT the indices}$$

As a general rule if numbers written in index form are **multiplied** together the resulting index is the **sum** of the indices:

$$5^3 \times 5^2 = 5^5 \qquad\qquad N.B. \; 3 + 2 = 5$$

if numbers written in index form are **divided** the resulting index number is the first index number **minus** the second:

$$5^4 \div 5^2 = 5^2 \qquad\qquad N.B. \; 4 - 2 = 2$$

Examples:
Simplify these numbers, if possible, leaving the answer in index form:

    a) $2^4 \times 2^6$: $2^4 \times 2^6 = 2^{10}$
    b) $6^7 \div 6^2$ $6^7 \div 6^2 = 6^5$

Simplify these numbers leaving the answer in index form:

4.   a) $3^3 \times 3^2$ b) $6^7 \times 6^4$ c) $4^3 \times 4^3 \times 4^3$
       d) $7^2 \times 7^5$ e) $3^2 \times 3^2 \times 3$ f) $7^3 \times 7 \times 7$

5.   a) $2^5 \div 2^2$ b) $4^7 \div 4^3$ c) $5^8 \div 5^7$
       d) $7^5 \div 7$ e) $3^5 \div 3^2$ f) $7^3 \div 7$

6.   a) $4^3 \times 4^3 \div 4^2$ b) $5^7 \times 5^2 \div 5^4$ c) $4^3 \times 4^3 \div 4^2$
       d) $7^2 \times 7^4 \div 7^5$ e) $3^2 \times 3^2 \div 3$ f) $7^3 \times 7^2 \div 7$

7.   a) $3^8 \times 3^3 \div 3$ b) $7^3 \times 7^2 \div 7^4$ c) $2^2 \times 2^3 \div 2^5$
       d) $5 \times 5^3 \div 5^2$ e) $3 \times 3 \div 3^2$ f) $7 \times 7^4 \div 7^5$

Note that the adding and subtracting rules are **only** true when considering powers of **similar** numbers.
$5^3 \times 2^3$ does not equal either 5^6 or 2^6 (but does equal 10^3)

---

8.   Simplify these numbers IF POSSIBLE and leave the answer in index form
       a) $3^3 \times 3^3$ b) $6^7 \times 5^5$ c) $6^7 \div 5^2$
       d) $8^5 \div 8^2$ e) $7^2 \div 2^2$ f) $4^3 \times 4$
       g) $2^2 \times 2^3 \times 2^2$ h) $3^2 \times 3^3 \div 3^2$ i) $4^8 \times 3^3 \times 5^2$
       j) $3^2 \times 5^3 \times 2^2$ k) $6^7 \times 5^5 \div 6^2$ l) $6^7 \times 6^5 \div 6^2$
       m) $7^3 \times 7^3 \times 3^2$ n) $5^5 \times 5^5 \div 5^3$ o) $2^4 \times 3^4 \div 6^2$

Also note that :

$5^3 + 5^3$ does not equal 5^6 but equals 2×5^3

and :

2×5^3 does not equal 10^3 ! $(2 \times 5^3 = 250)$ (which cannot be simplified
                                                           to index form.)

8.   Simplify these numbers leaving the answer in index form:
   a) $3^3 + 3^3$ b) $4^2 + 4^2$ c) $5^3 + 5^3$
   d) $7^2 + 7^2$ e) $5^2 + 5^2$ f) $7^3 + 7^3$

9.   Simplify these numbers IF POSSIBLE leaving the answer in index form:
   a) $2^3 + 3^3$ b) $3^2 \times 4^2$ c) $5^3 \times 5^3$
   d) $7^2 \div 7^2$ e) 5×5^2 f) 3×7^3

Negative Indices

What happens if we divide 5^3 by 5^6?
We can look at this in two ways:

$$5^3 \div 5^6 = 5^{3-6} \qquad\qquad\qquad 5^3 \div 5^6 = \frac{5^3}{5^6}$$

or

$$= 5^{-3} \qquad\qquad\qquad\qquad = \frac{1}{5^3}$$

Therefore: $5^{-3} = \dfrac{1}{5^3}$

As $5^3 \div 5^3 = 5^{3-3}$ and also $5^3 \div 5^3 = 1$
                      $= 5^0$
it follows that $5^0 = 1$

In fact any positive number to the power 0 is one.

The table of powers of 5 on page 48 can then continue:

$5^2 = 5 \times 5 = 25$
$5^1 = 5$
$5^0 = 1$

$5^{-1} = \dfrac{1}{5}$

$5^{-2} = \dfrac{1}{25}$

$5^{-3} = \dfrac{1}{125}$ etc.

Exercise 4B

Use a calculator when necessary with this exercise.

1.   Write these in index form:

   a) $\dfrac{1}{2 \times 2 \times 2}$ b) $\dfrac{1}{9 \times 9}$ c) $\dfrac{1}{3 \times 3 \times 3}$

   d) $\dfrac{1}{8 \times 8}$ e) $\dfrac{1}{2 \times 2 \times 2 \times 2 \times 2}$ f) $\dfrac{1}{4 \times 4 \times 4}$

2. Work out the actual fractions in question 1.

3. Write these in index form

a) $\dfrac{1}{9}$ b) $\dfrac{1}{8}$ c) $\dfrac{1}{49}$ d) $\dfrac{1}{144}$

e) $\dfrac{1}{128}$ f) $\dfrac{1}{27}$ g) $\dfrac{1}{216}$ h) $\dfrac{1}{625}$

4. a) $3^3 \div 3^6$ b) $6 \div 6^4$ c) $4^3 \div 4^7$
  d) $7^3 \div 7^5$ e) $3^2 \div 3^2$ f) $7 \div 7^5$

5. a) $2^5 \times 2^{-2}$ b) $4^{-7} \times 4^3$ c) $5^{-8} \times 5^7$
  d) $7^5 \times 7^{-1}$ e) $3^5 \times 3^{-2}$ f) $7^{-3} \times 7$

6. a) $4^3 \times 4^3 \times 4^{-2}$ b) $5^7 \times 5^2 \times 5^{-4}$ c) $2^3 \times 2^3 \times 2^{-2}$
  d) $7^2 \times 7^4 \times 7^{-9}$ e) $3^2 \times 3^2 \times 3^{-3}$ f) $7^3 \times 7^2 \times 7^{-5}$

7. a) $3^3 \times 3^{-3}$ b) $6^3 \times 6^{-5}$ c) $4^2 \times 4^{-3}$
  d) $4^2 \div 4^{-2}$ e) $3^2 \div 3^{-5}$ f) $7^3 \div 7^{-7}$

Solving Equations With x^2

Exercise 4C

Example: $$x^2 = 9$$ $$x = 3$$

Solve these equations:

1. $x^2 = 1$ 6. $a^2 = 64$
2. $a^2 = 100$ 7. $x^2 = 0.09$
3. $b^2 = 49$ 8. $a^2 = 1600$
4. $c^2 = 8$ 9. $b^2 = 0.16$
5. $y^2 = 4$ 10. $y^2 = 400$

Squares And Square Roots

Since x^2 is $= x \times x$, we say that x is the SQUARE ROOT of x^2.

1 is the square of 1, and of -1 1 and -1 are the square roots of 1
4 is the square of 2, and of -2 2 and -2 are the square roots of 4
9 is the square of 3, and of -3 3 and -3 are the square roots of 9
16 is the square of 4, and of -4 4 and -4 are the square roots of 16

In reality we rarely need to use the negative square root and for the rest of this chapter we are only going to consider positive square roots.

The positive square root of 4 is written: $\sqrt{4} = 2$

Exercise 4D

Find these squares and square roots:

1. $\sqrt{16}$

2. $\sqrt{25}$

3. $\sqrt{10\ 000}$

4. 0.4^2

5. 1.2^2

6. $\sqrt{0.25}$

7. $\sqrt{144}$

8. 100^2

9. 0.1^2

10. $\sqrt{121}$

11. $\sqrt{0.0036}$

12. $\sqrt{1.21}$

13. 0.01^2

14. $\left(\dfrac{0.3}{0.2}\right)^2$

15. $\sqrt{0.01}$

16. $\left(\dfrac{1}{10}\right)^2$

17. $\sqrt{\dfrac{1}{25}}$

18. $\left(\dfrac{1}{2}\right)^2$

19. $\left(\dfrac{2}{3}\right)^2$

20. $\sqrt{\dfrac{1}{9}}$

21. $\sqrt{\dfrac{4}{25}}$

22. $\sqrt{\dfrac{4^2}{2^2}}$

23. $\left(\dfrac{\sqrt{16}}{\sqrt{36}}\right)^2$

24. $\sqrt{\dfrac{16^2}{2^2}}$

Using Prime Factors to Find Square Roots

Consider the numbers: $2 \times 2 \times 2 \times 2 \times 3 \times 3 \times 3 \times 3$
this could be written: $(2 \times 2 \times 3 \times 3) \times (2 \times 2 \times 3 \times 3)$

or:
$$2^4 \times 3^4 = \left(2^2 \times 3^2\right) \times \left(2^2 \times 3^2\right)$$
$$= (2^2 \times 3^2)^2$$

therefore $2^2 \times 3^2$ is the square root of $2^4 \times 3^4$

Exercise 4E

Write these numbers as the product of their prime factors and hence find their square root:

Example: Find the square root of 441   1

$$3\overline{)441}$$
$$3\overline{)147}$$
$$7\overline{)\ 49}$$
$$7\overline{)\ \ 7}$$
$$1$$

$441 = 3^2 \times 7^2 = (3 \times 7) \times (3 \times 7)$

$\sqrt{441} = 3 \times 7 \quad = 21$

1. 144	**5.** 2025	**9.** 1089
2. 225	**6.** 196	**10.** 3969
3. 576	**7.** 324	**11.** 3136
4. 1521	**8.** 1225	**12.** 7056

Other Roots

$2 \times 2 = 4$ and so 2 is the square root of 4

$2 \times 2 \times 2 = 8$ and so 2 is the cube root of 8 and is written: $\sqrt[3]{8} = 2$

$2 \times 2 \times 2 \times 2 = 16$ and so 2 is the fourth root of 16 and is written: $\sqrt[4]{16} = 2$

Exercise 4F
Find these powers and roots:

1. 3^6	**6.** 2^8	**11.** $\sqrt[8]{256}$
2. 6^4	**7.** $\sqrt[4]{81}$	**12.** $\sqrt[4]{256}$
3. $\sqrt[3]{125}$	**8.** 3^5	**13.** $\sqrt[3]{729}$
4. 9^3	**9.** $\sqrt[6]{729}$	**14.** $\sqrt[4]{625}$
5. $\sqrt[4]{16}$	**10.** 4^4	**15.** Try $5^2, 6^2, 25^2$

You should notice that the three numbers that have been squared appear as the last figure, or figures, in the answer. There are only three other numbers between 25 and 100 which do this, can you work out what they are?

16. Think of a number, square it. (e.g. 42^2)
Now add 1 to the number and square that (e.g. 43^2)
Now take the original square away from the 1st square (e.g. $43^2 - 42^2$)
Subtract 1 and divide your answer by 2. What do you have?
Try this with some other numbers and see if you always get the same result!

Roots As Indices

We now know that $\quad 5^3 \times 5^2 = 5^5 \qquad N.B.\ 3 + 2 = 5$
but $\quad 5 \times 5 = 25$ and therefore 5 is the square root of 25

What is the square root of 5?

Let x be the square root of 5.

$$5^x \times 5^x = 5$$
$$x + x = 1$$
$$2x = 1$$
$$x = \frac{1}{2}$$
$$and \qquad 5^{\frac{1}{2}} \times 5^{\frac{1}{2}} = 5$$

Therefore $5^{\frac{1}{2}}$ is another way of writing $\sqrt{5}$.

Calculating With Roots And Powers

Exercise 4G

Examples:

$$7^{\frac{1}{2}} \times 7^{\frac{1}{2}} \times 7^{\frac{1}{2}} \times 7^{\frac{1}{2}} = 7^{\frac{1}{2}+\frac{1}{2}+\frac{1}{2}+\frac{1}{2}}$$

$$= 7^2$$

$$\left(\sqrt{2}\right)^4 = \sqrt{2} \times \sqrt{2} \times \sqrt{2} \times \sqrt{2}$$

$$= 2 \times 2$$

$$= 2^2$$

1. $\sqrt{3} \times \sqrt{3}$ **5.** $\sqrt{3} \times \sqrt{3} \times \sqrt{3}$ **9.** $(5^{\frac{1}{2}})^2$

2. $7^{\frac{1}{2}} \times 7^{\frac{1}{2}}$ **6.** $\sqrt{7} \times \sqrt{7} \times \sqrt{7} \times \sqrt{7}$ **10.** $(3^{\frac{1}{2}})^4$

3. $\sqrt{11} \times \sqrt{11}$ **7.** $5^{\frac{1}{2}} \times 5^{\frac{1}{2}} \times 5^{\frac{1}{2}} \times 5^{\frac{1}{2}}$ **11.** $(\sqrt{7})^2$

4. $2^{\frac{1}{2}} \times 2^{\frac{1}{2}}$ **8.** $\sqrt{5} \times \sqrt{5} \times \sqrt{5}$ **12.** $(3^{\frac{1}{2}})^8$

Usinge The Index Functions On The Calculator

The square roots we have calculated so far come out to be either a whole number or a limited number of decimal places.

However most square roots do not come out so easily,

For example we know that $2^2 = 4$ and so $\sqrt{4} = 2$

and that $20^2 = 400$ and so $\sqrt{400} = 20$

but what about $\sqrt{40}$?

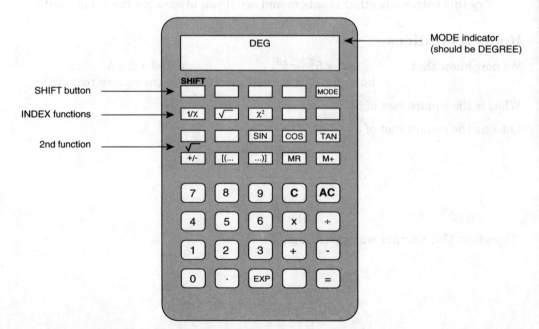

We cannot just work this out by looking at it, we have to use a calculator.

Find the Index Functions and the Second Function buttons on your calculator.

Find the $\sqrt{}$ button, it may be a second function.

On older models enter **4** **0** then; $\boxed{\sqrt{}}$ with a VPAM calculator enter $\boxed{\sqrt{}}$ then.
4 **0** Your calculator will read 6.324553 etc.
As this is not an exact amount we should round it up to one or two decimal places:
6.324553 = 6.3 (to 1 d.p.) or 6.32 (to 2 d.p.)

Second Function

Second functions are the functions written above the actual function button. Typically the cube root button: $\sqrt[3]{}$ is a second function. To find a cube root you have to push the 2nd function button (often marked SHIFT) and then the cube root button (often the +/– button).

Index Functions

Index functions refer to functions that find the square, the cube, the square root, the cube root, the reciprocal and other such functions. Exactly how they work depends on your calculator. Many are second functions. Let us start by finding the cube root of 8.

For older models enter 8, second function (or shift) then cube root. You should have the answer 2. If you get no answer or 0 you probably have a VPAM calculator. Press 2nd function (or shift) then the cube root and then 8. Your answer should be 2. If you cannot find this cube root then ask your teacher or refer to the manual.

Exercise 4H

1. Find these squares: $5^2, 15^2, 23^2, 125^2$

2. Find these square roots: $\sqrt{25}, \sqrt{289}, \sqrt{576}, \sqrt{262144}$

3. Calculate $\frac{1}{5}$. (Use the reciprocal button that is $\frac{1}{x}$) Now push the reciprocal button again, then again and again. What do you notice? Try this with some other numbers.

4. Look for this button: $\boxed{x^y}$. This will find you any power of any number.
    To find 3^5 you should enter 3 then the x^y button, then 5, and then enter. You should see the number 243. Now try these:
    $$2^7, 5^7, 7^4, 2^{20}.$$

5. Find the cube roots of the following:
    $$216, \quad 1728, 8000, \ 1\,953\,125$$

6. Look for this button: $\boxed{\sqrt[y]{x}}$. This is probably a second function and finds any
    root of any number. Use this button to find the cube roots of all the numbers above in question 12. Now try these:
    $$\sqrt[4]{16}, \sqrt[5]{243}, \sqrt[7]{78125}$$

Using The Memory

For harder calculations you may need to use the memory, particularly when your answers are not whole numbers.

Try subtracting the square root of 37 from the square root of 56. You should obtain the answer 1.005522. If not ask your teacher.

(For VPAM calculators the key sequence to try is $\sqrt{\ }$, 56, M+ , $\sqrt{\ }$, 37, M–, MR, for older models the key sequence to try is 56 , $\sqrt{\ }$, M+, 37, $\sqrt{\ }$, M–, MR.)

7.   Calculate $\sqrt[3]{39} - \sqrt{20}$.

These are much harder, see if you can get the right answers:

8. $\sqrt{\dfrac{3.1 \times 0.9}{1.5 \times 2.1}} + \sqrt{\dfrac{2.5 \times 1.9}{1.5 \times 0.7}}$

9. $\sqrt{(31^5 - 27^4)}$

10. $\dfrac{\sqrt{352 \times 612}}{\sqrt{295 \times 176}}$

11. $\dfrac{\sqrt{423} + \sqrt{132}}{\sqrt{645} - \sqrt{312}}$

12 $\dfrac{\sqrt[3]{27}}{\sqrt[4]{256}} - \dfrac{\sqrt[5]{243}}{\sqrt[7]{128}}$

13. $\sqrt[4]{\dfrac{317 \times 212}{412 \times 126}}$

14. $\dfrac{\sqrt[3]{321 \times 712}}{\sqrt[4]{211 \times 552}}$

15. $\sqrt[3]{\dfrac{105 \times 75}{136 - 73}}$

16. $\sqrt[4]{\dfrac{10^4 + 7^4}{3^5 + 4^3}} - \sqrt[7]{\dfrac{5^6 - 4^5}{3^3 + 2^4}}$

17. Use Worksheet 4/1 to help Captain H2O on his second space adventure. This time there is an added catch. You have to work out the names of the p l a n e t s written *upside-down*. The calculations all come out to an upside down word, so if yours do not then you have gone wrong - try again!

EARTH

$$\dfrac{5^2 (6284 - 4015)}{\sqrt[8]{390\ 625}}$$

Captain
H2O

Writing Answers

In the above calculations answers have been written to a full display of your calculator. Some problems require quite lengthy working, with final answers given to 3 significant figures or 2 decimal places. It is important that each stage of working is clearly shown and that **only** the final answer is rounded off - never calculate with rounded off answers, use the full display on your calculator. This will be covered in full in the relevant chapters.

Extension Exercise 4   More About Square Roots

Consider $\sqrt{4}$.

What number multiplied by itself makes 4?

$2 \times 2 = 4$ but also $-2 \times -2 = 4$

and so we can say $\sqrt{4} = \pm 2$

Find BOTH square roots of these numbers:

1.	1	**5.**	121	**9.**	361
2.	9	**6.**	289	**10.**	625
3.	16	**7.**	256	**11.**	324
4.	81	**8.**	144	**12.**	225

While it is important to be aware that a number has a positive and a negative square root for the rest of this exercise we are going to consider the POSITIVE square root only. Consider $\sqrt{3}$. There is no whole number answer to $\sqrt{3}$ and so it is often easier to leave the number as $\sqrt{3}$. This is particularly true when calculating with roots.

Consider $\sqrt{3} \times \sqrt{3}$ $\sqrt{3} \times \sqrt{3} = \sqrt{9} = 3$

similarly $\sqrt{3} \times \sqrt{12} = \sqrt{36} = 6$

Work out these products of square roots. Some come out to a whole number answer, and some do not. If not then leave the answer in root firm.

13. $\sqrt{3} \times \sqrt{48}$	**17.** $\sqrt{2} \times \sqrt{2} \times \sqrt{2}$	**21.** $\sqrt{3} \times \sqrt{18}$
14. $\sqrt{8} \times \sqrt{32}$	**18.** $\sqrt{5} \times \sqrt{25}$	**22.** $\sqrt{8} \times \sqrt{18}$
15. $\sqrt{3} \times \sqrt{7}$	**19.** $\sqrt{12} \times \sqrt{27}$	**23.** $\sqrt{3} \times \sqrt{27}$
16. $\sqrt{3} \times \sqrt{2} \times \sqrt{6}$	**20.** $\sqrt{7} \times \sqrt{28}$	**24.** $\sqrt{6} \times \sqrt{54}$

The numbers that you ended up with that are written in root form include:
$$\sqrt{8}, \sqrt{125}, \sqrt{48}.$$

Although these are not whole number square roots they are multiples of square numbers:

$$\sqrt{8} = \sqrt{2 \times 4} \qquad \sqrt{125} = \sqrt{5 \times 25} \qquad \sqrt{48} = \sqrt{3 \times 16}$$
$$= \sqrt{2} \times \sqrt{4} \qquad\quad = \sqrt{5} \times \sqrt{25} \qquad\quad = \sqrt{3} \times \sqrt{16}$$
$$= 2\sqrt{2} \qquad\qquad\quad = 5\sqrt{5} \qquad\qquad\quad = 4\sqrt{3}$$

Simplify these:

25. $\sqrt{2} \times \sqrt{3} \times \sqrt{10}$	**29.** $\sqrt{21} \times \sqrt{14}$	**33.** $\sqrt{6} \times \sqrt{18} \times \sqrt{4}$
26. $\sqrt{2} \times \sqrt{4} \times \sqrt{8}$	**30.** $\sqrt{6} \times \sqrt{12}$	**34.** $\sqrt{3} \times \sqrt{12} \times \sqrt{15}$
27. $\sqrt{3} \times \sqrt{5} \times \sqrt{15}$	**31.** $\sqrt{8} \times \sqrt{24}$	
28. $\sqrt{8} \times \sqrt{12}$	**32.** $\sqrt{12} \times \sqrt{15}$	

Expressions with square roots can be factorised and simplified :

Examples:

$$\sqrt{3} \times \sqrt{6} + \sqrt{72} = \sqrt{18} + \sqrt{72} \qquad simplify$$

$$= \sqrt{2} \times \sqrt{9} + \sqrt{2} \times \sqrt{36} \qquad factorise$$

$$= 3\sqrt{2} + 6\sqrt{2} \qquad extract\ squares$$

$$= 9\sqrt{2} \qquad simplify$$

$$\frac{1}{\sqrt{2}} + \sqrt{2} = \frac{1 + \sqrt{2} \times \sqrt{2}}{\sqrt{2}} \qquad find\ common\ denominator$$

$$= \frac{1 + 2}{\sqrt{2}}$$

$$= \frac{3}{\sqrt{2}} \times \frac{\sqrt{2}}{\sqrt{2}} \qquad make\ denominator\ a\ whole\ number$$

$$= \frac{3\sqrt{2}}{2} \qquad simplify$$

Simplify these:

35. $\sqrt{72} \times \sqrt{50}$

41. $\dfrac{1}{\sqrt{8}} + \dfrac{1}{\sqrt{12}}$

36. $\sqrt{12} \times \sqrt{27}$

42. $\dfrac{1}{\sqrt{5}} + \sqrt{5}$

37. $\sqrt{20} \times \sqrt{45}$

43. $\dfrac{7}{\sqrt{7}} - \sqrt{7}$

38. $\sqrt{20} \times \sqrt{10} + \sqrt{15} \times \sqrt{5}$

44. $\dfrac{3}{\sqrt{2}} - \sqrt{2}$

39 $\sqrt{8} \times \sqrt{10} + \sqrt{9} \times \sqrt{20}$

45. $\dfrac{\sqrt{3}}{\sqrt{2}} + \dfrac{\sqrt{2}}{\sqrt{3}}$

40. $\dfrac{\sqrt{3}}{3} + \sqrt{3}$

46. $\dfrac{\sqrt{6} + \sqrt{6}}{\sqrt{3}}$

Summary Exercise 4

1. Write these in index form:
   a) $3 \times 3 \times 3$
   b) $4 \times 4 \times 4 \times 4 \times 4$
   c) $2 \times 2 \times 2 \times 2 \times 2 \times 2$
   d) $7 \times 7 \times 7$

2. Now write down the answers to question one .

3. Write these numbers in index form:
   a) 8
   b) 125
   c) 64
   d) 81

4. Write these as fractions in index form:
   a) 2^{-2}
   b) 3^{-5}
   c) 7^{-3}

5. Simplify these, if possible, leaving your answer in index form:
   a) $3^2 \times 3^4$
   b) $5^3 \times 5^7$
   c) $7^5 \div 7^2$
   d) $5^4 \div 5$
   e) $3^2 \div 3^5$
   f) $2^2 \div 2^8$
   g) $3^3 + 3^3$
   h) $3^3 + 2^3$
   i) $5^2 \div 3^3$
   j) $6^4 \div 2^4$
   k) $3^3 \times 5^2$
   l) $5^3 - 4^2$

6. Simplify these leaving your answers in index form:
   a) $4^2 \times 4^{-3}$
   b) $2^7 \times 2^{-5}$
   c) $3^{-2} \div 3^3$
   c) $5^{-2} \div 5^2$
   d) $4^{-2} + 4^{-2}$
   e) $7^2 \times 7^{-2}$

7. Solve these equations:
   a) $x^2 = 16$
   b) $a^2 = 100$
   c) $b^2 = \frac{1}{4}$
   d) $y^2 = 0.25$
   e) $c^2 = 40\ 000$

8. Give these square roots to (i) one decimal place and (ii) two decimal places:
   a) $\sqrt{45}$
   b) $\sqrt{0.35}$
   c) $\sqrt{135}$

9. Find these:
   a) $\sqrt{3136}$
   b) 9^4
   c) $\sqrt[3]{512}$
   d) $\sqrt[5]{\frac{412+321}{129 \times 63}}$
   e) $\frac{\sqrt[4]{8^5 - 5^4}}{\sqrt[5]{9^3 - 7^5}}$

10. a) Can you find two numbers x and y so that x^y is the same as y^x ?
    b) What does that tell you if anything about $\sqrt[y]{x}$ and $\sqrt[x]{y}$?

Activity 4 - Investigation Chain Letters

Investigation Chain Letters

You may well have received a letter reading something like this:

> "How do you like receiving letters? Most of us do, and this letter is to guarantee that you receive hundreds of letters. All you have to do is to send a letter to the person at the top of the list below. Then copy out this letter 5 times, take off the top person from the list and add your name at the bottom. Then send the five copies to five of your best friends."
> 1. John Smith
> 2. Sara Ing
> 3. Pete Black
> 4. Imran Patel
> 5. Claire Jones

P.S. Don't break the chain and don't tell the post office - they think this is illegal!

Let us consider how true is the claim that you will receive hundreds of letters. This letter takes 5 stages to move you up to the top of the list.

Therefore your 5 friends will send letters to 5 friends who will send letters to 5 friends who will send letters to 5 friends who will send letters to 5 friends who will all send me a letter.

1.   How many letters will I receive if the chain has not been broken? (not 25 !)

2.   How many letters should I receive if their were 6 people on the list and I had sent letters to 6 friends?

3.   How many letters would I receive if there were 5 people on the list but everybody in the chain sent out ten copies to friends?

4.   Investigate this for different numbers of people on the list and different numbers of copies. Can you find a rule for the number of letters that you receive in theory and the number of copies that you send out?

5.   One of the most famous chain letter "scams" (and one of the reason that these are illegal) asked you to sent £10 to the person at the top of the list and then "sell" your letters for £1 each to ten other people. This time there was a list of 10 people before you were sent the £10's. How may people should have been in the chain by then? How does this compare to the population of Britain?

A great many people lost their £10 this time because everybody else had heard of it first - and most broke the chain!

Chapter 5

Percentages

A percentage is another way of writing a hundredth,

and so 7% is equivalent to $\dfrac{7}{100}$ or, as a decimal, 0.07

There is such an important connection between percentages, fractions and decimals that it is important to be fully confident in converting from one to the other.

Remember:

To turn fractions to decimals:
  Divide the top number (numerator)
  by the bottom number (denominator)

$$\frac{3}{8} = 3 \div 8 = 0.125$$

To turn decimals or fractions into percentages:

  Multiply by 100

$$0.125 = 01.25 \times 100\%$$
$$= 12.5\% \text{ or } 12\tfrac{1}{2}\%$$

To turn percentages into decimals:
  Divide by 100

$$85\% = 85 \div 100$$
$$= 0.85$$

To turn percentages into fractions:
  Write as a fraction with 100
  as the denominator
  and simplify if possible.

$$72\% = \frac{72}{100} = \frac{18}{25}$$

To turn decimals into fractions:
  Write a fraction with the
  correct denominator (10, 100, 1000 ...)
  and simplify if possible.

$$0.64 = \frac{64}{100} = \frac{16}{25}$$

It is also important to be able to form a percentage and to find a percentage of an amount.

Forming A Percentage

For example:

My Maths result was 24 out of 40, what is this as a percentage?

$$\text{Percentage} = \frac{\overset{6}{24}}{\underset{1}{40}} \times 10\cancel{0}$$

$$= 60\%$$

Finding A Fraction Of An Amount

Example:

Everything is marked down 20% in the Sale.

What is the Sale price of a Discman previously marked at £88?

$$\text{Discount} = \frac{20}{100} \times 88$$

$$= \frac{176}{10}$$

$$= £17.60$$

$$\text{Sale Price} = £88.00 - £17.60$$

$$= £62.40$$

This exercise is to revise these concepts. When using the fraction method the numbers should cancel down and you should not need a calculator. Check the answers with a calculator to verify your arithmetic.

Exercise 5A

1. Write the following fractions as (i) percentages: and then (ii) decimals.

   a) $\frac{1}{5}$ b) $\frac{3}{10}$ c) $\frac{5}{8}$ d) $\frac{4}{25}$

2. Write these percentages as (i) decimals and then (ii) fractions.
   a) 14%   b) 65%   c) 33%   d) 44%

3. These percentages all contain a fraction, but you should recognise their fraction equivalents. Write them as (i) fractions and then (ii) decimals:

   a) $12\frac{1}{2}\%$ b) $66\frac{2}{3}\%$ c) $16\frac{1}{6}\%$ d) $37\frac{1}{2}\%$

4. Here are some recurring decimals.
   Write them as (i) fractions and then (ii) decimals.

   a) $0.\dot{3}$ b) $0.8\dot{3}$ c) $0.\dot{2}$

5. 88% of my class had a BCG inoculation. What percentage did not?

6. 64% of people fail their driving test first time. What percentage pass?

7. What is 10% of £35?

8. What is 60% of 3m?

9. What is 25% of two hours?

10. What is 35% of £5 ?

11. What is 63% of 500km ?

12. In my class of 25 , 11 of us had flu. What percentage of the class is that?

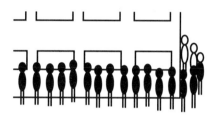

13. The cost of cat food has risen 5%. If it was 40p per can, what is it now?

14. In the sale, prices are marked down 12%. What is the sale price of:
    a) A pair of trainers normally costing £20?
    b) A jacket normally costing £35?
    c) A CD player normally costing £90 ?

15. We picked 65 apples but 26 of them had maggots in them. What percentage did not?

16. A have negotiated a rise of 15% in my pocket money. If it was £5 per week what is it now?

17. If income tax is 25% how much tax do I pay on earnings of £2 500?

18. My father made 120 bottles of home made wine. Only 35 bottles were drinkable! What percentage is that?

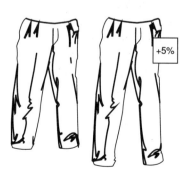

19. Extra long jeans cost 5% more than standard length ones. If standard jeans are £25 how much are extra long jeans?

20. My friend and I were cleaning cars to raise money. When we had finished we worked out our costs as £2 per car, and realised we had made a 15% loss. What were we charging?

21. I cooked 144 mince pies for the Christmas Fayre, but 48 of them burnt. What percentage of them did not burn?

22. Service charge at our local Hamburger Restaurant is 15%. How much service was added on to our food bill of £25?

23. There is 10% discount from our computer suppliers for orders over £100. If boxes of ten discs usually cost £12, how many boxes must we buy before we qualify for the discount and how much will we save?

24. What percentage of this pie chart is:
    a) red?
    b) blue?
    c) yellow?

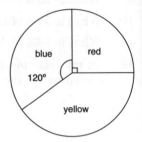

25. In a survey of 300 pupils in the school 120 came to school by car, 50 walked , 70 came on a school bus and the rest came by public transport.
    a) What percentage came by public transport?
    b) Show this information on a pie chart?

Percentage as a Decimal

The first exercise was done without a calculator and therefore used the fraction method so that the numbers would cancel to give easier arithmetic. However you will usually have more complicated numbers - and a calculator. While you can use the fraction method using a calculator it is more efficient to convert the percentage to a decimal.

For example:

Value Added Tax is currently $17\frac{1}{2}$ %. Find the V.A.T. on a computer costing £599.

V.A.T.	$= 17\frac{1}{2}$ % of £599	$17\frac{1}{2}$ %= 0.175
	$= 0.175 \times £599$	*(write down the calculation you are entering)*
	$= £104.825$	*(write the full answer from your calculator)*
	$= £104.83$ (to 2 d.p.)	*(money is usually written to the nearest penny)*

Note the way that the answer is structured. It is important that your calculations are clearly written. You need to write out the full answer given on the display in case you need to use it in a subsequent calculation. Work on building up good habits and you will not have to unlearn bad ones!

Finding a percentage using a calculator is done in the same way as before:

For example:

I had £120 in my building society and a year later, after interest has been added, I have £129. What rate of interest was applied?

Interest earned = 129 − 120 = £9

Interest Rate $= \dfrac{9}{120} \times 100$

$= 7.5\%$

Exercise 5B

Use a calculator for this exercise. Write down all working carefully.
You need Worksheet 5/1 for question 1.

1. Work through Worksheet 5/1 using your calculator. You will find it helpful to record your routes and the values calculated on the way to your targets.

2. V.A.T. is currently $17\frac{1}{2}\%$. Find the V.A.T. on these articles:

Teddy bear £12

Fax Machine £279

Tennis Racquet £49

Bicycle £150

Baseball Cap £2.50

Footbal £16

3. Find the selling price of the articles in question 1.

4.   All prices are marked down 15% in a sale. What discount is there on these articles:

Kite £15   Beach Ball £4   Walkman £35

Alarm Clock 12

Stereo System £150

Kettle £25

5.   What is the selling price of these articles in the sale?

6.   My grandfather opened a building society account for me and put in £80. If the interest rate is 6% how much interest did I earn in one year?

7.   A computer was marked at £699, but we bought it in the sale for £550. By what percentage was the computer marked down?

8.   Tennis balls are normally sold for 99p each. In the sale there are two 'bargain packs'; I can either buy 4 balls for £3.60 or 6 balls for £5.50. Which pack gives the larger percentage discount?

9.   Theatre tickets are normally £12, but if you have a party of 10 or more people you save 15%. How many tickets do we have to buy to get two people in for free?

Percentage Increase And Decrease

In the above exercises there have been several examples of amounts rising or falling through a percentage increase or decrease. It can be quite confusing to work out whether some charges result in a rise or fall. These are the ones that you are most likely to meet:

Decrease	**Increase**
Discount	Premium
Sale Price	Surcharge
Income Tax	Value Added Tax (VAT)
Devaluation	Service Charge
No-Claims Bonus	Commission
Loss	Profit

When we are talking about percentage problems we are frequently talking about money. Some decreases are good things in that we save money, for example discounts, sale prices and no-claims bonus; while others mean that we have less money or need to spend more, for example income tax and devaluation.

Most increases cost us money, if we are **buying** services. Commission, VAT, and service charges are all added to the bill and therefore increase the cost. However if we are **selling** services then these percentages make up our earnings. Some professions rely entirely on percentage commissions for their income.

Calculating Percentage Increase And Decrease

In the last exercise you calculated VAT as a percentage and then added it to the original price to find the selling price.
This can be done in one calculation. Consider the original price as being 100% of itself, you then add VAT as $17\frac{1}{2}$ % of the original price and that gives you $117\frac{1}{2}$ %

Original Price	VAT		New Price
100%	+ $17\frac{1}{2}$ %	=	$117\frac{1}{2}$ % or 1.175

The number 1.175 is known as the **multiplying factor**. If you multiply all the prices in Question 2 of the last exercise by 1.175 you should get the prices in question 3.

A sale price involves a percentage decrease and so the percentage sum looks like this:

Original Price	Discount		New Price
100%	− 15%	=	85% or 0.85

The number 0.85 is known as the **multiplying factor**. If you multiply all the prices in Question 4 of the last exercise by 0.85 you should get the prices in question 5.

Example:
A service charge of 12% is added to my restaurant bill of £52.50.
a) What is the total amount of my bill?

  Total amount = 1.12 × 52.50
          = £58.80

b) The value of my car has dropped 12% over the last year.
If it was worth £5 000 last year what is its current value?

  New value = 0.88 × 5 000
        = £4 400

Exercise 5C

1. Multiply all the prices in Question 2 of the previous exercise by 1.175 and check that you get the answers in Question 3.

2. Multiply all the answers in Question 3 of the previous exercise by 0.85 and check that you get the answers in Question 4.

3. Write down the **multiplying factor** in the following examples:

    a) an increase of 4%   h) service charge of $12\frac{1}{2}$%
    b) a surcharge of 5%   i) a premium of 10%
    c) a discount of 8%   j) commission at 8%
    d) income tax at 20%   k) a devaluation of 16%
    e) a saving of 18%   l) a decrease of 32%
    f) a no-claims bonus of 15%   m) supertax at 40%
    g) commission at 2%

4. Trainers are normally sold at £35 a pair. In the sale they are marked down 12%. What is the sale price of the trainers?

5. A service charge of 12% is added on to my bill. If the bill was £25 what is the amount I have to pay?

6. My local pizza take away is offering 10% off all orders over £15 this week. If I order two pizzas at £8.25 each what will I have to pay?

7. We are trying to sell our house for £150 000. The estate agents commission will be 2%. How much money would be actually received from the sale?

8. A new car is said to devalue 15% in its first year and 10% in its second year. If my mother bought a new car costing £8 500 two years ago what was its value at the end of one year? What was its value at the end of two years?

9. A length of 'bungy jumping' elastic is said to stretch up to 22% of its original length. If its original length is 20m what is its maximum stretched length?

10. The instructions for cooking roast lamb tell me to roast it for 40 minutes per kg but to reduce the time by 15% if the joint is boned. For how long should I roast a 4kg boned leg of lamb?

11. Water increases in volume by 4% when it freezes and becomes ice. What is the frozen volume of 4 litres of water? Give your answer in cubic cm. (1 litre = 100 c.c.)

12. Our household insurance is normally £350, but we have earned a 12% no claims bonus. What is the new insurance premium?

Income Tax

Income Tax is worked out as a percentage of your earnings although you are allowed to earn a certain amount without having to pay tax at all.

Tax is paid to the government and different governments change the actual rate of tax depending on how much revenue they wish to raise. This is not a new practice. Your study of history should have shown many occasions when rulers, kings, and governments have raised taxes to pay for a variety of expenses - most notably to pay for wars, and for the repairs caused by war. A large part of present government expenditure goes on the National Health, Defence and Social Services.

At present income tax is charged at 20% of the first £3000 of your taxable earnings and then at 25% of all higher earnings until a threshold of £40 000. Earnings above £40 000 are taxed at 40%. All these amounts are per year.

For example: A Single man earning £16 000 p.a. has a tax free allowance of £3525. What does he earn per year after paying tax?

Taxable earnings   = 16 000 – 3525
                   = £12 475
                   = £3000 + £9475

80% of £3000   = 0.8 x 3000
               = £2 400

75% of £10 000   = 0.75 x 9475
                 = £7106.25

Earnings after tax = £3525 + £2400 + £7106.25
                   = £13 031.25

Exercise 5D

1. A single persons allowance is £3525. Work out the annual earnings for these single people:
    a) A shop assistant earning £12 000 per year.
    b) A teacher earning £20 000 per year.
    c) A nurse earning £15 000 per year.
    d) A solicitor earning £50 000 per year.

2. A married coupleÕs allowance is £4557. Work out the annual earnings for these married people:
    a) A mechanic earning £16 000 per year.
    b) A manager earning £25 000 per year.
    c) A salesman who earned £10 000 in the first six months and £8 000 in the second six months.
    d) A company chairman earning £65 000.

Percentage Change

In all the examples the percentage has meant a change of value. At times the change has been caused by a percentage such as tax, or commission or a bonus, at other times the percentage records the change in values.

A percentage is a useful way of recording change because it does not look at the actual values themselves, but at the proportion that has changed.

The percentage change can be seen from the multiplying factor:

        1.20 means a percentage increase of 20%

        0.72 means a percentage decrease of 28%

We found new values by using the calculation:

        New amount = Original amount × Multiplying factor

This can be rearranged so that :

$$\text{Multiplying factor} = \frac{\text{New Amount}}{\text{Original Amount}}$$

For example: A car dealer buys in a car for £1250, spends £200 on repairs and then sells the car for £2750. What is his percentage profit?

$$\text{Multiplying factor} = \frac{\text{New Amount}}{\text{Original Amount}}$$

$$= \frac{2750}{1250 + 200}$$

$$= 1.896...$$

$$= 1.90 \ (\text{to 3 s.f.})$$

The dealer made a 90% profit.

Exercise 5E

In each of these situations say which is the **Original Value** and which is the **New Value**, and thus whether there has been an **increase** or a **decrease**:

1. The shirt cost £15 before the sale and £12 in the sale.

2. The bill was £52.50. After VAT and service were added it was £67.86

3. I bought a car for £2500 and sold it for £1750

4. There were 416 pupils in the school last year. This year there are 395.

5. The account was £300, with commission and tax we paid £423

6. I earn £18 000 per year. I take home £1200 per month.

7. A wholesaler buys 100 discs for £50. He sells five discs for £8.

8. We paid premiums of £220 last year. We pay premiums of £190 this year.

9. The tickets cost £15 each. We paid £240 for 20 of us.

10. Now work out the percentage change in each of the above.

Finding The Original Amount

Many of the prices that we see are the result after tax has been added and deducted. If you go shopping during the sales you just see the sale price. Most shop prices have already had VAT added on. If you are running your own business it is important to know how much of a price is VAT that will go to the government and how much is the actual price that you receive.

We found new values by using the calculation:

New value = Original value x Multiplying factor

By substituting into this expression when we know the amount after a percentage increase or decrease we can find the original value.

For example: Find the original price of an article to which VAT
at $17\frac{1}{2}$ % has been added and is now marked at £23.50

New value	= Original value × Multiplying factor
£23.50	= Original value × 1.175
Original Value	= 23.50 ÷ 1.175
	= £20

Exercise 5F

The first ten of these questions ask you to find the original amount. In the next questions you must decide if you are required to find the original amount or the new amount. Give answers to 2 d.p. if they are not whole numbers.

1. A second hand car dealer makes 20% profit when he sells a car for £2640. How much did he pay for the car?

2. A stereo being sold for £58.75 includes VAT at $17\frac{1}{2}$ %. What is the price without VAT?

3. The value of our house has dropped 8% in the last year. It is now worth £147 000. What was it worth last year?

4. Our local MP won 42% fewer votes this election than the last election. If he won 14 500 votes this time how many did he win the time before?

5. A music shop is selling off last month's Top 10 CD's to make room for this month's new Top 10. By selling each CD at £9.85 the shop is giving an 18% discount. What was the price of a CD last month?

6. The volume of water increases by 4% when it freezes and becomes ice. What volume of water in litres is equivalent to a block of ice 10cm × 10cm × 25cm?

7. I have grown 5% this year and I now measure 1.60m. What was my height last year?

8. The number of pupils boarding at my school has dropped 8% in the last five years. If there are 142 pupils boarding now, how many were boarding five years ago?

9. A wholesaler buys in 25kg bags of potatoes and sells the potatoes to the public in bags of 10kg to make 25% profit. If he sells the 10kg bags at £1.20 each what did he pay for the 25kg bags?

10. A car is said to devalue 15% in its first year and then 10% in its second. If our two year old car is worth £6120 now what was it worth last year? What did we pay for it new?

11. I pay £300 premium for my car insurance after a no-claims bonus of 20%. What is my premium without the no-claims bonus?

12. An art dealer paid £4000 for a painting and sold it at a 15% loss. What was the selling price?

13. Tax at 25% is paid on our company's profits of £90 000. How much tax do we pay?

14. My accountant charges me 45% of the amount that he saves my company over the year. If I paid him £675 this year how much has he saved my company?

15. The bill including service at 15% came to £48.30. What was the bill without service?

16. In hot weather the volume of air can expand by up to 10%. If I need a maximum of 16 litres of air in my tyres when they are hot, how many cubic cm of cold air should I put in?

BILL
andg abj
shdfgu8
laidjhfr
15% service:...

17. My building society paid 8% interest in 1994 and 6% interest in 1995. If I had £237.60 in my account in January 1995 what did I have in my account in January 1996? What did I have in January 1994?

18. VAT increased from 15% to 17½%. The VAT on a television set thus increased by £10. What was the original selling price (including VAT) of the Television?

19. I found that I had had £100 put in a building society account for me when I was born, and that then everyone had forgotten about it. The money has been earning 6% interest per year. How much money do I have in my account on my thirteenth birthday?

20. I find that, as I am under 18 and not earning, I am entitled to extra interest of 2% per annum. What is the amount that I actually receive on my 13th birthday?

Extension Exercise 5

Compound Interest

Did you get the last two questions of the previous exercise right?

Let us look at the situation in more detail.

If I invest £100 for a year at 6% at the end of the year I will have £100 × 1.06 in my account.

If I keep that amount in my account for another year at the same interest rate I will have [(£100 × 1.06) × 1.06] in my account.

This amount can be re-written as £100 × 1.06^2.

If I keep this amount in my account for a third year at the same interest rate I will then have [(£100 × 1.06^2) × 1.06] in the account.

This amount can be re-written as £100 × 1.06^3.

If this then continues for 13 years then the amount in the account will total:

$$£100 × 1.06^{13}.$$

How do we work that out? Find the button $\boxed{x^y}$ on your calculator . (It may be y^x and it may be a second function)

1.06^{13} is found by entering 1.06 then pressing the $\boxed{x^y}$ button and then enter 13 and then =.

To do the whole calculation in one go enter 100, then × and then open brackets. Enter 1.06, then press the $\boxed{x^y}$ button and then enter 13.

Close the brackets and then press =. You should have £213.292 83

In the next question the interest rate has increased by 2% and is now 8%. Do the calculation again using 1.08 instead of 1.06. Your answer should be £217.962 37.

A common mistake is to increase the answer 213.292 83 by 2%, but you can see that this does not give the correct answer - **it is important to always work out percentage problems from first principles**.

This calculation of the interest gained over several years is called compound interest. If C is the capital invested, at x% for n years then the formula for the amount received at the end of that period is:

$$\text{New amount} = C \times \left(1 + \frac{x}{100}\right)^n$$

For example:

If £150 is invested for 10 years at 5%, how much is in the bank after that time?

$$\text{New amount} = C \times \left(1 + \frac{x}{100}\right)^n$$

$$= 150 \times 1.05^{10}$$

$$= £244.334\ 19$$

$$= £244.33 \ (\text{to 2 d.p.})$$

1. £50 is invested at birth for a baby. The interest rate is fixed at 8%.
    How much will be in the bank when the baby becomes:
    a) five years old?   c) ten years old?
    b) 18 years old?   d) 21 years old?

2. Banks pay higher interest for larger deposits. If I invest £5000 in a bank at a
    fixed interest rate of 12% what will be in the bank after:
    a) one year?   b) three years?   c) five years?

3. A car reduces in value by 12% each year. If A car cost £12 000 when it was new
    what will it be worth when it is:
    a) two years old   b) five years old c) ten years old.
    d) What does the car actually lose in value in its first year?
    e) What does the car actually lose in value in its tenth year?

4. I receive an annual salary of £20 000.
    a) If my pay increases at a steady rate of 5% per annum what should I be earning
    in 5 years time?
    b) How many years will it take for my salary to double to £40 000 per annum?
    c) If I am 30 years old now and my salary continues to increase at the same rate
    will I ever receive £60 000 before I retire at 65 years old?
    d) What salary will I be receiving before I retire?

5. a) The population of China was expanding at 10% per annum. How many years
    does it take for the population to double?
    b) After strict population controls the population of China has started to fall by
    2%. How many years will it take to halve the size of the population?

6. Assuming an average inflation rate of 5% what will be the probable cost in ten
    years time of:
    a) a family car (now £6 500)   b) A television (now £350)
    c) a kg of best rump steak (now £10)
    Assuming the same rate of inflation what would the cost of these items have
    been ten years ago?

7. Draw the graph of $y=1.05x$, taking values of x from −10 to 10.
    How could you use your graph to answer question 6?

Summary Exercise 5

1. I scored 63 marks out of 80 for my maths test. What is this as a percentage?

2. Last year I spent 1 hour and 30 minutes on my homework each night. This year I have to spend 25% longer. How much time do I now spend on homework?

3. We have 12% fewer apples from our garden this year. Last year we collected 308kg. How many did we collect this year?

4. Fred estimated that there were 500 words in his English essay. He then counted and found there were 524 words. What was the percentage error of his estimate?

5. a) If the price of a leather jacket was normally £175 what would be the price in the sale?
   b) The price of a jumper in the sale was £11.80. What was the original price?

Sale! Sale!

25% off all marked prices

6. a) The value of the Classic Macintosh has dropped by 25%. If the old price was £630 what is the new price?
   b) When the Classic first came out VAT was 15%. It is now 17.5%. If the price before VAT was £500 what difference did the change in VAT make to the price?
   c) The new model LCII is sold for £999.99. How much of this is VAT at 17.5%? Give your answer to the nearest penny.

7. My monthly allowance has risen by 40%. If it is now £28 per month what was it before?

8. The value of my house has dropped by 12% in the last year. I am told that it is worth £140 800 now. What was my house worth a year ago?

9. My journey to work at my usual speed takes 20 minutes. How long will my journey take if I increase my speed by 25%?

10. I have £2000 in the bank. Last year the interest rate was 8% and this year it has dropped to 6%. How much money will I have in the bank at the end of this year?

Activity 5 - The Trading Game

The Trading Game

On Worksheets 5/2, 5/3, 5/4 and 5/5 you will find the playing board, the nets of two dice and the money and the goods cards you need. You will probably need at least two copies of Worksheet 5/3 as you need lots of money! Start by making up the two Trading Dice. You will also need a normal dice.

The Rules of the Game

1. This game is for two players.

The Bank

2. The players take it in turn to run the bank. The older player starts by being bank but any player who changes from being a customer to being a shopkeeper or vice versa takes over the running of the bank

To Start the Game

3. Place the goods cards on the corresponding squares on the board.

4. The banker gives each player £500.

5. The playing board is in two sections. Both players start at the top left hand corner of the outer board (Budget Day) and play the game as a customer.

6. Throw a normal dice to move clockwise round the outer Board.

7. Any player landing on a special 'Become a shopkeeper' square transfers to the inner board. Shopkeepers move anticlockwise round the board.

Playing as a Customer

8. A customer moves clockwise round the outer board. The number of moves is given by throwing a normal dice. Every time you pass a budget square you receive £50.

9. If a customer lands on a 'goods square' with a goods card he is obliged to purchase the goods if he has enough money. Throw the two Trading Dice and work out what you must pay for the goods.

The price is the marked price plus or minus the percentage increase or discount given by the two dice. Pay the price of the goods into the bank and receive a goods ticket. (All prices are worked out to the nearest £1)

10. If you land on a 'Sale Square' throw again and move as before. This time if you then land on a 'Goods Square' you roll the percentage dice only and pay the marked price less **double** that percentage.

11. If you land on a 'Budget Square' throw again and move as before. This time if you then land on a 'Goods Square' you roll the percentage dice only and pay the marked price plus **double** that percentage.

12. If you land on a special 'Cash Square' then you pay or receive money from the bank.

Playing as a Shopkeeper

13. The shopkeeper moves round the board in an anticlockwise direction. When he lands on a 'Goods Square' with a goods card he is obliged to sell those goods.

14. The marked price of the goods is your selling price after your profit or loss. The trading dice represent the profit or loss that you have made. Calculate your cost price and thus your actual profit or loss.

15. If you have made a profit you receive that amount from the bank, if you have made a loss you pay that amount to the bank.

16. If you land on a 'Become A Customer Square' you cross to the outer board and play as a customer as before.

The Winner

17. The winner is the player with the most money at the end of the time allowed for the game. If any player runs out of money then he is the loser.

HAPPY TRADING!

Chapter 6

Equations And Inequalities

You should by now be quite confident at solving equations that require one or two stages to solve them. Try this first exercise to remind yourself.

Example	$\dfrac{x}{2} - 5 = 2$
	$\dfrac{x}{2} = 7$ (+5)
	$x = 14$ (×2)

Exercise 6A

1. $3x = 12$

2. $x + 5 = 7$

3. $x - 2 = 5$

4. $\dfrac{x}{3} = 2$

5. $5 + x = 9$

6. $9 - x = 7$

7. $x + 8 = 5$

8. $3 - x = 12$

9. $3x + 1 = 7$

10. $2 = 12 + 5x$

11. $\dfrac{x}{4} + 1 = 3$

12. $4 - 2x = 7$

13. $3 = 7 - 3x$

14. $4(2x - 2) = 7$

15. $4 = 3(7 + 2x)$

16. $\dfrac{x}{2} - 3 = 5$

17. $\dfrac{x + 1}{4} = 3$

18. $3 = 1 - 6x$

19. $\dfrac{1}{3}(x + 3) = 2$

20. $4 - 2x = 7$

More Equations

If I am told:

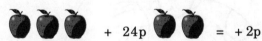 + 24p = + 2p

The cost of "2 apples and 24 pence is the same value as 3 apples and 2 pence ,"
I should be able to write an equation to find the price of an apple.
If the price of an apple is x pence

Then $2x + 24 = 3x + 2$

We solve an equation in this form in the same manner as we solved the simpler equations, we want to simplify the equation until we end up with a value of x equal to a number.

To simplify this equation we must first take $2x$ from both sides and then continue as before. It is always a help if we explain what we are doing all the way through we could have taken $3x$ from both sides, but that would leave $-x$ on the left hand side. We want to avoid negative numbers and therefore eliminate $2x$ and not $3x$

Example:	$2x + 24 = 3x + 2$
	$\qquad\qquad (-2x)$
	$24 = x + 2$
	$\qquad\qquad (-2)$
	$22 = x$
or	$x = 22$

Exercise 6B

Solve these equations:

1. $2x + 4 = x + 8$
2. $2x + 14 = 3x + 8$
3. $4x + 12 = 5x + 5$
4. $6x + 10 = 7x + 6$

5. $7x + 9 = 8x + 4$
6. $3x + 2 = x + 8$
7. $4x + 2 = x + 11$

8. $2x + 14 = 6x + 6$
9. $2x + 12 = 6x + 8$
10. $7x + 4 = 5x + 8$

In the above examples we only had to subtract numbers, in the following you may have to add them:

Example:	$4x + 12 = 7x - 3$
	$\qquad\qquad (-4x)$
	$12 = 3x - 3$
	$\qquad\qquad (+3)$
	$15 = 3x$
	$\qquad\qquad (\div 3)$
	$5 = x$
or	$x = 5$

11. $2x - 4 = x + 1$
12. $4x - 7 = 3x + 3$
13. $5x - 3 = 4x + 2$
14. $3x + 3 = 2x + 7$

15. $4x + 1 = 5x - 6$
16. $7x + 9 = 9x - 5$
17. $8x - 5 = 5x + 1$

18. $2x + 1 = 4x - 9$
19. $2x - 3 = 15 + 4x$
20. $7x - 7 = x + 11$

Sometimes when one x term has been removed a negative number is left. It is very important that this is written down clearly. Some of the following equations contain brackets, remember to multiply out the brackets before you try and solve the equation.

Example: $5(x - 2) = 5 + 8x$

            (brackets)

            $5x - 10 = 5 + 8x$

            $(-5x)$

            $-10 = 5 + 3x$

            (-5)

            $-15 = 3x$

            $(÷3)$

            $-5 = x \ or \ x = -5$

21. $3x + 1 = 2(x - 2)$ **25.** $7 + 6x = 5x - 3$ **28.** $5x + 7 = x - 1$
22. $3x - 1 = 4x - 5$ **26.** $3(3x + 2) = 4(x - 1)$ **29.** $7x + 1 = 2(x - 2)$
23. $5x + 7 = 4(x - 1)$ **27.** $2(1 + 2x) = 7(x - 1)$ **30.** $3x - 1 = 7 + 5x$
24. $4x - 1 = 5x - 7$

Remember that although all the answers so far have been whole numbers there is no reason why the answer should not be a fraction, or even a negative fraction:

Example: $3x - 1 = 3(1 + 2x)$

                (brackets)

            $3x - 1 = 3 + 6x$

                $(-3x)$

            $-1 = 3 + 3x$

                (-3)

            $-4 = 3x$

                $(÷3)$

            $x = -\dfrac{4}{3} = -1\dfrac{1}{3}$

31. $4x - 1 = x + 1$ **35.** $3x - 7 = 4(1 + 2x)$ **38.** $3 + 2x = 8x + 9$
32. $5x - 6 = 3x + 1$ **36.** $3 + 2x = 2(2x - 1)$ **39.** $3x - 10 = 7x + 4$
33. $x - 1 = 2 + 3x$ **37.** $7x - 1 = x + 4$ **40.** $5 + 6x = 3x - 2$
34. $3(1 + 2x) = x + 7$

In the above equations there was a "rhythm" to the solving, as long as you followed the rhythm you should arrive at the solution, there are some special cases where things may look a little peculiar:

1. The vanishing x term:

    Consider: $3x + 2 = x$

                    $(-x)$

        $(2x + 2 = ?)$ *(Help! No x! Write 0)*
        $2x + 2 = 0$

                    (-2)

            $2x = -2$

                    $(÷2)$

        $x = -1$

2. The negative x term:

Consider: $\quad 2x + 2 = 4 + 3x$

$$(-3x)$$
$$-x + 2 = 4$$
$$(-2)$$
$$-x = 2 \quad or \quad x = -2$$

To avoid the negative x term (and it is easy to make mistakes with negative numbers) it is a good idea to find the x term with the smallest coefficient and eliminate that term first. This will ensure that the remaining x term is positive. This needs particular care when one or more of the x terms have a negative coefficient.

Exercise 6C

Solve these equations:

Example: $\quad x + 3 = 4 - 2x$

The x terms are x and $-2x$, eliminate $-2x$

$$x + 3 = 4 - 2x$$
$$(+2x)$$
$$3x + 3 = 4$$
$$(-3)$$
$$3x = 1$$
$$(\div 3)$$
$$x = \frac{1}{3}$$

1. $3x + 4 = 2x$
2. $4x = 7x - 5$
3. $8 + 3x = 2x$
4. $2(3x + 2) = 3x$
5. $7 - 3x = 4x$
6. $2(2 - x) = x$
7. $4x = 5 - 7x$
8. $3x = 7 - 2x$
9. $2(4x - 1) = 2x$
10. $5x = 3 - 7x$
11. $7x - 4 = 8 - x$
12. $3x - 7 = 3 - 2x$
13. $2(2x + 1) = 6 - 5x$
14. $3 - 2x = 8 + 3x$
15. $4x - 1 = 6 - x$
16. $2(2 - x) = 3x + 1$
17. $11 - 2x = 3 + 2x$
18. $5 + 2x = 7 - 3x$
19. $7 - x = 4x - 3$
20. $13 - 4x = 1 + 5x$

Equations With Fractions

We are used to the rule 'multiply out brackets first' when solving equations, but what happens when the bracket is multiplied by a fraction?

For example: $\quad \frac{1}{3}(2x + 1) = 5$

The brackets could be multiplied by the fraction but that would give:

$$\frac{2x}{3} + \frac{1}{3} = 5$$

which is not very inviting, it is better to multiply both sides of the equation by the denominator (×3) first:

$$2x + 1 = 15$$

which gives a much simpler equation to solve.

Exercise 6D

Solve these equations with fractions. Remember to multiply BOTH SIDES OF THE EQUATION by the denominator first.

1. $\dfrac{x}{3} = 4$ 5. $\dfrac{x+2}{3} = 4$ 8. $\dfrac{3-4x}{2} = x$

2. $\dfrac{1}{4}x = 3$ 6. $\dfrac{2x-3}{5} = 2$ 9. $\dfrac{1}{4}(2-x) = x$

3. $\dfrac{2x}{5} = 4$ 7. $\dfrac{1}{5}(4-3x) = 4$ 10. $\dfrac{2(2x+1)}{3} = x$

4. $\dfrac{3}{4}x = 6$

The equations above have only had one term each side of the equal sign. What happens when there is more than one term?

$$\text{For example:} \qquad \frac{x}{4} + 3 = 2x$$

The general rule, multiply both sides by the denominator is still the correct rule to follow; but be careful to multiply **EVERY TERM** on each side by the denominator.

Example: $\dfrac{x}{4} + 3 = 2x$ $(\times 4)$

$\dfrac{4 \times x}{4} + 4 \times 3 = 4 \times 2x$ *(cancel out fraction)*

$x + 12 = 8x$

$\qquad\qquad 12 = 7\text{x}$ $(-x)$

$\qquad\qquad \dfrac{12}{7} = x$ $(\div 7)$

$\qquad\qquad x = 1\dfrac{5}{7}$

---

11. $\dfrac{x}{3} + 1 = 4$ 15. $4 + \dfrac{x}{2} = 3$ 18. $\dfrac{1}{3}x = 4 - 2x$

12. $\dfrac{x}{5} - 3 = 1$ 16. $4 - \dfrac{x}{5} = x$ 19. $\dfrac{2x}{5} + 3 = 2$

13. $\dfrac{x}{2} + 3 = x$ 17. $\dfrac{x}{3} = 4 + x$ 20. $4 - \dfrac{3x}{5} = 2x$

14. $\dfrac{x}{7} - 3 = x$

Some equations with fractions may need brackets:

$$\frac{2}{3}(x+4)=3x-4$$

Example

$(\times 3)$

$2(x+4)=3(3x-4)$
$2x+8=9x-12$

$(-2x)$

$8=7x-12$

$(+12)$

$20=7x$

$(\div 7)$

$\frac{20}{7}=x=2\frac{6}{7}$

21. $\frac{1}{3}(x+3)=x+2$ **23.** $\frac{2(3+2x)}{5}=3x-2$ **25.** $\frac{2x}{5}=x+2$

22. $\frac{3}{5}(2x+3)=2-3x$ **24.** $3x=\frac{2x}{7}-2$ **26.** $\frac{3}{4}=3x-5$

The equations so far have only had one fraction and thus only one denominator, but there will often be occasions when you will have two fractions. Consider this example:

$$\frac{3x}{4}=\frac{2}{5}$$

We only need to get rid of the fraction on the same side as the x term, and so we multiply both sides of the equation by 4:

$$\frac{4\times 3x}{4}=\frac{2\times 4}{5}$$

(simplify)

$3x=\frac{8}{5}$

$(\div 3)$

$x=\frac{8}{15}$

27. $\frac{2x}{3}=\frac{1}{4}$ **29.** $\frac{3}{7}x=\frac{2}{5}$ **31.** $\frac{3}{4}=\frac{4x}{9}$

28. $\frac{3x}{4}=\frac{2}{5}$ **30.** $\frac{2}{3}=\frac{3x}{5}$ **32.** $\frac{x}{3}=\frac{5}{6}$

When there are two fractions in an equation plus other terms then you need to multiply **EVERY TERM** by both denominators, and then cancel:

Example:

$$\frac{x}{4} + 3 = \frac{2}{3}$$

$(\times 4, \times 3)$

$$\frac{3 \times 4 \times x}{4} + 3 \times 4 \times 3 = \frac{3 \times 4 \times 2}{3}$$

(now multiply)

$$3x + 48 = 8$$

(-48)

$$3x = -40$$

$(\div 3)$

$$x = -\frac{40}{3} = -13\frac{2}{3}$$

Now that the equations are more complex it really helps to write down what you are doing at each stage in the brackets to the right.

33. $\frac{x}{4} + 2 = \frac{1}{3}$ **36.** $5 - \frac{x}{2} = \frac{3}{5}$ **39.** $\frac{3}{4} - 2x = \frac{x}{5}$

34. $5 + \frac{2x}{3} = \frac{1}{5}$ **37.** $\frac{x}{4} = 2x + \frac{1}{3}$ **40.** $\frac{3x}{5} = \frac{1}{3} - 4x$

35. $\frac{3x}{4} - 2 = \frac{2}{3}$ **38.** $\frac{x}{4} + 2 = \frac{x}{3}$

You have now solved equations in various different forms, and so time yourself through this exercise of **20 QUESTIONS:**

Exercise 6E

1. $4 + x = 6$

2. $2 = 5 - x$

3. $9x = 15$

4. $\frac{x}{4} = 5$

5. $2x + 1 = 7$

6. $9 - 3x = 3$

7. $3(x + 1) = 2$

8. $7 = 2(x - 3)$

9. $\frac{1}{3}(x + 4) = 2$

10. $7 = \frac{2x - 5}{3}$

11. $\frac{3}{4}(x - 2) = 1$

12. $3x + 3 = 2x + 7$

13. $5x - 5 = 6x + 9$

14. $3x - 1 = 4 + x$

15. $7x + 4 = 5 + 2x$

16. $5x + 3 = 2x$

17. $7 - 4x = 9 + 2^x$

18. $\frac{4x}{5} = \frac{6}{7}$

19. $\frac{2x}{3} - 4 = x$

20. $3 - \frac{2x}{5} = \frac{3x}{4}$

You have now become proficient in solving equations in various forms, but why is this such a useful skill? We often have to solve problems that involve an unknown quantity, and the neatest way to do this is to let the unknown be x and then to form an equation.

Make sure that you define x carefully at the beginning of your solution, and at the end check your answer to make sure that it makes sense within the context of the original problem. Remember to answer the actual question, putting in the correct units if these are required.

Exercise 6F

Example:
I get the same amount of pocket money each week. One week I bought 4 tennis balls and then I had 27p left over. The following week I bought 2 tennis balls and had £1.45 left over. How much are tennis balls and how much pocket money do I get each week?

Let tennis balls cost x pence
One week I had : $4x + 27$ Next week I had : $2x + 145$

$$4x + 27 = 2x + 145$$
$$(-2x)$$
$$2x + 27 = 145$$
$$(-27)$$
$$2x = 118$$
$$(\div 2)$$
$$x = 59$$

Tennis balls cost 59 pence each and I get £2.63 pocket money.

1. I have just enough money to buy 4 packets of Jelloes or to buy two packets of Jelloes and 15 sticks of licorice at 2p a stick.
   a) If a packet of Jelloes costs x pence, what is the cost of 4 packets in terms of x?
   b) What is the cost of 2 packets of Jelloes and the 15 sticks of licorice, in terms of x?
   c) Form an equation in x and solve it .
   d) How much does a packet of Jelloes cost and how much money did I have to start with?

2. Buns cost 12 p. The cost of 4 cakes and 6 buns is the same as the cost of 3 buns and 5 cakes.
   a) If cakes cost xp write an expression in x for the cost of 4 cakes and 6 buns?
   b) Write an expression in x for the cost of 3 buns and 5 cakes.
   c) Write an equation in x and solve it.
   d) What is the cost of 5 cakes?

3.   Here are two angles on a straight line:
      Form an equation in x and solve it to find
      the two angles.

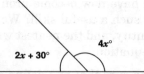

4. What is the angle sum of this triangle ?
   Form an equation in x and solve it to find
   the three angles in the triangle.

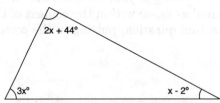

5.   My grandfather gave me some
money. He gave my elder brother ten pounds more than he gave me and he gave
my younger sister two pounds less.
a) If my grandfather gave me £x how much, in terms of x, did he give my brother
and my sister?
b) How much did my grandfather give us altogether?
c) If the total amount that my grandfather gave us was four times the amount
that I received how much, in terms of x, did my grandfather give us?
d) Form an equation in x and solve it to find out how much we each received.

Some equations need brackets:

Example:
My mother is twice my age now. 10 years ago she was 3 times my age.
How old am I and how old is my mother?

Let my age now be x years
Then my mothers age now is $2x$ years

8 years ago I was $x - 10$ years old
My mother was $2x - 10$ years old

$$3(x - 10) = 2x - 10 \quad \text{(brackets)}$$
$$- 30 = 2x - 10$$
$$\quad\quad (- 2x)$$
$$x - 30 = - 10$$
$$\quad\quad (+ 30)$$
$$x = 20$$
I am 20 years old and my mother is 40
(check 10 years ago I was 10 and my mother was 30)

---

7.   My sister is 2 years older than me, and my father is four times as old as my
      sister. If I am x years old find in terms of x:
      a) My sister's age.
      b) My father's age.
      c) My father is five times as old as I am. Form an equation in x and solve it to
      find my age.

8. My mother is 3 times as old as I am and my father is four times as old as I am. If I am x years old find, in terms of x:
a) My mother's age
b) My father's age
c) My father is 9 years older than my mother. Form an equation in x and solve it to find my age.

9. A farmer goes to market and buys some chickens. The following week he goes to market again and buys four more chickens than the previous week, he also buys lots of ducklings, in fact he bought twice as many ducklings as chickens. If the number of chickens that he bought the first week is x find, in terms of x:
a) The number of chickens he bought the second week.
b) The number of ducklings he bought the second week.
c) If the total number of chickens and ducklings he bought the second week is four times the total number he bought the first week form an equation in x and solve it to find how many ducklings he bought.

11. In a bag of marbles there are four more red marbles than yellow marbles, and three times as many green marbles as red marbles. If the number of yellow marbles is x find, in terms of x:
a) The number of red marbles
b) The number of green marbles
c) If there are 36 marbles in the bag form an equation in x and solve it to find the number of yellow marbles.

12. My brother is four years younger than me. Four years ago I was twice his age. If my age now is x years find, in terms of x:
a) My brother's age now.
b) My age 4 years ago
c) My brothers age 4 years ago.
d) Form an equation in x and solve it to find my brothers age now..

13. My brother and sister and I were picking strawberries. I picked 3 kg more than my sister but my brother picked twice as many kg as I did. If the number of kg that I picked was x find, in terms of x:
a) The number of kg my sister picked.
b) The number of kg my brother picked
c) If we picked 21 kg altogether form an equation in x and solve it to find how many kg of strawberries my sister picked.

14. A company makes Widgets and Wotsits. They make 4p more profit on Widgets than they do on Wotsits. If the profit on a Wotsit is x pence find, in terms of x:
a) The profit on one Widget.
b) The profit on 100 Wotsits.
c) The profit on 200 Widgets.
c) For every batch of 100 Wotsits and 200 Widgets the company makes £23. Form an equation in x and solve it to find the profit on each Widget and Wotsit.

15. On Mother's day my son gave me one red rose for each year of his age, and my daughter gave me two white roses for each year of her age. My son is 4 years older than my daughter received 28 roses.

a) If my son is x years old how many roses did he give me?

b) How old is my daughter in terms of x ?

c) How many roses did my daughter give me, in terms of x ?

d) Form an equation in x and solve it to find the ages of my two children.

For these questions form an equation in x and solve it to find the answer to the question:

16. I think of a number, double it and add 7 and I have three times the number that I first thought of. What was that number ?

17. In 12 years time I will be twice as old as I am now. How old am I now ?

18. I have to write 1000 lines. I have written most of them and now I have to write one third of the amount that I have actually written plus 20 lines. How many lines have I actually written?

19. Kola Cola costs 6p more per can than Perli Cola. I can buy 4 tins of Perli Cola for the same as I can buy 3 cans of Kola Cola. What is the cost of each brand of Cola?

20. My father is 3 times as old as my sister and four times as old as me. My sister is 3 years older than I am. How old is my sister?

Inexact Answers

Most problems in mathematics have an exact answer: $4 \times 7 = 28$.
But some answers give a range , for example :
'It takes me between 10 and 15 minutes to get to school.'

I could write this as: $10 \leq \text{time} \leq 15$

Remember that > means 'greater than', and < 'less than'.
Consider this inequality: $2 < x < 5$

x is greater than 2 and less than 5

This can be shown on the number line:

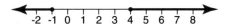

The values of x that satisfy this inequality are 3 and 4.

Remember that $\geq$ means "greater than or equal to" and $\leq$ means "less than or equal to".

Consider this pair of inequalities: $x < -1$ $x \geq 4$.

x is less than -1, and x is greater than or equal to 4

This can be shown on the number line. Note the hollow circle for < or > and the solid circle for $\leq$ or $\geq$:

Note that there are NO VALUES of x that satisfy this pair of inequalities.

Exercise 6G

Give all the possible whole numbers of x for these inequalities, show the range on a number line:

> For example: $4 \leq x < 7$
>
> $x = 4, 5$ or 6

1. $3 \leq x < 6$
2. $1 \leq x \leq 4$
3. $5 < x \leq 8$
4. $0 < x < 5$

5. $-2 \leq x < 3$
6. $-5 > x \geq -7$
7. $3 \geq x > -1$

8. $2 \geq x > -2$
9. $x \geq 4$ and $x < 8$
10. $x < 10$ and $x \geq 5$

Solving Inequalities

An inequality, or an inequation, is written like an equation, but using a greater than or less than sign instead of an equal sign. It is then solved using some of the same techniques that you have learnt to use when solving equations.

For example:

a) $4x > 24$

$(\div 4)$

$x > 6$

b) $x - 4 > 6$

$(+ 4)$

$x > 10$

Exercise 6H

Solve these inequalities:

1. $3x < 6$

2. $5x \geq 15$

3. $7x \geq 21$

4. $14 < \dfrac{x}{2}$

5. $21 \geq 3x$

6. $x + 4 < 6$

7. $\dfrac{x}{3} - 2 \leq 7$

8. $3 + \dfrac{x}{4} > 3$

9. $4 + x < 5$

10. $3x + 7 > 9$

11. $3 + 2x \geq 5$

12. $7 < x - 4$

13. $14 \geq 6 + \dfrac{x}{3}$

14. $5 \leq \dfrac{x}{5} + 3$

The inequalities above have been solved by adding, subtracting or dividing by a positive value of x . Now consider the inequality :

$$4 > 1$$

What happens when we add, subtract, multiply or divide the inequality by the constant 2?

$4 > 1$	$4 > 1$	$4 > 1$	$4 > 1$
$(+2)$	(-2)	$(\times 2)$	$(\div 2)$
$6 > 3$	$2 > -1$	$8 > 2$	$2 > \dfrac{1}{2}$

All the new inequalities are **true**.

Now do the same again but with the negative constant -2:

$4 > 1$	$4 > 1$	$4 > 1$	$4 > 1$
$(+(-2))$	$(-(-2))$	$(\times(-2))$	$(-(\div 2))$
$2 > -1$ $6 > 3$		$-8 > -2$	$-2 > -\dfrac{1}{2}$

This time the resulting inequalities are **not** all true.

-8 is **less** than -2, and -2 is **less** than $-\dfrac{1}{2}$.

Multiplying or Dividing an inequality by a negative constant <u>reverses</u> the inequality:

If $-x > 4$ then $x < -4$

However we have already seen in solving equations that it is better to keep the x term positive. This is particularly true when solving inequalities, as by keeping the x term positive we do not have to worry about reversing the inequality.

For example: Solve these inequalities:

a) $7 - 2x > 6$

$\qquad$ (+2x)

$7 > 6 + 2x$

$\qquad$ (−6)

$1 > 2x$

$\qquad$ (÷2)

$\frac{1}{2} > x$

$x < \frac{1}{2}$

b) $3 - \dfrac{x}{4} \le 4$

$\qquad$ (×4)

$12 - x \le 16$

$\qquad$ (+x)

$12 \le 16 + x$

$\qquad$ (−16)

$-4 \le x$

$x \ge -4$

However it is worth noting that if the x term had not been positive the last line of each inequation would have been:

$$-x > -\tfrac{1}{2} \quad \text{and} \quad -x \ge -4$$

when multiplied by −1 these become:

$$x < \tfrac{1}{2} \quad \text{and} \quad x \ge -4$$

Solve these inequalities:

15. $3 + 2x < 4$

16. $5 > 3 - 4x$

17. $3 - 2x \le 7 + 3x$

18. $3 + 4x > 7x - 5$

19. $16 \ge 4 - \dfrac{x}{3}$

20. $4 + \dfrac{3x}{4} > 9$

21. $7 - 2x \le 5x - 1$

22. $\dfrac{x}{4} - 1 > 6$

23. $8 - \dfrac{x}{3} \ge 5$

24. $5 < 6 - \dfrac{x}{2}$

25. $\dfrac{2x}{3} + 5 \le 2$

26. $7 - \dfrac{3x}{5} < 3$

27. $4 + 2x < 9 - 2x$

28. $3 + 4(x - 3) > x$

29. $5 - 2(x + 5) \le 3x$

30. $3(x - 4) > 5(4 - 2x)$

31. $2 - (x - 1) \ge 2(3 - x)$

Sometimes the inequation is written with two inequalities:

$$3 < 3x - 2 \le 5$$

and each part solved separately:

For example: $3 < 3x - 2 \le 5$

$$3 < 3x \qquad\qquad\qquad 3x - 2 \ge 5$$
$$\qquad (+2) \qquad\qquad\qquad\qquad (+2)$$
$$5 < 3x \qquad\qquad\qquad 3x \le 7$$
$$\frac{5}{3} < x \qquad\qquad\qquad x \le \frac{7}{3}$$

$$1\frac{2}{3} < x \le 2\frac{1}{3}$$

Solve these inequalities, and give all the whole number integers that satisfy each one:

32. $3 + x < 2 - x < 5$

33. $7 \le 3x + 4 < 13$

34. $6 \le \dfrac{x}{2} + 1 < 8$

35. $5 > 6 - \dfrac{2x}{3} \ge \dfrac{1}{2}$

36.   (i) Solve this inequality:
$$7 - 3x > 2 - x$$
   (ii) Give two prime numbers that satisfy this inequality.

37.   (i) Solve this inequality $2(3x + 2) < 4 - 3(2 - x)$
   (ii) Which of these numbers satisfies the inequality:

$$-3 \qquad -1 \qquad 2 \qquad 4$$

38.   (i) Solve the inequality $\dfrac{x}{3} - \dfrac{2(x - 3)}{4} \ge \dfrac{1}{6}$

   (ii) What is the lowest prime number that satisfies the inequality?

39.   (i) Solve the inequality $4 - \dfrac{x}{3} > 2x + 1 > 3$

   (ii) Give all the whole number integer values of x that satisfy the inequality

40.   Find all the whole number values of x that satisfy the inequality:

$$\frac{x}{2} + 1 < 6 - x \le 2x$$

41.   Why are there no values of x that satisfy the inequality:

$$\frac{1}{2} > \frac{x}{3} - 4 > \frac{3}{4}$$

Extension Exercise 6

In the exercises in Algebra and Arithmetic that we have done so far the symbols all have distinct meaning. There is no reason why we cannot have other symbols to which we allocate a special meaning.

For example: If # means "4 more than" then:

$$12 \text{ \# } 8 \qquad 4 \text{ \# } 0 \qquad 2^3 \text{ \# } 2^2 \quad \text{etc.}$$

If $x \text{ \# } 7$ then $x = 11$ (*11 is 4 more than 7*)

If $20 \text{ \# } x^2$ then $x^2 = 16$
and $x = 4$ or -4

1.   a) If # means "4 more than" which of these statements are true:
    i) $6 \text{ \# } 10$ ii) $7 \text{ \# } 3$ iii) $4^3 \text{ \# } 4^2$

   b) Find a value of x that makes each of these statements true:
    i) $7 \text{ \# } x$ ii) $x \text{ \# } 15$ iii) $x^2 \text{ \# } x$
    iv) $5 \text{ \# } \dfrac{1}{x}$ v) $\dfrac{20}{x} \text{ \# } 0$ vi) $\dfrac{24}{x} \text{ \# } \dfrac{x}{2}$

2.   If ‡ means "3 more than the square of" then
         $4 \ddagger 1$ (*4 is more than 1 and 1 is the square of 1*)
         $12 \ddagger -3$ (*12 is 3 more than 9 and 9 is the square of –3*)
   a) Which of these statements are true:
    i) $52 \ddagger 7$ ii) $13 \ddagger 10$ iii) $61 \ddagger 8$

   b) Find all the values of x that make these statements true:
    i) $39 \ddagger x$ ii) $x \ddagger 5$ iii) $4x \ddagger x$
    iv) $13 x \ddagger 2 x$ v) $\dfrac{13}{2x} \ddagger \dfrac{1}{x}$ vi) $x^4 + x \ddagger x^2$

3.   If the symbol Δ between two numbers means " is one more than half of"
   Thus $5 \Delta 8$ (*5 is one more than 4 which is half of 8*)
   a) Which of these statements is true:

    i) $4 \Delta 10$ ii) $3 \Delta 1$ iii) $\dfrac{3}{2} \Delta 1$

   b) Find all the values of x that make these statements true:

    i) $x \Delta 4$ ii) $6 \Delta x$ iii) $\dfrac{1}{2} \Delta x$
    iv) $x \Delta \dfrac{1}{2}$ v) $\dfrac{1}{x} \Delta \dfrac{-4}{x}$ vi) $\dfrac{3}{2x} \Delta -\dfrac{1}{x}$

4. If the symbol ◊ means "3 times half of" and so :

    3 ◊ 2   *(3 is 3 times 1 which is half of 2)*

a) Which of the following is true:

i) 6 ◊ 2   ii) 12 ◊ 8   iii) 4.5 ◊ 3

b) Write the values of x which make these statements true:

i) x ◊ 6   ii) 24 ◊ x iii) 0.9 ◊ x

iv) $\frac{1}{3}$ ◊ x v) $1 = \frac{1}{x}$

c) What is the ratio of the first number to the second number?

d) If the first number is x what is the second number, in terms of x?

5. The symbol † between two numbers denotes the highest common factor of the two numbers and the symbol • between the two numbers denotes the lowest common multiple of the two numbers, the smaller number is always written first.

Therefore 4 † 6=2 and 4•6=12

a) Which of these statements is true:

i) 4 † 7=1   ii) 8 •12 = 48   iii) 2^3 † 3^2=6

b) Find all the possible values of x that could make these statements true:

i) 3 † 6 = x ii) 5 •15 = x iii) x † 36=9

iv) x • 24 = 48   v) x † 12= x

c) Consider: 3 † 6 • 4 . Can you find two different answers to the expression.? Write down clearly your reasons for each answer. (i.e. do (3† 6) • 4 then 3† (6 • 4))

d) Repeat this for 8 † 6 • 3 .

e) Take the three digits 8,6, and 3 in as many different orders as is possible (remembering the rule!) and see if you get any different answers.

f) Try other sets of three numbers. Can you find a rule for the sets of three numbers that give you a single solution?

Summary Exercise 6

1. Solve these equations:
   a) $3x + 2 = 5$ b) $6 - 2x = 3$ c) $3(2x - 1) = 7$

2. Solve these equations:
   a) $2x + 4 = 3x + 1$ b) $4x + 1 = 4 - 2x$ c) $3x - 1 = x + 9$

   d) $5x - 4 = 4x$ e) $3 - 5x = 2x - 11$ f) $\frac{1}{3}(2 - 3x) = 4$

3. Solve these equations:

   a) $\frac{x}{3} + 5 = 2$ b) $6 - \frac{x}{2} = 1$ c) $\frac{1}{3}(2x + 4) = 3$

   d) $4 - \frac{2x}{3} = 1$ e) $3 + \frac{x}{2} = x$ f) $\frac{2x}{5} + 4 = x$

   g) $\frac{x}{4} = \frac{2}{3}$ h) $2 + \frac{2x}{3} = \frac{x}{4}$ i) $\frac{3}{4} = 3 - \frac{2x}{5}$

4. My mother is three times as old as I am. Four years ago my mother was four times as old as I am. If my age is x years now find, in terms of x :
   a) My mother's age now.
   b) My age 4 years ago.
   c) My mother's age 4 years ago.
   d) Now form an equation in x and solve it to find my mother's age now.

5. For the same amount of money I can either buy 5 sticks of liquorice and 8 penny sweets or 4 sticks of licorice and 12 penny sweets.
   a) If the cost of a stick of licorice is x pence what is the cost , in terms of x, of 5 sticks of licorice and 8 penny sweets?
   b) What is the cost, in terms of x, of 4 sticks of licorice and 12 penny sweets?
   c) Write an equation in x and solve it to find the cost of a stick of licorice.

6. Find all the whole number values of x that fit these inequalities, show the range on a number line:
   a) $1 \le x < 5$ b) $-3 < x \le 1$ c) $\frac{2}{3}(4 - 2x) \ge 5$

7. Solve these inequalities:
   a) $2x - 7 < 1$ b) $\frac{x}{5} \ge 3 - x$
   c) $3(2 - 3x) \ge 2 - (3x + 1)$

8. Find all the whole number values of x that satisfy this inequality:

$$\tfrac{1}{4}x + 1 > \tfrac{2}{3}x > 1 - x$$

Revision Exercises 1

In this exercise you may not use a calculator for the first 10 questions.

1.   The school is buying a new football strip for the 1st, 2nd, 3rd and 4th elevens. They need enough for the 11 players and two reserves in each team.

a) How many players will need a new football strip?

b) If each strip costs £21.40 how much money must the school raise?

2.   There are 63 teaching rooms in the school and every one is getting a new rotary white board. If the total cost is £4473 how much does one rotary white board cost?

3.   Give the following numbers as the product of their prime factors:

a) 224   b) 405   c) 420   d) 2225

4.   Find two prime numbers less than 25 whose mean is also a prime number.

5.   a) If $51 \times 72 = 3672$ without using a calculator give the answer to:

(i) 5.1×7.2 (iii) 510×0.072

(ii) 0.51×720 (iv) $36.72 \div 7.2$

b) If $\dfrac{1.6 \times 29}{5 \times 2.5} = 3.712$ without using a calculator give the answer to:

(i) $\dfrac{1.6 \times 29}{5 \times 25}$ (ii) $\dfrac{160 \times 29}{0.5 \times 2.5}$ (iii) $\dfrac{1.6 \times 2.9}{0.5 \times 0.25}$

6.   Calculate:

a) $3\dfrac{4}{5} + 1\dfrac{2}{3}$ b) $2\dfrac{4}{7} \times 4\dfrac{2}{3}$ c) $\dfrac{3\frac{1}{5} - 1\frac{5}{6}}{4\frac{7}{9} \div 1\frac{5}{6}}$

7.   a) Solve these equations:

(i) $5 - 2x = 7$ (ii) $5 + 2x = 7 - 5x$ (iii) $\dfrac{3}{4}(x - 5) = 2x$

b) Simplify giving your answer in index form:

(i) $3^7 \div 3^4$ (ii) $5^2 \times 5 \times 5^3$ (iii) $3^3 \times 2^3$

8.   In my school we are awarded credits for good pieces of work. This term I have 5 more credits than my best friend Henry but the top credit winner has twice as much as Henry and I together.

a) If I have x credits how many, in terms of x, does Henry have?

b) How many, in terms of x, does the top credit winner have?

c) If the top credit winner has a total of 54 credits form an equation in x and solve it.

d) How many credits does Henry have?

9. a) Find all the whole number values of x that fit these inequalities, show the range on a number line:
(i) $3 \leq x < 7$ (ii) $x < -3$

b) Solve these inequalities, show the solutions on a number line:
(i) $3x - 2 < 1$ (ii) $\dfrac{x}{3} \geq 4 - x$ (iii) $2(3 + x) \geq x \geq 3x - 4$

c) List all the whole number values of x that fit this inequality:
$$\dfrac{x}{2} + 3 \leq 2x < \dfrac{3x}{4} + 5$$

10. The number 10 to the power 100 is called a "Googol".
a) Write this in index form.
b) If it takes of a second to write each digit how long will it take to write to Googol in full.
c) If each digit is 3mm wide, and spaces are written in the correct places (and are also 3mm wide) how long a distance will one Googol take when the number is written out in full?
d) A "Googolplex" is 10 to the power of a Googol. How many times more digits are there in a Googolplex than a Googol?

11. a) Simplify these, if possible, leaving your answer in index form:
(i) $4^2 \times 4^4$ (ii) $7^2 \times 7^5$
(iii) $3^3 \div 3$ (iv) $5^2 \div 4^4$
(v) $3^2 \times 3^{-4}$ (vi) $5^{-3} \times 2^{-5}$
(vii) $4^{-2} \div 4^4$ (viii) $2^{-5} \div 5^{-3}$

b) Write these index numbers out in full:
(i) 3^7 (ii) 2^5 (iii) 5^3

c) Write these index numbers out in full, using correct decimal notation:
(i) 2^{-3} (ii) 3^{-2} (iii) 4^{-4}

12. a) The manufactures of tomato sauce have a special offer. You now get an extra 20% of sauce absolutely free. If the bottle size was originally 350ml, how much extra tomato sauce are you now getting?
b) In a sale the price of all kitchen appliances has been dropped by 15%. If a cooker cost £350 before the sale what does it cost now?
c) I am going to a discount centre to do some shopping. I buy a pair of trainers that were £35 but is now £28, a CD that was £15 and is now £12 and a T shirt that was £12 but is now £9. What percentage saving did I make on each article, and what is my total percentage saving?

13. a) Estimate the answer to these, give your answer to one significant figure:

(i) $\dfrac{3.52}{23.6 \times 5.27}$ (ii) $\dfrac{3.7}{218} + \dfrac{0.34}{0.0534}$

b) Now use a calculator to work out the exact answers.
   Give each answer correct to :   (i) 2 decimal places   (ii) 3 significant figures

14. a) I am 4 years older than my sister. If I am x years old how old, in terms of x is my sister?
b) My mother is three times as old as I am, write an expression in x for my mothers age.
c) My mother is also four times as old as my sister. Write another expression in x for my mother's age.
d) Write an equation in x and solve it.
e) How old is my mother?

15. a) My monthly allowance has risen from £20 per month to £22.50. What percentage increase is this?
b) Last year I saved £150 and I invested it in an account at 8.5% interest. How much will I receive at the end of ten years?
c) This year I spend, on average, $2\frac{1}{2}$ hours a day doing my homework. This is an increase of 50% from last year. How long, on average, did I spend each night doing my prep last year?

16. Use a calculator to work out these, for each answer write out the full display as given on your calculator:

a) (i) $(3.7)^2 - (0.92)^2$ (ii) $\sqrt{(3.7)^2 - (0.92)^2}$

b) (i) $24.5^2 \times 5.75^2$ (ii) 6.72×0.0537 (iii) $\sqrt[3]{\dfrac{24.5^2 \times 5.75^2}{6.72 \times 0.0537}}$

17. (a) My father bought a new car last year. Over the year the value of the car has dropped by 15%. If it is now worth £10,200, what was the original value of the car.
(b) This year and the next , the value of the car will drop by a further 12% each year from the value at the beginning of each year. What will the car be worth at the end of the third year.
c) Over the three years what percentage of the car's original value has been lost?

18. The Babylonians had a very efficient numbering system that was based on 60 rather than on base 10 like our decimal system. The Babylonian system is still used today to calculate time (60 seconds in a minute and 60 minutes in an hour). However their way of writing numerals made some calculations difficult. They did many calculations by looking up squares of numbers from a table. Try this Babylonian calculation:
a) Take any two digits (for example 3 and 4)
b) Calculate their sum and their difference (7 and 1)
c) Square the sum and the difference (49 and 1)
d) Take the difference of those numbers and divide by 4. What is your answer?
e) Try this with three other pairs of numbers. What mathematical calculation are you doing?

19. a) My father is four years older than my mother and I am one third of my mothers age. If my father is x years old write an expression in x for my age.
b) I am 14 years old. Form an equation in x and solve it. How old is my mother?

20. 9 is a very special number and produces several interesting number patterns.
Consider the powers of 9, i.e. $9^1, 9^2, 9^3, 9^4$, and so on. Make a table and record only the last digit of each power. What do you notice? Repeat the experiment with powers of 4 and powers of 3, use your tables to find the last digit of: a) 4^{2325} b) 3^{5678}.

Chapter 7

Indices and Algebra

In Chapter 3 we looked at indices numerically.
This chapter will look at using algebra with indices.

Multiplying

Consider: $\qquad 2^3 \times 2^2 = (2 \times 2 \times 2) \times (2 \times 2)$
$$= 2^5$$
$$= 32$$

Similarly: $\qquad x^2 \times x^4 = x^6$
We can see a general rule:
$$x^a \times x^b = x^{a+b}$$

Exercise 7A

Calculate these leaving your answer in index form:

1. $x^2 \times x^5$
2. $b^3 \times b^2$
3. $a^4 \times a^3$
4. $2^2 \times 2^3 \times 2^4$
5. $3^a \times 3^b$

6. $3^2 \times 3^3$
7. $a^2 \times b^3$
8. $3^a \times 3^a$
9. $x^a \times y^a$
10. $3^2 \times 3^3 \times 3^4$

11. $x^2 \times x^3 \times x$
12. $b^2 \times b^3 \times b$
13. $a \times a^5 \times a^2$
14. $6^x \times 6^y \times 6$
15. $a \times a^x \times a^x \times a$

Division

Consider $\qquad 16 \div 4 = 4 \qquad\qquad\qquad 81 \div 3 = 27$
or $\qquad\qquad 2^4 \div 2^2 = 2^2 \qquad\qquad\quad 3^4 \div 3^1 = 3^3$
as a general rule:
$$x^a \div x^b = x^{(a-b)}$$

Exercise 7B

Calculate these, giving your answers in index form:

1. $a^4 \times a^2$
2. $b^7 \div b^3$
3. $x^6 \div x^3$
4. $2^6 \div 2^3$
5. $3^a \div 3^b$

6. $5^3 \div 5^2$
7. $x^7 \div x^3$
8. $a^4 \div a$
9. $y^4 \div y$
10. $x^5 \div x$

11. $5^x \div 5$
12. $x^a \div x^3$
13. $a^x \div a^y$
14. $x^a \div x$
15. $a^b \div a^c$

Consider the case $5^3 \div 5^3$. Using the above rule would give us :

$$5^3 \div 5^3 = 5^{3-3}$$
$$= 5^0$$

We know that if you divide a number by itself the answer is always 1. Thus $5^0 = 1$

In general terms: $x^a \div x^a = x^{a-a}$
$$= x^0$$
$$= 1$$

Sometimes the index number may be negative, remember that:

$$10^{-2} = \frac{1}{10^2} = \frac{1}{100} \quad \text{similarly} \quad x^{-3} = \frac{1}{x^3}$$

Calculate these, giving your answer as a fraction, if appropriate.

16. $x^2 \div x^5$ 21. $2^4 \div 2^7$ 26. $2x^2 \div x^3$
17. $a^3 \div a^6$ 22. $x^4 \div x^2$ 27. $2x^2 \div 4x^3$
18. $b \ddot{o} b^3$ 23. $a^2 \div b^2$ 28. $a^3 \div 5a^3$
19. $x^7 \div x^7$ 24. $x \div x^5$ 29. $y^a \div 3y^b$
20. $7^a \div 7^b$ 25. $x \div x^a$ 30. $4x^3 \div 16x^5$

Powers

An expression containing an idex number may itself be raised to a power

$$(2^4)^2 = 2^4 \times 2^4$$
$$= 2^8$$
$$(x^2)^3 = x^2 \times x^2 \times x^2$$

In general terms:
$$(x^a)^b = x^{ab}$$

Exercise 7C

Express in index form:

1. $(3^2)^3$ 6. $(x^m)^n$ 11. $(2^2)^2 \div (4^2)^3$
2. $(2^3)^2$ 7. $(3^2)^3 \times (3^2)^4$ 12. $(2x^3)^3 \times (x^2)^2$
3. $(x^4)^2$ 8. $(x^2)^2 \times (x^3)^3$ 13. $(2x^3)^4 \div (3x^2)^3$
4. $(x^3)^3$ 9. $(4^4)^3 \div (4^2)^2$ 14. $(3a^3)^3 \div (9^2)^2$
5. $(4^a)^b$ 10. $(x^4)^2 \div (x^2)^3$ 15. $(2x^4)^2 \times (a^2)^2$

Using the fact that $(x^a)^2 = x^a \times x^a = x^{2a}$
then $(x^{\frac{1}{2}})^2 = x^{\frac{1}{2}} \times x^{\frac{1}{2}} = x$

and $x^{\frac{1}{2}} = \sqrt{x}$

similarly $x^{\frac{1}{3}} = \sqrt[3]{x} \quad \text{and} \quad x^{\frac{1}{4}} = \sqrt[4]{x}$

Express these either as whole numbers or in index form

16. $9^{\frac{1}{2}}$

17. $81^{\frac{1}{4}}$

18. $25^{\frac{1}{2}}$

19. $27^{\frac{1}{3}}$

20. $16^{\frac{1}{4}}$

21. $125^{\frac{1}{3}}$

22. $8^{\frac{1}{3}}$

23. $(x^2)^{\frac{1}{2}}$

24. $(2x^2)^2$

25. $(9x^2)^{\frac{1}{2}}$

26. $(x^2)^{\frac{1}{2}} \times (x^2)^{\frac{1}{3}}$

27. $(2x)^2 \div (3x)^2$

Combining Multiplication And Division

We may need to combine expressions in algebra, for example:
$$2x^2 \times 3x^3 = 2 \times x \times x \times 3 \times x \times x \times x$$
$$= 6x^5$$
$$3ab^3 \times 4a^2 = 12a^3b$$

It is important not to confuse adding and multiplying:
$$a^3b + a^3b + a^3b = 3a^3b \qquad\qquad a^3b \times a^3b \times a^3b = a^9b^3$$

Exercise 7D

Simplify these expressions, if possible:

1. $a \times a^2 \times a^3$

2. $3a \times 2a^2 \times a^3$

3. $3b + b^2 + 2b^3$

4. $2b^2 + b^2 + 3b^3$

5. $2ab + a^2b + 3b^2$

6. $4x^2y + x^2y + 3x^2y$

7. $4xy + x^2y - xy$

8. $4xy + x^2y - xy^2$

9. $3ac \times a^2b + 4ac$

10. $2bc + a^2b + 4ac$

A fraction in algebra may be cancelled down in the same way as a numerical fraction. These algebraic fractions may have common factors in the same way as ordinary fractions:

$$3x^3y^2 \div 6xy \;=\; \frac{3x^3y^2}{6xy} \qquad (3, x, \text{ and } y \text{ are all common factors})$$
$$= \frac{3 \times x \times x \times x \times y \times y}{6 \times x \times y}$$
$$= \frac{x^2y}{2}$$

Simplify these, and if possible, check that your answer is in the simplest form possible:

11. $\dfrac{3a^2b}{a}$

12. $\dfrac{3a^2b}{b}$

13. $\dfrac{6a^2b}{2b}$

14. $\dfrac{8xy^2}{2xy}$

15. $\dfrac{3a^2b}{5b}$

16. $\dfrac{3a^2b}{24b^3}$

17. $\dfrac{2mn}{8m^2n}$

18. $\dfrac{24x^2y^3}{15x^3y}$

19. $\dfrac{12x^3y^2}{4x^2y}$

20. $\dfrac{18a^3b^2}{6ab^3}$

21. $\dfrac{6x^2y^2}{4x^3y^2}$

22. $\dfrac{15a^2bc^3}{10ab^2c}$

Indices And Brackets

When there is a number outside a bracket we know that we multiply through the brackets by the number:

$$2(3x + 4) = 6x + 8$$

When there is x outside the bracket then you multiply through by x.

For example:

$$x(x + 2) = x^2 + 2x$$
$$x(x^2 + 2x) = x^3 + 2x^2$$
$$x^2(x^2 + 2x) = x^4 + 2x^3$$

Exercise 7E

Multiply out these brackets:

1. $x(2x + 1)$
2. $x(3x - 2)$
3. $x(4 - 3x)$
4. $2x(x + 4)$

5. $3x(2x - 5)$
6. $x^2(x + 1)$
7. $x^2(x^2 + x - 1)$
8. $x^2(4 - 3x)$

9. $2x^2(3x - 2)$
10. $2x^2(2x^2 + 3x - 2)$
11. $x^3(x^2 + 1)$
12. $4x^3(2x^2 - 4x + 3)$

Now try multiplying these out and simplifying. **Remember** that multiplying by a negative number changes the sign of the original number. **Therefore a minus outside the brackets changes the sign when the brackets are removed:**

For example:
$$x(3x + 2) - 2x(x - 4) = 3x^2 + 2x - 2x^2 + 8x$$
$$= x^2 + 10x$$

13. $x(2x^2 + 1) + 2x(x - 3)$

14. $x^2(2x + 1) - x(x + 3)$

15. $2x(2x^2 + x) + 3x^2(2x - 2)$

16. $2x(x^2 - 3) - x^2(3x + 1)$

17. $x^2(3x^3 + 4) + 2x^2(3 - 2x)$

18. $4x(3x - x^2) - 2x^2(4 - 3x)$

Try these with x and y:

For example:
$$2x(3x + y) - y(2x + y) = 6x^2 + 2xy - 2xy - y^2$$
$$= 6x^2 - y^2$$

21. $x(x + y) + y(x + y)$

22. $2x(3x + y) - 2y(x + 2y)$

23. $x^2(2x - y) + y(3x^2 + 2y)$

24. $xy(2x + y) - y(3x^2 + y^2)$

25. $x^2(3y - x^2) + 2x(3x^3 - xy)$

26. $xy^2(3x + 2) + x^2y(4 - 2y)$

27. $x^2(4 + 3y) - 4x(2x + 2xy)$

28. $xy(3y - 2x) - x^2(4y + y^2)$

29. $3x^3(2x - 3y + 1) - 2y(3x^3 + 4)$

30. $2x^2y(3x + 4y) - 3xy^2(2x + 3y)$

Factorising

The last exercise concerned multiplying brackets by a factor outside the brackets. Factorising is when a common factor is taken outside the brackets - the reverse process.

For example:
$$3x^2 + 2x = x(3x + 2)$$
$$8x^2 + 4xy = 4xy(2x + 1)$$

Exercise 7F

Factorise these expressions where possible:
These six questions have a number as a common factor

1. $3x + 6$ **3.** $6 + 9x$ **5.** $24x + 16$
2. $8y - 4$ **4.** $18 - 4y$ **6.** $7x - 6$

These six questions have a letter as a common factor
7. $x^2 + 5x$ **9.** $3x + x^2$ **11.** $x^3 + 8x$
8. $x^2 - 7x$ **10.** $5x - x^2$ **12.** $x^3 - 6x$

These six questions have both a number and a letter as common factors

13. $2x^2 + 4x$ **15.** $9xy + 6y^2$ **17.** $6y^2 - 12xy$
14. $6x - 9x^2$ **16.** $12x^2 - 9xy$ **18.** $8xy - 4x^2$

Now try these:
19. $3xy + 16x^2 + 4x$ **26.** $14x^2 + 8xy + 2y^2$
20. $8x^2y - 14xy$ **27.** $10xy + 14y^2 - 4$
21. $8x^2 - 6xy^2$ **28.** $16x^2 - 14xy - 6$
22. $12y^2 - 9y + 3x$ **29.** $16x^2 - 14xy - 6x^2$
23. $12y + 8x^2y - 16y^2$ **30.** $20a^2b - 4b^2$
24. $3x^2y + 4xy^2 + 2xy$ **31.** $20a^2b - 4ab^2 + 2ab$
25. $12xy - 16x^2y - 4xy^2$ **32.** $16ac^2 + 8a^2$

Trial And Improvement

In the problems we met earlier in the last chapter we were able to make an equation in x, and then solve it. For other problems the equation may not be simple to solve,

For example:
My garden is rectangular. The length is 5 m longer than the width and the area is 130 sq. m.. Find the length and the width of the garden to the nearest 10 cm. If the width is x then the length will be $x+5$, an expression for the area would be $x(x+5)$ and the equation :
$$x(x+5) = 130$$
$$x^2 + 5x = 130$$

As there is an x^2 in the equation it cannot be solved in the usual way – a different method is needed. Trial and improvement methods work in the opposite way to normal equation solving, first you make an estimate of the answer, substitute that answer into the equation and see how accurate it is, then make a better estimate and try again. Continue doing this until you have the correct answer, or close to the correct answer. It is very important that all the results are recorded so that earlier results

Width	Length	Area	Note
8 m	13 m	104 sq m	too small
9 m	14 m	126 sq m	too small
10 m	15 m	150 sq m	too big

can be used to help to find the correct answer more quickly.

Width	Length	Area	Note
9.1	14.1	128.31	too small
9.2	14.2	130.64	too small
9.15	14.15	129.47	too big
9.16	14.16	129.7056	too small
9.17	14.17	129.9389	too small
9.18	14.18	130.1724	too big

First make a table and try whole numbers until you can find the closest values:
Now try to find a value to the nearest 10 cm, or to one decimal place, and then to two decimal places.
Remember you can only approximate to one decimal place from an answer to two decimal places.

The width is between 9.17m and 9.18m and so to the nearest 10cm the garden is 9.2m by 14.2m.

Exercise 7G

Worksheet 7/1 may be used with this exercise.

1. The length of my bedroom is 2m longer than the width, and the floor area is 70 sq. metres. Find the length and width of the room by trial and improvement. Give your answer to the nearest 10cm.

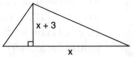

2. The height of a triangle is 3cm more than the base. The area of the triangle is 60 sq. cm. Find the base and height of the triangle using trial and improvement methods. Give your answer correct to one decimal place.

3.   A square photograph is surrounded by a border that is 5cm wide. If the area of the border is 182 sq. cm. use trial and improvement methods to find the dimensions of the photograph correct to the nearest millimetre.

4.   a) A rectangle has its base 6cm longer than its height. If the height is h cm long draw a sketch of the rectangle and write an expression for the base.

b) Write an expression for the area of the rectangle.

c) The area of the rectangle is 118cm^2. Copy and continue the table below and, using trial and improvement methods, find the height and the base of the rectangle correct to 2 decimal places.

Height	Base	Area	Note
8	14	112	too small
9	15		

5.   The height of this triangle is two thirds the length of its base, and its area is 31 sq. metres What is the length of the base correct to the nearest 10cm?

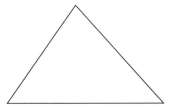

6. The height of a parallelogram is 5cm less than its base:
a) Write an expression in b for the area of the parallelogram:
b) The area of the parallelogram is 40cm^2. Copy and continue the table below to find the value of b to 2 decimal places using trial and improvements methods.

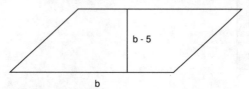

7. a) Given that the formula for the area of a trapezium is $Area = \dfrac{h(a + b)}{2}$, write an expression for the area of this trapezium:

b	b-5	b(b-5)
10	5	

b) The area of the trapezium is 24 cm^2. Copy and complete this table and continue it to find, by trial and improvement, the value of x correct to 2 decimal places:

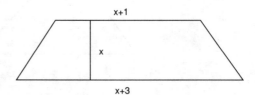

x	x+1	x+3	Area of Trapezium
3	4	6	36
2	3	5	...
2.5	...	...	...
...	...	...	...

Extension Exercise 7

More About Square Roots

Before the advent of the modern electronic calculator it was quite a lengthy problem to find a square root.

Heron of Alexandria, who lived around 75AD, was a Greek mathematician and engineer. As an engineer he frequently needed to find square roots and his method for finding square roots was used for many centuries. It is surprisingly accurate, especially when you consider the Greek system for recording numbers made it difficult even to multiply.

Heron's method works on a system of repetitive calculations and is accurate after 5 approximations to 17 decimal places. The method is frequently used by computers and calculators to give square roots.

Heron's Method

1. Find the approximate square root of a number x call it y_1

2. Calculate $\dfrac{x}{y_1}$.

3. Find the average of y_1 and $\dfrac{x}{y_1}$. Call this answer y_2.

4. Find the average of y_2 and $\dfrac{x}{y_2}$ Call this answer y_3.

5. Continue in this way until you have the accuracy that you need.

For example: To find the square root of 10

1. Let y_1 be 3

2. $\dfrac{x}{y_1} = \dfrac{10}{3}$

3. The average of $3 + \dfrac{10}{3} = \frac{1}{2}\left(3 + 3\frac{1}{3}\right)$

$$= \frac{1}{2} \times 6\frac{1}{3}$$
$$= 3.16666...$$
$$= 3.17 \text{ (to 2 d.p)}$$

Use fraction or decimal arithmetic to find the square root of these by Heron's approximation. Calculate y_2 and then round off to 2 d.p.

1.	8	**5.**	27	**9.**	85
2.	17	**6.**	105	**10.**	21
3.	23	**7.**	13	**11.**	55
4.	15	**8.**	22	**12.**	72

Now check your answers with a calculator.

Summary Exercise 7

1. Simplify these expressions, leaving your answer in index form:
   a) $a^3 \times a^2$ b) $b^4 \times b^3$ c) $c^3 \times c$

2. Simplify these expressions, leaving your answer in index form:
   a) $a^4 \div a^2$ b) $b^6 \div b^3$ c) $c^4 \div c$

3. Simplify these expressions, leaving your answer in index form:
   a) $a^2 \div a^4$ b) $b^3 \div b^3$ c) $c \div c^5$

4. Simplify these expressions, if possible:
   a) $a^4 \times a^2 \times a^5$ b) $3b^3 + 2b^3 - b^3$
   c) $c^4 + c + c^2$

5. Simplify these expressions, if possible:
   a) $\dfrac{3 \times a^2 \times b^3}{6 \times a \times b}$ b) $\dfrac{15ab^2c}{3bc^2}$ c) $\dfrac{8a^2b}{4b}$

6. Multiply out these brackets:
   a) $x(x+3)$ b) $2x(3x-5)$ c) $x^2(6-x)$

7. Multiply out these brackets, and simplify:
   a) $x^2(x + 3) + x(3x - 2)$
   b) $3x(2x^2 - 6) - 2x(5 - 2x^2)$

8. Factorise the following expressions, if possible:
   a) $3x + 9$ d) $12x - 8$ g) $4xy + 2y^2$
   b) $3x^2 - 12$ e) $3x^2 + 12x + 3x$ h) $4x^2y + 8y^2 - 6x$
   c) $9x^3 + 5x^2y - 7xy$ f) $12x^2y + 5y^2 - 7x$

9. This rectangle has a width 7cm less than its length and an area of 55cm². Copy and complete this table to find the length and width of the table to 2 d.p. by trial and improvement:

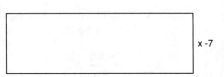

x	$x - 7$	$x(x - 7)$	
12	5	60	Too big
11	4	44	

Activity 7 - Compound Interest with a Spreadsheet

Compound Interest problems can be looked at in detail by using the spreadsheet application on a computer. The instructions here refer to ClarisWorks, but instructions are similar for most programmes.

Consider this problem:

Your grandfather put £100 in the bank for you on the day you were born. How much is it worth on your 10th birthday, your 14th birthday and your 20th birthday?

1. Open a new Claris Works spreadsheet.
    Give the first five columns these headings:
    Year no, Capital at start, Interest rate, Interest, Capital at end.

2. Type 1 in the year number column, then press return, now type in the first formula =A1+1 and press return or click on the tick sign. Click back on the cell A2 and hold the mouse button down and drag down until all 10 cells are highlighted:
    Typing Command + D will copy the formula down the A column and the number series 1 to 10 will appear. Click on box A5, you will see the formula has become =A4 + 1.

3. Your screen should look like this:

	A	B	C	D	E
1	Year No	Capital	Interest rate	Interest	Capital at end
2	1				
3	2				
4	3				
5	4				
6	5				
7	6				
8	7				
9	8				
10	9				
11	10				

Type 100 in cell B2, 10% in C2, and the formula =B2*C2 in cell D2, and the formula = B2 + D2 in E2.

You might like to change the colour of the interest rates to red. Do this by selecting cell D2 and then selecting Text Colour from the Format menu

4. Note that as you typed 10% the computer changed this to 0.1. Why?

5. Change B3 back to 10%.Your spreadsheet tells you that you now have £110 in your savings account at the end of year one and therefore at the start of year two. Roughly how much interest do you think you will earn in
    a) The second year?   b) The whole ten years?
    How much do you think you will have in your savings account after 10 years?.

6. Now type =E2 into cell B2, and then copy the formulae in B3 down to cell B11, do the same with the formula or value C2, D2 and E2. As you push the Command +D for the E column all the columns will magically change. If you do this successfully you will have the value 259.3742460 in cell E11. If not ask for help.

7. Is the amount in E11 the same as you predicted?.
    If not what did you do wrong in your prediction?

8. Roughly how much do you think you will have in your savings account at the end of::   a) 14 years? b) 20 years?

9. Copy the values or formulae in cells A11, B11, C11, D11 and E11 down to row 21 and see the correct answer to the question above. You will have far too many decimal places. To correct this highlight column B, pull down the format menu, select format number and click on the radio button against 'currency'. You will now have only two decimal places. Repeat this with columns D and E in turn. Now write the correct answers: a) 14 years?   b) 20 years?

10. Highlight column E. Go to the Options menu and select 'make chart'. Choose an area graph and push return. You should have a graph like this:

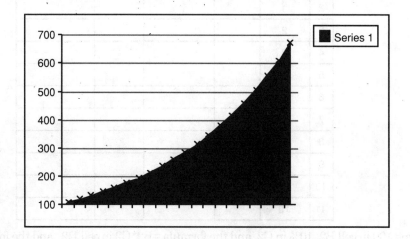

11. Why do you think the graph curves upwards?

12. Click on your graph and drag it up near to your spreadsheet. Arrange the spreadsheet and graph on the screen so that you can see them both. Now change the interest rate on the spreadsheet to 6%. Copy this rate for all 20 years and watch the graph. Try some other interest rates of your own. What happens if the interest rate changes? Try years 1-5 at 15%, 6-10 at 12%, 11-15 at 10% and 16-20 at 8%.

Chapter 8

Sequences

(The first exercises in the chapter are repeated from Chapter 23 in Book 1)

A sequence is a succession of terms with some rule connecting them.

For example:

2, 4, 6, 8, 10, ...　　　is the sequence of even numbers.

Each term is found by adding 2 to the previous term.

Some sequences follow numerical rules, while others, such as prime numbers, do not.

Exercise 8A

Fill in the next three numbers in these sequences. If you can find a numerical rule write that down:

1. 1, 3, 5, 7, 9, ...
2. 1, 4, 9, 16, 25, ...
3. 3, 6, 9, 12, 15, ...
4. 1, 3, 6, 10, 15, ...
5. 1, 2, 4, 8, 16, ...
6. 0, 3, 8, 15, 24, ...
7. 1, 1, 2, 3, 5, 8, 13, ...
8. 1, 2, 4, 7, 11, ...
9. 2, 6, 10, 14, 18, ...
10. 1, 6, 11, 17, 23,......

11. 8, 4, 2, 1, ...
12. 0.1, 0.5, 0.25, 0.125, ...
13. 1, 4, 7, 10, 13, ...
14. 1, 8, 27, 64, ...
15.　　　　　　2, 3, 5, 7, 11, ...
16. 2, 5, 10. 17, 26, ...
17. 100, 10, 1, 0.1, ...
18. 1, 3, 2, 4, 3, ...
19. 25, 5, 1, 0.2, ...
20. 0, 7, 26, 63, 124, ...

The missing terms in the above sequences could be found by looking at the previous term, but this makes it very difficult to find. For example the 100th term in the sequence in question 4:

1, 3, 6, 10, 15, 21, 28, 36, 45, 55, ... the sequence of triangle numbers.

To do this we have to look at the pattern of the numbers and try to find a rule which works for all the terms in that sequence.

Sometimes this is easier to think about if we have a series of drawings or patterns to help us.

Exercise 8B

1.　Look at this pattern:

b) Complete this table.

Tile colour:	
White	Grey
1	
2	
3	
4	
5	
n	

Can you fill in the rule for the *n*th pattern?

2.   Look at these patterns:

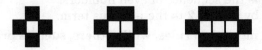

Make a table like the one above and fill it in. Can you find the rule for the *n* th pattern?

3.   Look at these patterns:

Make a table of values as in question 1 and thus find a rule for the number of black tiles when you have *n* white tiles.

4.   Look at these patterns:

Draw the next two patterns in the series.
Make a table for the number of white circles and the number of black circles.
What is the rule for the number of black circles when you have *n* white circles?

5.   Look at these patterns:

Draw the next two patterns in the series.
Make a table for the number of white circles and the number of black circles.
What is the rule for the number of black circles when you have *n* white circles?

6.   Look at these patterns:

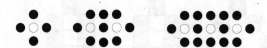

Draw the next two patterns in the series.
Make a table for the number of white circles and the number of black circles.
What is the rule for the number of black circles when you have *n* white circles?

From Functions To Sequences

Consider a function, for example, $y = 2x + 1$,
There is a value of y for each value of x, we usually put these in a table:

x	1	2	3	4	5
y	3	5	7	9	11

We can write this in a different way, and say that the y numbers are a **sequence** and the values of x tell us what number in the sequence we are looking at.

> If the 1st number is when $n = 1$,
> the 2nd number is when $n = 2$,
> the 3rd number is when $n = 3$,
> and thus the k th number is when $n = k$.

If we say that the number in the sequence is represented by S then in the above example:

$$\text{If} \quad \begin{array}{ll} n = 1 & S_1 = 3 \\ n = 2 & S_2 = 5 \\ n = 3 & S_3 = 7 \\ n = 4 & S_4 = 9 \end{array}$$

and so the rule for n th term in the series is $S_n = 2n + 1$

In the previous exercise the patterns help us to understand the relationship between the pattern number and the rule.

Without the drawn patterns it helps us to think about series in the same way as we thought about 'What's in the box?'

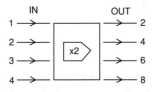

This machine represents the function
$T_n = 2n$,
and so
$$\begin{array}{ll} T_1 = 2 & T_2 = 4 \\ T_3 = 6 & T_4 = 8 \end{array}$$

Exercise 8C

1. Copy and complete the terms T_1, T_2, T_3, T_4, for this function machine and try and write a rule for T_n:

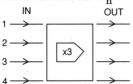

$$T_1 = \\ T_2 = \\ T_3 = \\ T_4 =$$

2. Copy and complete the terms T_1, T_2, T_3, T_4, for this function machine and try and write a rule for T_n:

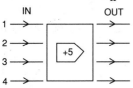

$$T_1 = \\ T_2 = \\ T_3 = \\ T_4 =$$

3.   Copy and complete the terms T_1, T_2, T_3, T_4, for this function machine and try and write a rule for T_n:

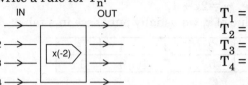

$T_1 =$
$T_2 =$
$T_3 =$
$T_4 =$

4.   Copy and complete the terms T_1, T_2, T_3, T_4, for this function machine and try and write a rule for T_n:

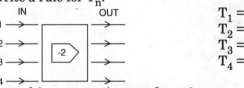

$T_1 =$
$T_2 =$
$T_3 =$
$T_4 =$

The next machines contain two functions:

5.   Copy and complete the terms T_1, T_2, T_3, T_4, for this function machine and try and write a rule for T_n:

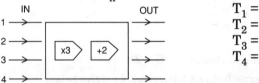

$T_1 =$
$T_2 =$
$T_3 =$
$T_4 =$

6.   Copy and complete the terms T_1, T_2, T_3, T_4, for this function machine and try and write a rule for T_n:

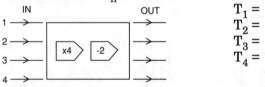

$T_1 =$
$T_2 =$
$T_3 =$
$T_4 =$

From your answers above you should notice that when the terms of the sequence go up in 3's there is a 3n in the nth term, when the terms of the series go up in 4's there is a 4n in the nth term. and so on. Now try these without the function machines:

7.   If the nth term of the series is $S_n = 3n - 2$ what is the:
      a) 1st term   b) 2nd term   c) 3rd term   d) 4th term ?

8.   If the nth term of the series is $T_n = 1 + n$ what is T_n when:
      a) $n = 1$ b) $n = 2$ c) $n = 3$ d) $n = 4$

9.   If the nth term of the series is $V_n = 5n + 1$, what is :
      a) V_1 b) V_2 c) V_3 d) V_4

10.   If the nth term of the series is $S_n = 4 + 2n$, what is :
      a) S_1 b) S_2 c) S_3 d) S_4

To find the rule it can help to draw a relationship diagram . Then look at whether the terms go up in a fixed number.

11. Can you find the next three terms in the series and hence the rule for T_n :
    $T_1 = 3$ $T_2 = 6$ $T_3 = 9$ $T_4 = 12$ $T_5 = 15$
    i.e if $1 \to 3$
    $2 \to 6$
    $3 \to 9$
    $4 \to 12$
    then $n \to$?

12. Can you find the next three terms in the series and hence the rule for Tn :
    $T_1 = 2$ $T_2 = 5$ $T_3 = 8$ $T_4 = 11$ $T_5 = 14$
    (draw a relationship diagram to help!)

13. Can you find the next three terms in the series and hence the rule for Sn:
    $S_1 = 3$ $S_2 = 8$ $S_3 = 13$ $S_4 = 18$ $S_5 = 23$

14. Can you find the next three terms in the series and hence the rule for T_n :
    $T_1 = 6$ $T_2 = 10$ $T_3 = 14$ $T_4 = 18$ $T_5 = 22$

In all the above examples the sequences have gone *up* by a fixed number. Now consider sequences that go *down* by a fixed number:

15. If the *n*th term of the series is $S_n = 3 - n$ what is the:
    a) 1st term   b) 2nd term   c) 3rd term   d) 4th term   e) 10th term ?

16. If the *n*th term of the series is $T_n = 1 - 3n$ what is T_n when:
    a) $n = 1$ b) $n = 2$ c) $n = 3$ d) $n = 4$ e) 10 ?

17. If the *n*th term of the series is $V_n = 5 - 2n$, what is :
    a) V_1 b) V_2 c) V_3 d) V_4 e) V_{10} ?

18. Can you find the next three terms in the series and hence the rule for Sn:
    $S_1 = 16$ $S_2 = 12$ $S_3 = 8$ $S_4 = 4$ $S_5 = 0$

19. Can you find the next three terms in the series and hence the rule for Tn:
    $T_1 = 8$ $T_2 = 3$ $T_3 = -2$ $T_4 = -7$ $T_5 = -12$

20. Look at this pattern of matches:

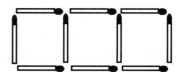

How many matches will be needed in the fourth pattern?
How many matches will be needed in the tenth pattern?
What is the rule for the number of matches that will be needed for the *n*th pattern?

Quadratic Sequences

All the sequences in the above exercise followed a **linear** rule. That is, if you were to plot the pattern number against the corresponding term you would have a straight line.

However some sequences do not have a linear rule.

Consider this sequence:

$T_1 = 1$
$T_2 = 1 + 3$
$T_3 = 1 + 3 + 5$
$T_4 = 1 + 3 + 5 + 7$

If you add up the numbers you should find that $T_1 = 1$, $T_2 = 4$, $T_3 = 9$, $T_4 = 16$

And so the sequence $T = 1, 4, 9, 16, 25 ...$ or the sequence of square numbers
and $T_n = n^2$

Exercise 8D

1. Draw the next two patterns in this sequence:

    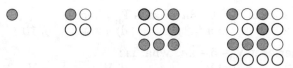

    Explain why the pattern of adding odd numbers gives the sequence of square numbers.

2. Look at these rectangle numbers.
    In each rectangle the length is always one more than the width:

    a) Draw the next two rectangle numbers.

Rectangle Number	Number of Dots
R_1	$1 \times 2 = 2$
R_2	$2 \times 3 =$
R_3	$3 \times$
R_4	
R_5	
R_6	

    b) Copy and complete this table, and hence find the rule for R_n:

3. Here are the triangle numbers.
a) Draw the next two triangle numbers.
b) Copy and complete the table from question 2.
Compare the number of dots in the rectangle numbers with the number of dots in the triangle numbers. What do you notice?
c) Now write the rule for T_n.

Use the results for square, rectangle and triangle numbers to find the rule for the nth term of these sequences:

4. A square with a bite out of it:

5. A rectangle with width 2 units less than the length:

6. A truncated triangle:

7. Two truncated triangles:

Now try to write the rule for these sequences. Look at the patterns, see if the terms go up in a fixed number, do they compare to square numbers, triangle numbers, rectangle numbers, or are the terms formed by a pattern of products (e.g. 1×2, 2×3, 3×4)?

8. 2, 5, 10, 17, ...

9. 2, 4, 7, 11, ...

10. 3, 9, 18, 30, ...

11. 2, 6, 10, 14, ...

12. 4, 10, 18, 28, ...

13. 2, 7, 14, 23, ...

14. What sequence do you get if you add a square number to the pattern number (e.g. $1 + 1, 4 + 2, 9 + 3$) . What is the rule?

15. What sequence do you get if you multiply the triangle numbers by 8, and then add 1? What is the rule for this sequence?

16. What sequence do you get if you multiply the triangle numbers by 2 and subtract the pattern number? What is the rule for this sequence?

17. What sequence do you get if you multiply the triangle numbers by 3 and subtract the pattern number? What is the rule for this sequence?

18. What sequence do you get if you multiply the square numbers by 2 and subtract the corresponding triangle numbers ? What is the rule for this sequence?

Geometric Sequences - An Introduction To FRACTALS

When using number or algebra to generate a sequence we apply the same operation over and over again.

For example:

$2, 5, 8, 11, 14, 17, ...$ We add 3 to each previous term

$2, x + 2, 2x + 2,\ 3x + 2, 4x + 2, ..., ...$ we add x to each term.

The same can be done in Geometry. If we apply the same rule over and over again we can make a repeating pattern within a pattern. This is a <u>fractal</u>.

In 1975 Polish mathematician Benoit Mandelbrot introduced Fractal Geometry. He coined the word fractal to signify certain complex geometric shapes. The word is derived from the Latin *fractus*, meaning 'fragmented' or 'broken' and refers to the fact that these objects are self-similar, that is, their component parts are similar to the whole shape. These forms repeat themselves on an increasingly smaller scale, so that if each component is magnified it will look basically like the object as a whole.

For example:
a) Divide a line into three equal parts:

b) Replace the central section with two sides of an equilateral triangle:

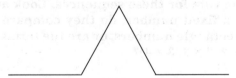

(c)   Divide the lines into three equal parts:

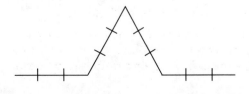

d) Replace the central sections with two sides of an equilateral triangle:
   Second generation

Exercise 8E

You will need worksheets 8/1, 8/2, 8/3 and 8/4 for this exercise.

1. The first pattern on Worksheet 8/1 is a triangle with sides of 9 units. What is its perimeter? What is its area in triangular units?

2. To produce the first generation of this fractal you have to divide each side of the triangle into three parts and then build an equilateral triangle on the central part, just like the previous example.
    a) Copy your triangle into the second box on the worksheet and do this to each side of the triangle.
    This is your <u>first generation fractal</u>.
    b) What is the perimeter of this pattern?
    c) What is its area?

3. a) Copy your first generation fractal into the third box on the worksheet and repeat the 'divide and build' to each side of the pattern. (That will be 12 times in all).
    This is your <u>second generation fractal</u>.
    b) What is the area of this pattern?
    d) To find the perimeter it is now simplest to count the number of sides, and to multiply this by the length of one side.

4. Now fill in this table at the bottom of Worksheet 8/2

Generation number	Area	No of sides	Length of each side	Perimeter
0	81	3	9	27
1	108	12	3	36
2	...	...	...	...
3				

5. Now draw a 3 × enlargement of your first triangle on Worksheet 8/2. The sides will be of length 27 units triangle with sides of 27 units. This time you can draw a <u>third generation fractal</u>.

6. Fill in the column for the number of sides of each generation. Can you find a rule for the number of sides in the nth generation?

7. The 3rd generation fractal is a ×3 enlargement and so you must divide the length of each side by 3 before filling in the 'Length' column and thus finding the perimeter. Can you find a rule for the perimeter of the nth pattern?

8. As the 3rd generation fractal is a × 3 enlargement you must divide the area of this pattern by 9 before filling in the 'Area' column . Can you find a rule for the area of the *n*th pattern?

9. As the number of sides becomes larger and larger what can you say about the area? What can you say about the perimeter? A cross section through your lungs would be rather like this - they have a relatively small area and a huge perimeter.

Geometric Sequences And Numbers

10. <u>Serpinski's Gasket</u>.
    You are going to have to shade and then rub out in this sequence, so do the first shading very lightly.
    a) Take the equilateral triangle of side 16 units on Worksheet 8/3.
    Divide it into 4 equal triangles. Remove (or do not shade in) the central one
    b) Divide each remaining triangle into four and remove (rub out) the central one. This is the second generation gasket.
    c) Repeat this procedure as many times as you can. Shade the final result carefully.
    d) Complete this table:

Generation Number	1	2	3	4	5
No. of Triangles	4	13	...	...	...
Fraction of whole triangle removed	1/4	...	...	...	...

11. Now take the other equilateral triangle with sides of 16 units.
    a) Pascal's triangle has been started for you. Note that the numbers are formed by adding the number above 0 the left to the number above on the right. (3 + 3 = 6, 4 + 6 = 10, 5 + 10 = ?) Finish it off so that all the 16 rows are completed. (Use a calculator!)
    b) Now shade all the odd numbers.
    c) Compare your two triangles. What do you notice? Can you explain your answer at all?

12. Pascal's triangle contains several of the sequences that you have studied in this chapter. Try adding up each row of the triangle like this:

$$
\begin{array}{ccccccccc}
 & & & & 1 & & & & & & 1 \\
 & & & 1 & + & 1 & & & & & 2 \\
 & & 1 & + & 2 & + & 1 & & & & 4 \\
 & 1 & + & 3 & + & ... & + & 1 & & & ... \\
 1 & + & ... & + & 6 & + & ... & + & 1 & & ...
\end{array}
$$

    a) Can you find a rule for the sum of the *n*th row?
    b) Can you find the pattern of triangle numbers? (It is a sloping 'diagonal' not a row or column.

c) What pattern is there in the next diagonal?

d) Can you find a rule for the 4th term in the *n*th row?

Extension Exercise 8

Pentagonal And Hexagonal Numbers

We have looked at the patterns produced by dots of triangles and squares, which give us triangle numbers and square numbers.

Copy and complete this table for the number of dots in each pattern number:

Number	1st	2nd	3rd	4th	5th	*n*th
Triangular	.1	3	6	...	...	...
Square	1	4	...	...	...	...

The next two shapes in this sequence are <u>pentagons</u> and <u>hexagons</u>. Let us look at the patterns that these produce:

Pentagonal

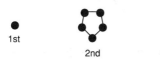
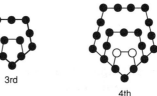

Hexagonal

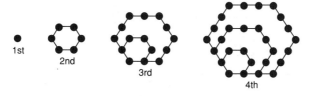

Now add to the above table to record these numbers.

Number	1st	2nd	3rd	4th	5th	nth
Triangular	1	3	6	...	...	...
Square	1	4	9	...	...	...
Pentagonal	1	5	12	...	...	...
Hexagonal	1	6	...	...	...	...

Can you work out the rule for the *n*th number of each polygon number?

Without drawing patterns can you extend the table for Heptagonal and Octagonal Numbers?

Summary Exercise 8

1.   Write down the next three terms of these series:
     a) 2, 7, 12, 17, ...
     b) 16, 4, 1, 0.25, ...
     c) 4, 2, 0, –2, ...

2.   Look at this series of patterns:

     a) Draw the next three patterns in the series.
     b) How many black dots will there be if there are 10 white dots?
     c) How many white dots will there be if there are 44 black dots?

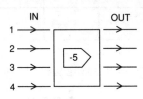

3.   Copy and complete the terms T_1, T_2, T_3, T_4, for this function machine and try and write a rule for T_n:
     $T_1 =$
     $T_2 =$
     $T_3 =$
     $T_4 =$

4.   Copy and complete the terms T_1, T_2, T_3, T_4, for this function machine and try and write a rule for T_n:

     $T_1 =$
     $T_2 =$
     $T_3 =$
     $T_4 =$

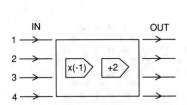

5.   If the nth term in the series is $S_n = 20 - 3n$, what is:
     a) S_1 b) S_3 c) S_6 d) S_{12}

6.   Can you find the next three terms in the series and hence the rule for T_n :
     $T_1 = 4$ $T_2 = 7$ $T_3 = 9$ $T_4 = 12$ $T_5 = 15$

7.   Can you find the next three terms in the series and hence the rule for T_n :
     $T_1 = 2$ $T_2 = 7$ $T_3 = 14$ $T_4 = 23$ $T_5 = 34$

8.   Can you find the next three terms in the series and hence the rule for T_n :
     $T_1 = 5$ $T_2 = 3$ $T_3 = 1$ $T_4 = -1$ $T_5 = -3$

Activity 8 - 3D Fractals

We can see fractals in 3D by repeating a pattern of cuts. This pattern is a bit like the snowflake except that we are going to turn the middle thirds into 3D squares:

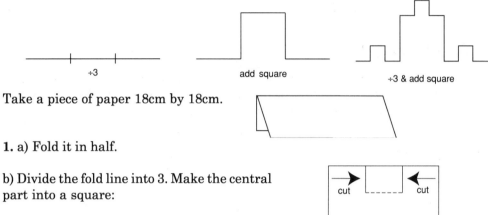

Take a piece of paper 18cm by 18cm.

1. a) Fold it in half.

b) Divide the fold line into 3. Make the central part into a square:

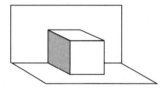

c) Score the lines as shown ....

d) Cut the solid lines and fold out your first generation pattern.

2. a) Flatten the sheet again and divide all the lines that have been folded IN into 3 parts. Make the central part into a square.

b) Fold and cut like the diagram. Now fold out your second generation pattern.

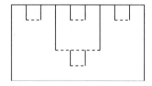

3. Flatten the diagram and divide, square, score and cut for your third generation pattern.

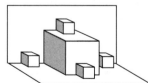

4. If you stick your 3D fractal on to folded coloured card it really shows up the repeating pattern.

5. Now design some of your own, or buy Tarquin Publications's book 'Fractal Cuts' and make some of those.

Chapter 9

Using Formula

What Is A Formula?

A formula is a mathematical statement, in the form of an equation, of a rule or principle. When you found the rule for the nth term of a sequence in the last chapter you were finding the formula for that sequence.

Formulae are written using symbols, and without any units in them. Being in the form of an algebraic equation they should not contain × or ÷ signs, but use brackets and fractions.

> For example: Write a formula for A, where A is the average, in kg, of three masses, x kg, y kg, and z kg
>
> $$A = \frac{x + y + z}{3}$$

Exercise 9A

1. Write a formula for N, where N is the total amount of money that I have, in pounds, if I start with £x and am given £y more.

2. Write a formula for N, where N is the total amount of money that I have, in pounds, if I start with £a and spend £b.

3. Write a formula for A when Am is the average of four lengths, wm, xm, ym and zm

4. Write a formula for P, where P is the perimeter of this rectangle:

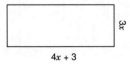

$3x$

$4x + 3$

5. Write a formula for A, where A is the area of the above rectangle.

6. Write a formula for P, where P is the perimeter of this triangle:

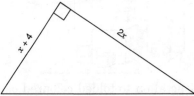

$x + 4$ $2x$

$3x - 2$

7. Write a formula for A, where A is the area of the above triangle.

8. Write a formula for N, where N is the total amount of money that I have, in pence, if I start with £x and am given £y more.

9. Write a formula for N, where N is the total amount of money that I have, in pounds, if I start with x pence and am given y pence more.

10. Write a formula for N, where N is the cost, in pounds, of buying 10 articles at £y each.

11. Write a formula for N, where N is the cost, in pounds, of buying n articles at £y each.

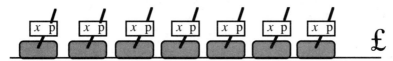

12. Write a formula for N, where N is the cost, in pounds, of buying n articles at x pence each.

13. Write a formula for P, where P is the perimeter of this shape:

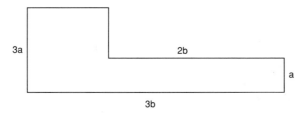

14. Write a formula for A, where A is the area of the above shape.

15. Write a formula for P, where P is the perimeter of this shape:

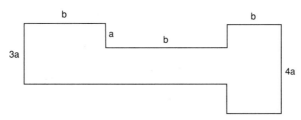

16. Write a formula for A, where A is the area of the above shape.

17. Write a formula for A, where A is the area of this shape:

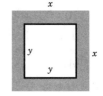

18. Write a formula for A where Acm^2 is the area of a frame where the outside of the frame is $x$cm by $y$cm and the frame is 5cm wide.

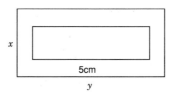

Substituting Into Formulae

When using a formula, numbers have to be substituted into the formula and then the answer calculated. While this process may be done with a calculator and appear to be simple it is important that certain rules are followed to avoid careless mistakes and to enable someone else to follow the working.

Particular care needs to be taken when substituting negative numbers into a formula, as it is very easy to make a mistake with one sign which then invalidates the answer.

$$
\begin{aligned}
\text{For example: If } a = -2, b = -3 \text{ and } c = 2 \text{ calculate } N \text{ if } N = ab^2 - bc \\
N &= ab^2 - bc && \text{Formula} \\
&= (-2 \times (-3)^2) - (-2 \times 2) && \text{Substitute} \\
&= (-2 \times 9) - (-4) && \text{Calculate} \\
&= -18 + 4 \\
&= -14 && \text{Answer}
\end{aligned}
$$

The stages **1. Formula**
            2. Substitute
            3. Calculate
            4. Answer
plus   **5. Units**

All need to be conscientiously performed and written down. The calculation may be done using a calculator but it is important that the actual calculation being performed is written down.

Most mistakes using formula occur in substituting carelessly. Do not try and combine substitution and calculation.

One common mistake is to confuse ab^2 with $(ab)^2$.

$$ab^2 = a \times b \times b \quad \text{whilst} \quad (ab)^2 = a \times b \times a \times b$$

and $\quad 2a^2 = 2 \times a \times a \quad$ whilst $\quad (ab)^2 = 2 \times a \times 2 \times a$

also note that $-a^2 = -a \times a = -a^2 \quad$ but $\quad (-a)^2 = (-a) \times (-a) = a^2$

Exercise 9B

1. If $a = -2$, $b = -1$ find N when:
    a) $N = a + b$ b) $N = a - b$ c) $N = b - a$
    d) $N = ab$ e) $N = 3a + 2b$ f) $N = 3a - 2b$

2. If $a = -3$, $b = 2$ and $c = -4$ find N when:
    a) $N = a^2$ b) $N = a^2 + b^2$ c) $N = 3a^2 - 2c^2$
    d) $N = ab - bc$ e) $N = a(b - c)$ f) $N = a^2(2b + 3c)$

3. If $a = -0.5$, $b = -2$ and $c = 0.2$ find N when:
    a) $N = ac$ b) $N = ab + c^2$ c) $N = abc$
    d) $N = ab - bc$ e) $N = a(b - c)$ f) $N = b(a^2 - c^2)$

4. If $x = -3, y = 4$ and $z = -1$ Find M when :

a) $M = \dfrac{x}{y}$

b) $M = \dfrac{xy}{z}$

c) $M = \dfrac{xyz}{4}$

d) $M = \dfrac{(x+y)}{(y-z)}$

e) $M = \dfrac{(x^2 - z^2)}{(x+y)}$

f) $M = \dfrac{(3x^2 - 2y^2)}{(3y - 2z)}$

5. If $a = -1, b = -2$ and $c = 3$ find N when:

a) $N = ab^2$

b) $N = (ab)^2$

c) $N = abc$

d) $N = ab - bc$

e) $N = a^2b - b^2c$

f) $N = a^2(4b^2 - 3bc)$

6. If $a = 0.24, b = 2.1$ and $c = 0.3$ find N when:

a) $N = ab^2$

b) $N = (ab)^2$

c) $N = abc$

d) $N = ab - bc$

e) $N = a^2b - b^2c$

f) $N = a^2(4b^2 - 3bc)$

7. If $a = -3, b = 2$ and $c = -2$ find N when:

a) $N = ab^2$

b) $N = (ab)^2$

c) $N = abc$

d) $N = \dfrac{a^2}{c}$

e) $N = \dfrac{a(c - b)}{2b}$

f) $N = \sqrt{b^2 - 4ac}$

8. If $x = 3.1, y = -0.07$ and $z = -1.25$ Find A when :

a) $A = x^2 + y^2$

b) $A = x(x + y)$

c) $A = x^2 - yz$

d) $A = \dfrac{xy - z^2}{4}$

e) $A = \dfrac{2x(y^2 - z^2)}{2z}$

f) $A = \dfrac{(2x - 3z)(3y^2 + xz)}{3y}$

9. If $x = -0.5, y = 2.5$ and $z = -1.2$ Find V when :

a) $V = x^2y$

b) $V = x(y^2 + z^2)$

c) $V = x^2z - y^2z$

d) $V = \dfrac{z^2(x^2 - y^2)}{4y}$

e) $V = \dfrac{2xy^2 - 3yz^2}{2}$

10. If $a = -0.25, b = 2.1$ and $c = -0.8$ find N when:

a) $N = ab^2 - bc^2$

b) $N = (ab - bc)^2$

c) $a^2(b - c)^2$

Area And Volume Formula

You are familiar with some formulae for length, area and volume.
For example: Find the area of a trapezium with parallel sides of 4cm
and 7cm and height 6cm.

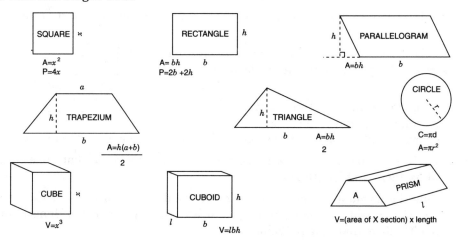

For example: Find the area of a trapezium with parallel sides of 4cm
and 7cm and height 6cm.

$$A = \frac{h(a+b)}{2}$$

$$= \frac{\cancel{6}^3(4+7)}{\cancel{2}_1}$$

$$= 3 \times 11$$

$$= 33\text{cm}^2$$

Exercise 9C

**Choose the correct formula from those above to answer the following
questions. You may use a calculator but you must write down the four
stages of working, and remember the units. Use π button on your calculator
and give non-exact answers to 3 s.f.**

1. Find the area of a triangle of base 5.6cm and height 2.8cm.

2. Find the perimeter of a rectangle of base 45cm and height 1.4m. Give your
    answer in metres.

3. Find the volume of a cube of side 1.2m

4. Find the area of a parallelogram of base 1.3m and height 55cm. Give your
    answer in sq. m.

5. Find the volume of a cuboid in m^3 of length 5.2m, breadth 45cm and height
    45cm.

6. Find the circumference of a circle of radius 15cm.

7. Find the area of a circle of diameter 20cm.

8. Find the volume of a prism in m^3 with cross sectional area of 12cm^2 and length
    1.2m.

9. Find the area of a trapezium in m^2 with parallel
    sides of lengths 55cm and 1.4m and height
    65cm.

10. Using the formula for the area of a triangle find
    the formula for the area of a kite in terms of its
    diagonals and hence find the area of a kite with diagonals of 12cm and 15cm.

11. Find the volume of a prism with a cross sectional area in the shape of a circle of
    radius 12cm and length 20cm.

12. Using the formula for the area of a rectangle derive a formula for the surface
    area of a cuboid and hence find the surface area of a cuboid of length 14cm,
    breadth 20cm and height 12cm.

Finding An Unknown Quantity

In the above examples you had to find the Area , Perimeter or Volume when you were given the lengths. There are times when you know the Volume, Area or Perimeter and you have to find a length.

This is done by following exactly the same steps as before.

For example: The area of a triangle is 24cm² and its base is 12.4cm. Find the height of the triangle.

$$A = \frac{bh}{2} \qquad \text{1. Formula}$$

$$24 = \frac{\overset{6.2}{\cancel{12.4}} \times b}{\cancel{2}} \qquad \text{2. Substitute}$$

$$\frac{24}{6.2} = 6.2 \times b \qquad \text{3. Calculate}$$

$$= b \qquad\qquad (\div 6.2)$$

$$b \;\; = 3.870....$$

$$= 3.87 \text{ (to 3.s.f)} \qquad \text{4. \& 5. Answer and units}$$

Note that once you have substituted into the formula you now have an equation with one unknown quantity. Treat this exactly like any other equation.

Exercise 9D

Using the formula given earlier find these quantities. Use π button on your calculator and give non-exact answers to 3 s.f.

1. Fine the side of a square of area 289cm².

2. Find the height of a rectangle of base 12cm and area 228cm².

3. Find the base of a parallelogram of height 14cm and area 238cm².

4. Find the base of a triangle of height 5.5cm and area 132cm².

5. Find the length of a side of a cube of volume 343cm³.

6. Find the diameter of a circle of circumference 14cm.

7. Find the radius of a circle of area 100cm².

8. Find the radius of a circle of circumference 12m.

9. Find the diameter of a circle of area 250cm².

10. Find the radius in cm of a circle of area 4m.

11. Find the height of a trapezium with parallel sides of 10cm and 12cm and area 132cm².

12. Find the height of a trapezium with parallel sides of 55cm and 1.2 m , and area of 4m².

13. A trapezium has one parallel side twice as long as the other and height 5cm. If the area is 12cm² find the length of the parallel sides.

14. Find one parallel side of a trapezium if the other is 20cm, the height is 12cm and the area is 50cm².

15. Find one parallel side of a trapezium if the other is 1.4 m, the height is 60cm and the area is 5m.

16. A prism has a volume of 288cm³ and a cross sectional area of 24cm² , what is its height?

17. A prism has a volume of 100cm³ and a cross sectional area of 15cm² , what is its length?

18. A prism has a cross section in the shape of a triangle of base 12cm and height 8cm, and the volume of the prism is 720cm³ , what is its length?

19. A prism has a cross section in the shape of a circle of radius 8cm, the volume of the prism is 200cm³ , what is its height?

20. A prism has a cross section in the shape of a circle of circumference 15cm. The volume of the prism is 268cm³ , what is the length of the prism?(Clue – find r from the circumference first).

21. A parallelogram has a base twice as long as its height, and area 30cm² , how long is the base?

22. A triangle has a height three times as long as its base and area 25cm², what is the height?

23. The sides of a rectangle are in the ratio 3 : 4 and the area of the rectangle is 100cm² . What are the lengths of the sides?

24. The base and height of a triangle are in the ratio 3 : 5 and the triangle has an area of 150cm² , what is the length of the base and the height?

25. A cuboid has sides in the ratio 5 : 7 : 8 and a volume of 1m , what are the lengths of the sides?

Polygon Formula

You are familiar with some formulae for finding interior and exterior angles of polygons:

Exercise 9E

1. Find the sum of the interior angles of a pentagon.

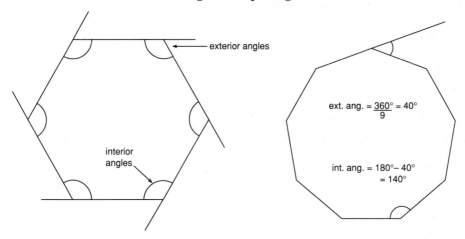

exterior angles

interior angles

ext. ang. $= \frac{360°}{9} = 40°$

int. ang. $= 180° - 40°$
$= 140°$

2. Find the sum of the interior angles of a nonagon.
3. Find the sum of the interior angles of an octagon.
4. Find the exterior angle of a regular hexagon.
5. Find the exterior angle of a regular heptagon.
6. Find the exterior angle of a regular decagon.
7. Find the interior angle of a regular pentagon.
8. Find the interior angle of a regular octagon.
9. How many sides has a regular polygon whose exterior angles are all 18°?
10. How many sides has a regular polygon whose exterior angles are all 24°?
11. How many sides has a regular polygon whose interior angles are all 150°?
12. How many sides has a regular polygon whose interior angles are all 160°?
13. ABCDE is a regular pentagon. O is the centre of the pentagon
    such that AO = BO = CO = DO = EO.
    Find (a) ∠AOB   (b) ∠OBC   (c) ∠ABC

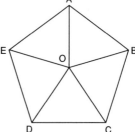

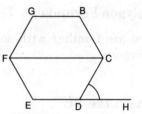

14. BCDEFG is a regular hexagon.
Find, giving reasons for your answers:
(i)   ∠CDH
(ii)   ∠CDE
(iii)   ∠DCF
(iv)   What can you say about CF and DE

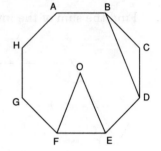

15. ABCDEFGH is a regular octagon with centre O.
Find giving reasons for your answers:
(i)   ∠EOF
(ii)   ∠FED
(iii)   ∠OED
(iv)   ∠BCD
(v)   ∠CDB
(vi)   ∠BDE
(vii) What can you say about BD and OE?

16. ABCDE is a regular pentagon and EDFGHI is a regular hexagon. Find, giving
reasons for all your answers:
(i)   ∠CDE
(ii)   ∠EDF
(iii)   ∠CED
(iv)   ∠DEF
(v)   ∠CDF
(vi)   ∠ECF

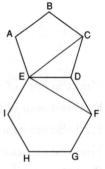

17. Here is the base of a regular polygon. The exterior
angle is 11 times bigger than the interior angle. How
many sides has the polygon.

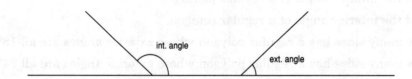

Distance, Speed and Time Formula

The formula for the distance travelled given the speed and time is $d = s\,t$

From this can be derived the formula for time : $\quad t = \dfrac{d}{s}$

and the formula for speed: $\quad s = \dfrac{d}{t}$

For example: I walk for 4 hours at 3km per hour. How far do I walk?

$$\text{Distance} = \text{speed} \times \text{time}$$
$$= 3 \times 4$$
$$= 12\text{km}$$

As the units of time do NOT follow the metric system. There are 60 seconds in a minute and 60 minutes in an hour it is a good idea to always convert time to a fraction or decimal fraction of the unit. Therefore if speed is in km per hour then $2\,\tfrac{1}{2}$ hours and 30 minutes would be 2 hours or 2.5 hours. If you calculated time to be 3.3333.... hours then this is 3 hours or 3 hours and 20 minutes.

For example : If I travelled 12 miles in 12 minutes what is my speed?

$d = 12$ miles $\qquad\qquad$ time $= 12$ minutes $= \dfrac{12}{60}\ (=\dfrac{1}{5})$ hour $= 0.2$ hours

$d = st$ and therefore $\qquad\qquad s\ =\ \dfrac{d}{t}$

$$=\ \dfrac{12}{0.2}$$

$$=\ 60 \text{ mph}$$

Exercise 9E

1.   I travel at 60mph for 45 minutes. How far do I go?

2.   A space rocket travels at 3000km per hour for 5 minutes. How far does it go?

3.   I walk three quarters of a mile in twenty minutes. What is my speed in miles per hour?

4.   A comet travels 100km in 10 minutes. What is its speed in km/h ?

5.   I drive for 90 miles at a speed of 60mph. How long does the journey take?

6.   My mother drives at 40mph for 30 minutes, and then she drives at 30 mph for 40 minutes. How far does she go?

7.   It took us three hours and twenty minutes to travel 300km. What was our speed?

8.   We travelled for 12 miles on the M25 at 10mph, but then we went on the M4 for 80 miles at 60mph. What was our total journey time?

9.   An aeroplane left Heathrow at 1034 and arrived at Newark, USA at 1624. If the distance is 3605 miles what is the speed of the aeroplane?

10. A ship travelled for 6 days and 4 hours on a journey from Southampton to Gibraltar, a distance of 3219 kilometres. What was the average daily distance covered, and what was the speed?

11. If a car travels twice the distance from A to B at the same speed it travelled from A to B how much longer or shorter is the journey time?

12. If a car travels three times the distance from A to B in the same time it travelled from A to B how much faster or slower is the speed?

13. If a car travels three times the distance from A to B in half the time it travelled from A to B how much faster or slower is the speed?

Average Speed

Although the examples above talk about 'speed' it is hard in practice to drive 60 miles at a constant speed, and so this should really be thought of as 'average speed' such that:

$$\text{average speed} = \frac{\text{total distance}}{\text{total time}}$$

However, unlike most averages, you cannot find the average of two speeds by simply adding them together and dividing by two. Look at the next example:

We travelled at 40km per hour for 15 minutes and then travelled at 60km per hour for 20 minutes. What was our average speed?

$\text{Speed}_1 = 40\text{km/h}$ $\text{Time}_1 = 15 \text{ mins} = 0.25\text{h}$

$d = s\,t$

$d_1 = 40 \times 0.25$

$= 10\text{km}$

$\text{Speed}_2 = 60\text{km/h}$ $\text{Time}_2 = 20 \text{ mins} = \frac{1}{3}\text{h}$

$d = s\,t$

$d_2 = 60 \times \frac{1}{3}\text{h}$

$= 20\text{km}$

Total distance $= 30\text{km}$ Total time $= 35$ minutes $= \frac{35}{60}$ hour

$\text{average speed} = \frac{\text{total distance}}{\text{total time}}$

$= 30 \div \frac{35}{60}$

$= 51.428....$

$= 51.4\text{km/h}$ (to 3 s.f.)

14. A car travels for 45 minutes at 40km/h and then for 30 minutes at 60km/hour.

   a) What distance did the car travel?
   b) What was the average speed?

15. A man walked for 15 minutes at 4km/h and then for 12 minutes at 5km/hour.
   a) What distance did the man walk?
   b) What was his average speed?

16. A train travelled at 60km per hour for 20 minutes and at 120km per hour for one hour and forty minutes.
   a) What distance did the train travel?
   b) What was its average speed?

17. An aeroplane travelled at 250km/h for one and a half hours and then at 350km/h for two and a half hours.
   a) What distance did the aeroplane travel?
   b) What was the average speed?

18. A car travelled at an average speed of 55mph for 2 hours, the first part of the journey was in town travelling at 30mph for 20 minutes. What was the speed of the second part of the journey?

19. A car travelled at an average speed of 100km/h for 80km, the first part of the journey the speed was 40km/h for 15 minutes. What was the speed of the second part of the journey?

20. A London to Paris train travels from London to Dover, a distance of 120km, at 100km/h. If the train travels the 40km under the channel at 80km/h, before travelling the 250km to Paris at 125km/h.
   a) What is the total journey time?
   b) What is the average speed of the train?

21. Work out the answers to 14a), 15a) 16a) 17a) and 20a) using the fraction method and check that you get the same answers as before.

22. An aeroplane sets of from London at 1145 and reaches Glasgow at 1320. The aeroplane spends 40% of the total flight time travelling at 120mph. If the distance from London to Glasgow is 400 miles?
   a) What is the average speed of the aeroplane?
   b) At what speed and for what distance does the plane travel for 60% of the time?

23. A motor bike courier spends part of his
day in traffic and part of his time on a
motorway. On the motorway he travels
at an average speed of 60mph, and in
town his speed is an average of 20mph.
a) On Monday he had to do a delivery
of 40 miles of which 30 miles were on
the motorway.

(i)   What distance did he travel in town?
(ii) What was the total time?
(iii) What was his average speed?
b) On Tuesday he has to make the same trip in the same time, but he was held
up in town and travelled at an average speed of 15mph. Was he able to make
the delivery without breaking the speed limit on the motorway of 70mph?

Rearranging Formulae

When we had to find the lengths in the earlier exercise we substituted numbers into
the formula and then solved the resulting equation. However there are times when
we need to rearrange the formula, such as in the previous exercise when we
rearranged the formula $d = s\,t$ to give :

$$t = \frac{d}{s} \text{ and } s = \frac{d}{t}$$

This is done in exactly the same way as solving an equation, keep thinking along
the lines of 'do the same thing to both sides' and write what you are doing on the
right hand side:

For example: Rearrange the formula $y = \dfrac{x}{4} + 7$ to give x in terms of y.

$$y = \frac{x}{4} + 7$$

$$(-7)$$

$$y - 7 = \frac{x}{4}$$

$$(\times 4)$$

$$4(y - 7) = x$$
$$x = 4(y - 7)$$

Note the use of brackets, and the correct use of algebra. No × signs or ÷ signs in the
actual formula.

Exercise 9G

Make x the subject of the following formulae:

1. $y = x + 3$

2. $y = x - 5$

3. $y = 4 + x$

4. $y = 8 - x$

5. $y = x + a$

6. $y = x - b$

7. $y = c + x$

8. $y = d - x$

9. $y = 2x$

10. $y = ax$

11. $y = \dfrac{x}{2}$

12. $y = \dfrac{x}{b}$

13. $y = 2x + 3$

14. $y = 3x - 4$

15. $y = 5 + 3x$

16. $y = 5 - 2x$

17. $y = 3x + a$

18. $y = 2x - b$

19. $y = c + 3x$

20. $y = d - 3x$

21. $y = ax + b$

22. $y = cx - d$

23. $y = a - bx$

24. $y = \dfrac{2x}{3}$

25. $y = \dfrac{3x}{a}$

26. $y = \dfrac{ax}{b}$

27. $y = \dfrac{2a}{x}$

28. $y = \dfrac{3b}{2x}$

29. $y = \dfrac{ab}{x}$

30. $y = \dfrac{x}{2} + 1$

31. $y = \dfrac{x}{3} - 5$

32. $y = 6 - \dfrac{x}{5}$

33. $y = \dfrac{x}{a} + b$

34. $y = \dfrac{ax}{b} - c$

35. $y = a - \dfrac{bx}{c}$

36. $A = \dfrac{x(a+b)}{2}$

37. $A = \dfrac{h(a+x)}{c}$

38. $A = \dfrac{h(a-x)}{2c}$

39. $A = \dfrac{h(a+b)}{x}$

40. $A = \dfrac{h(a+b)}{ax}$

41. $y + a = \dfrac{x}{3}$

42. $y = \dfrac{b}{3+x}$

43. $y + c = \dfrac{a}{b-x}$

44. $y + a = \dfrac{b}{ax}$

45. $y + a = \dfrac{x+b}{c}$

Units Of Formulae

When writing formulae or working with several formulae put together it is important that we keep asking ourselves 'does this look right' 'does this seem sensible'. It is as easy to do this with letters as it is with numbers, and if we bear in mind the units of a formula this can help to check the validity of what we are doing.

If D = Density in g/m³, M = mass in g and V = Volume in cm³ find the units of the following and hence the quantity, if any, being found:

a) DV

b) $\dfrac{V}{M}$

$DV = \dfrac{g}{cm^3} \times cm^3$

$\dfrac{V}{M} = \dfrac{cm^3}{g}$

$= g$

$= ?$

$= $ mass

$= $ wrong formula

Exercise 9H

1. If d is a length in m, t is a time in seconds and s is a speed in m/s what are the units of the following and what quantity, if any, do they represent?

   a) st b) $\dfrac{t}{d}$ c) $\dfrac{d}{s}$ d) dt

2. If D = Density in g/m³, M = mass in g and V = Volume in cm³ find the units of the following and hence the quantity, if any, being found:

   a) MV b) $\dfrac{M}{V}$ c) MD d) $\dfrac{M}{D}$

3. If a, b, c and d are units of length in cm for which quantity, length, area or volume, if any, are the following formulae:

   a) $a(b+c)$ b) $\dfrac{\pi a^2}{b}$ c) $\pi a^2(b+c)$ d) $\dfrac{abc}{\pi}$

   e) $\sqrt{a^2+b^2}$ f) $\pi a(b^2+c)$ g) $\sqrt[3]{abc}$ h) $\dfrac{\pi a^2 b + c}{2a}$

4. If u and v are units of speed in m/s, t is a unit of time in secs, m of mass in g and a, b, c, and s units of length in cm what are the units of the following formulae:

   a) $A = \dfrac{m}{abc}$ b) $B = s\sqrt{u^2 - v^2}$ c) $C = t\sqrt{u^2 - v^2}$ d) $D = \dfrac{s}{u+v}$

Extension Exercise 9

Rearranging Formulae with Factorising and Roots

In the previous exercise on rearranging formulae the only operations used were $\times$, $\div$, $+$, and $-$. However there are times when you have more than one x term and need to factorise:

For example: Make x the subject of the following formula

$$y - x = \frac{a + x}{b}$$

$$(\times b)$$

$$b(y - x) = a + x$$

$$(\times brackets)$$

$$by - bx = a + x$$

$$(+bx)$$

$$by = a + x + bx$$

$$(-a)$$

$$by - a = x + bx$$

$$(factorise)$$

$$by - a = x(1 + b)$$

$$(\div (1 + b))$$

$$\frac{by - a}{1 + b} = x$$

$$x = \frac{by - a}{1 + b}$$

Note that the rearrangement is made simpler if you keep the x term positive, just as you have done for equations and inequations. Do not miss out any stages of working, this tends to lead to mistakes.

Make x the subject of the following formulae:

1. $y = \dfrac{a + x}{b + x}$

2. $y = \dfrac{a + x}{x - b}$

3. $b - x = \dfrac{a + x}{c}$

4. $ax = \dfrac{a + x}{b + c}$

5. $y(a - x) = b(a + x)$

6. $y(a - x) = b(a + x)$

7. $x - y = \dfrac{a + x}{b}$

8. $c(y + x) = a(x - b)$

9. $y = \dfrac{a(a - x)}{b + x}$

10. $y(a - x) = \dfrac{x(a - c)}{b}$

There are times when formulae contain squares and square roots. Square roots usually need to be multiplied out before you can rearrange the equation. Look at this example:

Make x the subject of this formula:

$$y = \sqrt{x^2 + a^2}$$

(square both sides)

$$y^2 = x^2 + a^2$$

$(-a^2)$

$$y^2 - a^2 = x^2$$

($\sqrt{}$ both sides)

$$\pm\sqrt{y^2 - a^2} = x$$

$$x = \pm\sqrt{y^2 - a^2}$$

It is important to realise that $\sqrt{x^2 + y^2}$ is not equal to $x + y$.

11. If $x = 3$ and $y = 4$ calculate

    a) $x + y$ b) $x^2 + y^2$ c) $\sqrt{x^2 + y^2}$

12. If $x = 13$ and $y = 12$ calculate

    a) $x - y$ b) $x^2 - y^2$ c) $\sqrt{x^2 - y^2}$

Now make x the subject of the following formula:

13. $y = \sqrt{x^2 - a^2}$ **17.** $y = \dfrac{\sqrt{x^2 + b^2}}{a}$

14. $y = \sqrt{a^2 - x^2}$ **18.** $y = \dfrac{\sqrt{x^2 + b^2}}{x}$

15. $\dfrac{y}{b} = \sqrt{x^2 - a^2}$ **19.** $y^2 = \sqrt{x^2 + b^2}$

16. $\dfrac{x}{a} = \sqrt{x^2 + b^2}$ **20.** $y = \sqrt{\dfrac{x^2 - a^2}{b}}$

Summary Exercise 9

Use your calculator but show all stages of working. Take π as the value given by the π button on your calculator. Give any non-exact answers to 3 s.f.

1. Write a formula for P, where P is the perimeter of this shape:

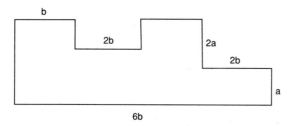

2. Write a formula for A, where A is the area of the above shape.
3. If $a = -1$, $b = 2$ and $c = -4$ find N when:
    a) $N = a - b$ b) $N = abc$ c) $N = c^2 - a^2$

    d) $N = \dfrac{a^2}{c}$ e) $N = \dfrac{a(c-b)}{2b}$ f) $N = \dfrac{a(c-b)}{2b}$

4. Find the area of a circle of radius 8cm.
5. Find the volume of a prism in m^3 with cross sectional area of $15cm^2$ and length 1.2m.
6. One parallel side of a trapezium is three times the length of the other, the height is 60cm and the area is $2m^2$. Find the lengths of the parallel sides.
7. a) A prism has a volume of $500cm^3$ and a cross sectional area of $81cm^2$, what is its height?
    b) If the cross section is in the shape of a triangle of base 18cm what is the height of the triangle?
8. I drive for 750 miles at a speed of 60 miles per hour. How long does the journey take?
9. A car travelled at 40km/h for 10 minutes and then at 60km/h for 50 minutes.
    a) What was the average speed?
    b) What distance did the car travel?
10. Make x the subject of the following formula :

    a) $y = a + x$ b) $y = c + ax$ c) $y = \dfrac{h(a-x)}{b}$

Activity 9 - Perigal's Dissection

Take a sheet of A3 plain paper.
In the middle of it draw a right angled triangle, it does not matter exactly what its dimensions are but make each side a different length. If a group of you are doing this then choose different dimensions. Draw your triangle askew like this.

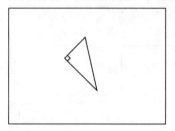

Now you are going to make each side of the triangle into a square like this:

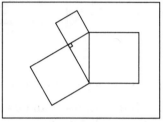

You now have three squares, a big one, a little one and a middle sized square. We are now going to dissect the middle sized square. First of all **very lightly** find its centre by drawing the two diagonals:

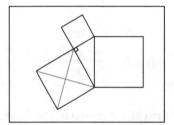

The longest side of a right angled triangle is the side opposite the right angle and is called the HYPOTENUSE. You now draw a line **parallel to the Hypotenuse** through the centre of the middle sized square, use a set square to draw the parallel line:
Slide your set square along a ruler to draw a parallel line

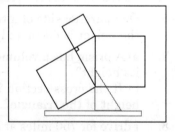

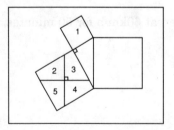

Now draw a line at right angles to the line you have just drawn also passing through the centre of the middle sized square:

Now trace over the little square and cut it out, trace over the middle sized square and cut out the four pieces. Now can you fit all five pieces together in the big square? Does the square on the hypotenuse equal the sum of the other 2 squares?

Chapter 10

Pythagoras's Theorem

Pythagoras was a Greek Philosopher and Mathematician. He was born on the island of Samos c 560 BC and travelled extensively as a young man. His contribution to mathematics was enormous. He was the first in the Western world (rather than the Eastern world of Ancient China and the Arabic world) to use letters on geometric shapes, and this enabled him to deduce and prove many geometric and algebraic theorems.

Pythagoras equated the beauty of numerical properties with religion and his followers became a secret brotherhood following religious rites as well as mathematical and philosophical studies.

Pythagoras demonstrated the construction of the five regular solids, and from his philosophical studies also asserted that this proved that the world must be round - a concept that took centuries to be accepted!

While Pythagoras's exploration into number theory has been the starting point for much mathematical development he is best known for being the first to prove that:

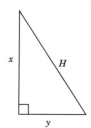

For any right angled triangle the square on the hypotenuse is equal to the sum of the squares on the other two sides.

or $$H^2 = x^2 + y^2$$

(Note the capital H for Hypotenuse – this avoids confusion with a lower case h, commonly used for height. Many problems concerning right angled triangles involve the height and the Hypotenuse - and they will not be the same side!)

Exercise 10A

In a right angled triangle the hypotenuse is the longest side - the side opposite the right angle. Copy each of these triangles with a neat sketch and mark the hypotenuse with a capital H:

1.
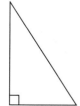

2.
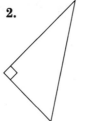

3.
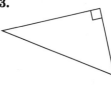

4. 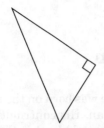   **5.** 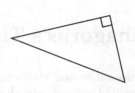   **6.**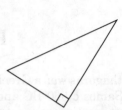

Finding The Hypotenuse

To find the hypotenuse of any right angled triangle we can use Pythagoras's theorem. As this is in the form of a formula we use the normal five stages for solving each problem:

        1. Formula
        2. Substitute
        3. Calculate
        4. Answer
        5. Units

For each question you should draw a sketch of the two dimensional triangle and label the Hypotenuse with a capital H.

For example: Find the hypotenuse of this triangle:

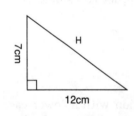

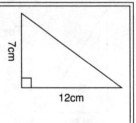

$$H^2 = x^2 + y^2$$
$$= 7^2 + 12^2$$
$$= 49 + 144 = 193$$
$$H = \sqrt{193}$$
$$= 13.892$$
$$= 13.9\text{cm (to 3 s.f.)}$$

Note that when writing down your calculations $H^2 = 193$

        but $H = \sqrt{193}$

Exercise 10B

Find the hypotenuse of these right angled triangles, give non - exact answers to 3 s.f. :

   1. 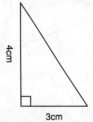   **2.** 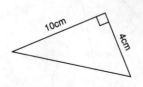   **3.**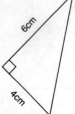

4.

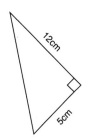

5.

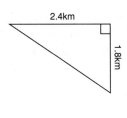

6.

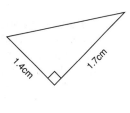

7.

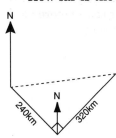

8.

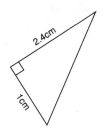

9.

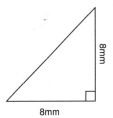

Example: A man walked 400m due North and then 500m due West. How far was he then from his starting point?

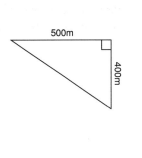

$H^2 = x^2 + y^2$ (Pythagoras' Theorem)
$$= 400^2 + 500^2$$
$$= 1600 + 2500$$
$$H = \sqrt{4100}$$
$$= 64.0312...$$
$$= 64.0m \text{ (to 3 s.f.)}$$

---

10. A plane flew 6 miles due East and then 8 miles due south. How far is the plane from its starting point?

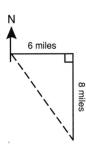

11. A ship sailed 240km South East and then 320km North East. How far was the ship then from its starting point?

12. A hunter set out from home at A and walked 1.4km on a bearing of 030° to a joint B and then walked 2.7km on a bearing of 120° to a point C. How far did he have to walk back home? (You must calculate angle ABC first!)

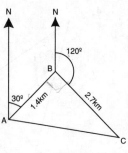

13. A school playground is in the shape of a rectangle 100m by 50m. John has to run around the whole perimeter of the rectangle and Janet has to run along the diagonal three times. Who runs further, Janet or John?

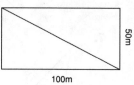

14. Find the length of the diagonals of a square of side 5cm.

15. A doorway is 2m tall and 1m wide. Can I get a square piece of wood with sides 2.3m square through the doorway? If not by how much must I shave off one side ?

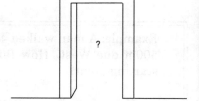

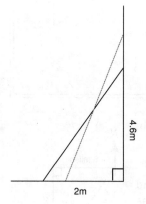

16. Fred and Bert have a new ladder. Fred reads the instructions and puts the foot of the ladder 2 m away from the foot of the wall so that the top of the ladder reaches a point 4.6 m above the ground.
a) How long is the ladder?
b) Bert complains that he cannot reach high enough up the wall. He decides to nove the foot of the ladder 0.5 metres towards the foot of the wall. Bert says that the top of the ladder will now be 0.5 m higher than before as the ladder stays the same length. Is Bert right?.

Finding A Side Other Than The Hypotenuse

If we know the hypotenuse and one other side of a right-angled triangle we can use Pythagoras's Theorem to find the third side. However, take care to substitute correctly into the equation.

For example: Find x in this triangle:

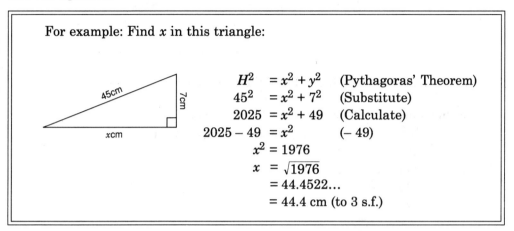

$$
\begin{aligned}
H^2 &= x^2 + y^2 \quad \text{(Pythagoras' Theorem)} \\
45^2 &= x^2 + 7^2 \quad \text{(Substitute)} \\
2025 &= x^2 + 49 \quad \text{(Calculate)} \\
2025 - 49 &= x^2 \quad\quad\ (-\ 49) \\
x^2 &= 1976 \\
x &= \sqrt{1976} \\
&= 44.4522... \\
&= 44.4 \text{ cm (to 3 s.f.)}
\end{aligned}
$$

Exercise 10C

Find x in these triangles:

1.

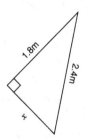

2.

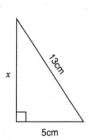

3.

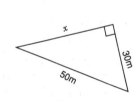

4.

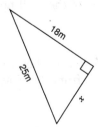

5.

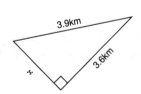

6.

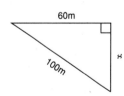

7.

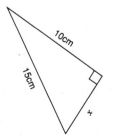

8.

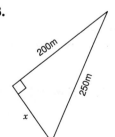

9.

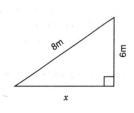

Example: A rectangle of base 24cm has diagonals of 32cm long.

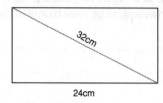 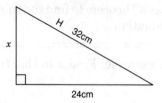

What length are the other sides of the rectangle?

Let the other side of the rectangle be $x$cm long.

$$H^2 = x^2 + y^2 \qquad \text{(Pythagoras' Theorem)}$$
$$32^2 = x^2 + 24^2$$
$$1024 = x^2 + 576$$
$$1024 - 576 = x^2$$
$$x^2 = 448$$
$$x = \sqrt{448}$$
$$= 21.168...$$
$$= 21.2 \text{ cm (to 3 s.f.)}$$

10. A rectangle of base 15cm has diagonals of 18cm. What length are the other sides of the rectangle?

11. A ship sails 15miles due North , and then sails due East until she is 30miles from her starting point, how many miles did she sail due East?

12. A rambler walked 1.5km North West dropped his handkerchief and then walked South West before he noticed. If he was now 2.4km from his starting place how far did he have to walk back to collect his handkerchief?

13. A ladder 4m long is leaning against a wall. If the foot of the ladder is 1m from the base of the wall how far up the wall does the ladder reach?

14. Another ladder is 3m long and reaches 2m up the wall. How far is the base of this ladder from the base of the wall?

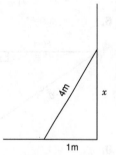

15. The bracket for a hotel sign is in the shape of a right angle triangle. How long is the top of the bracket?

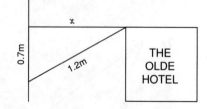

16. A square has diagonals of 5cm. What is the length of a side of the square?

Pythagoras's Theorem can be used to find the height of an isosceles triangle:

Find the height of an isosceles triangle ABC

$$H^2 = x^2 + y^2 \quad \text{(Pythagoras' Theorem)}$$
$$12^2 = x^2 + 5^2$$
$$144 = x^2 + 25$$
$$144 - 25 = x^2$$
$$x^2 = 119$$
$$x = \sqrt{119}$$
$$= 10.908...$$
$$= 10.9\text{cm (to 3 s.f.)}$$

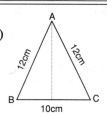

Exercise 10D

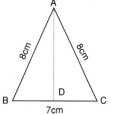

1. Find the height AD of an isosceles triangle ABC where
    AB = AC = 8 cm and BC = 7 cm

2. Find the height of an equilateral triangle of side 6cm.

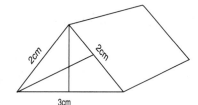

3. The sides of a line tent are 2 m long, and the
    corners are 3m apart. What is the height of the tent
    pole?

4. An isosceles triangle XYZ has height AX = 12cm and sides XY = XZ = 13cm.
    What is the length of YZ?

5. An equilateral triangle has a height of 8cm. What is the length of its sides?

Special Triangles

In the last few exercises a very few triangles came out with sides that were an exact
number or to an exact number of decimal places. These were

3cm, 4cm, 5cm   1.8 km, 2.4 km, 3.0.km,
5cm, 12cm, 13cm,   6 miles, 8 miles, 10miles,
30m, 40m, 50m,   60m, 80m, 100m,
3.9km, 3.6km, 1.5km,   150,m 200m, 250m.

Consider $3^2 + 4^2 = 9 + 16$ and $5^2 + 12^2 = 25 + 144$
                     $= 25$ $= 169$
Both 25 and 169 are perfect squares.

               $25 = 5 \times 5$ and $169 = 13 \times 13$

This makes the 3:4:5 - and the 5:12:13 $\triangle$ very special, and they frequently crop up in problems, either in this form or scaled up or down. In the examples above

1.8km, 2.4km, 3.0.km is a 3:4:5 $\triangle$ × 0.6,
6miles, 8miles, 10miles is a 3:4:5 $\triangle$ × 2,
30m, 40m, 50m is a 3:4:5 $\triangle$ × 10,
60m, 80m, 100m is a 3:4:5 $\triangle$ × 20,
150,m 200m, 250m is a 3:4:5 $\triangle$ × 50,
and 3.9km, 3.6km, 1.5km is a 5:12:13 $\triangle$ × 0.3,

Spotting a 3:4:5 $\triangle$ or a 5:12:13 $\triangle$ can save a lot of time and so it is worth taking a little bit of time to look and check whether or not a triangle is 'special'.

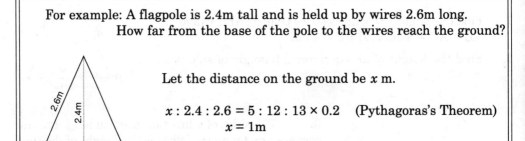

For example: A flagpole is 2.4m tall and is held up by wires 2.6m long.
         How far from the base of the pole to the wires reach the ground?

Let the distance on the ground be x m.

$x : 2.4 : 2.6 = 5 : 12 : 13 \times 0.2$ (Pythagoras's Theorem)
$x = 1m$

Exercise 1E

State whether or not these triangles are either 3:4:5 $\triangle$ or 5:12:13$\triangle$. If they are give the scale factor and find x.

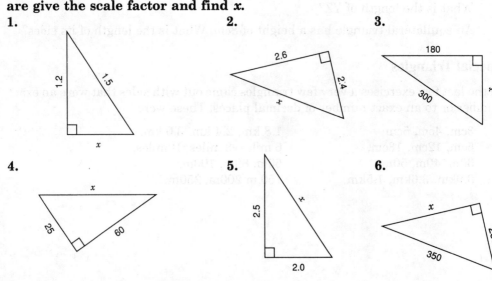

1.

2.

3.

4.

5.

6.

7.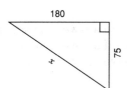

8.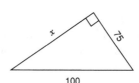

9. This is cross section through a porch. How long is the roof section AD?

10. This is a radio aerial. It is held up by three wires attached to its top. The wires are 15m long, how far are the wires from the base of the aerial?

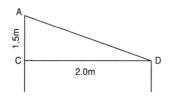

11. a) A flagpole 18m high is held up by wires that come $\frac{2}{3}$ up the pole.

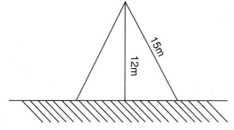

How high up from the ground is this?
b) The wires meet the ground 5m from the pole. How long are the wires?

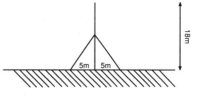

12. A hunter sets out from home. He follows tracks 1200m to the North and then 500m West. The tracks then disappeared! How far has he got to walk home?

13. The hunter's wife tracks a bear 600m to the North East and then 800m South East. She then shot the bear, how far does she have to drag it home?

14. Their son is out collecting firewood. He walked North West for a while and then walked 600m North East before walking 650m home. How far to the North East did he walk?

15. Find the height AX of an isosceles triangle where AB=AC=15cm and BC=18cm.

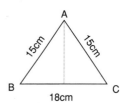

Mixed Problems

There are times when you have to use an earlier answer to answer the second part of a question. Remember not to calculate with a rounded off answer, but to use your full calculator display. It can sometimes be useful to leave answers in square root form.

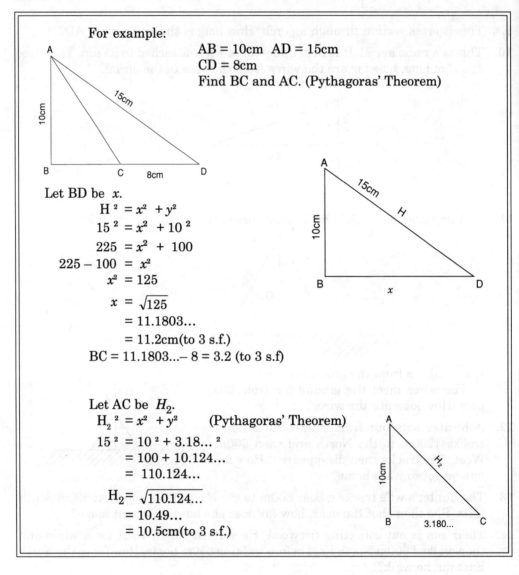

For example:

AB = 10cm AD = 15cm
CD = 8cm
Find BC and AC. (Pythagoras' Theorem)

Let BD be x.

$$H^2 = x^2 + y^2$$
$$15^2 = x^2 + 10^2$$
$$225 = x^2 + 100$$
$$225 - 100 = x^2$$
$$x^2 = 125$$
$$x = \sqrt{125}$$
$$= 11.1803...$$
$$= 11.2\text{cm (to 3 s.f.)}$$
$$BC = 11.1803... - 8 = 3.2 \text{ (to 3 s.f)}$$

Let AC be H_2.

$$H_2{}^2 = x^2 + y^2 \qquad \text{(Pythagoras' Theorem)}$$
$$15^2 = 10^2 + 3.18...^2$$
$$= 100 + 10.124...$$
$$= 110.124...$$
$$H_2 = \sqrt{110.124...}$$
$$= 10.49...$$
$$= 10.5\text{cm (to 3 s.f.)}$$

Exercise 10F

Give all non exact answers to 3 s.f.

1.

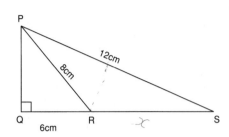

PR = 8cm   PS = 12cm and QR = 6cm.
Find PQ and RS

2. The diagonals of a kite are 40cm and 60cm, and the shorter diagonal cuts the larger one, one third of the way along its length.
Calculate the lengths of the sides of the kite.

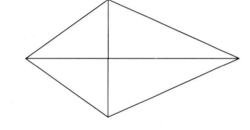

3.

∠ABC=90° and ∠ADB = 90°

AB = 24cm

AD = 19cm

BC = 12cm.

Find BD and CD.

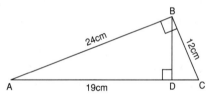

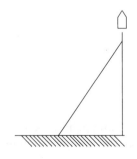

4. a) A prince has a ladder 5m long and instructions that the base of the ladder must be 2m away from the base of the wall. Is he able to rescue the princess whose cell is 4.7m above the ground?

  b) How far forward must the prince move the base of the ladder if he is to reach the window?

5. ABCD is a square with diagonal AC 10cm long.
E bisects CD and F bisects BC.
G is the point where EF cuts AC.
Calculate:
a) CD
b) CF
c) EF
d) CG

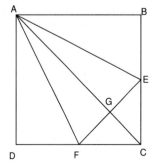

6. Consider this cuboid, it is an open topped box with a base 10cm by 7cm and height 5cm:

A spider sitting at A spies a bug tucked inside the corner of the box at B. The spider wants to take the most direct route to the bug.

To find out the spider's route you have to draw a net of the box. Mark the positions A and B and then draw the spider's route. How far does the spider have to go?

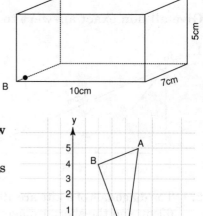

7. If A is the point (5, 5), B is the point (2, 4) and C is the point (4, –1):

a) Calculate AB, AC and BC

b) Is ABC a right angled triangle?

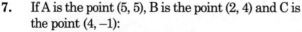

8. The mists came down on the moor in the middle of our Duke of Edinburgh expedition.

My group had walked 5km from our starting point on a bearing of 310° and then we walked another 3.75km on a bearing of 220°.

It was lucky that we had Amy with us. She managed to work out the distance that we were from our starting point without using a calculator. How did she do it and what was her answer?

9. The square ABCD has sides of 12cm. F is the mid point of AD. Calculate:

a) AC

b) FC

c) The areas of the triangles AFB, BCF, and AFC.

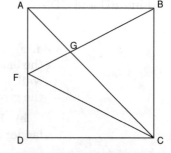

10. ABCD is a rectangle with AB = 12cm and CD = 8cm and F the mid point of AD. If G is the point where BF crosses AC what can you say about the area of triangle ABC and triangle FCG?

Extension Exercise 10

Pythagorean Triplets

The 3 : 4: 5 Δ and the 5 : 12 : 13 Δ were special because the squares of the smaller two numbers equalled the square of the larger number.

Groups of three numbers that have this property are known as 'Pythagorean Triplets'.

How many more can you find (excluding multiples of 3 : 4 : 5 and the 5 : 12 : 13) ? You might like to use the spreadsheet application on a computer to investigate this problem. If so you will need to find the correct formulae for finding squares and square root. If using microsoft Excel or Claris squares are given by typing ^ 2 and square roots by =SQRT(number or cell ref.). If you are using a different application you may need to look these up in the manual,

1. Start by making a table of numbers and their squares, you will need to go quite far, up to 40 or even 50:

Number	Square	Subtract	Answer
1	1		
2	4	4 − 1	3
3	9	9 − 4	5
4	16	16 − 9	7
5	25	25 − 16	$9 = 3^2$
6			
7			
8			
9			
10			

2. Then look at the difference between consecutive squares: for example $17^2 - 16^2 = 33$. See if any of these are perfect squares.

3. Next try looking at the differences between non- consecutive squares and see if any of those are perfect squares.

4. Look for a pattern in your answers, can you find and repeat a pattern or is this a random property of certain sets of numbers.

You are using your calculator or a computer to do this search, but spare a moment for the ancient Greeks who found their triplets without such aids to calculation!

Summary Exercise 10

1. Write out Pythagoras's Theorem, in words.

2. A hunter starts from home and travels 4km East and then 2.5km North. She then shoots a bear. How far does she have to carry the bear home?

3. An isosceles triangle ABC has base BC = 32cm and two equal sides AB = AC = 63cm. Calculate its height and thus its area.

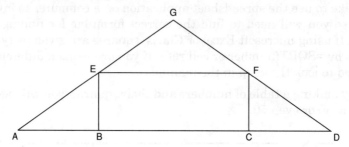

4. This diagram shows the cross section of our roof:
    The total height of the roof is 2.6m, and the heights BE and CF are both 1.3m. The sloping lengths AG and GC are both 4m.
    Calculate:
    a) The length AD.
    b) The total cross sectional area of the roof.
    c) The length AE and thus the length AB(compare the total height to height BE).
    d) The area of usable rectangle of roof space BCFE.

5. A similar roof of height CF of 2.6m and base AB of 7m has a dormer window inserted. The height of the window DE is 1.5m and the length CD is 2m.

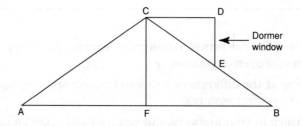

Calculate the length BE.

6. A company logo is in the form of two triangles as shown. The total width of the logo is 5cm and the height is 3cm. The ratio of BC:CE, and thus the lengths AB:DE is 3:2.
    Calculate:
    a) The length AD
    b) The area of the two triangles ABC and CDE

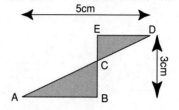

Activity 10 - Truthful Twins?

There is a famous set of twins where one on them always tells the truth and the other always lies. This is very difficult for anyone talking to the twins because they are identical twins and, it is impossible to tell them apart, so no one ever knows which one they are talking to.

1. Which twin, the liar or the truthful one, (or both or neither) could make these statements:
   a) "I always tell the truth."
   b) "I always tell lies."
   c) "I never tell lies."
   d) "My brother always tells the truth."
   e) "My brother always tells lies."
   f) "I always tell lies but my brother always tells the truth."

2. What question could you ask one twin to decide which one is the truth teller and which is the liar?

3. In this conversation which twin tells the truth and which one lies?
   A : "I always tell the truth."
   B: "If you are telling the truth, then I am lying".

4. And in this conversation can you tell which twin tells the truth and which one lies?
   A :"It is not true that I always tell lies".
   B: "My brother always tells lies".

5. Can I tell which is the truthful twin if I ask twin A;
   "Do you always tell the truth?" and A replies: "Yes."
   To which B says: "A said "Yes" but he always lies."

A useful way to solve these next problems is to make a truth table, like this:

	True	False
A	✓	
B		
C		

Assume A is telling the truth and then work through and see if B and C are truthful or not.
If this does not work then cross off the tick for A and see what happens if A is lying.

Another way is to use a Truth Tree:

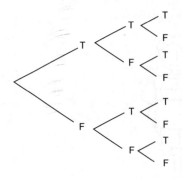

Follow the branches of the tree,

For example
"If A is lying then B is telling the truth and so is C lying or not?".

These triplets are even more difficult as one always tells the truth, one always lies and the other one sometimes tells the truth and sometimes lies.

In these conversations can you work out which triplet is which:

6.   A: "B sometimes tells the truth."
     B: "A always tells the truth."
     C: "I sometimes tell the truth."

7.   A: "Of the three of us two are telling the truth"
     B: "If I always tell lies then A sometimes tells lies."
     C: "I do not always tell the truth."

8.   A: "B sometimes tells the truth, and I always tell lies."
     B: "A always tells the truth and C sometimes tells the truth."
     C: "I always tell the truth."

9.   A: "B sometimes tells the truth."
     B: "A sometimes tell the truth."
     C: "I sometimes tell the truth."

10. A: "I always tell the truth."
     B: "I always tell lies."
     C: "B sometimes tells lies."

Can you make up some more truth and liar puzzles of your own?

Chapter 11

Area and Volume

Circles

Remember some of the special names for parts of the circle.
The circumference is the distance around the outside.
The radius is the length from the centre to the circumference.
The diameter is the length across the middle.
Diameter = 2 x radius.

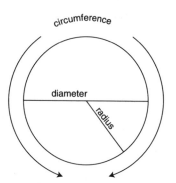

Remember the formulae for finding the Circumference and Area of a circle:

$$C = \pi d \quad \text{or} \quad C = 2\pi r \qquad A = \pi r^2$$

If you have trouble remembering which formula is which remind yourself of the dimensions:

$C = \pi d$ or $C = 2\pi r$ have one length so are formulae for length.
$A = \pi r^2$ has a length squared and so is a formula for area. (cm^2 or m^2 etc.)

Exercise 11A

Use the π button on your calculator for this exercise and give non - exact answers to 3 s.f.

> For example : Find the circumference of a circle of diameter 14cm.
> $$d = 14cm$$
> $$C = \pi d$$
> $$= \pi \times 14$$
> $$= 43.982...$$
> $$= 44.0cm \text{ (to 3 s.f.)}$$

1. Find the circumferences and areas of these circles:
   a) diameter of 8cm   b) radius of 31cm   c) diameter of 1.2m
   d) radius of 4.5m   e) diameter of 50cm   f) radius of 12m.

2. If the diameter of the earth is 12 756km use the π button on your calculator to find the length of the equator.

3. I am making a circular table cloth with a diameter of 2.5m. What length of ribbon must I buy in order to trim the circumference of my tablecloth?

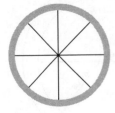

4. My bicycle has wheels of diameter 95 cm. How far will my bicycle go in one turn of the wheels

5. This table mat has a diameter of 14cm. Find its area and its circumference.

6. I have a glass with a base diameter of 7cm. Find the area of the base of my glass.

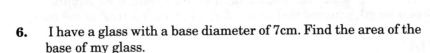

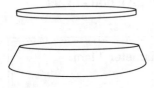

7. My mother has just cut a wooden lid to my baby sister's sand pit. The lid has a radius of 1.4m. Calculate the area of the lid. As the lid is made of blockboard it needs a length of wooden trim round the circumference What length of wooden trim does my mother need ?

8. We have a round table of circular diameter 3m, and we have just bought a tablecloth which is big enough to give a drop of 0.5m all the way round. What is the area of the tablecloth?

9. I have bought a large sheet of MDF (medium density fibreboard)1.25m by 2.5m. I cut out of the board the largest circle that I can. What area of MDF is left?

10. I have a length of wooden trim of 2m, what is the radius of the largest circle that I could trim with it?

11. I have a circular table cloth of area 5m². What is the radius of the largest table that it could cover?

12. I have made two identical lumps of modelling clay. I fashion one lump into a circular mat of diameter 9 cm. I think I will now turn the other lump of clay into a table mat. What is the length of a side of the square if the mats are the same thickness?

More Circle Problems

Some questions need a little more thought. You may need to use Pythagoras's theorem,make sure your working is clearly set out.

Exercise 11B

Use the π button on your calculator for this exercise and give non - exact answers to 3 s.f.

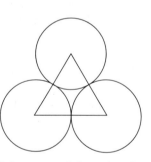

1. An equilateral triangle of side 4cm is drawn between the centres of three adjacent circles as shown.
   a) What is the height of the triangle?
   b) What is the area of the triangle?
   c) What is the area of one circle?
   d) What is the area of the part of one circle that is in the triangle?
   e) From your answers to b) and d) find the percentage of the area of the triangle that does **not** lie in a circle.

2. **Take π to be for this question, and do not use a calculator.**
   There are two cog wheels, A of diameter 21cm, and B of diameter 14cm.

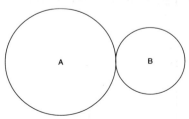

   a) Work out the circumferences of the two cogwheels.
   b) How many times will B turn for one turn of A?
   c) If B turns 100 times how many full turns will A have made?
   d) In fact A is driven by B, and B is driven by a motor that turns at 110 revolutions per minute. How many turns will A make in a minute?
   e) A turns a long conveyor belt of length 20m. How many times will the conveyor belt go round a full turn in an hour?

3. A quarter circle is folded round to make
    a cone. If the radius of the circle is 5cm
    what is :

    a) the curved surface area of the cone?
    b) The curved length of the quarter circle
    and thus the diameter of the cone?
    c) From c) find the radius of the base of
    the cone.
    d) The slanting side of the cone will be
    equal to the radius of the quarter circle. Draw a cross section of the cone and
    thus find its height.

4. Milk bottle tops of diameter 5cm are stamped out of a strip of metallic foil.
    Assuming there is minimum waste how many milk bottle tops can be stamped
    out of a strip of 1m of foil, and what is the percentage of foil wasted?

5. a) A bicycle wheel has a diameter of 35cm.
    How far does the bicycle travel in one
    revolution of the wheel?
    b) How far does the bicycle travel in 1000
    revolutions?
    c) How many revolutions does the wheel
    make if the bicycle travels 1km?
    d) If I am travelling on the bicycle at 30km
    per hour, how many revolutions does the
    wheel make in one minute?

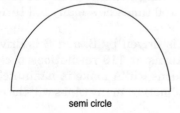

6. A racing bicycle is travelling at 50km per hour, and the cyclist is using a gear
    ratio of 1:5. That is one turn of the pedals makes the wheel turn 5 times.
    a) How many turns of the pedals makes the wheel turn 100 times?
    b) If the wheel has a diameter of 45cm how far does the bicycle travel in 10
    turns of the pedals?
    c) How many turns of the pedals does the cyclist make when he is travelling at
    50km per hour?

Parts Of Circles

Perimeter

Often there are shapes that are not whole circles but parts of circles:

To find the perimeter of a **semicircle** we have to first find **half** the circumference
and then **add** on the length of the straight side:

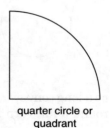

semi circle

quarter circle or
quadrant

Exercise 11C

Example: Find the area and perimeter of this semicircle:

$\pi = \frac{22}{7}$ d = 14cm   r = 7cm

Area = πr^2   **Perimeter:**

$= \dfrac{22 \times 7 \times 7}{7}$ Curved Part $= \dfrac{\pi d}{2}$

$= 22 \times 7$ $= \dfrac{22 \times 14}{7 \times 2}$

$= 154cm^2$ $= 22cm$

Perimeter $= 22 + 14$

$= 36cm$

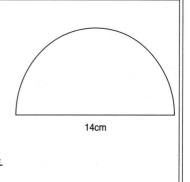

14cm

Take $\pi = \dfrac{22}{7}$ for questions 1 - 4

1.   Find the perimeter of this semicircular carpet :

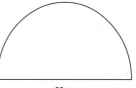

98cm

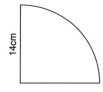

14cm

2. Find the perimeter of this quadrant.

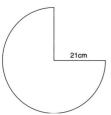

21cm

3. Find the perimeter of this three quarter

4. Find the areas of the three shapes in questions 1-3.

Use the π button on your calculator for questions 5-7:

5.   Here is the remains of a thin and crispy pepperoni pizza. I had carefully cut it into six equal slices, the I went to pour myself a glass of cola, and when I came back my dog had eaten a whole slice ! What area of my pizza did the dog eat and what area is left?

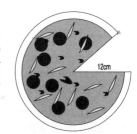

12cm

6. Calculate the distance around the outside of this running track.

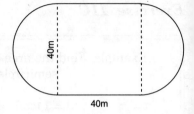

40m

40m

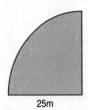

25m

7. This is a plan of a pond in the local park. What is the area of the pond ?

Take π = $\frac{22}{7}$ for question 8 - 9

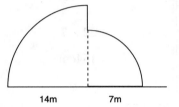

14m   7m

8. Here is the cross section of the building that won this year's architectural prize. Calculate the area of the cross section.

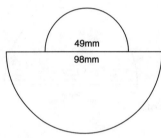

49mm

98mm

9. This is the cross section through a spinning toy. The top semicircle has a diameter of 49 mm and the bottom a semi circle of 98 mm. What is the area of the cross section?

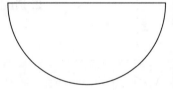

10. The perimeter of this shape is 20 cm. What is the radius of the semicircle?

Surface Area And Volume Of A Cylinder

The volume of a prism is given by the formula
   Volume = (Area of Cross Section) x height (or length or breadth)

h

As the cross section of a cylinder is a circle this formula can be written:
   Volume of cylinder = πr²h

The surface area has to be calculated in two parts, if you think about unwrapping the label from a tin can you will see that it is a rectangle whose length is equal to the circumference of the cylinder:

And therefore the curved surface area of a cylinder is given by the formula:

$$S.A. = 2\pi rh$$

but a solid cylinder has two ends and so the formula for the surface area of a solid cylinder is:

$$S.A. = 2\pi rh + 2\pi r^2$$

or $\quad S.A. = 2\pi r(h + r)$

For example: Find the Volume of a cylinder of radius 5cm and height 10cm. Give your answer in litres.

$$r = 5\text{cm} \qquad h = 10\text{cm} \qquad 1000\text{cm}^3 = 1 \text{ litre}$$

$$
\begin{aligned}
Volume &= \pi r^2 h \\
&= \pi \times 5^2 \times 10 \\
&= 785.398.. \\
&= 785\text{cm}^3 \\
&= 0.785 \text{ litres}
\end{aligned}
$$

Exercise 11D

Use the π button on your calculator for this exercise. Give non exact answers to 3 s.f.:

1. Find the volume of these cylinders in litres:
   a) radius 3cm and height 5cm
   b) diameter 60cm and height 50cm
   c) diameter 15cm and height 8cm
   d) radius 4m and height 5m
   e) height 20cm and radius 9cm.
   f) height 1.2m and radius 0.75m

2. Which has the larger volume, a cylinder with radius 5cm and height 6cm or a radius of 6cm and a height 5cm? Can you answer the question without actually calculating the volumes of the two cylinders?

3. A can of tomato juice has a radius of 5cm and a height of 12cm. What volume of tomato juice is contained in a tray of 24 tins? Give your answer in litres.

4. My little sister has a cylindrical paddling pool of radius 1.2m, and filled to a depth of 14cm. I had to fill up the pool using a cylindrical bucket of radius 12cm and height 30cm. How many bucket loads did I have to carry?

5.   Here is my birthday cake, before and after it was iced:

a) The cake without the icing is in the shape of a cylinder 10cm high and of diameter 24cm. What is its volume?

b) The icing is 0.5cm thick and is made in two parts, a circle on the top, and a long rectangle to go round the sides. What is the diameter of the circle of icing?

c) What is the height and length of the rectangle of icing?

d) What is the total volume of the icing?

e) If I mix icing sugar and water in the ratio 10:1 what volume of icing sugar was used?

6.   Here is a can of "Woof" dog food: The radius of the can is 6 cm and the height is 15cm.

a) The labels round the can overlap by one cm. Sketch a label and calculate its dimensions.

b) In the dog food factory several labels are printed on each sheet of A0 paper and then cut up by machine before the individual labels are stuck on the cans of "Woof". If a sheet of A0 paper is 840mm by 1188mm, how many labels are there on every sheet?

7.   A cube, 1m by 1m by 1m, is filled with water. A cylinder with diameter 1m contains the same amount of water. How high is the cylinder?

8.   A cylinder of radius 5cm and height 10cm is filled with water. The water is then poured into a hollow cube, which it fills exactly. What is the length of a side of the cube?

9.   A cylindrical glass of radius 4cm and height 8cm is filled with water. All the water is poured into an empty cylindrical jug of radius 8cm. What depth of water is now in the jug?

Units of Area And Volume

All the calculations we have done so far have used one unit of area, either mm^2, cm^2, m^2 or km^2. There are times when we start out with one unit of area and then need to change to another. This is more complicated than it looks. Look at these two squares. We know that 1m = 100cm.

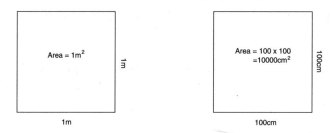

Therefore $1m^2 = 10\ 000cm^2$

There are also occasions when we need to change units of volume.
Look at these two cubes:
The volume of the second cube is $100 \times 100 \times 100 = 1\ 000\ 000cm^3$.

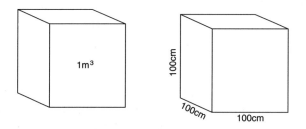

Therefore $1m^3 = 1\ 000\ 000cm^3$

Exercise 11E

1. Draw squares like the two above to find how many:
   a) square millimetres in a square centimetre
   b) square millimetres in a square metre
   c) square metres in a square kilometre.
   d) square metres in square centimetres
   e) square metres in square millimetres

2. Draw cubes like the two above to find how many:
   a) cubic millimetres in a cubic centimetre
   b) cubic millimetres in a cubic metre
   c) cubic metres in a cubic kilometre.
   d) cubic metres in cubic centimetres
   e) cubic metres in cubic millimetres

3. a) How many litres are there in a cubic metre?
   b) How many cubic mm are there in a litre?

More Volume Problems

In these problems you should not need to draw a 3D diagram but you may need to use Pythagoras's Theorem and so you should draw 2 dimensional sketches of a triangle when necessary.

When calculating with π leave π in your answer until the last possible moment - it frequently cancels out. It is perfectly acceptable to leave a length or volume in the form 100π, for example, and only multiply out the final answer.

For example:
A cylindrical glass of radius 4cm and height 8cm is filled with water.
All the water is poured into an empty cylindrical jug of radius 8cm.
What depth of water is now in the jug?

$$\text{Vol of glass} = \pi r^2 h$$
$$= \pi \times 4^2 \times 8$$
$$= 128\pi \text{cm}^3$$

$$\text{Vol. in jug} = \pi r^2 h$$
$$= \pi \times 8^2 \times h \text{cm}^3$$

$$\text{Therefore } 128\pi = 64\pi h$$
$$h = 2\text{cm}$$

Exercise 11F

1. A cylindrical jug of radius 9cm and filled with squash to a depth of 20cm. All the squash is to be equally divided between 10 small cylindrical glasses of internal diameter 6cm. What depth of squash should be poured into each glass?

2. This cylindrical glass of radius 5 cm has a volume of one litre. What is the length of the glass stick that juts fits across the inside of the glass.

3. This parallelogram of cardboard rolls into a cyllindrical tube and is then filledwith pastry dough. The cylindrical tube has a radius of 4cm and contains 800cm³ of dough.
    a) What is the height and length of the parallelogram?

b) You will notice that the top corner of the parallelogram is immediately above the bottom corner. How long is the sloping side?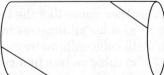

4. This fish tank has a rectangular base 20cm by 35cm and was filled with water from two cylindrical buckets of diameter 24cm and depthof water of 15cm. How deep is the water in the fish tank?

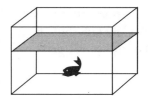

5 A rectangular block of clay, 5cm by 6cm by 10cm is fashioned into a cylinder of diameter 6cm. How long is this cylinder?

6. A cylindrical glass vase has an outer radius of 7cm and height of 15cm. The vase is 8 mm thick.
   a) Calculate the radius and height of the inside of the vase and hence its volume.
   b) Calculate the volume of glass used in making the vase.

7. A cylinder has a volume of 1 litre. Another cylinder has the same height as the first but twice the radius. What is its volume?

8. 100m of rope is wrapped around a barrel of diameter 2m.
   a) What length of rope is taken up by one turn around the barrel?
   b) How many turns are needed to take the whole 100m?
   c) The rope is 10cm in diameter, and the turns must lie flat on the barrel (i.e. a single thickness). What is the volume of the barrel?
   d) In fact a barrel of the correct size could not be found. The manufacturer supplied a barrel of diameter 2m but volume 7.5m^3. What length of rope is taken up by one turn around this barrel?

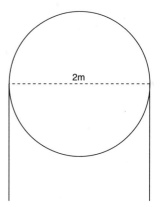

9. A cylindrical bucket is being used to fill up a rectangular water tank. The bucket has diameter 30cm and height 50cm. The rectangular tank has a base of 1m by 1.5m. How many buckets are needed to fill the rectangular tank up to a height of 50cm?

10. a) A cylinder has a volume of 5 litres and the diameter of the cylinder is equal to its height. What is the radius of the cylinder?
    b) The contents of that cylinder are poured into a rectangular tank whose base is a square of side equal to the diameter of the cylinder. What is the depth of water in the tank?

Volumes Of Right Prisms

In this chapter we have looked at the volumes of cubes, cuboids and cylinders. However it is important not to forget the general formula for the volume of a right prism:

A prism is a shape that has a <u>*constant cross section*</u>

This means that the shape can be sliced into slices of the same area:
These are all prisms. Note that the slices are perpendicular to the ends of each

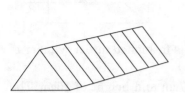 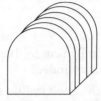

prism. "Perpendicular" means "at right angles" to, which is why these shapes are
called **right prisms**. It follows that if we know the area of one slice then we can
work out the volume of the prism by multiplying the area by the number of slices:

Volume of a prism = area of cross section × length (or height or depth)

For example: Find the volume of a right prism of length 10cm with
cross section an equilateral triangle of side 5cm.

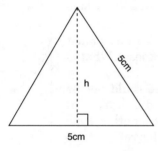 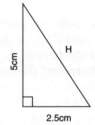

$$H^2 = a^2 + b^2 \qquad \text{(Pythagoras's Theorem)}$$
$$5^2 = 2.5^2 + h^2$$
$$h^2 = 25 - 6.25$$
$$= 18.75$$
$$h = 4.330127...$$
$$= 4.33\text{cm (to 3 s.f.)}$$

Vol.= Area of X section × length

$$= \frac{b \times h}{2} \times 10$$

$$= \frac{5 \times 4.330127}{2} \times 10$$

$$= 20.825....$$
$$= \underline{20.8\text{cm}^3} \text{ (to 3 s.f.)}$$

Exercise 11G

Solve these problems, remembering that you may need to use Pythagoras's theorem to find some lengths. You may also need to use some of the area formulae on page in chapter 9. If the answer is not exact give it correct to three significant figures.

1.-3. Find the volume of these prisms:

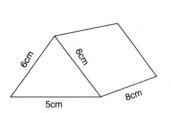 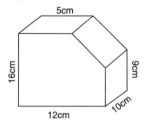 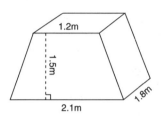

4. For each of the prisms above sketch the net and then work out the total surface area.

5. I have to pack a cylindrical tube of circumference 21.5cm and length 1.2m into a rectangular box.
a) What is the volume of the smallest box that I could use.
b) Sketch the net of the box and work out the surface area.

 **6.** A fly walks around the inside of a cylindrical glass of height 12cm and diameter 8cm. The fly finishes at the top of the glass immediately above its starting point, but it has travelled twice around the glasss. How far has the fly walked?

7. 6 cylindrical cans are tightly packed into a base 12cm by 18cm and height 10 cm. rectangular box of base 12cm by 18cm and height 10cm.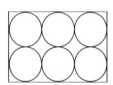
a) What is the volume of one can?
b) What percentage of the volume of the box is filled with air?

8. A chocolate bar is manufactured in the shape of a triangular prism. Each prism has length 15cm, and an equilateral triangular cross section of sides 4cm. Six of these bars are then packaged together to form a prism whose cross section is a hexagon. Sketch the net of the hexagonal package that the six bars fit into, calculate its surface area and its volume.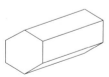

Extension Exercise 11

Using Area And Volume Formulae

There are times when we need to look at the theory behind circles and cylinders and not need to worry too much about the actual size. In these situations it helps to leave the lengths as letters and then manipulate the expressions. It can also help to leave a square root sign in the answer.

In problems like these it is perfectly acceptable to "invent" your own abbreviations as long as these are clear, using suffixes can help. It is always a good idea to define your abbreviations first.

For example:

Circle B has three times the area of circle A. What is the ratio of the radius of circle A to the radius of circle B?

Let radius A be r_a and radius B be r_b

If Area A $= \pi r_a^2$ Then Area B $= 3\pi r_a^2 = \pi r_b^2$

$$\text{Therefore} \qquad \frac{r_a^2}{r_b^2} = \frac{\pi}{3\pi} = \frac{1}{3}$$

$$\frac{r_a}{r_b} = \frac{1}{\sqrt{3}}$$

$$r_a : r_b = 1 : \sqrt{3}$$

---

1. Cylinder B has twice the radius and twice the height of cylinder A. How much greater is the volume of cylinder B?

2. A cogwheel A has twice the radius and thus twice the cogs as cogwheel B. How many more revolutions per minute does cogwheel B make?

3. a)(i) I have two containers, one a cube and the other a cylinder. Both are the same height both are full and contain one litre of water. What is the ratio height and of their base areas?

ii) One tenth of a litre is drawn off each container Which now contains the greater height of liquid and by how much?

b) The diameter of another cylinder is equal to the height of the cube.

(i) What is the ratio of their base areas? ii) One tenth of a litre is drawn off each container. Which now contains the greater height of liquid and by how much?

4. A cylindrical glass contains water. One quarter of the water is drunk and the glass is then filled with orange squash and stirred. One quarter of the liquid in the glass is then drunk, and the glass is topped up again with orange squash and stirred. What is the ratio of squash to water in the glass now?

5. Another cylindrical glass contains water. This time one tenth of the water is drunk and the glass is then filled up with orange squash. One tenth of the liquid in the glass is then drunk, and the glass is topped up again with orange squash. How many times must this be repeated until there is more squash in the glass than water?

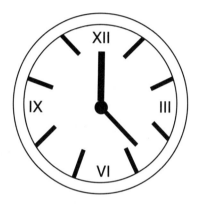

6. A housefly sitting on the minute hand of a clock travels 20m further in one day than a spider sitting on the end of the hour hand. If the hour hand is 10cm long what is the length of the minute hand?

7. a) A spider is sitting on the end of the hour hand of a different clock, and a fly is sitting on the end of the minute hand. The minute hand is twice the length of the hour hand which is rcm long. How far in terms of r is the spider from the fly at

   (i) 3 o'clock?
   (ii) 6 o'clock?

b) In theory the hour hand of a clock should travel 30° in one hour and thus 0.5° in one minute. However in practice the hour hand actually moves one degree every second minute. At what time after 3 o'clock will the spider be the same distance from the fly as it was at 3 o'clock? (Give your answer to the nearest second)

8. At 10:45 our spider has grown tired of not catching the fly and starts to crawl towards him at a rate of 1cm per minute, the spider can only walk along the hands of the clock. If the minute hand is 12cm long and the hour hand 6cm long when does the spider catch the fly? State clearly any assumptions that you have made.

9. Repeat question 8 but this time the spider sits on the end of the minute hand and the fly on the end of the hour hand. Is your answer different?

Summary Exercise 11

Use a calculator to solve these problems, but show all formulae and working. Use the value of π given by the π button of your calculator. Give non - exact answers to 2 decimal places.

1.   Find the area and circumference of a circle of diameter 1.3m.

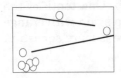

2. I put a 10 pence coin in a charity box. The coin rolls down two slopes each of 15 cm before it falls into a hole. How many times down the coin rotate on its journey?
(The diameter of a 10 pence coin is 24 mm.)

3.   Here is a new logo for a record company. The outside square has sides 25cm long.
Calculate:
i) The area of one whole circle.
ii) The blue area of one circle.
iii) The total blue area of the logo.
iv) The percentage of blue area in the whole logo.

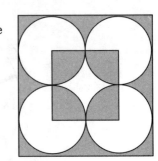

4.   Find the areas and perimeters of these shapes:

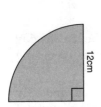
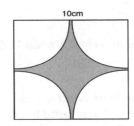
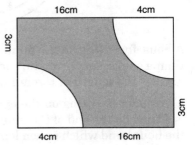

5.   Gasometers are large cylindrical containers holding domestic gas to feed the domestic supply. Gasometers are actually constructed so that as the gas is drawn out of the gasometer the height of the whole cylinder drops.
a) A gasometer is a cylinder with a diameter of 18m and when it is full it stands 12m high. What volume of gas is contained in it when it is full. Give your answer in litres.
b) 2million litres of gas are drawn off the gasometer during the week and so its height decreases accordingly. How tall is it now?
c) The rest of the gas is drawn out of the gasometer but it does not get smaller! Something has gone wrong! The gas repair man has to put a ladder across the inside of the gasometer, how long is the ladder?

6.   a) 4 litres of chocolate is melted in a pan whose radius is 9cm. How deep is the melted chocolate in the pan?
b) The chocolate is poured into a mould in the shape of an equilateral triangle of side 9cm. How deep is the chocolate in this mould?

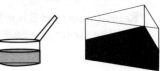

Activity 11 - Investigation

Packaging the Litre

The litre is the most common unit of volume that we now use. If you look at petrol stations you will see petrol sold in litres, in the supermarket you will see orange juice, milk, wine, shampoos and other fluids measured in litres or millilitres.

How many different packages with volume of exactly one litre can you find?

Although the cube is an obvious shape it is not usually used. Can you think why not?

Can you design some right prisms with a volume of exactly one litre?
These could be cylindrical, rectangular, triangular, trapezoid or any regular or irregular shape that you like.

First decide what it is that you are going to package :
The latest bright green fizzy drink
The latest herbal shampoo
The latest chocolate bar
Orange juice
Talcum powder
Or just a pretty container to keep on your bedside table.

Next think about the shape you want your package to be -

    long and thin?
    small and squat?

Now think about putting hundreds of these packages together. To do this efficiently and economically it is a good thing if they fit closely together. In fact this could be part of your design - put several together and make a new shape (like those triangular prism chocolate bars we looked at earlier!).

The net of your package is important too. How are you going to cut hundreds of these off one long strip of cardboard?

Now calculate the dimensions of your shape - you could use the spreadsheet programme of your computer to help you - making sure that you include the printout with your finished design.

Chapter 12

Simultaneous Equations

What Is An Equation?

Equations can come in various forms, for example:

$$y = x^2 \quad a + 3 = 5 \quad 4 - 2x = 3x - 1 \quad 3(t + 1) = 1 - 2(2t + 4) \quad 2u + 3v = 2$$

What the equations all have in common is that they all contain an equals sign. This means that the equation is *balanced* .

The expression on the left hand sign *is equal in value to* the expression on the right hand side.

In mathematics you have been used to looking at one equation on its own. This equation would contain one variable, often x, but it could equally be $y, a, t, r,$ or h. You know that you can solve this equation by simplifying, then adding and subtracting, multiplying and dividing values on both sides of the equation.

Most equations that we have been used to solving have had only one variable, or unknown quantity.

Writing Equations In Two Variables

As with any equation it is important to define your unknown quantities first.

For example:
I am thinking of two number whose sum is 12. Write this as an equation.

Let the numbers be x and y

$$x + y = 12$$

Exercise 12A

1. I am thinking of two numbers greater than 0 whose sum is 24. Write this as an equation.

2. I am thinking of two numbers greater than 0 whose difference is 8. Write this as an equation.

3. I am thinking of two numbers greater than 0. I double one and add this to the other and the answer is 20. Write this as an equation.

4. My mother sends me to buy 15 cans of drink. I can buy either Cola or Orangeade. Show this as an equation.

5. I have £3 to buy some pencils and rulers. Pencils cost 25 pence and rulers cost 30 pence each. Show this as an equation.

Using Graphs To Solve Problems With Two Variables

Example:
I want to buy some avocados and some mangoes. Avocados cost 60 pence each and mangoes cost 80 pence each.

a) Let the number of avocados I buy be a and the number of mangoes I buy be m. I spend exactly £12 altogether. Show how this can be given by the equation $3a + 4m = 60$.

b) Draw a graph of $3a + 4m = 60$ and use it to show how many of each fruit I can buy.

a) The cost of a avocados at 60 pence each = $60a$
    The cost of m mangoes at 80 pence each = $80m$
    The total cost is £12 or 1200 pence.
    Therefore $60a + 80m = 1200$
                                                    ($\div 20$)
                   $3a + 4m = 60$

b) $3a + 4m = 60$
    When $a = 0$ $m = 15$, when $m = 0$ $a = 20$

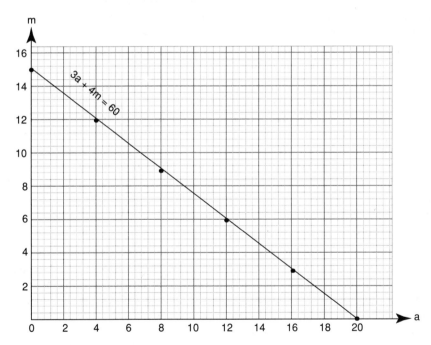

From the graph I could buy either:

0 mangoes and 20 avocados	9 mangoes 8 avocados
3 mangoes 16 avocados	12 mangoes 4 avocados
6 mangoes 12 avocados	15 mangoes 0 avocados

Exercise 12B

1. Draw a graph of $3x + 5y = 15$. Draw a table of the whole number values of x and y that lie on the line.

2. Draw a graph of $2x + 7y = 28$. Draw a table of the whole number values of x and y that lie on the line.

3. I am thinking of two numbers greater than 0. If I double one of them and add it to the other the answer is 20. If my numbers are x and y this can be shown by the equation $2x + y = 20$. Draw a graph of $2x + y = 20$ and use the graph to show all the possible numbers that I could be thinking of.

4. I am thinking of two numbers greater than 0. If I double one of them and add it to half the other the answer is 12. If my numbers are x and y this can be shown by the equation $4x + y = 24$. Draw a graph of $4x + y = 24$ and use the graph to show all the possible numbers that I could be thinking of.

5. My Mother send me out shopping with £8. I have to buy some milk, which costs 80 pence a litre, and some juice, which costs £1.60 a litre. Unfortunately I have forgotten how many litres of milk and juice I was supposed to buy.
    a) If I let the amount of milk that I buy be m and the amount of juice that I buy be j show that the total amount that I spend can be given by the equation $m + 2j = 10$.
    b) Draw a graph of $m + 2j = 10$ and use your graph to show the numbers of litres each of milk and juice that I could buy for exactly £8.
    c) I suddenly remember that I should buy exactly 6 litres altogether. How many litres each of milk and juice is this?

6. I have £3 and I am going to buy some oranges and some lemons. Oranges cost 25 pence each and lemons cost 15 pence each.
    a) If I let the number of lemons I buy be x and the number of oranges that I buy be y show that the total cost of my shopping can be shown by the equation: $3x + 5y = 60$.
    b) Draw a graph of $3x + 5y = 60$ with a scale of 1 cm to 1 unit on both the horizontal and the vertical axes.(You may turn the graph paper round)
    c) From your graph draw up a table of the number of oranges and lemons that I could buy.
    d) In fact my recipe calls for twice as many oranges as lemons. How many of each did I buy?

7. I have to buy some more batteries. Extra-Long life batteries cost £4.50 per pack of 5, while normal batteries cost £1.50 per pack of 3. I have £13.50 to spend.
    a) Let the number of packs of Extra – Long Life batteries I buy be x and the number of packs of normal batteries that I buy be y. Show that the total amount that I spend can be shown by the equation : $3x + y = 9$.
    b) Draw a graph of $10x + 3y = 30$.
    c) Use your graph to show how many packs of each type of battery I could buy for exactly £15.
    d) I decide to buy as near as possible the same number of batteries. How many of each pack do I buy?

What Are Simultaneous Equations?

When we get a problem which involves two unknown quantities.

      For example :   The sum of two numbers is 13.

If we let the two numbers be x and y then we can write an equation: $x + y = 13$.

We cannot solve this equation with a unique solution, we do not have enough information. As we have seen there are several pairs of values of x and y which can satisfy this equation.

However if we are also told that the difference between the two numbers is 3 then we can write another equation: $x - y = 3$

Now consider the graphs of both these equations:

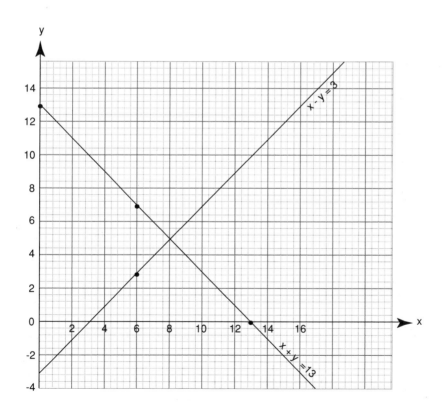

$x + y = 13$

x	0	13	6
y	13	0	7

$x - y = 3$

x	0	3	6
y	−3	0	3

From the graph we can see that there is one, and only one, point that lies on both lines (8, 5). The solution to our equations is $x = 8$ and $y = 5$.

Our two equations were solved by considering them together. These are called **simultaneous equations**. The solution to the previous problem shows that the solution to a pair of simultaneous equations is a point which lies on the graph of both equations.

There are various ways of solving simultaneous equations, the exact method depending on the wording of the question and the format of the equation. It is often easiest to understand things that can be seen and, although the graphical method of solving equations can take quite a long time, it is a good place to start.

The Graphical Method

Exercise 12C

Use worksheets 12/1 and 12/2 for question 2 of this exercise.

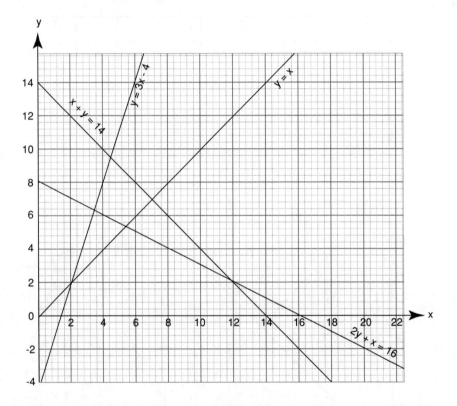

1. Use the graph to find the solutions to the following pairs of simultaneous equations:

    a) $x + y = 14$ b) $2y + x = 16$ c) $2y + x = 16$ d) $x + y = 14$
       $y = x$ $x + y = 14$ $x = 0$ $y = 0$
    e) $y = 3x - 4$ f) $2y + x = 16$ g) $y = 3x - 4$ h) $y = 3x - 4$
       $x + y = 14$ $y = x$ $2y + x = 16$ $y = x$

Remember: When drawing a straight line graph you need two points, but it is better to have three to check that your points are correct. It **does not matter** which three points you choose - they are only used for drawing the line. Any pair of points that fits that equation will lie on the line that you have drawn.

If your equation is in a simple form it can help to choose $x = 0$ for your first point and $y = 0$ for your second, then choose a third point that is not too close to the first two. Alternatively you could choose three points an equal distance apart such that $x = -3, 0, 3$. Either method is perfectly acceptable.

You must draw the line that represents your equation as long as possible since it does not stop at the limit of the points that you have chosen.

2. Solve these pairs of simultaneous equations graphically. (Use Worksheets 2/1 and 2/2)

a) $x + y = 12$ b) $x + y = 10$ c) $x + 2y = 10$ d) $3x + y = 10$
   $x - y = 4$ $2x + y = 4$ $x - y = 7$ $2x - y = 0$

3. Draw a pair of axes with values of both x and y from –5 to 5 to solve each of these pairs of equations:

a) $x + y = 3$ b) $x - 2y = 2$ c) $2x + 3y = 10$ d) $3x + y = 10$

   $x - y = -5$ $2x + y = 4$ $x - y = -5$ $2x - y = 7$

4. The answers to these equations may not always be a whole number. Using a scale of 1cm to 1 unit draw pairs of axes with values of x from – 8 to 8, and values of y from – 5 to 12. Read off your graph carefully and give your answers in decimal form.

a) $x + 2y = 6$ b) $7x + 2y = 5$ c) $2x - y = -8$ d) $x + y = 4$
   $3x - 4y = 4$ $x - 4y = 11$ $x + 2y = 4$ $6x - 4y = 1$

5. Choose your own scale and axes for these pairs of equations:

a) $2x + y = 1$ b) $x - 3y = 9$ c) $3x + 2y = -3$ d) $3x + 2y = 10$
   $x - y = -7$ $x + y = -5$ $4x - y = 7$ $5x - 2y = 2$

6. Draw graphs of each of these pairs of equations, what is different about them:

a) $x + y = -1$ b) $3x - 3y = 3$ c) $y = 2x + 1$ d) $3x + y = 4$
   $x + y = 3$ $x - y = 1$ $2x - y = 3$ $2y = 8 - 6x$

The Elimination Method

Drawing graphs accurately takes time. Most of the answers to the above equations were either whole numbers or quite simple decimals. There must be a quicker way to solve them.

Look at our original pair of equations:

$$x + y = 13$$
$$x - y = 13$$

You may notice that there are the same number of x's in each equation and the same number of y's. If we add y to $-y$ we get nought. Therefore if these two equations are added together the y terms cancel each other out and we will have:

$$2x = 16$$

and so
$$x = 8$$

As always in mathematics it is very important to explain clearly to anyone reading your work exactly what you are doing. There is a conventional way of writing out the solution to a pair of simultaneous equations. It is important that you follow these conventions as it then means that your work will be understood.

In the following examples you will see that in the first the equations are added to eliminate the x terms, and in the second the equations are subtracted to eliminate, in this case, the y terms. The next step is to substitute the first solution back into one of the equations to find the other variable, and then finally the answer is checked.

Example 1:

$$2x + y = 5 .... (1)$$
$$3x - y = 10 .... (2)$$
$(1) + (2)$ $5x = 15$
                                          $(\div 5)$
                 $x = 3$

Substitute
in (1) $6 + y = 5$
                          (-6)
              $y = -1$

Check in (2) $9 - (-1) = 10$

Example 2:

$$2x + 3y = 10 .... (1)$$
$$2x - y \; = 2 \; .... (2)$$
$(1) - (2)$ $4y = 8$
                                          $(\div 4)$
                 $y = 2$

Substitute
in (1) $2x + 6 = 10$
                              (-6)
              $2x = 4$
                                  $(\div 2)$
              $x = 2$

Check in (2) $4 - 2 = 2$

Exercise 12D

Solve these pairs of simultaneous equations using the elimination method.

1. $3x + y = 7$
    $x - y \; = 1$

2. $x + 2y = 7$
    $x + y = 4$

3. $x + 2y = 7$
    $x - y \; = 1$

4. $2x + y = 10$
    $3x - y = 5$

5. $3x + 2y = 15$
    $x + 2y = 9$

6. $x + 2y = 10$
    $3x - 2y = 6$

7. $2x + y = 12$
    $2x - 3y = 4$

8. $3x - y = 8$
    $3x + y \; = 10$

9. $3x + y = \; 7$
    $3x - 2y = -5$

Frequently the pairs of simultaneous equations are not as straightforward as this and do not have the same number of x's or y's in each equation. Another stage of working is then necessary to multiply either one or both of the equations by a scale factor in order to have an equal x or y term in both equations.

The Scale Factor Method

In the first example only one of the equations has to be multiplied by a scale factor. In the second both equations do. Note the convention of showing your working method by numbering each equation.

Example 1:

$$2x + y = 5 \dots\dots\dots\dots \quad (1)$$
$$3x - 2y = 4 \dots\dots\dots\dots \quad (2)$$
$(1) \times 2 \quad 4x + 2y = 10 \dots\dots\dots\dots \quad (3)$

$(3) + (2) \qquad 7x = 14$
$$(\div 7)$$
$$\underline{x = 2}$$

Substitute
in (1) $\qquad 4 + y = 5$
$$(-4)$$
$$\underline{y = 1}$$

Check in (2) $\quad 6 - 2 = 4$

Example 2:

$$2x + 7y = 10 \dots\dots\dots\dots \quad (1)$$
$$3x - 2y = -10 \dots\dots\dots\dots \quad (2)$$
$(1) \times 3 \quad 6x + 21y = 30 \dots\dots\dots\dots \quad (3)$
$(2) \times 2 \quad 6x - 4y = -20 \dots\dots\dots\dots \quad (4)$
$(3) - (4) \qquad 25y = 50$
$$(\div 25)$$
$$\underline{y = 2}$$

Substitute
in (1) $\qquad 2x + 14 = 10$
$$(-14)$$
$$2x = -4$$
$$(\div 2)$$
$$\underline{x = 2}$$

Check in (2) $\quad -6 - 4 = -10$

It is important that you substitute and check in the original equations, not in one that has been multiplied. Not only does this give you easier numbers it also means that if you have made a mistake then it will be shown up by checking the original problem.

Exercise 12E

Solve these pairs of simultaneous equations:

1. $3x + y = 5$
$\quad x + 3y = 7$

2. $3x + 2y = 8$
$\quad 2x + y = 5$

3. $5x - 2y = 11$
$\quad x + 4y = 11$

4. $2x - y = 5$
$\quad x + 3y = 13$

5. $5x - 3y = 15$
$\quad 2x + y = 9$

6. $5x + 2y = 22$
$\quad 3x + y = 6$

7. $3x + 2y = 7$
$\quad 2x + 3y = 3$

8. $2x + 3y = 5$
$\quad 3x + 4y = 14$

9. $5x - 2y = 1$
$\quad 3x + 5y = -18$

10. $3x + 4y = -6$
$\quad 2x - 9y = 24$

11. $2x + 3y = 5$
$\quad 4x + 2y = 0$

12. $7x - 3y = 27$
$\quad 4x + 4y = -6$

The Rearrangement And Substitution Methods

There are times when the equations are not in the same form. In these situations there are two options: either the equations can be rearranged so that they are in the same form, or one equation can be substituted into another.

These two examples show the same pair of equations. In the first, one equation is rearranged, in the second, one equation is substituted into the other.

Example 1:

$$3x + 2y = 6 \quad \dots\dots(1)$$
$$y = 5 - 2x \quad \dots\dots(2)$$
$$(1) + 2x: \quad 2x + y = 5 \quad \dots\dots(3)$$

$$(3) \times 2 \quad 4x + 2y = 10 \quad \dots\dots(4)$$
$$3x + 2y = 6 \quad \dots\dots(1)$$

$$(4) - (1) \qquad \underline{x = 4}$$
substitute
in (1) $\qquad 12 + 2y = 6$
$$(-12)$$
$$2y = -6$$
$$(\div 2)$$
$$\underline{y = -3}$$

Check in (2) $-3 = 5 - 8$

Example 2:

$$3x + 2y = 6 \quad \dots\dots\dots (1)$$
$$y = 5 - 2x \quad \dots\dots. (2)$$
sub (2) in (1):
$$3x + 2(5 - 2x) = 6$$
$$3x + 10 - 4x = 6$$
$$(+ x)$$
$$10 = 6 + x$$
$$(- 6)$$
$$\underline{4 = x}$$
substitute in (2)
$$y = 5 - 8$$
$$\underline{y = -3}$$

Check in (2) $12 - 6 = 6$

Exercise 12F

Solve these pairs of simultaneous equations:

1. $3x + y = 6$
$\quad\ y = x + 2$

2. $2x + 3y = 25$
$\quad\ x = y - 5$

3. $3x = y - 9$
$\quad\ 2y = 4 - x$

4. $y - 4x = 1$
$\quad\ 3x = y$

5. $15 = 3x - 2y$
$\quad\ 4x = 3 - y$

6. $2x + y = 1$
$\quad\ -2y = 2 + 7x$

7. $3y - 2x = 12$

$\quad\ 2y = 18 + 4x$

8. $\dfrac{x}{2} = -4 - 3y$

$\quad\ x + 2y = 2$

9. $4y - 2x = 15$

$\quad\ y = \dfrac{x}{4} + 3$

10. $x - y = 4$
$\quad\ 3y = -6 - 2x$

11. $5x - y = 3$
$\quad\ 4y = 10x - 1$

12. $2x + y = 3$
$\quad\ 3y = 2 - 3x$

Solving Problems With Simultaneous Equations

Many story problems are made easier by using simultaneous equations. It is particularly important to explain every step of your working as you solve these problems otherwise it will be very difficult for anyone else to follow what you are doing. Start by defining your variables, e.g. x and y.

For example:

I buy 15 pencils. Coloured pencils cost 35p each and ordinary graphite pencils cost 22p each. If I receive 92p change from a £5 note then how many of each type of pencil did I buy?

Let the number of coloured pencils be x and the number of graphite pencils be y.

$$\text{Total cost} = £5 - £0.92$$
$$= £4.08 = 408\text{p}$$

$$x + y = 15 \quad \ldots\ldots\ldots\ldots(1)$$
$$35x + 22y = 408 \ldots\ldots\ldots\ldots(2)$$

$(1) \times 22$

$$22x + 22y = 330 \ldots\ldots\ldots\ldots(3)$$

$(2) - (3)$

$$13x = 78$$
$$(\div 13)$$
$$\underline{x = 6}$$

Sub. in (1)

$$6 + y = 15$$
$$(-6)$$
$$\underline{y = 9}$$

Check in (2) $210 + 198 = 408$

Coloured pencils cost 35p and graphite pencils cost 22p each.

When you have finished your solution do check the original problem to make sure that you have answered the question.

Exercise 12G

1. The sum of two numbers is 25, and the difference between the two numbers is 5. What are the numbers?

2. I have two brothers. One of them is 4 years older than the other. The sum of their ages is 28. How old are they?

3. I have saved up £25 more than my sister. We decided to pool our money to buy a CD player and found that we had £145 between us. How much had we each saved?

4. On a walking holiday I walked 4 miles further on the first day than I did on the second. If I walked a total of 17 miles in two days how far did I walk on each day?

5. a) Solve this pair of simultaneous equations: $c + g = 20$ *and* $12c + 15g = 282$.
    b) I have to buy 20 apples. I buy some Cox's at 12p each and some Granny Smiths at 15p each. If I spent £2.82 in total use your answers to part (a) to find out how many of each I bought.

6. a) Solve this pair of simultaneous equations: $3p + s = 84$ and $2p + 2s = 84$
    b) My little sister collects stickers. For 84p she can either buy 4 sheets of plain stickers and one sheet of shiny ones, or she can buy 2 sheets of plain stickers and 2 sheets of shiny ones. Use your answers to part (a) to find what it would cost her to buy 3 sheets of plain stickers and 2 sheets of shiny ones.

7. a) Solve this pair of simultaneous equations: $3c + m = 127$ and $2c + 3m = 136$.
    b) If I buy 3 cans of Cola and one munchy bar that will cost me £1.27.
    If I buy 2 cans of Cola and 3 munchy bars that will cost me £1.36.
    Use your answers to part (a) to find the cost of one can of Cola and one munchy bar.

8. a) Solve this pair of simultaneous equations: $y = x + 4$ ans $2y + 2x = 56$.
    b) The length of a rectangle is 4cm longer than its width. The perimeter is 56cm^2. What are the length and width of the rectangle?

9. On my new computer game I have to zap aliens called Troggles and Gruggles. Zapping a Troggle scores 15 points and zapping a Gruggle scores 20 points. Last round I zapped a total of 20 aliens and scored 365 points. Form a pair of simultaneous equations and solve them to find how many Troggles and Gruggles I zapped.

10. This is a new game. I have to avoid hitting the Minkies, but try to hit the Tankies. On my first go I hit 5 Minkies and 9 Tankies, and scored 83 points. On my second round I hit 2 Minkies and 12 Tankies and scored 134 points. Form a pair of simultaneous equations and solve them to find out how many more points I score for hitting a Tankie than a Minkie.

11. A straight line given by an equation in the form $y = mx + c$ passes through a point A (2,4) and a point B (1,1). Form a pair of simultaneous equations and solve them to find m and c. Write down the equation of the line.

12. I have to buy a total of 15 Christmas cards. I buy some at 33p each for my relations and the rest at 25p each for my friends. If I spent a total of £4.15 how many of each type did I buy?

13. My mother only lets me spend 2 hours a day playing computer games. Last Sunday I spent three times as long playing "Prince of Persia" as I did playing "Lemmings". How long did I spend on each?

14. I have to buy 20 cans of drinks for my party. I buy 12 cans of Cola and 8 cans of lemonade and the total cost is £3.84. What would be the cost of 10 cans of Cola and 10 of lemonade?

15. On my new computer game I have to shoot down asteroids and alien star ships. I shot 12 asteroids and 5 alien ships and scored 465 points on level one, and then shot 15 asteroids and 4 alien ships and scored 480 points on level 2. How many points did I receive on level three when I shot down 20 asteroids and 6 alien ships ?

Extension Exercise 12

In the examples in this chapter you have had to solve two simultaneous equations to find two unknown quantities. There is no reason why you cannot have three unknown quantities, but you will have to have three equations. Each equation need not necessarily have all three variables in it.

Consider this problem:

The sum of two numbers is 15. One of these numbers added to a third makes 17 the other number added to the same third number makes 14.

Let us call our numbers a, b, c.

The three facts above give us three equations:

$$a + b \quad = 15 \dots\dots\dots (1)$$
$$a \quad + c = 17 \dots\dots\dots (2)$$
$$b + c = 14 \dots\dots\dots (3)$$

Note that the equations are written such that the letters stay in the same column.

It does not matter which pair of equations we take first. In this case I am going to take (3) from (2) to eliminate c.

(2) − (3)	$a - b = 3 \dots\dots\dots$ (4)
(1)	$a + b = 15 \dots\dots\dots$ (1)

$$(4) + (1) \qquad 2a \quad = 18$$
$$(\div 2)$$
$$a = 9$$

Substitute in (1)

$$9 + b = 15$$
$$(-9)$$
$$b = 6$$

Substitute in (2)

$$9 + c = 17$$
$$(-9)$$
$$c = 8$$

Check in (3) : $\quad 6 + 8 = 14$

---

1. Solve these three simultaneous equations:

$$x + y \quad = 4$$
$$x \quad + z = 8$$
$$y + z = 2$$

2. Solve these three simultaneous equations:

$$a + b + c = 7$$
$$a + b - c = 6$$
$$a - b - c = 2$$

3.   Solve these three simultaneous equations:
$$2a + b - c = 1$$
$$4a + b - 3c = 5$$
$$a - c = 2$$

4.   I have two brothers. The sum of our three ages is 40. The difference between the eldest and the youngest of us is 14. I am closer to my younger brothers age than my elder brothers age by two years. How old am I?

5.   My mother sent me out to buy ten pieces of fruit, of 3 different varieties.
If I buy 3 apples and 6 bananas and 1 coconut it will cost me £1.59.
However if I buy 2 coconuts and 7 bananas and 1 apple it will cost me £2.18.
If I buy 1 coconut, 2 apples and 7 bananas it will cost me £1.55.
a) Write 3 simultaneous equations and solve them to find the cost of the 3 types of fruit.
b) How can I buy my ten pieces of fruit at the minimum cost?

6.   I am thinking of three numbers. The sum of two of them is 24.
If I multiply the smallest number by the remaining number I have 91.
If all my numbers are prime numbers what numbers are they?

7.   a)   (i) Show that it is impossible to solve the simultaneous equations:
$$x + 2 = y \qquad y - 1 = z \qquad z - 1 = x$$
      (ii) Is there a limit to the possible solutions of these three equations?
      b) Show that it is impossible to solve the simultaneous equations:
$$x - 3 = y \qquad y + 6 = z \qquad z - 4 = x$$
      (ii) Is there a limit to the possible solutions of these three equations?

8.   Solve these three simultaneous equations:
$$y = 2^x \qquad x = 2y^z \qquad x = 3^z$$

Summary Exercise 12

1. Use the above graph to solve the following pairs of simultaneous equations:
    a) $x + y = 6$
       $2y - x = 10$
    b) $3y + x = 36$
       $2y - x = 10$
    c) $x + y = 6$
       $3y + x = 6$
    d) Explain why you cannot find a solution to this pair of simultaneous equations:

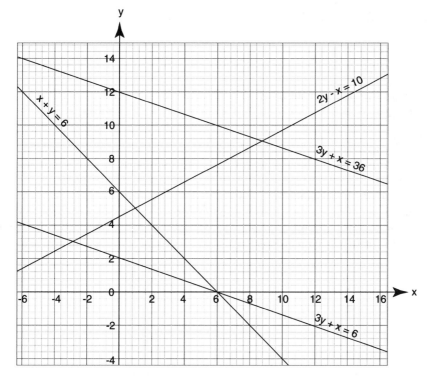

$$3y + x = 36$$
$$3y + x = 6$$

2. Solve these pairs of simultaneous equations:
    a) $x + 2y = 3$
       $x - y = 6$
    b) $x - y = 6$
       $x + y = 4$
    c) $3x + 2y = 0$
       $2x - y = 7$

    d) $x + 4y = 10$
       $4x - 5y = -23$
    e) $2x - 3y = 7$
       $5x + 2y = 8$
    f) $3x - 4y = 12$
       $2x + 6y = -5$

    g) $y = 1 - 2x$
       $x + 2y = -1$
    h) $y = 2 - x$
       $x = y + 4$
    i) $y = 2x - 2$
       $y = 4 - 3(x + 1)$

3. I was supposed to buy my mother 3 clear light bulbs and 4 pearl light bulbs, which would have cost £3.10. By mistake I bought 4 clear bulbs and 3 pearl bulbs, and that cost me £3.20. What is the cost per bulb of each sort of light bulb?

4. We buy 10 packets of sparklers for Guy Fawkes Day. Plain sparklers cost £1.20 per packet and coloured sparklers cost £1.50 per packet. If I spent £12.90 in all how many packets of coloured sparklers did I buy?

Revision Exercises 2

If the answer is not exact correct your answer to 3 significant figures unless otherwise instructed.

1. a) Write the answers to these in index form:

a) $2^2 \times 2^5$ b) $5^7 \div 5^2$ c) $x^5 \div x^3$ d) $\dfrac{3x^2y^3}{6x^3y}$

e) $\dfrac{24a^2bc^2}{16b^3c}$

b) Find the square root of (i) $3^3 \times 3^5$ (ii) $a^7 \div a^3$ (iii) $\dfrac{x^6}{y^2}$

c) Factorise:

(i) $2x^2 + 12xy$ (ii) $12ab^2 + 8a^2b + 4a$ (iii) $6x^2y - 3y^2 + 9x$

2. A rectangle has its base 6 cm longer than its height. If the height is h cm draw a sketch of the rectangle and write an expression for the base.

b) Write an expression for the area of the rectangle.

c) The area of the rectangle is 118 cm^2. Copy and continue the table below using trial and improvement methods to find the value of h to two decimal places and thus find the base of the rectangle.

height	base	Area
8	14	112
9	15	

3. a) Write down the next three terms of these series:

(i) 1, 4, 7, 10, ...

(ii) 2, 5, 10, 17, ...

(iii) 8, 5, 2, −1, ...

b) If the nth term in the series is $S_n = 9 - 2n$, what is:

(i) S_1 (ii) S_3 (iii) S_6 (iv) S_{10}

c) Can you find the next three terms in the series and hence the rule for T_n:

$T_1 = 3$ $T_2 = 8$ $T_3 = 13$ $T_4 = 18$ $T_5 = 24$

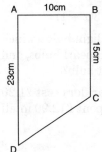

4. This is the cross section of a nesting box, angles DAC and ABC are right angles, and AD is parallel to BC:

a) Calculate the length of CD.

b) Calculate the cross sectional area ABCD.

c) If the top of the nesting box is a square, calculate the volume of the nesting box.

Here is the piece of wood that forms the front of the nesting box.

d) There are 2 cm of wood on each side of the circular hole. Calculate the area of the hole.

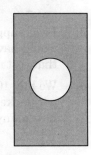

5. (a) Factorise $15st - 5t^2 - 30s^2t$

(b) If a = 4, b = 5 and c = −17, evaluate the expressions:

(i) $\sqrt{b^2 - 4ac}$ (ii) $\dfrac{-b + \sqrt{b^2 - 4ac}}{2a}$

6. a) This equailateral triangle has sides of 10cm. Calculate the height and thus the area of the triangle.

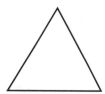

b)

(i) A painter has the base of his ladder 2.4 metres from the foot of the wall. It then touches the wall at a point 6 metres above the ground. How long is his ladder?

(ii) In order to reach a little higher the painter moves the ladder 60 cm closer to the wall. How high up the wall does his ladder reach now?

7. a) If $x = 1.2$ $y = -2.4$ and $z = 1.8$ Evaluate the expressions:

(i) $x^2 - 2yz$ (ii) $(x^2 - 2yz)^2$ (iii) $\dfrac{xyz}{(x^2 - 2yz)^2}$

b) A trapezium has parallel sides of 12 cm and 8 cm and Area 60 cm². What is the perpendicular distance between the parallel sides?

8. A car travels for 20 minutes at 60 km/h and then for 30 minutes at 70 km/hour.
a) What distance did the car travel?
b) What was the average speed?

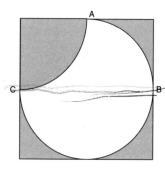

9. A piece of decorative ironwork has this cross section composed of a semicircle, a quadrant and an inverted quadrant. The whole piece is stamped out of a square of side 60cm.
a) Find the area enclosed by the semicircle BC.
b) Find the area enclosed by the quadrant AB.
c) Find the area of the square.
d) Find the area of the decorative shape.
e) Find the shaded area, that is the area that is wasted.
f) Calculate the percentage of the original shape that is wasted.

10. A company makes Widgets and Plunkets. Each Widget makes a profit of W pounds and each Plunket makes a profit of P pounds.
a) One week the company made 15 Widgets and 60 Plunkets and made a profit of £246. Write an equation in W and P to show this information.
b) The following week the company made 50 Widgets and 24 Plunkets and made a profit of £204. Write another equation in W and P to show this information.

c) Solve the two equations simultaneously to find the value of W and P and find out the profit the company made in the third week when they made 20 Widgets and 40 Plunkets.

11. a) Factorise these expressions:
(i) $4ab - 3a$ (ii) $2x^2y + 6y^2 - 3y$
b) Make x the subject of these formula:

(i) $y = ax + 4$ (ii) $a = bc - dx$ (iii) $c = \dfrac{a+b}{ax}$

c) If a = 2.1, b=1.5 and c= –1.8 find x if:
$$b = \frac{c^2 - a^2}{ax}$$

12. Here are two squares each with side 10 cm.

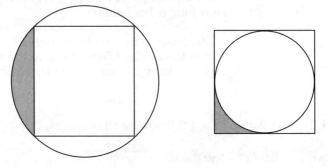

a) The first square is inscribed inside a circle. Calculate the radius of the circle and hence find the shaded area.
b) The second square has a circle inscribed within it. Calculate the radius of this circle and thus find the shaded area.

13. The height of a triangle is 5 cm less than its base:
a) Write an expression in b for the area of the triangle:

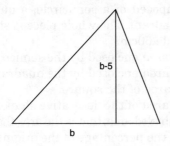

b-5

b

b) The area of the triangle is 40 cm^2. Copy and continue the table below and find the value of b to 2 decimal places using trial and improvements methods:

base	height	Area
12	7	
11	6	

c) Write down the base and height of the triangle correct to 2 decimal places.

14. Here is a pattern of rhombuses:
The second pattern contains 4 little rhombuses and 1 larger rhombus of side 2 units. Pattern number three contains 9 little rhombuses, 4 rhombuses of side 2 units and 1 rhombus of side 3 units.
a) Draw the next two patterns in the series and count the number of rhombuses in each.
b) Find a rule for the series and hence find the number of rhombuses in the 10th pattern.

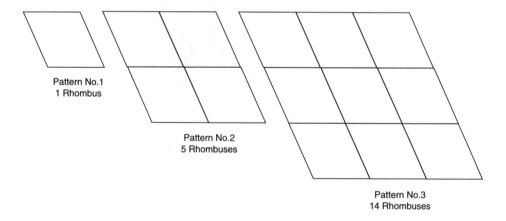

Pattern No.1
1 Rhombus

Pattern No.2
5 Rhombuses

Pattern No.3
14 Rhombuses

194

Chapter 13

Large And Small Numbers

Most problems that we have to work out have quite ordinary numbers, but as we explore the world of Science, Geography and Astronomy we start to get some very large numbers and some very small numbers.

Consider these facts about the Earth and its Elements:

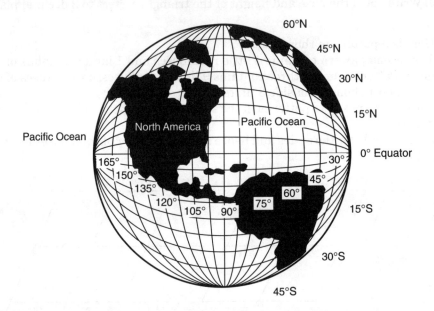

The Earth is the fifth largest of the planets and is on average 149 700 000km from the sun.

The total mass of the Earth is 6 694 000 000 000 000 000 000 tonnes (i.e. 6 694 million million million).

The population of China was approximately 1 115 000 000 in 1990.

The relative density of Hydrogen is about 0.000 089 9.

The distance between atoms in copper is about 0.000 000 000 34m.

Now if you look at your calculator you will see that the display can only show 8 or 10 digits. This makes it very difficult to calculate with these large and small numbers. We have to find a way of writing them in *shorthand* so that we can use the calculator.

Writing these numbers in shorthand also makes it easier to compare their relative size, and to calculate with them. It is also quicker to write shorthand.

The shorthand system we use is based on the fact that our number system is the decimal system and the powers of ten can be written with indices:

- one thousand is 10^3
- one hundredth is 10^{-2}

Exercise 13A

Write these numbers as powers of ten:

> Example: $10\ 000 = 10^4$
> $0.000\ 001 = 10^{-6}$

1. 100 000	**5.** 100 000 000	**9.** 1 000 000 000
2. 100	**6.** 0. 000 000 001	**10.** 0.000 01
3. 0.01	**7.** 10 000	**11.** 0.1
4. 0.000 1	**8.** 0.001	**12.** 1

Write these numbers as a single figure multiplied by a power of 10:

> For example: $4\ 000 = 4 \times 1000$ $0.007 = 7 \times 0.001$
> $= 4 \times 10^3$ $= 7 \times 10^{-3}$

13. 200 000	**20.** 0.000 02
14. 0.000 002	**21.** 500 000 000 000 000
15. 0.3	**22.** 200
16. 0.005	**23.** 0.007
17. 0.000 000 006	**24.** 0.000 000 000 000 8
18. 400 000 000	**25.** 5 000
19. 0.000 009	**26.** 30 000

Write these numbers out in full, remember to put the space in the correct position after each group of three numbers:

> For example: $3 \times 10^4 = 3 \times 10000$
> $= 30\ 000$
> $7 \times 10^{-5} = 7 \times 0.000\ 01$
> $= 0.000\ 07$

27. 7×10^2	**32.** 3×10^1	**37.** 6×10^6
28. 8×10^6	**33.** 2×10^{-3}	**38.** 2×10^{-2}
29. 9×10^{-1}	**34.** 7×10^7	**39.** 7×10^8
30. 5×10^2	**35.** 8×10^{-5}	**40.** 1×10^{-7}
31. 9×10^5	**36.** 4×10^{-3}	

Standard Index Form

This way of writing numbers, that is as a number multiplied by a power of ten is called "standard index form".
The definition of standard index form is :

A number between one and ten multiplied by a power of ten.

The numbers we have just looked at have all been just single numbers, but there is no reason why we cannot have decimals, and often we have to have decimals:

$3.4 \times 10^3 = 3.4 \times 1000$ *note the 3 is × 1000 so the answer will be three thousand*
$\qquad\quad = 3400$ *and something not thirty four thousand*

Exercise 13B
Write these numbers out in full:

1. 4.5×10^2
2. 2.3×10^3
3. 1.82×10^4
4. 7.34×10^5
5. 9.02×10^{-1}

6. 3.71×10^{-2}
7. 4.1×10^{-3}
8. 6.72×10^{-4}
9. 5.45×10^3
10. 3.65×10^{-2}

11. 4.302×10^7
12. 9.104×10^{-5}
13. 4.235×10^2
14. 6.025×10^{-3}
15. 7.123×10^2

Write these numbers in standard index form:

For example:	230 000	$= 2.3 \times 100\ 000$
		$= 2.3 \times 10^5$
	0.000 305	$= 3.05 \times 0.000\ 1$
		$= 3.05 \times 10^{-5}$

16. 420
17. 12 000
18. 234 000 000
19. 102 000
20. 3000

21. 55
22. 600 000 000 000
23. 0.003
24. 0.004 51
25. 0.000 056

26. 0.000 000 705
27. 0.12
28. 0.305
29. 67 900 000
30. 0.000 045 56

Exercise 13C
Give your answers to these in standard index form:

1. Write 4km in millimetres.
2. Write 6kg in grams.
3. How many seconds are there in a day?
4. What is 5 millimetres in km?
5. What is 5g in tonnes?
6. Write 4.24 millimetres in km.
7. "Mega" is the prefix for one million. A megabuck is one million dollars. Write 150 megabucks in standard index form.

8. "Micro" is the prefix for one millionth. One microsecond is one millionth of a second. Write 90 microseconds in Standard Index Form.

9. Dinosaurs roamed the Earth 150 million years ago. Write the number of years in Standard Index Form.

10. A pico is a million millionth. Write 15 picoseconds in standard index form.

11. The Big Bang is supposed to have taken place 1010 years ago. How many years is that?

12. The total mass of the Earth is 6 694 000 000 000 000 000 000 tonnes (i.e. 6 694 million million million) Write this mass in Standard Index Form.

13. The relative density of Hydrogen is 0.000 089 9. Write this in Standard Index Form.

14. The distance between copper atoms is about 3.4 x 10^{-10}m. Write this distance out in full.

Standard Index Form And The Scientific Calculator

Try this sum on your Scientific Calculator.

450 000 × 250 000

If you have an **older style** calculator the display showing the answer will look something like this:

$$1.125 \quad {}^{11}$$

This is the calculator's own shorthand for 1.125×10^{11} or 112 500 000 000

If you have a newer style VPAM calculator the display will look something like this:

$$1.125 \; {}^{\times 10 \; 11}$$

which is the calculator's way of saying 1.125×10^{11}.

Now do the sum 0.000 004 ÷ 500 000. If you have an **older style** calculator the answer on the display should be something similar to:

$$8.00 \quad {}^{-12}$$

This is the calculator saying 8×10^{-12}, or 0.000 000 000 008

If you have a newer style VPAM calculator the display will look something like this:

$$8.00 \, {}^{\times 10 \; -12}$$

When you write your answers you must write the sum correctly and **must not** write the calculator shorthand, as 8^{-12} is in fact $\frac{1}{8^{12}}$ not 8×10^{-12}.

Now repeat *Exercise 13C* using your calculator and check your answers.

Exercise 13D

Do these using your calculator. Give your answers first in standard form and then written out in full.

Example: How many millimetres are there in 250 000km?

$$250\ 000\text{km} = 250\ 000 \times 1000 \times 1000\text{mm}$$
$$= 2.5 \times 10^{11}\text{mm}$$
$$= 250\ 000\ 000\ 000\text{mm}$$

---

1. The circumference of the Earth is 40 000km. What is this in millimetres?

2. A Kilobyte of computer memory is different to a normal kilo unit. It is not one thousand but 2^{10} bytes. A megabyte is 2^{10} Kilobytes. The bit is the smallest particle of memory storage and there are eight bits in a byte. How many bits are there in 4 megabytes?

3. How many seconds are there in a century?

4. "Micro" is the prefix for one millionth. For example one microsecond is one millionth of a second. How many minutes is 9 microseconds?

5. "Mega" is the prefix for 1 million. For example one megabuck is one million dollars. The current rate of exchange is 1.75 American dollars to the English pound. What is 5.5 megabucks in pounds

6. Radio frequency is measured in Hertz, or more usually kilohertz.(1000 Hz) or mega Hertz (I million Hertz). To find the wavelength of the frequency you divide 300 000 by the frequency. If the frequency of a radio station is 200 kHz what is its wavelength?

7. The average wage is £15 000 per year. If the health service employs 2.4 million people, estimate the amount that they must pay out in wages every year. (Assume every employee receives the average wage).

8. Of the 2.4 million employees each one has four weeks holiday, or 20 working days. How many man-days is that in total?

9. The circumference of the Earth is 40 000km. The diameter of a 10p coin is 24mm. How many 10p coins would be needed to completely cover the Equator? What would this be worth?

10. The biggest dinosaur was Ultrasaurus, the name "Ultrasaurus" means the largest lizard. One Ultrasaurus found in Colorado was more than 30 metres long, stood 18 metres high and weighed 136 tonnes. What are these dimensions in millimetres, and milligrams?

11. The dinosaurs roamed the Earth during the Jurassic period, which ended 135 million years ago. Roughly how many days ago is this?

12. Ornithominus was probably the fastest dinosaur and could run at 80km per hour. How many millimetres an hour is this?

13. a) Very large distances are measured in light years. Light travels at 300 000km per second. The distance that it travels in a year is then a "light year". From this information show that one light year is equal to 9.5×10^{12} kilometres.
b) The nearest star (apart from the sun) is Proxima Centauri and this is 4.3 light years away. How far is this in kilometres?

14. A newer unit of astronomical measurement is the parsec. One parsec is roughly 3.25 light years. How many kilometres is this?

15. The maximum speed of a Harrier Jet is 1186km/hour. How many mm/hour is this?

16. How far would a Harrier Jet go in metres, at maximum speed, in 4 hours?

17. The moon takes 27 days, 7 hours 43 minutes and 11 seconds to go round the Earth. How many seconds is this in total?

18. a) 1 nautical mile is 1 853.18m. How many millimetres are there in 1000 nautical miles.
b) From the distance for the circumference of the earth above find the length of the equator in nautical miles.

19. The dimensions of an atom are measured in Angstroms. One Angstrom (1Ä) is equal to 10^{-10} m.
Write 1 Ä in (i) cm   (ii) mm   (iii) micrometers where one micrometer (µm) $=10^{-6}$ m.

20. An aeon is 10^9 years. The sun was formed 4.5 aeons ago. How many years ago is that?

Calculating In Standard Index Form Using A Calculator

On your calculator you should find a button marked EXP. EXP is short for 'exponent' which is another way of describing a number written to the power of another number. Try this calculation:

$$(4.1 \times 10^7) \times (5.3 \times 10^9)$$

On the calculator key in the following sequence, look carefully at the display as you follow the calculation through:

You should get the answer 2.173×10^{17}, if not consult the manual for your calculator.

Exercise 13E

Now use your calculator to solve these problems; you will need to use the EXP button to calculate in standard index form and give your answers in standard index form. Some of these problems involve figures used in astronomy. When we look at the stars we are actually seeing light that was emitted by the star millions of years ago. It has taken that long for the light to travel across the universe to us. In one second light travels 300 000km.

1.   The distance between the sun and the earth is 1.5×10^9km, and the speed of light is 3×10^5km per second. How long is it from the time light is emitted by the sun before we see it on earth? Give your answer in a) seconds and b) minutes.

2.   Let us see how big our galaxy is. The Big Bang that created the galaxy is supposed to have occurred 10×10^{10} years ago. How far has light travelled since then? (This should give us the limit of the size of the galaxy)

3.   The most distant objects that we can see are galaxies at distances at over 10^{10} light years away.
a) As 1 light year is 9.5×10^{12} km How many years old is the light that we are seeing?
b) How many times older than our own universe must those galaxies be?

4.   A galaxy 3 million light years away from us moves at between 50 and 100 km per second. How far would it travel in one year?

5.   Astronomers believe that the galaxy expanded very rapidly just after its creation. When it was between 10^{-33} and 10^{-30} seconds old it is believed to have expanded 101 000 000 times. This number 10 to the power of one million, is written as 1 followed by one million noughts.
a) If this number was to be written in a book the same size as this one How many noughts could you get on one page?
b) How many pages would there have to be in the book?

6.   Quasars were first found in the 1960's and appear as blue star-like objects, and are sources of intense radio waves, (hence their name **quas**i **s**tellar **r**adio **s**ource). These are 10 000 times brighter than a normal galaxy and are visible at distances of 10^{10} light years or more. How old is the light that we are seeing?

7.   A space craft re-entering the Earth's atmosphere travels at 10 metres per second. What is this in km per hour?

8.   Dinosaurs roamed the earth 150 million years ago. If we are seeing light today from a star that exploded then how far away is that star?

Approximate Answers

The Continuous Nature of measurement

When working with very large and very small numbers we cannot always be sure of **exactly** what the figure is, the numbers are approximate. We are used to giving answers corrected to either a certain number of significant figures or to a certain number of decimal places.

Consider the length 3.5cm:

This could either be a number rounded off to 2 significant figures or to one decimal place.

If the length has been 'rounded off' what is the largest possible length that this could have been?

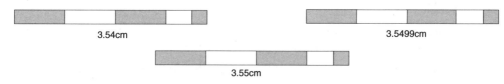

	3.54cm			3.5499cm

	3.55cm

3.54cm   would round off to 3.5cm (to 2 s.f. or 1 d.p.)
3.5499cm   would round off to 3.5cm (to 2 s.f. or 1 d.p.)
3.55cm   would round off to 3.6cm (to 2 s.f. or 1 d.p.)

Of these three lengths 3.5499cm is the largest, but the largest possible length is 3.5499...cm . In fact we know that 3.5499... is so nearly 3.55 that it makes sense to use that figure.

Similarly what is the smallest possible length that could be rounded up to 3.5cm?

3.44cm   would round off to 3.4cm (to 2 s.f. or 1 d.p.)
3.45cm   would round off to 3.5cm (to 2 s.f. or 1 d.p.)
3.4999cm   would round off to 3.5cm (to 2 s.f. or 1 d.p.)

Of these three lengths 3.45cm is the smallest.

The length 3.5cm could therefore lie between 3.45cm and 3.55cm (but could not actually equal 3.55). We write this as:
$$3.54 \le 3.4 < 3.55$$

Exercise 13F

1. Give the range of values that the following rounded lengths lie within:
    a) 4.72m   b) 4km   c) 3.2cm   d) 4.2mm   e) 3.50cm

2. Give the range of values that the following rounded masses lie within:
    a) 325 g   b) 4.7kg   c) 43mg   d) 450g   e) 8.00kg

3. Give the range of values that the following rounded volumes lie within:
    a) 4.0 litres   b) 75.0 litres   c) 3.25ml

4.   Look at these three areas of 6m²:

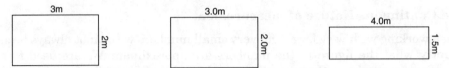

For each rectangle work out the maximum and minimum width and length and thus calculate the maximum and minimum possible values of the areas of the rectangle.

5.   Consider some other rectangles of area 6m² and work out the maximum and minimum possible values of the area of the rectangle. What is the smallest possible value for a rectangle of area 6m² and what is the largest ?

6.   Consider several rectangles of area 8m² and calculate the largest possible value of the area of the rectangle and the smallest possible value of the area of the rectangle.

7.   Consider several rectangles of area 10m² and calculate the largest possible value of the rectangle and the smallest possible value.

8.   Work out The maximum and minimum possible areas of this rectangle:

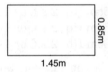

9.   a) We have a new electronic bell to mark the beginning and end of our lessons. It is accurate to the nearest 0.5 of a second. Our maths lesson today is supposed to be exactly 40 minutes. What is the shortest time the lesson could last, in seconds?

b) Something has gone wrong with our new electronic bell. In fact it has proved to be accurate only to the nearest 0.5 of a minute. What is the shortest time our maths lesson could last now, in seconds?

10.   A train journey is reported to take 1 hour and 15 minutes, to the nearest minute. What is the shortest and longest time that this journey could actually take?

11.   A rivet and a corresponding rivet hole are specified to be exactly 6mm in diameter. However the machine can only be precise to a hundredth of a mm, how much larger could the rivet be than the rivet hole exactly?

12.   A bricklayer is building a wall 8.0m long by 2.0m tall with bricks that are 22.5cm long and 7.5cm high. He lays mortar 1.25cm wide between the bricks. What are the maximum and minimum numbers of bricks he needs to build the wall?

Extension Exercise 13

Working With Rounded Numbers

We frequently use rounded numbers when talking about figures in every day life. You would not say to a friend – "I'll be there in 7 minutes and 30 seconds", you would say either 'I'l be there in five minutes' or "I'll be there in 10 minutes".

1. a) My maths teacher complains that I am always late for his lesson. He says that I am 5 minutes late every time. He makes me work out how many whole maths lessons I miss over the school year because of my lateness. We have 5 lessons of maths every week and there are 30 weeks of school in a school year. Can you answer the maths teacher's question?
    b) What is wrong with the maths teacher's question?

2. a) Four of us are practising for the school sports day. We measure how far each of us could run in a one minute sprint. The distances we recorded were:
    A: 202.5m   B: 171.2m   C: 182.3m   D:195.2m
    Which of A, B, C or D is the fastest?
    b) Four of us are practising for the school sports day 1500 metre race. The times that we record are (in minutes: seconds: hundredths of a second):
    A: 5: 15: 20   B: 5: 16: 45   C: 6: 21: 08   D: 6: 05: 04
    Which of A, B, C or D is the fastest?
    c) If you had to time a measured km who would be the fastest, the person with the shortest time or the one with the longest time?

Consider what happens when using rounded off values in a formula:

For example : If $a = 20$ and $b = 50$ correct to the nearest ten calculate the upper values of:

    a) $a + b$ b) $\dfrac{a}{b}$

       $a + b < 25 + 55$ $\dfrac{a}{b} < \dfrac{25}{45}$

           < 55 < 0.5

---

3. If $a = 6$ and $b = 8$ correct to one significant figure calculate the upper and lower possible values of:

    a) $a + b$ b) $a - b$ c) ab d) $\dfrac{b}{a}$ e) $\dfrac{b}{a}$

4. If $a = 2.1$ and $b = 4.5$ correct to one decimal place calculate the upper and lower possible values of:
    a) $a + b$ b) $a - b$ c) ab d) $\dfrac{b}{a}$ e) $\dfrac{b}{a}$

5. If $a = 0.35$ and $b = 2.45$ correct to one decimal place calculate the upper and lower possible values of:

    a) $3a + 4b$ b) $a^2 - b^2$ c) $a^2 b$ d) $\dfrac{a^2}{b}$

Summary Exercise 13

1.   Write these numbers as powers of 10:
     a) 100 000   b) 0.000 01   c) 100 000   d) 0.000 000 01

2.   Write these numbers in Standard Index Form:

     a) 4000   b) 500 000   c) 45 000 000   d) 39 800 000 000

3.   Write these numbers in Standard Index Form:
     a) 0.05   b) 0.000 009   c) 0.000 045 6   d) 0.007 54

4.   Write these numbers out in full, remembering to put the spaces in the correct
     places after each group of three numbers:
     a) 4×10^4 b) 7.5×10^6 c) 2.75×10^6 d) 5.09×10^3

5.   Write these numbers out in full, remembering to put the spaces in the correct
     places after each group of three numbers:
     a) 3×10^{-6} b) 6.7×10^{-4} c) 8.05×10^{-6} d) 8.13×10^{-6}

6.   Write 40 000km in mm. Give your answer in Standard Index Form.

7.   Write 6mg in kg. Give your answer in Standard Index Form.

8.   If you blink 5 times a minute while you are awake how many times have you
     blinked by your fourteenth birthday? Give your answer in Standard Index Form.

9.   Calculate the following, giving your answers in Standard Index Form:
     a) 47 million multiplied by 235 thousand million.
     b) 375 millionths divided by 342 thousand.
     c) $8.09 \times 10^{12} \times 7.52 \times 10^8$
     d) $1.05 \times 10^{-10} \div 7.52 \times 10^{-12}$

10. A virus spreads infection **exponentially**; that is, the number of infected people
     doubles each day.
     a) If 20 people are infected on the first day of The month How many are
     infected 10 days later? (Give your answer in Standard Index Form)
     b) In fact the virus only causes infection for 3 days on average, and so on the
     4th day the original 20 people are not infected by the virus any longer. How
     many people are there actually infected 10 days later?

11. Give the range of values that these lengths could lie between:
     a) 7m   b)   10.5cm   c)   3.45mm   d)   4.0km

12. Give the range of values that these masses could lie between:
     a) 10kg   b)   3.05g   c)   345mg   d)   3.0g

13. Work out the maximum and minimum areas of a square with sides of 5.2cm, to
     one decimal place.

Activity 13 - Investigation Binary Arithmetic

You should now have a good appreciation of how our decimal number system works on the base of 10. This number system has stood us very well for centuries; however at the end of the twentieth century something changed - not only were humans able to speak to each other they also started to talk to machines - to telephones, calculators and computers. As technology advanced the machines started to talk to each other, and then to talk back to humans. How is this possible?

Machines 'talk' to each other by a series of electronic pulses; these pulses have two states 'on' and 'off', we could write these as 1 and 0.

When a machine needs to transmit a number it can only transmit a pulse; it would be very inefficient to transmit 1000 pulses to represent the number 1000, so how do they do it?

If you consider our number system with 10 digit figures, the value of each figure is represented by its position:

H T U	or	10^2	10^1	10^0
3 7 5		3	7	5	three hundred and seventy five.

A machine only has 2 digit figures, 1 and 0, and so to use the same idea of the value of the digit being represented by the column that it is in the column headings must be in the powers of 2:

2^2	2^1	2^0	
1	0	1	$(1 \times 4) + (1 \times 1) = 5$

This system of using 1's and 0's is known as the <u>binary system</u>. It was of interest to mathematicians before technology came into use, but now is an essential part of any system design.

Here are some numbers written in binary; can you convert them to decimal numbers:

1. 110
2. 1101
3. 11
4. 111
5. 1011
6. 1010
7. 10 101
8. 11 101
9. 11 001
10. 111 111

Now convert these decimal numbers to binary:

11. 8
12. 16
13. 19
14. 20
15. 50
16. 100
17. 324
18. 171
19. 429
20. 245

Now investigate binary arithmetic - adding, subtracting, multiplication and division. Can you write an arithmetic book explaining how to use these numbers and calculate with them, include any 'algorithms' or rules that you can find?

Chapter 14

Graphs of Linear Functions

A graph is a pictorial representation of a relationship. It can be a bar graph, a column graph, a line graph or a curve. In this chapter we are going to look further at graphs that are a straight line.

If a graph is a straight line then that represents a relationship between the two **variables** on the **axes** that is linear. If the graph goes through the origin, (0, 0) this means that the two variables are directly proportional to one another. Examples of this type of relationship are conversion graphs; for example foreign exchange or miles to kilometres.

Conversion Graphs

Consider the currency conversion, £1= 8.5 French Francs.
This conversion can be shown on a graph:

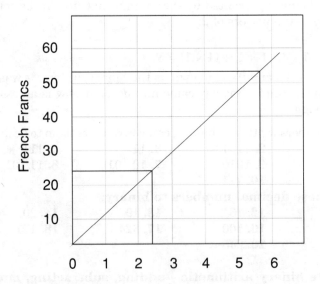

On this graph we need to look carefully at the scale.
   Horizontally one small square is equal to £0.20.
   Vertically one small square is equal to 2 FF.

   From the graph we can see that £2.60 is equal to 22 FF
                      and 46 FF is equal to £5.40

Note that when you read off the graph you should draw lines parallel to the axes to read off the scales exactly. This is very important with conversion graphs to make sure that your answer is as accurate as possible.

Exercise 14A

Use Worksheet 14/1 with Q1 and Q2 of this exercise

1. 1 kilogram is equal to 2.2lb. (pounds weight).
   a) What are these weights in pounds:
   (i) 0kg   (ii) 5kg
   b) On graph paper draw a pair of axes, the horizontal axis from 0 to 6kg on a scale of 1cm to 1 kg, the vertical axis from 0 to 14lb on a scale of 1cm to 2lb.
   c) Plot the three points from part (a) on your graph and draw a long straight line through the points.
   d) Write the title of your graph:
   "Graph to show the conversion of Kilograms to pounds"
   e) Rule off lines on the graph to find
   (i) 1.4kg in lb   (ii) 4.5kg in lb   (iii) 3.0lb. inkg   (iv) 10.5lb. in kg
   and write down the answers.

2. 1 litre is equal to 0.22 gallons
   a) What are these amounts in gallons: (i) 0 litres   (ii) 5 litres   (iii) 20 litres ?
   b) On graph paper draw a pair of axes.
   Let the horizontal axis represent litres from 0 to 30 litres on a scale of 1cm to 5 litres and the vertical axis represent gallons from 0 to 12 gallons on a scale of 1cm to 2 gallons.
   c) Draw a conversion graph of litres to gallons and use your graph to find:
   (i) 12 litres in gallons   (ii) 25 litres in gallons
   (iii) 3 gallons in litres   (iv) 8.2 gallons in litres.

3. £1 = 3.6 DM (German Deutsche Marks)
   a) How many DM are there in
   (i) £50   (ii) £100 ?
   b) Use this information to draw a conversion graph of Pounds Sterling to DM, with the Pounds Sterling from 0 to £200 on the horizontal axis on a scale of 4cm to £50, and DM from 0 to 750 DM on the vertical axis on a scale of 2cm to 100 DM.
   c) Use your graph to calculate
   (i) 100 DM in £   (ii) 500 DM in £
   (iii) £125 in DM   (iv) £90 in DM

4. £1 = $1.6 (United States Dollars)
   Use this information to draw a conversion chart of Pounds Sterling from 0 to £500 to United States Dollars. Use the horizontal axis for Pounds Sterling, to a suitable scale. Use your graph to find the value of
   (i) £450 in US$ (ii) £225 in US$ (iii) $700 in £   (iv) $425 in £.

5. The cooking time for a pot roast of lamb is as "45 minutes per lb plus 45 minutes."

calculated a) How long would it take to cook:
(i) a 2 lb joint   (ii) a 5 lb joint ?
b) Draw a conversion graph for cooking time against axis with a scale of 2 cm to one hour and a suitable scale for weight on the vertical axis.(Think carefully about what happens to your line between 0 hours and 1 hour!).
c) Use your graph to find:
(i) The time taken for to roast a joint of (i) 3½lb. (ii) 4½lb
(iii) How heavy is a joint that takes 2½ hours to roast?

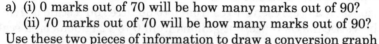

6. The final Maths exam mark is out of 100. The mark out of 20 for the mental arithmetic is halved to give a mark out of 10. This mark is added to the mark for the written paper for a final percentage. The actual marks for the written paper were out of 70 and so they have to be converted to a mark out of 90.

a) (i) 0 marks out of 70 will be how many marks out of 90?
(ii) 70 marks out of 70 will be how many marks out of 90?
Use these two pieces of information to draw a conversion graph of the original mark to the new mark.

b) Use your graph to find the mark out of 90 for (i) $\dfrac{35}{70}$ (ii) $\dfrac{60}{70}$

c) If I scored 15 out of 20 for the mental arithmetic test and 55 out of 70 for the written paper what will be my final percentage?

7. 10 km is equal to 6.2 miles
Draw a conversion chart to convert kilometres from 0 to 100 into miles.
(Let the horizontal axis be kilometres.)
Use your chart to find:
a) 25 miles in kilometres
b) 70 kilometres in miles
c) The equivalent of the 60 mph speed limit in kilometres per hour.
d) The equivalent of the French speed limit of 60 km per hour in mph.

Travel Graphs

A travel graph shows the relationship between distance travelled and time taken.

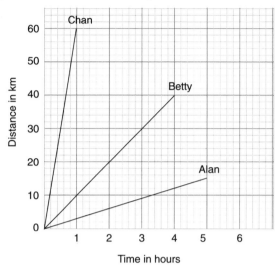

This graph shows that Alan travelled 15 km in 5 hours, Betty travelled 40 km in 4 hours and Chan travelled 60 km in one hour.

From this we can see that as Alan travelled 15 km in 5 hours his speed was 3 km per hour, and he was probably walking. Similarly Betty was travelling at 10 km per hour, possibly on a bicycle and Chan was travelling at 60 km per hour, probably by car.

Exercise 14B

1. Here is a graph showing a car journey.

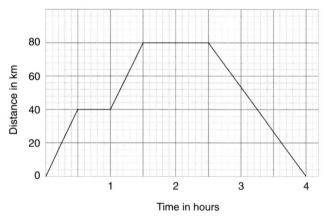

    a) At what speed was the car travelling for the first hour?
    b) What did the car do after one hour of its journey?
    c) What speed did the car travel after that?
    d) What did the car do for the last hour of the journey?
    e) Describe what you think the purpose of this car journey was.

2.   Here is the graph of another journey:
Describe this journey including the time and different speed for each part of the journey.

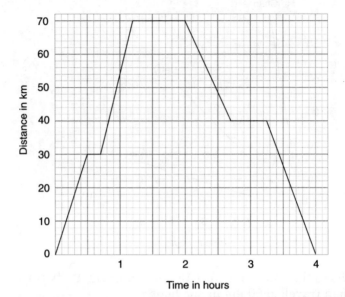

3.   This graph shows two trains leaving Adamstown and Beesville at the sametime.
a) What is the difference between the two trains?
b) How long after the start of the journey do the two trains cross?
c) How far from Beesville is this?
d) At what speed does the Adamstown to Beesville Express travel?
e) What is the fastest speed that the Beesville to Adamstown travels?

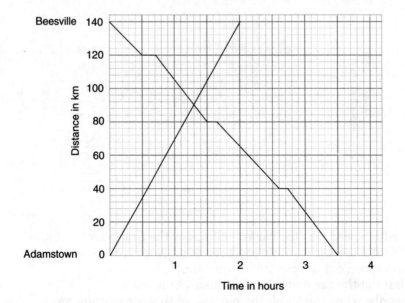

4. A car travels at 100 km per hour along the motorway for one and a half hours. The car then stops at a Jolly Muncher restaurant for 45 minutes before continuing its journey. The traffic is now heavier and so the car travels for 30 minutes at 40 km per hour before coming off the motorway and travelling for 15 minutes at 60 km per hour.

Draw a travel graph to show the journey, take 1cm to represent 30 minutes on the horizontal axis and 1cm to represent 20 km on the vertical axis. How far was the journey?

5.   a) A car leaves

point A at 10 a.m. and travels 100 km at 80 km per hour, it then stops for 30 minutes before travelling another 80 km at 60 km per hour to point B. Draw a travel graph to show the journey and use the graph to find out at what time the car reaches its destinationat B?

b) Another car leaves point B at 10.45 a.m. and travels at a steady 70 km per hour to point A. Add a graph of this cars journey. Use the graph to find out when the second car reaches point A and at what time the two cars crossed.

6. A boy leaves home at 9a.m.; he walks for 30 minutes at 4 km per hour then he takes a bus into town which travels at 40 km per hour for 45 minutes. He spends 1 and a quarter hours in town doing his Christmas shopping. He then starts to walk home at a speed of 5 km per hour. His mother leaves home at 11.15 a.m. and drives to town to pick him up, driving at 60 km per hour. Draw a travel graph to show these two journeys and find out at what time the boy meets his mother.

7. Asram and Ben set off from school at 4.00 p.m. to visit the local museum. Asram wakls at 4 km per hour for 5 minutes and then catches a bus which travels at 30 km per hour for 20 minutes, directly to the museum. Ben cycles at 15 km per hour for 42 minutes until he gets to the museum.

Draw a travel graph of these two journeys and use your graph to find out at what time the bus overtakes the bicycle.

Straight Lines

In the first two exercises we looked at straight line graphs representing real situations, now we are going to look at straight lines that represent equations.

Graphs Parallel To The Axes

Let us look at a graph. Any point on the graph has a pair of co-ordinates:

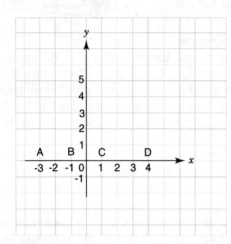
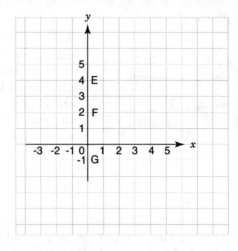

All the points on the x axis have a y co-ordinate of 0.
Therefore the x axis is the line $y = 0$

All the points on the y axis have an x co-ordinate of 0,
and the x axis is the line $x = 0$

Similarly a line parallel to the x axis will have all its y co-ordinates the same and thus will be of the form $y =$ a constant, and a line parallel to the y axis will have all its x co-ordinates the same and be of the form $x =$ a constant.

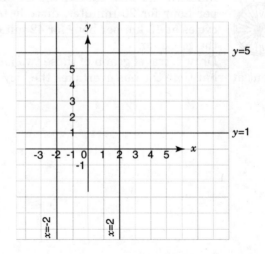

Exercise 14C

Write down the equations of lines 1. - 6.

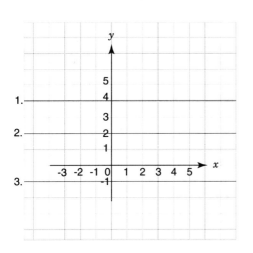

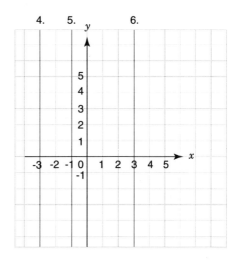

Now on graph paper draw a pair of axes taking values of x and y from -5 to 5 and draw the following lines:

7. $x = 3$ **10.** $y = 0$ **13.** $y = -2$
8. $y = 5$ **11.** $y = -4$ **14.** $x = -3$
9. $x = -1$ **12.** $x = 0$

15. On graph paper draw a pair of axes taking values of x and y from -5 to 5 and draw the following points on the grid: $(-2, -2), (0, 0), (1, 1), (4, 4)$. Join up the points to make a line. On this line all the values of x equal the values of y. Label the line $y = x$.

16. On the same pair of axes plot the following points on the grid: $(2, -2), (0, 0)$, $(-1, 1), (3, -3)$. Join up the points to make a line. On this line all the values of x equal the negative values of y. Label the line $y = -x$.

17. On graph paper draw a pair of axes taking values of x and y from -5 to 5 and draw the following lines on the grid: $x = 4, y = -3$ and $y = x$. Calculate the area of the triangle made by the three lines.

18. On graph paper draw a pair of axes taking values of x and y from -5 to 5 and draw the following lines on the grid: $x = 2, y = 3$ and $y = -x$. Calculate the area of the trapezium made by the four lines.

19. On graph paper draw a pair of axes taking values of x and y from -5 to 5 and draw the following lines on the grid: $x = 5$ ans $y = -x$. Draw a third line such that the three lines make a triangle of area 32 square units.

20. On graph paper draw a pair of axes taking values of x and y from -5 to 5 and draw the following lines on the grid: $y = 3$, $y = -2$ and $y = x$. Draw a fourth line such that the four lines make a trapezium of area 27.5 square units.

Graphs That Are Not Parallel To The Axes

The graphs of straight lines that we have looked at have either been parallel to the axes or have been sloping; some graphs have a greater slope than others.

Exercise 14D – For discussion

1. On graph paper draw a pair of axes taking values of x and y from –5 to 10. Copy and complete these tables of values for the following functions:

a) $y = 2x$

x	–5	0	5
y			

b) $y = -3x$

x	–3	0	3
y			

c) $y = \dfrac{x}{2}$

x	–10	0	10
y			

d) $y = 5x$

x	–2	0	2
y			

e) $y = -\dfrac{x}{4}$

x	–8	0	8
y			

Now draw and label the graphs of these 5 functions on your co-ordinate grid.
Add the graphs of $y = x$, $y = -x$

2. What do you notice about the graphs that you have drawn?
    You should notice that all the functions with a negative coefficient of x slope down from left to right and all those with a positive coefficient of x slope up from left to right.
    You should also notice that the larger the coefficient of x the steeper the slope

    so that $y = 5x$ has a very steep slope and $y = -\dfrac{x}{4}$ has a very gentle slope.

The amount of slope is called the **Gradient**, and it can be calculated by measuring the vertical and horizontal units on the grid.

It is important to remember that the steeper the line then the larger the gradient. Look at the graphs of $y = x$, $y = -x$, these are at 45° to the horizontal and have a gradient of 1 and –1 respectively.

Gradient

If you look at a sloping line on a co-ordinate grid you can see that the horizontal and vertical lines of the grid form a right angled triangle with the line. To measure the gradient we need to look at that triangle:

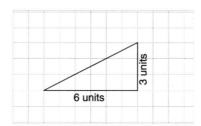

This triangle has a height of 3 and a base of 6 and so the gradient = $\frac{3}{6} = \frac{1}{2}$.

Notice that it does not matter where we draw the right angled triangle , the gradient will always be $\frac{1}{2}$.

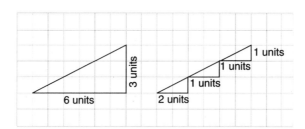

As a general rule to find the gradient of a line draw a right angle triangle (make it large enough so that you can measure accurately) measure the base and height of the triangle and thus:

$$\text{Gradient} = \frac{\text{height}}{\text{base}}$$

Do remember that if you are measuring a line sloping from left to right then the base measurement will be negative and thus the gradient will be negative. Example:

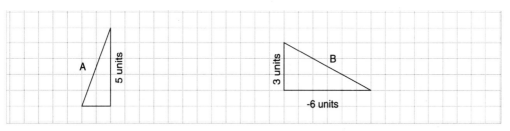

Gradient A = $\frac{5}{2} = 2\frac{1}{2}$ Gradient B = $\frac{3}{-6} = -\frac{1}{2}$

Exercise 14E

1. Calculate the gradient of these lines:

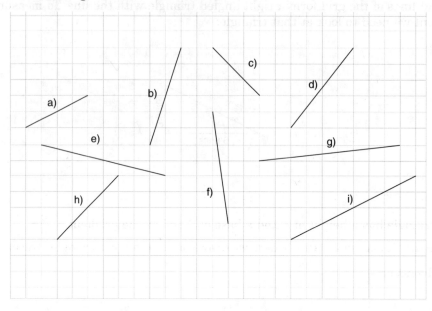

2. On centimetre squared paper draw the following lines:

a) 10cm long and a gradient of 5   f) 10cm long and a gradient of 2

b) 7cm long and a gradient of $\frac{1}{2}$ g) 10cm long and a gradient of $-\frac{1}{4}$

c) 6cm long and a gradient of 3   h) 10cm long and a gradient of –1

d) 4cm long and a gradient of 1   i) 4cm long and a gradient of –4

e) 6cm long and a gradient of $\frac{2}{3}$ j) 8cm long and a gradient of $1\frac{1}{2}$

When the line is on a co-ordinate grid where the *x* and *y* axes have different scale then it is important to calculate with the correct number of units:

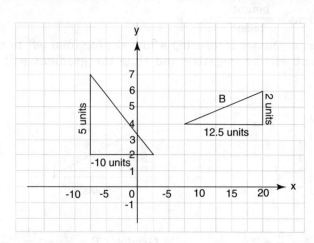

3. Find the gradients of these lines:

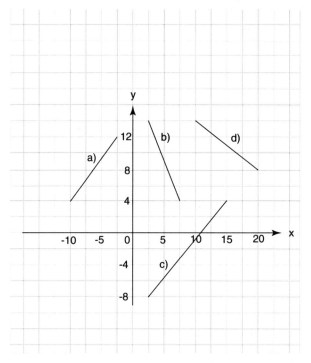

4. Find the gradients of these lines (a) to (e):

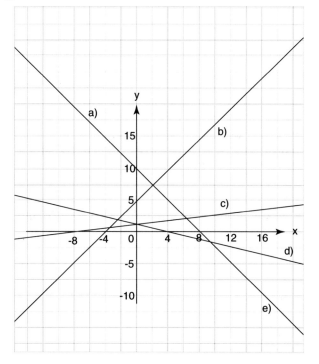

If you are given the co-ordinates of two points the gradient can be found by joining up the points, drawing a right angle triangle and calculating the length of the base and the height of the triangle and thus calculating the gradient.

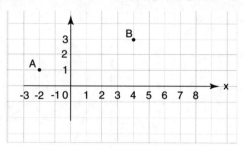

However it is not actually necessary to draw the line:

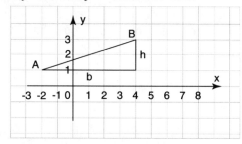

If we consider any two points $A(x_1, y_1)$ and $B(x_2, y_2)$

The height $h = y_1 - y_2$

The base $b = x_1 - x_2$

The gradient $= \dfrac{y_1 - y_2}{x_1 - x_2}$

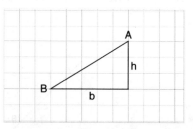

It does not matter whether we take $x_1 - x_2$ or $x_2 - x_1$ as long as we take the same difference in the y co-ordinates, since one corresponds to travelling from A to B and the other from B to A.

For example: Find the gradient of a line AB with A (3, 5) and B(–1, –3)

$$\text{Gradient} = \frac{5 - - 3}{3 - -1}$$

$$= \frac{8}{4}$$

$$= 2$$

5. Find the gradients of the lines joining the following pairs of points:
a) A (3, 2) and B (1, 0)   d) C (4, 3) and D (10, 1)
b) E (–1, –3) and F (5, –1)   e) G (–6, 5) and H (1, –1)
c) I (102, 95) and J(88, 102)   f) K (65, –42) and L (–35, – 17)

6. Find the missing numbers a, b, c and d in these lines:
a) PQ with P(a , 4) and Q(7, 5) and a gradient of 1
b) RS with R (3 , 1) and S(–9, b,) and a gradient of 3
c) TU with T(– 1, c) and U(7, –3) and a gradient of –2
d) VW with V(–5 , –4) and W(d, 8) and a gradient of –4

7. On graph paper draw a pair of axes with values of x and y from –5 to 10.
Draw graphs of the following equations:
a) $y = x$ d) $y = -x$ g) $y = 3x + 1$

b) $y = 1 - 2x$ e) $y = \dfrac{x}{2} - 4$ h) $y = 2x - 8$

c) $y = 6 - \dfrac{x}{3}$ f) $y = 7 - x$ i) $y = 3x - 5$

Calculate the gradient of each line.

8. Look again at the lines that you drew for question 7. Which pairs of lines are parallel? What do you notice?

9. Look again at the lines that you drew for question 7. Give the co-ordinates of the point where each line crosses the y-axis. What do you notice?

General Equation Of A Line : $y = m\,x + c$

The last three questions of the previous exercise demonstrated a very important relationship between the equation of the line, its gradient and the point where it crosses the y axis.

The point where the line crosses the y axis is known as the y–intercept.

$y = 3x + 1$ has a **gradient** of 3 and a **y - intercept** of 1.

$y = \dfrac{x}{2} - 4$ has a **gradient** of $\dfrac{1}{2}$ and a **y - intercept** of –4.

$y = 2x - 8$ has a **gradient** of 2 and a **y - intercept** of –8.
$y = 1 - 2x$ can be rewritten as $y = -2x + 1$
$y = -2x + 1$ has a **gradient** of –2 and a **y- intercept** of 1.

In general terms:
For an equation of the form **y = mx + c**

the **gradient** is **m** and the **y- intercept** is **c**.

> For example: Write down the gradient and the y-intercept of the following:
>
> a) $y = x + 4$ b) $y = -\dfrac{x}{3} + 1$
>
> Gradient $= 1$ Gradient $= -\dfrac{1}{3}$
>
> y intercept $= 4$ y intercept $= 1$

Exercise 14F

1. Write down the gradient and intercept of the following:
    a) $y = 2x + 4$ d) $y = -x - 3$

    b) $y = \dfrac{x}{5} + \dfrac{2}{5}$ e) $y = \dfrac{2x}{3} - 7$

    c) $y = 2x - \dfrac{1}{2}$ f) $y = -3x + 1$

2. On graph paper draw a pair of axes with values of x and y from -5 to 10.
    Draw graphs of the lines in question 1.

3. Write down the gradient and y-intercept of each of these lines, and hence write
    down an equation for each line:

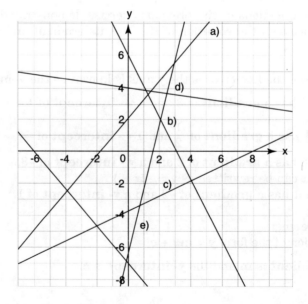

4. Write down the gradient and intercept of the following, (the equations may need to be rearranged first):

a) $y = 3 + 2x$

b) $y = \dfrac{x - 3}{4}$

c) $y + x = \dfrac{1}{2}$

d) $\dfrac{2x - y}{3} = 1$

e) $y = 5 - x$

f) $x = 3 + 4y$

g) $2(y + x) = 5$

h) $2(y + 2x) = 8$

i) $5x = 3 + 4y$

5. On graph paper draw a pair of axes with values of x and y from –5 to 10. Draw graphs of these lines :

a) $y = 5 + 2x$

b) $y = 3 - x$

c) $y = \dfrac{x - 1}{2}$

d) $y = \dfrac{2 - x}{3}$

e) $x + y = \dfrac{1}{4}$

f) $2y + x = 3$

The last two equations were written in the form: $ax + by = d$
What general rules can we find about the equation of a line written in this form?

The y-intercept is found when $x = 0$
Substituting $x = 0$ into the equation gives $by = d$

and so the y-intercept $= \dfrac{d}{b}$

The x-intercept is found when $y = 0$
Substituting $y = 0$ into the equation gives $ax = d$

and so the x-intercept $= \dfrac{d}{a}$

The graph looks like this:

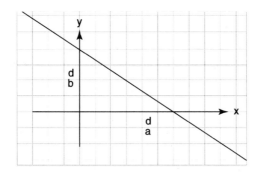

5. Write down the points where the following lines cross the x and y axes and the gradient of each line:

a) $x + y = 6$ f) $x - y = 2$
b) $2x + y = 4$ g) $2x + 6y = 2$
c) $x + 3y = 2$ h) $4x + 3y = 6$

d) $\dfrac{x}{2} + \dfrac{y}{3} = 1$ i) $\dfrac{2x}{3} - \dfrac{3y}{4} = 6$

e) $\dfrac{2x + 5y}{3} = 2$ j) $\dfrac{2}{3}(x + y) = 5$

6. On graph paper draw a pair of axes with values of x and y from –5 to 10. Draw graphs of the lines a) to f) in question 1.

7. In the following equations of straight lines write down all the pairs of parallel lines and then any pairs that have the same y-intercept:

a) $2x + y = 6$ e) $x - y = 2$
b) $y = x + 6$ f) $3x - 6y = 2$

c) $y = \dfrac{3}{4}x + \dfrac{3}{2}$ g) $2y = 3 - 4x$

d) $y = \dfrac{x}{2} - 2$ h) $\dfrac{3x}{5} - \dfrac{4y}{5} = 4$

Finding The Equation Of A Line

For example:
Find the equation of a line which passes through $(2, 4)$ and $(-1, 10)$

Method 1:

Gradient $= \dfrac{10 - 4}{-1 - 2}$ $= \dfrac{6}{-3}$ $= -2$

As the line passes through $(2,4)$ substitute $x = 2, y = 4$ and $m = -2$ in $y = mx + c$
$4 = -2 \times 2 + c$
$4 = -4 + c$
$c = 8$
The equation is $y = -2x + 8$

Method 2
Substitute the pairs of values of x and y into the general equation of a line:
$$4 = 2m + c ....(1)$$
$$10 = -m + c ....(2)$$

$(2) - (1)$ $6 = -3m$
                   $m = -2$
Sub in (2) $10 = 2 + c$
                   $c = 8$
The equation is $y = -2x + 8$

Exercise 14G

1. Find the equation of the line which:
    a) Passes through (0, 5) with a gradient of 2.
    b) Passes through (4, 0) with a gradient of 6.
    c) Passes through (3,3) with a gradient of 1.

2. Find the equations of the following lines:
    a) Passes through (–3, –5) with a gradient of 2
    b) Passes through (3, –4) with a gradient of –3
    c) Passes through (–2, –5) with a gradient of –4
    d) Passes through (100, –95) with a gradient of 1

3. Find the equation of the following lines:
    a) Joining (3,4) and (1,6)
    b) Joining (4, –5) and (2, 1)
    c) Joining (10, –8) and (–2, –4)
    d) Joining (0, 0) and (20, 100)

4. I have been carrying out an experiment with a variable Y against time and I have plotted my results and joined the points together with a line of best fit:

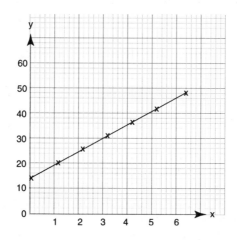

    a) What is the gradient of the line?
    b) Where does the line meet the Y- axis?
    c) Suggest an equation linking Y and t.

5. Here are some experimental results for a variable X against time t:

X	0	11	25	36	45	60
t	0	5	10	15	20	25

    a) Draw a suitable pair of axes on graph paper, taking t as the horizontal axis.
    b) Plot the points and join them up with a line of best fit.
    c) What is the gradient of the line?
    d) Where does the line meet the X axis?
    e) Suggest a possible equation linking X and t.

6. Here are some experimental results for a variable Z against time t:

Z	8	11	16	20	25	28
t	0	1	2	3	4	5

a) Draw a suitable pair of axes on graph paper, taking t as the horizontal axis.
b) Plot the points and join them up with a line of best fit.
c) What is the gradient of the line?
d) Where does the line meet the X axis?
e) Suggest a possible equation linking X and t.

7. Here are some experimental results for a variable W against another variable x:

W	120	106	91	75	9	
x	0	1	2	3	4	5

a) Draw a suitable pair of axes on graph paper, taking x as the horizontal axis.
b) Plot the points and join them up with a line of best fit.
c) What is the gradient of the line?
d) Where does the line meet the vertical axis?
e) Suggest a possible equation linking W and x.
f) What do you think the value of W will be when $x = 5$? What factors could affect your answer?

8. Here are some experimental results for a variable p against another variable q
It is obvious to the scientist that there is not a linear relationship between p and q.

p	5.2	6.3	10.15	18.4	35.12	67.2
q	0	0.9	2.2	2.85	4.06	5.3

He therefore decides to see if there is a relationship between p and q^2
a) Calculate the corresponding values of q^2.
b) Draw a suitable pair of axes on graph paper.
c) Plot the points and join them up with a line of best fit.
d) What is the gradient of the line?
e) Where does the line meet the vertical axis?
f) Suggest a possible equation linking p and q^2.

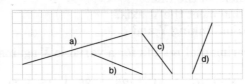

Extension Exercise 14

Harder Problems Involving Gradient

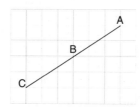

1. Three points ABC lie on a line and B is the mid-point of AC.
    a) If A (2,6) and C (10, 14) what are the co-ordinates of B?
    b) If A(5, –3) and B (–7, –7) what are the co-ordinates of C?
    c) If A (–x, 4), B (0, 7) and C(x , 2x) find x .
    d) If A (–8, 3x), B (–1, x) and C(2x , –x) find x.

2. Give the equations of each of the lines in question 1.

3. If three points A, B and C lie on a straight line (are collinear) then AB and BC
    (and, therefore, AC) must have the same gradient. Assuming these sets of three
    points are collinear find the value of x in each set:
    a) A (2, 5)   B (x, 8)   C (10, 17)
    b) A (x, 3)   B (2x, –3)   C (4, 1)
    c) A (x, 2x)   B (1, x)   C (7, –x)
    d) A (x, 13)   B (–2, –2x)   C (–x, –7)

4. Give the equations of each of the lines in question 3.

5. The lines AB and CD cross at a point P.
    If A (2, –5)   B(5, 1)   C (4, 3) and D (–2, 7) find, without drawing, the co-
    ordinates of P.

6. The lines AB and CD, neither of which goes through the origin, cross at a point P. If A
    (1, 2x)   B(3, x)   C (1, x) and D (3, 2x) and P(2, 6), find the value of x .

7. The lines AB and CD, neither of which goes through the origin, cross at a point P.
    If A (–1, 5)   B(x, x)   C (0, y) and D (2x, –y) and P(3x, –x), find the values of x and y.

226

Chapter 14: Graphs And Linear Functions

Summary Exercise 14

1. There are 163 Japanese Yen to £1 sterling.
    a) Calculate the value of (i) £100 and (ii) £500 in Japanese Yen.
    b) On graph paper draw a horizontal axis from 0 to £1000 taking 2cm to £100 and a vertical axis from 0 to 175 000 Yen taking 4cm and 25 000 yen .
    c) Draw a conversion graph of Pounds Sterling to Yen.
    d) Use your graph to convert (i) £250 and (ii) £680 to Yen.
    e) Use your graph to convert (i)25 000 Yen and (ii)150 000 Yen in Sterling.

2. The Smith family travelled by car at 50 km per hour for 40 km. They stopped for 2 minutes, then continued the journey for 20 km at 60 km per hour. The family then stopped for 45 minutes while they went shopping. They then drove straight back home at 55 km per hour. Draw a travel graph to show the car journey and use your graph to find out at what time the Smith family arrived home.

3. Find the gradients of these lines:

4. What is the gradient of line AB with A (3, –4) and B (6, 5) ?

5. Draw a pair of axes with values of x and y from – 5 to 5 and draw graphs of the following equations:

    a) $y = \dfrac{x}{3} - 3$ b) $y = 2 - x$ c) $2x + 5y = 10$ d) $\dfrac{x}{3} + \dfrac{y}{4} = 2$

6. Find the equations of the following lines:

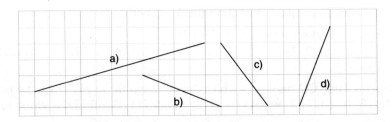

    a) AB with A(3,–2) with a gradient of 2.
    b) CD with C(4, –7) and D(–2, 5)
    c) OF with O (0, 0) and which is parallel to the line $2x - 6y = 5$.

7. Draw a pair of axes on graph paper, using a suitable scale, and plot these pairs of points:

    Draw a line of best fit and, by considering the gradient and intercept, suggest an equation connecting p and q.

Activity 14 - Experiments And Graphs

Are there any experimental results that will result in straight lines?

You know that if you draw a graph of time against distance travelled for a car travelling at a constant speed that the graph will be a straight line. Are there any other situations which can be measured over a period of time to give a straight line?

These are some that you could calculate or measure:

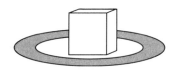

1. The distance travelled by the minute hand of a clock.
2. The length of your shadow on a sunny day.
3. The number of pupils in the school from an hour before school starts to the start of school.
4. The height of a bean plant over three weeks.
5. The temperature of a cup of tea in the 30 minutes from when it was first brewed.
6. The height of an ice cube when it is left out of the fridge.

We know that the minute hand of a clock travels at a constant rate and so we know that this will give a straight line graph, but what about the others?

Look at each experiment and state what other variables apart from those that you are recording might affect the result of your experiment, then write out a 'protocol' of your experiment to make it as 'fair' as possible.

Here is an example for Experiment 6 – Measuring the height of an ice cube

1. Make a big ice cube so that it is easier to measure. Take an clean empty yoghurt pot and fill it with tap water and place it in the freezer for 48 hours before you are planning to do the experiment.

2. Take the pot out of the freezer and turn it upside down on a flat plate. Let the plate be in a position so that any melted water can drain away.

3. Keep testing the pot every five minutes until you can lift the pot off the ice. Measure the height of the ice cube.

4. Measure the height of the ice cube every ten minutes until it is too small to be measured.

Draw a graph of height against time.

Chapter 15

Introducing Trigonometry

What Is Trigonometry

Simple trigonometry uses the relationship between the size of an angle and the length of the sides in a right angle triangle.

Look at these right angle triangles, all of base 5cm:

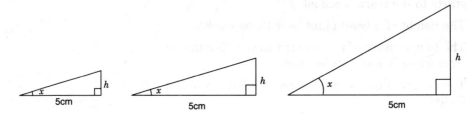

You can see that as the angle marked x increases so the height of the triangle increases. There would seem to be a relationship between the angle and the sides of the triangle. Let us investigate this further.

Draw a large right angled triangle ABC in your book, with the right angle at B. It does not matter what size the other two angles are. In fact for this investigation it is a good idea if everybody in the class draws different sizes of triangles.

Now divide your triangle into smaller triangles like this:

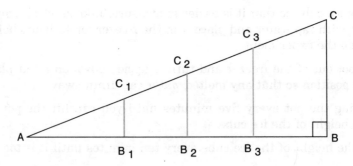

Now draw a table like this :

Triangle	AB	BC	$\dfrac{AB}{BC}$
AB_1C_1			
AB_2C_2			
AB_3C_3			
AB_1C_1			

The AB and BC columns can be filled in by measuring the lines in your drawing. When you have done that calculate AB ÷ BC. If you have measured accurately, all the values in this column will be the same.

Now measure the angle BAC.

To find the relationship between the ratio $\frac{AB}{BC}$ you will need a scientific calculator. When you turn it on make sure that the memory is clear and that it is in DEGREE mode, (shown by the word DEG at the top of the display). If it is not in this mode change it using the mode buttons.

The ratio we are investigating is known as the TANGENT of an angle - find the TAN button on your calculator.

If you have a new style VPAM calculator Key the TAN button and then the angle that you measured.

If you have an older style calculator key in the angle first and then enter TAN.

In either case the figure that you have should be about the same as your ratio $\frac{AB}{BC}$. If it is not check it again or ask your teacher.

Terminology

When looking at the sides of a right angle triangle we need to relate them to a marked angle. The angle here is marked with an arc. You are familiar with the HYPOTENUSE - the longest side opposite the right angle. The side opposite the marked angle is the OPPOSITE and the side touching the right angle and the marked angle is the ADJACENT.

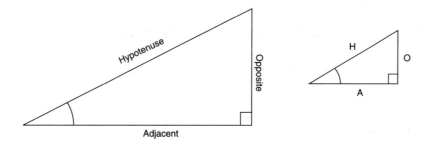

The sides of the triangle can then be marked H, O and A to determine which is which.

Now we can say   **The tangent of an angle = $\dfrac{\textbf{Opposite side}}{\textbf{Adjacent side}}$**

$$\textbf{or Tan A} = \frac{\textbf{opp}}{\textbf{adj}}$$

Calculating The Tangent

Use your calculator to find some tangents of various angles to 3 s.f.:

> For example: Find tan 30°
>
> $$\tan 30° = 0.57735....$$
> $$= 0.577 \text{ (to 3 s.f.)}$$

Exercise 15A

Use your calculator to find the tangents of these angles, give your answer to 3 s.f.:

1. 60°
2. 45°
3. 80°
4. 15°

5. 20°
6. 27.5°
7. 65°
8. 67.5°

9. 72.5°
10. 5°
11. 33.35°
12. 43.71°

Calculating The Angle

If you know the tangent and need to find the angle use the second function on your calculator marked $\tan^{-1}$ or possibly 'inverse tan'.

> For example: Find the angle whose tangent is 1.37.
> $$\tan x = 1.37$$
> $$x = 53.873..$$
> $$= 53.9° \text{ (to 1 d.p.)}$$

Exercise 15B

Use your calculator to find the angles whose tangents are given below, giving your answer to 1 d.p.

1. 1.5
2. 2.3
3. 0.72
4. 0.14

5. 0.5
6. 1.75
7. 0.89
8. 0.37

9. 4.5
10. 88.9
11. 0.05
12. 0.32

Finding The Opposite Side

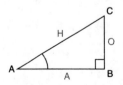

In the right angled triangle ABC:

$$\text{Tangent of angle A} = \frac{\textbf{Opposite side}}{\textbf{Adjacent side}}$$

$$\text{or } \tan A = \frac{\textbf{opp}}{\textbf{adj}}$$

For example:

$$\text{Tan A} = \frac{\text{opp}}{\text{adj}}$$

$$\text{Tan } 30° = \frac{x}{7}$$

$$x = 7 \times \tan 30°$$
$$= 4.04145...$$
$$= 4.04\text{cm (to 3s.f.)}$$

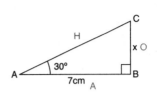

Exercise 15C

Find the side indicated by a letter in these questions. Always start by drawing the diagram and labelling the sides H, O and A. Give your answers correct to 3 significant figures:

1.

2.

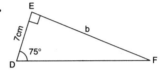

3.

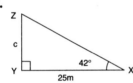

4.

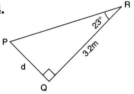

5.

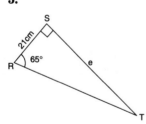

6.

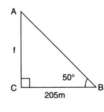

7.

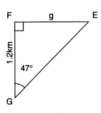

8.

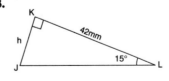

9.

10.

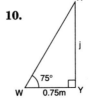

In the next 5 questions it is important to draw the triangle first, taking care when labelling the sides H, O and A.

11.   In △ ABC, ∠A = 42°, ∠B = 90° and AB = 7.2cm. Find BC.
12.   In △ DEF, ∠D = 83°, ∠F = 90° and DF = 105m, find EF.
13.   In △ XYZ, ∠Z = 90°, ∠X = 42° and XZ = 53m, find YZ.
14.   In △ PQR, ∠P = 21°, ∠R = 90° and PR = 4.1m, find QR.
15.   In △ STU, ∠S = 90°, ∠U = 71° and SU = 37m, find ST.

Finding The Adjacent Side

The simplest way to calculate the adjacent side is to calculate the third angle of the triangle and use that as the marked angle, and then label your triangle O, A and H as before. Alternatively you can use the method below:

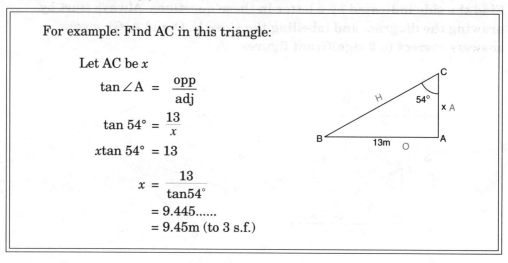

For example: Find AC in this triangle:

Let AC be x

$$\tan \angle A = \frac{\text{opp}}{\text{adj}}$$

$$\tan 54° = \frac{13}{x}$$

$$x\tan 54° = 13$$

$$x = \frac{13}{\tan 54°}$$

$$= 9.445......$$

$$= 9.45\text{m (to 3 s.f.)}$$

Exercise 15D

Find the side indicated by a letter in these questions. Always start by drawing the diagram and labelling the sides O, A and H. Give your answers correct to 3 significant figures:

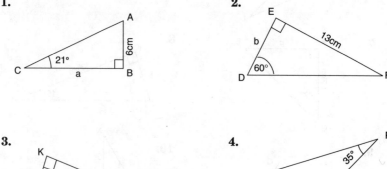

1.

2.

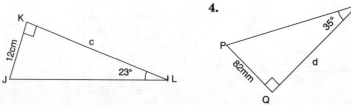

3.

4.

5.

6.

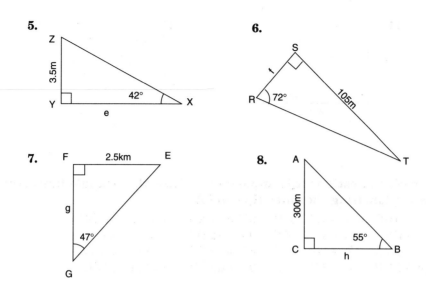

The remainder of the questions in this exercise are mixed, sometimes the side marked is the opposite side and sometimes the adjacent side. It is particularly important to take care when labelling O, A and H:

9.

10.

11.

12.

13.

14.

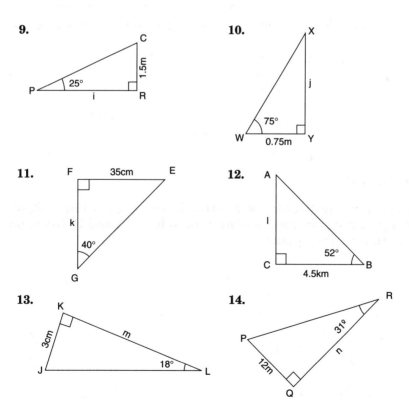

15.

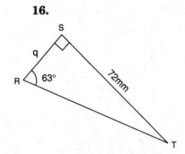

16.

In the next 4 questions it is important to draw the triangle first, taking care when labelling the sides H, O and A.

17. In △ ABC, ∠A = 75°, ∠B = 90° and AB = 25cm. Find BC.
18. In △ DEF, ∠D = 17°, ∠F = 90° and DF = 6m, find EF.
19. In △ XYZ, ∠Z = 90°, ∠X = 67° and XZ = 3.2km, find YZ.
20 In △ PQR, ∠P = 17°, ∠R = 90° and PR = 12m, find QR.

Finding The Angle

Remember to use the second function on your calculator to find the angle:

For example: Find ∠ A in this triangle, give your answer correct to 1 d.p.:

$$\tan \angle A = \frac{\text{opp}}{\text{adj}}$$

$$= \frac{13}{5}$$

$$\angle A = 68.962...$$

$$= 69.0 \ (\text{to 1 d.p.})$$

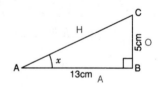

Exercise 15E

Find the angle indicated by a letter in these questions. Always start by drawing the diagram and labelling the sides O, A and H. Give your answers correct to 1 decimal place:

1.

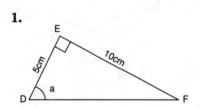

2.

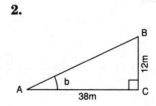

3.

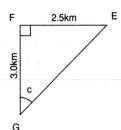

4.

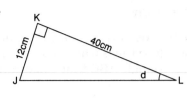

5.

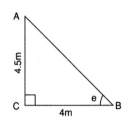

6.

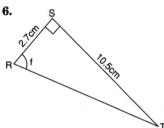

7.

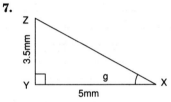

8.

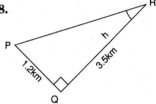

9.

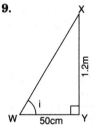

10.

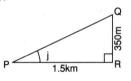

11. In △ABC, ∠B = 90° and AB = 2cm,   BC = 5cm, find   ∠A
12. In △DEF, ∠F = 90° and DF = 16m,   EF = 25m, find   ∠D
13. In △XYZ, ∠X = 90° and XZ = 1.2km, XY = 600m, find ∠X
14 In △PQR, ∠R = 90° and PR = 25mm, QR = 37mm, find ∠P
15. In △ABC, ∠A = 90° and AB = 12km, AC = 25km, find ∠C

Sine And Cosine

The tangent ratio only includes the opposite and adjacent sides, but it is apparent that there will be times when you may need to include the hypotenuse. Look back to the original triangle ABC that you drew:

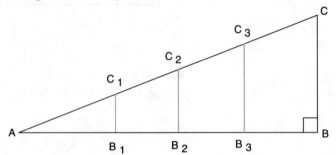

Now draw another table , like this :

Triangle	AB	BC	AC	$\dfrac{AB}{AC}$	$\dfrac{BC}{AC}$
AB_1C_1					
AB_2C_2					
AB_3C_3					
ABC					

The AB, BC and AC columns can be filled in by measuring the lines in your drawing. When you have done that calculate AB ÷ AC; if you have measured accurately all the values in this column will be the same. Then calculate BC ÷ AC. All the values in this column should be the same.

Now measure the angle BAC.

Find the SIN button on your calculator and calculate SIN of the angle BAC.

The figure that you have should be the same as your ratio $\dfrac{AB}{AC}$. If not check it again or ask your teacher.

$$\textbf{The sine of an angle } = \frac{\textbf{Opposite side}}{\textbf{Hypotenuse}}$$

$$\text{or} \quad \sin A = \frac{\textbf{opp}}{\textbf{hyp}}$$

Find the COS button on your calculator and calculate the COS of the angle BAC.

The figure that you have should be the same as your ratio $\dfrac{AB}{AC}$. If not check it again or ask your teacher.

$$\textbf{The cosine of an angle } = \frac{\textbf{Adjacent side}}{\textbf{Hypotenuse}}$$

$$\text{or} \quad \cos A = \frac{\textbf{adj}}{\textbf{hyp}}$$

Calculating The Sine And Cosine

Use your calculator to find the sine and cosine of various angles to 3 s.f.

> For example: Find sine 35° and find cosine 45°
>
> $\qquad$ sin 35° = 0.573576.... $\qquad\qquad$ cos 45° = 0.7071..
> $\qquad\qquad$ = 0.574 (to 3 s.f.) $\qquad\qquad\qquad$ = 0.707 (to 3 s.f)

Exercise 15F

Use your calculator to find the sine and cosine of these angles, giving your answer to 3 s.f.:

1. cos 60°	5. sin 20°	9. cos 12.5°
2. sin 15°	6. cos 37.5°	10. sin 5°
3. cos 80°	7. sin 85°	11. cos 73.25°
4. cos 25°	8. sin 77.5°	12. sin 63.71°

Calculating The Angle

If you know the sine and need to find the angle use the second function on your calculator marked $\sin^{-1}$ or possibly 'inverse sin'.

> For example: Find the angle whose sine is 0.45
> $\qquad\qquad$ sin x = 0.45
> $\qquad\qquad\quad$ x = 26.743....
> $\qquad\qquad\qquad$ = 26.7° (to 1 d.p.)

Exercise 15G

Use your calculator to find the angle whose sine is given below, give your answer to 1 d.p.

1. 0.7	5. 0.75	9. 0.567
2. 0.9	6. 0.12	10. 0.345
3. 0.5	7. 0.89	11. 0.055
4. 0.2	8. 0.37	12. 0.382

13. Now find the angles whose cosine is the value given above in Q 1π12.

14. Comparing the angles that you have obtained with the angles that you worked out before, what do you notice?

This leads to a useful fact about sine and cosine:

$$\mathbf{sin}\ x° = \mathbf{cos}\ (90 - x)°$$

Finding Opposite And Adjacent Sides Using Sine And Cosine

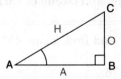

In the right angled triangle ABC:

$$\sin A = \frac{\text{opp}}{\text{hyp}} \qquad \text{and} \qquad \cos A = \frac{\text{adj}}{\text{hyp}}$$

The sides are calculated in the same manner as using tan. Note in the examples that the side **not** being used in the ratio is crossed out, this helps to avoid errors by using the wrong ratio.

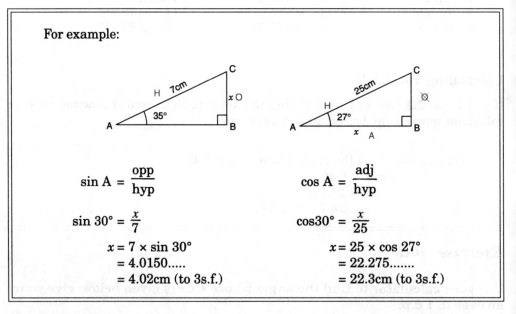

For example:

$$\sin A = \frac{\text{opp}}{\text{hyp}}$$

$$\sin 30° = \frac{x}{7}$$

$$x = 7 \times \sin 30°$$
$$= 4.0150.....$$
$$= 4.02\text{cm (to 3s.f.)}$$

$$\cos A = \frac{\text{adj}}{\text{hyp}}$$

$$\cos 30° = \frac{x}{25}$$

$$x = 25 \times \cos 27°$$
$$= 22.275.......$$
$$= 22.3\text{cm (to 3s.f.)}$$

Exercise 15H

Find the side indicated by a letter in these questions. Always start by drawing the diagram and labelling the sides H, O and A. Give your answers correct to 3 significant figures:

The first four questions all use the sine ratio:

1.   **2.**

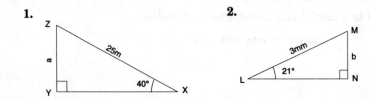

3.

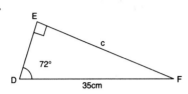

4.

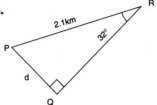

The next four questions all use the cosine ratio:

5.

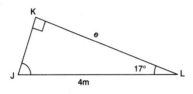

6.

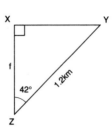

7.

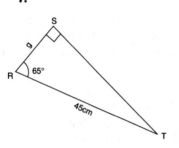

8.

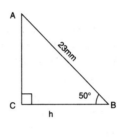

The next few questions are either sine or cosine:

9.

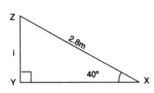

10.

11.

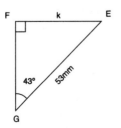

12.

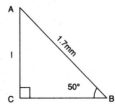

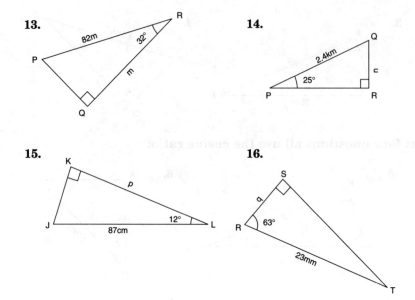

In the next 6 questions are a mixture of sine, cosine and tangent. It is important to draw the triangle first, taking care when labelling the sides O, A and H. Take time to make sure that you are using the correct ratio.

11. In $\triangle$ ABC, $\angle$A $= 37°$, $\angle$B $= 90°$, and AC $= 3.2$km, find AB.
12. In $\triangle$ DEF $\angle$D $= 83°$, $\angle$E $= 90°$, and DF $= 55$m, find DE.
13. In $\triangle$ XYZ, $\angle$Z $= 90°$, $\angle$X $= 65°$, and XZ $= 12$cm, find YZ.
14. In $\triangle$ JKL, $\angle$J $= 25°$, $\angle$K $= 90°$, and JL $= 104$m, find KL.
14. In $\triangle$ PQR, $\angle$P $= 71°$, $\angle$R $= 90°$, and PR $= 53$mm, find PQ.
15. In $\triangle$ STU, $\angle$S $= 90°$, $\angle$U $= 36°$, and TU $= 3$m, find SU

Finding The Hypotenuse

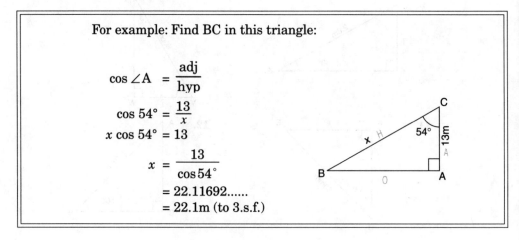

For example: Find BC in this triangle:

$$\cos \angle A = \frac{adj}{hyp}$$

$$\cos 54° = \frac{13}{x}$$

$$x \cos 54° = 13$$

$$x = \frac{13}{\cos 54°}$$

$$= 22.11692......$$

$$= 22.1\text{m (to 3.s.f.)}$$

Exercise 15I

Find the hypotenuse in these questions. They are a mixture requiring either sine or cosine; take time to make sure that you are using the correct ratio.

1.
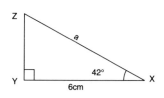

2.
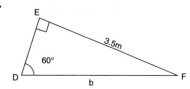

3.
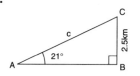

4.
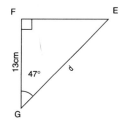

5.
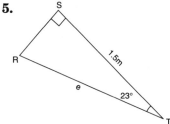

6.
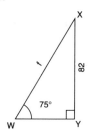

Give your answers correct to 3 significant figures.
7. In Δ ABC, ∠A = 12°, ∠B = 90° and AB = 45cm. Find AC.
8. In Δ DEF, ∠D = 65°, ∠F = 90° and DF = 12m, find DE.
9. In Δ XYZ, ∠Z = 90°, ∠X = 62° and XZ = 4.2km, find XY.
10 In Δ PQR ∠P = 37°, ∠R = 90° and PR = 27mm, find PQ.

Finding The Angle

Remember to use the second function on your calculator to find the angle:

For example: Find ∠A in this triangle. Give your answer correct to 1 d.p.

$$\tan \angle A = \frac{\text{opp}}{\text{adj}}$$

$$= \frac{13}{5}$$

∠A = 68.962...
= 69.0 (to 1 d.p.)

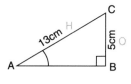

Exercise 15J

Find the angle indicated by a letter in these questions. Always start by drawing the diagram and labelling the sides H, O and A.
Give your answers correct to 1 decimal place:

The first four all use the sine ratio:

1.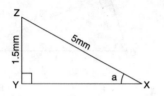

2.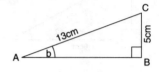

3.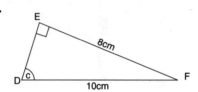

4.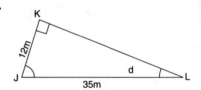

The next four all use the cosine ratio:

5.

6.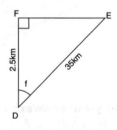

7.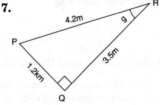

8.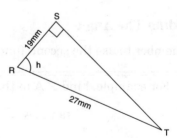

The remainder are a mixture of sine, cosine an tangent problems, it is particularly important now to take care when labelling O, A and H:

9.

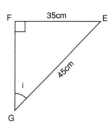

10.

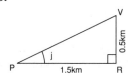

11.

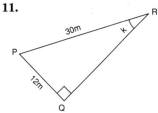

12.

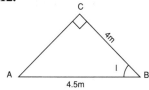

13.

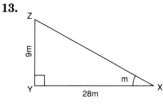

14.

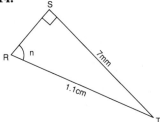

15.

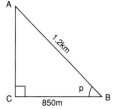

16.

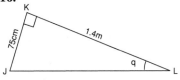

17. In △ ABC, ∠B = 90° and AB = 25cm. AC = 35cm, find ∠A.

18 In △ DEF, ∠F = 90° and DF = 12m, EF = 29m, find ∠D.

19. In △ XYZ, ∠X = 90° and YZ = 3.6km, XY = 700m, find ∠X

20. In △ PQR, ∠R = 90° and PQ = 52mm, QR = 25mm, find ∠P

Solving Problems Using Trigonometry

When dealing with problems in trigonometry it can be a help to use the mnemonic SOHCAHTOA, which is made up of the three ratios SOH CAH TOA

or $\quad \sin = \dfrac{\text{opp}}{\text{hyp}}$ and $\quad \cos = \dfrac{\text{adj}}{\text{hyp}}$ $\tan = \dfrac{\text{opp}}{\text{adj}}$

As with problems using Pythagoras's Theorem it is important to draw the right angled triangle in which you are working; some problems may require Pythagoras's theorem to solve the problem.

For Example: ABCD is a cross section through a roof truss.
              Find a) BD b) AC

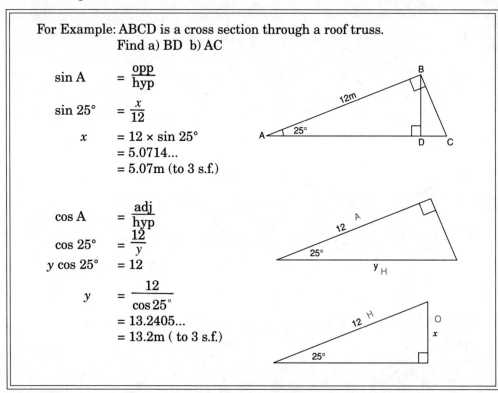

$$\sin A \quad = \dfrac{\text{opp}}{\text{hyp}}$$

$$\sin 25° \quad = \dfrac{x}{12}$$

$$x \quad = 12 \times \sin 25°$$
$$= 5.0714...$$
$$= 5.07\text{m (to 3 s.f.)}$$

$$\cos A \quad = \dfrac{\text{adj}}{\text{hyp}}$$

$$\cos 25° \quad = \dfrac{12}{y}$$

$$y \cos 25° \quad = 12$$

$$y \quad = \dfrac{12}{\cos 25°}$$
$$= 13.2405...$$
$$= 13.2\text{m (to 3 s.f.)}$$

Angles Of Elevation And Depression

If you are standing some distance from a tall object such as a building or a tree the angle of the line of sight to the top of the object and the ground is called the 'angle of elevation':

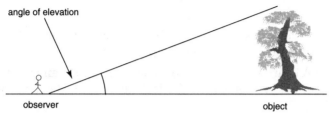

If you are standing above an object, when on top of a cliff for example, the angle of the line of sight with the horizontal is known as the 'angle of depression':

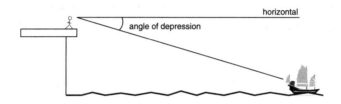

Exercise 15K

Give non- exact answers correct to 3 significant figures.

1. The princess is at the window 12m above the ground. The prince knows that it is unsafe to have a ladder at an angle with the ground more than 75°. What is the shortest ladder he will need to be able to reach the bottom of the window safely?

2. The angle of elevation of the top of the flagpole from a point 50m away from its base on horizontal ground is 5°. How tall is the flagpole?

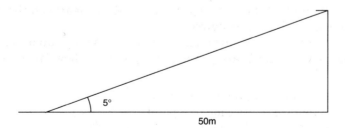

3. The angle of elevation of the top of a tree from a point 45m away on horizontal ground is 9°. Calculate the height of the tree.

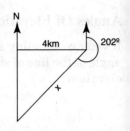

4.   A hunter walks 4km due East and then changes course to a bearing of   202°. How far must he walk until he is due South of his starting point?

5.   A plane flew 100km on a bearing of 125°. How far must he then fly to be due South of his starting point?

6.   From a point A a bird B can be seen on a bearing of 072° and a cat C can be seen on a bearing of 162°. AC is 5m and AB is 7.2m. Find the bearing and distance of C from B.

7.   A line passes through the points A (3, 5) and B (–2, 9). Find the angle the line makes with the *x* axis.

8.   Find the angle that the line $y = 3x - 4$ makes with the *y* axis.

9.   This is a section through a roof truss WXYZ, $\angle$XZY = $\angle$WXY = 90°, $\angle$XWZ=55° and XY = 7.5m

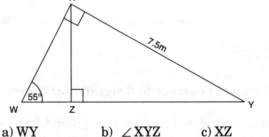

Find   a) WY   b) $\angle$XYZ   c) XZ   d) WX

10.   From a point on a cliff 17m above sea level the angle of depression of a yacht is 12°. How far is the yacht from the base of the cliff?

11.   a) A ship set sail on a bearing of 290° and sailed for 500 miles. Draw a sketch of this journey and calculate how far North and East the ship was from the starting point.
b) The ship then changed course and sailed another 500 miles on a bearing of 215°. Draw a sketch of this part of the journey and calculate how far the ship sailed East and South on this part of the journey.
c) Draw a diagram of the total voyage so far. Mark clearly on the diagram   all the distances you have calculated.
d) At this point the crew mutinied. They threw the captain overboard and set sail for home. On what bearing should they sail and how far from   home are they?

12.   A plane at A is flying at 500m above the ground, the angle of depression of a point C above the is 45° and of a point B is 23°. Calculate the distance between B and C.

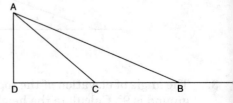

Exercise S15

1. a) Sketch an equilateral triangle of side 2 units.
   b) Use Pythagoras's Theorem to calculate the height of the triangle. Leave your answer as a square root.
   c) Use your answer to part b) to find the value of sin 30°, cos 30° and tan 30°. Leave your answers as a fraction with square roots if necessary.
   d) Use your answer to part b) to find the value of sin 60°, cos 60° and tan 60°. Leave your answers as a fraction with square roots if necessary.

2. a) Sketch an equilateral triangle with base angles of 45° and two equal sides of one unit.
   b) Use Pythagoras's Theorem to calculate the hypotenuse. Leave your answer as a square root.
   c) Use your answer to part b) to find the value of sin 45°, cos 45°and tan 45°. Leave your answers as a fraction with square roots if necessary.

3. Here are two special right angled triangles.

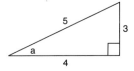 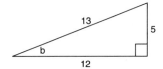

Write down the values of sin a, cos a and tan a and sin b, cos b and tan b. Leave your answers as fractions.

Now use your answers to the first three questions to solve these problems. You should calculate in fractions, leaving values as square roots if necessary:

4. Find all the remaining lengths in this cross section:

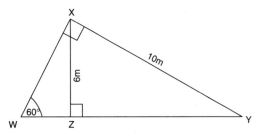

5. From a point A the angle of depression of a point C is 45°. AD is 100m and BD is 240m. Calculate the distance between B and C.

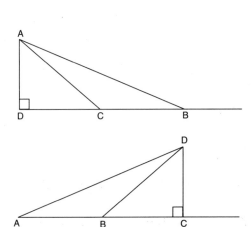

6. From a point B the angle of elevation of the top of a building D is 60°. If AC is 240m and CD is 100m. Calculate the distance between A and B, and the distance AD.

Summary Exercise 15

1. Find the value of these:
    a) tan 24°   b) sin 52°   c) cos 72°

2. Find x when:
    a) tan x = 3.5   b) sin x = 0.785   c) cos x = 0.632

3. Find BC:

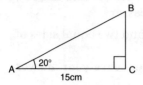

4. Find angle C:

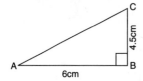

5. Find a) DF and b) QR

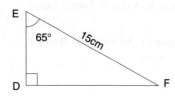 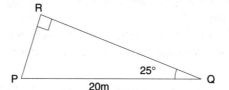

6. Find AC:

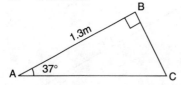

7. Find the angles marked x:

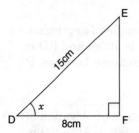 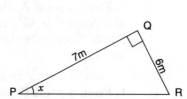 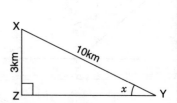

8. From a yacht the angle of elevation of a lighthouse 7m tall is 12°. How far is the yacht from the lighthouse?

9. A plane travels 200km on a bearing of 065° and then 150km on a bearing of 123°. Find the bearing and distance of the plane from its starting point.

Activity 15 - Investigation - Polyhedral Numbers

A tetrahedron is a triangular based pyramid, and a regular tetrahedron has a net of four equilateral triangles:

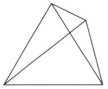 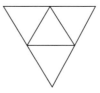

Tetrahedral numbers are made up from forming tetrahedrons from triangles:

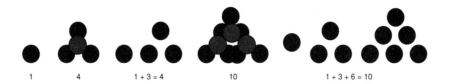

What are the set of numbers being added together called?

Copy and complete this table, extend it by another three rows:

n		tetra no:
1	1	1
2	1 + 3	4
3	1 + 3 + 6	10
4	1 + 3 + 6 + 10	
5	1 + ...	

What is the 10th tetrahedral number? The 100th ?

By considering the formula for the nth triangle number, or otherwise, find a formula for the nth tetrahedral number.

The next set of polyhedral numbers are those formed by square based pyramids, the 1st such number will be 1, the second $1 + 4 = 5$, the third $1 + 4 + 9 = ...$ etc.

The next set will be those formed by the sum of the pentagonal numbers.

Investigate sets of polyhedral numbers and see what rules you can find, you might find it interesting to include Pascal's Triangle as part of your investigation.

Chapter 16

Equations And Brackets

Brackets

In a calculation numbers in brackets indicate that that part of the calculation must be done first:

$$3 \times (4 + 5) = 3 \times 9 = 27$$

In algebra it is not always possible to actually calculate inside the bracket, but the number outside the bracket still indicates the number that **everything** inside the bracket must be multiplied by:

> For example:
> $$3(2 + x) = 6x + 12$$

Exercise 16A

Multiply out these brackets:

1. $3(3x + 1)$
2. $4(2x - 5)$
3. $2(5 - 3x)$
4. $7(3 + x)$
5. $6(2x + 5)$
6. $x(3x + 1)$
7. $2x(4x - 3)$
8. $a(5a - 2b)$
9. $a(5b + c)$
10. $3x(4 - 3x)$

Multiply out these brackets and simplify the answer if possible:

> For example:
> $$3(2x + 4) - 4(3 - x) = 6x + 12 - 12 + 4x$$
> $$= 10x$$

11. $2(x + 3) + 3 (2x - 2)$
12. $2(x + 2) - 3 (x - 2)$
13. $2(4x - 3) + 3 (2x + 1)$
14. $4(3 - x) - 3 (x - 3)$
15. $5(2x - 1) - 2 (2 - 5x)$
16. $2x(x + 5) + 3(3x - 1)$
17. $x(4x + 2) - (x + 5)$
18. $7(5 - 2x) - 3x(2x + 3)$
19. $3(x + 3) + x(2 - 5x)$
20. $5x(3 - 2x) - 3(x + 5x)$

Multiply out these brackets and simplify the answer if possible:

21. $4a(a + b) + b(2a - b)$
22. $2c(c + 3) + 5(4 - 2c)$
23. $3a(a + 3) + 5b(5 + b)$
24. $2a(a - 3b) - b(a - 4b)$
25. $p(2q - p) - q(p + q)$
26. $2(4 - 2c) + 2c(3c + 2d)$
27. $5b(2a - b) + 2a(2b - a)$
28. $3c(2c - 5) + 3(7 + 3c)$
29. $2(x + 3) + 2x(x + 3)$
30. $3(2x - 5) - x(2x - 5)$
31. $3c(4c + 3d) + 2(4c + 3d)$
32. $2a(3a + b) - (3a + b)$
33. $5x(1 - 2x) + 3(1 - 2x)$
34. $x(2x - y) + 2y(2x - y)$

Look carefully at the last six examples of the last exercise. The expression in both sets of brackets is the same: $5x(1 - 2x) + 3(1 - 2x)$

This could also be written: $(5x + 3)(1 - 2x)$

For example:
$$(3x + 1)(x + 5) = 3x(x + 5) + 1(x + 5)$$
$$= 3x^2 + 15x + x + 5$$
$$= 3x^2 + 16x + 5$$

$$(2x - 3)(x - 7) = 2x(x - 7) - 3(x - 7)$$
$$= 2x^2 - 14x - 3x + 21$$
$$= 2x^2 - 17x + 21$$

The first line of the working above can be omitted by remembering the following rule:

First pair   Outer pair   Inner pair   Last pair

Exercise 16B

Multiply out these brackets and simplify:

1. $(x + 1)(x + 4)$
2. $(x + 3)(x + 2)$
3. $(x + 6)(x + 4)$
4. $(x + 7)(x + 7)$
5. $(x + 1)(x + 1)$
6. $(x + 4)(x + 3)$
7. $(x + 2)(x + 4)$
8. $(x + 3)(x + 3)$
9. $(x + 8)(x + 3)$
10. $(x + 2)(x + 7)$

11. $(x + 1)(x - 2)$
12. $(x - 2)(x + 3)$
13. $(x + 2)(x - 5)$
14. $(x - 4)(x + 4)$
15. $(x - 1)(x + 3)$
16. $(x - 2)(x + 6)$
17. $(x + 5)(x - 3)$
18. $(x - 3)(x + 3)$
19. $(x + 5)(x - 4)$
20. $(x + 1)(x - 1)$

21. $(x - 2)(x - 1)$
22. $(x - 2)(x - 4)$
23. $(x - 3)(x - 5)$
24. $(x - 7)(x - 1)$

25. $(x - 2)(x - 2)$
26. $(x - 5)(x - 8)$
27. $(x - 1)(x - 1)$
28. $(x - 7)(x - 4)$

29. $(2x + 1)(x + 3)$
30. $(2x + 1)(3x + 2)$
31. $(2x + 1)(2x + 1)$
32. $(x + 4)(4x - 5)$
33. $(2x + 4)(2x - 4)$
34. $(5x + 1)(2x - 7)$

35. $(2x + 4)(2x - 3)$
36. $(2x + 5)(3x + 3)$
37. $(x - 4)(4x + 7)$
38. $(2x + 3)(2x + 3)$
39. $(3x + 2)(3x - 2)$
40. $(4x - 1)(2x + 3)$

Factorising Algebraic Expressions

A number can be written as a product of its prime factors, for example:

$$36 = 2^2 \times 3^3$$

An algebraic expression can also be written as a product of factors. Some expressions have common factors:

> For example:
> $$x^2 + 3x = x(x + 3)$$
> $$3xy^4 - 6xy + 12x^2y = 3xy(y^3 - 2 + 4x)$$
> $$8x^4 - 9y \text{ has no common factors.}$$

In the examples above common factors for each term in the expression were divided out and written outside the expression, but consider an expression such as:

$$a^2 + 3a + 4a + 12$$

Although there is no common factor for every term of the expression there are common factors for each pair of terms:

$$a^2 + 3a + 4a + 12 = a(a + 3) + 4(a + 3)$$

Now the expression in each pair of brackets is the same and the full factorisation looks like:

$$a^2 + 3a + 4a + 12 = a(a + 3) + 4(a + 3)$$
$$= (a + 3)(a + 4)$$

Exercise 16C

Factorise these expressions:

> For example:
> $$4ab + 6a + 10b + 15 = 2a(2b + 3) + 5(2b + 3)$$
> $$= (2a + 5)(2b + 3)$$
>
> $$x^2 - 5x + 2x - 10 = x(x - 5) + 2(x - 5)$$
> $$= (x + 2)(x - 5)$$

In all the above expressions the factors were positive, care must be taken when factors are negative. Note: $-3 + 9 = -3(x - 9)$

1. $a^2 + 3a + 3a + 9$
2. $x^2 + 4x + 2x + 8$
3. $9y + 6 + 6xy + 4x$
4. $a^2 - 2a + 3ab - 6a^2$
5. $x^2 - 2x + 3x - 6$
6. $12ab + 6a + 2b + 1$
7. $x^2 - 3x + 4x - 12$
8. $2a + 6a^2 + 3 + 9a$
9. $6ab + 9b + 3a + 9$
10. $1 - 3x + 4x - 12x^2$
11. $12y - 9 + 8y^2 - 6y$
12. $15t + 6t^2 + 10 + 4t$
13. $5s - 15st + 3 - 9t$
14. $10 - 25a + 8b - 20ab$

For example:
$$x^2 - 3x - 4x + 12 \quad = x(x-3) - 4(x-3)$$
$$= (x-4)(x-3)$$

$$8xy + 6y - 4x - 3 \quad = 2y(4x+3) - (4x+3)$$
$$= (2y-1)(4x+3)$$

15. $x^2 + 3x - 4x - 12$

16. $x^2 - 3x - 4x - 12$

17. $a^2 + 6a - 2a - 18$

18. $12xy + 9x - 8y - 6x$

19. $a^2 - 5a - 3a + 15$

20. $12xy - 3x - 4y + 4$

21. $9b + 15ab - 6 - 10a$

22. $x - x^2 + 16x - 2$

23. $2b^2 - 6b + 9 - 3b$

24. $2x^2 + 8x - x - 4$

25. $12xy - 3x + 1 - 4y$

26. $15t + 9 - 10st - 6s$

27. $12 - 3x - 16x - 4x^2$

28. $3x - 12x^2 - 4x + 1$

29. $10 - 2x - 3x^2 + 15$

30. $3y + 6 - 5xy - 10x$

Many of the above examples could have been simplified before factorisation:
$$3x^2 + 3x - 4x - 4 = 3x^2 - x - 4$$

How can the simplified form be factorised?

First look at these two examples when the number term is positive, and the two expressions in brackets will contain either two positive signs or two negative signs:

$$x^2 + 5x + 6 = x^2 + 3x + 2x + 6$$
$$= x(x+3) + 2(x+3)$$
$$= (x+2)(x+3)$$

$$x^2 - 7x + 6 = x^2 - 6x - x + 6$$
$$= x(x-6) - 1(x-6)$$
$$= (x-1)(x-6)$$

In the first example $5x$ was split into $3x$ and $2x$ because $3 \times 2 = 6$ and in the second $7x$ was split into $6x$ and x because $6 \times 1 = 6$

Now look at these two examples when the number term is negative, and the two expressions in brackets will contain one positive sign and one negative sign

$$x^2 + 5x - 6 \quad = x^2 + 6x - x - 1$$
$$= x(x+6) - (x+6)$$
$$= (x-1)(x+6)$$

$$x^2 - x - 6 \quad = x^2 - 3x + 2x - 6$$
$$= x(x-3) + 2(x-3)$$
$$= (x+2)(x-3)$$

In the first example $5x$ was split into $6x$ and $-x$ because $6 \times 1 = 6$ and in the second x was split into $-3x$ and $2x$ because $3 \times 2 = 6$

In general terms consider the expression that factorises into:
$$(x+m)(x+n) = x^2 + mx + nx + mn$$
$$= x^2 + bx + c$$

First split the number term c into a factor pair m and n and then consider the signs in the equation, these fit one of these four variations:

$x^2 + bx + c$	both factors +ve	*In these two expressions the*
$x^2 - bx + c$	both factors −ve	*factor pair must add up to b*
$x^2 + bx - c$	larger factor +ve	*In these two expressions the factor*
$x^2 - bx - c$	larger factor −ve	*pair must have a difference of b*

While an expression of the form $x^2 + bx + c$: factorises into $(x+m)(x+n)$ an expression in the form $c + bx + x^2$ will factorise into $(m+x)(n+x)$.

Exercise 16D

Factorise these expressions:

1. $x^2 + 3x + 2$
2. $x^2 + 4x + 3$
3. $10 + 7x + x^2$
4. $x^2 - 4x + 3$
5. $5 - 6x + x^2$

6. $x^2 - 6x + 8$
7. $6 - 7x + x^2$
8. $x^2 - 10x + 21$
9. $x^2 + 22x + 21$
10. $x^2 - 8x + 7$

11. $x^2 + x - 2$
12. $x^2 - 2x - 3$
13. $10 + 3x - x^2$
14. $x^2 - 4x - 5$
15. $7 - 6x + x^2$

16. $x^2 - 7x - 8$
17. $18 + 3x - x^2$
18. $x^2 - 4x - 21$
19. $x^2 - 10x - 14$
20. $x^2 - x - 12$

21. $x^2 + 11x - 12$
22. $x^2 - 9x + 8$
23. $12 + 7x + x^2$
24. $x^2 - 3x - 18$
25. $8 - 6x + x^2$

26. $x^2 - 6x - 16$
27. $18 + 3x - x^2$
28. $x^2 - 11x + 24$
29. $x^2 - 9x + 14$
30. $x^2 + 5x - 24$

Factorise these expressions, they will have to be rearranged into the $x^2 + bx + c$ or $c + b x + x^2$ form first:

31. $x^2 + 12 + 7x$
32. $12 + x^2 - 7x$
33. $4x - 12 + x^2$
34. $24 - 5x - x^2$
35. $14 - x^2 - 5x$

36. $x^2 + 15 + 8x$
37. $x^2 + 18 - 9x$
38. $7x - x^2 - 18$
39. $x^2 + 15 - 16x$
40. $8x + 9 - x^2$

When the x^2 term has a coefficient greater than one then the factorisation becomes harder. The rules for the signs still holds true but the factor pairs of the coefficient of x must be considered as well.

> For example: Factorise a) $2x^2 + x - 6$ and b) $6x^2 + 29x + 9$
>
> $$2x^2 + x - 6 = 2x^2 + 3x - 2x - 6$$
> $$= x(2x + 3) - 2(x + 3)$$
> $$= (x - 2)(2x + 3)$$
>
> $$6x^2 + 29x + 9 = 6x^2 + 2x + 27x + 9$$
> $$= 2x(3x + 1) + 9(x + 3)$$
> $$= (2x + 9)(3x + 1)$$

You may be able to go directly to the answer without needing the middle stages, that is perfectly acceptable and may be the quickest method.

Exercise 16E

Factorise these expressions:

1. $2x^2 + 11x + 12$
2. $3x^2 + 5x + 2$
3. $3x^2 + 19x + 6$
4. $2x^2 - 7x + 3$
5. $3x^2 + 14x + 8$

6. $3x^2 - 18x + 15$
7. $3x^2 + 5x - 12$
8. $3x^2 + 13x - 10$
9. $2x^2 + 31x - 16$
10. $3x^2 + x - 4$

11. $3x^2 - 17x - 6$
12. $4x^2 + 4x - 3$
13. $10x^2 + 15x + 5$
14. $6x^2 + 22x - 8$
15. $9x^2 - 29x + 6$

16. $8x^2 - 10x - 12$
17. $12x^2 + 56x + 9$
18. $9x^2 - 27x + 8$
19. $10x^2 + 27x - 9$
20. $12x^2 - x - 20$

Squares And The Difference Between Them

In all the examples that we have considered so far the expressions in the brackets have been different, but consider what happens when you square an expression:

For example: Expand these brackets: a) $(x + 3)^2$ and b) $(2x + 4)^2$

$$(x + 3)^2 = (x + 3)(x + 3)$$
$$= x^2 + 3x + 3x + 9$$
$$= x^2 + 6x + 9$$

$$(2x + 4)^2 = (2x - 4)(2x - 4)$$
$$= 4x^2 - 8x - 8x + 16$$
$$= 4x^2 - 16x + 16$$

Exercise 16F

Multiply out these brackets:

1. $(x + 2)^2$
2. $(x + 5)^2$
3. $(x - 6)^2$
4. $(x + 10)^2$

5. $(x - 8)^2$
6. $(2x + 1)^2$
7. $(3x - 2)^2$

8. $(2x + 5)^2$
9. $(4x - 3)^2$
10. $(3x - 5)^2$

Look at your answers above, you will see that the coefficient of x^2 and the number term are both squares, and the coefficient of x is always even. Use this pattern to factorise the following expressions:

11. $x^2 - 4x + 4$
12. $x^2 + 8x + 16$
13. $x^2 - 2x + 1$
14. $x^2 + 14x + 49$

15. $x^2 - 28x + 144$
16. $4x^2 - 12x + 9$
17. $9x^2 + 8x + 1$

18. $4x^2 - 28x + 49$
19. $25x^2 + 30x + 9$
20. $4x^2 - 36x + 81$

Multiply out these brackets:

21. $(x - 3)(x + 3)$
22. $(x - 2)(x + 2)$

23. $2x - 3)(2x + 3)$
24. $(3x - 1)(3x + 1)$

25. $(3x - 4)(3x + 4)$
26. $(ax - b)(ax + b)$

From these examples you can see that the middle term has cancelled itself out and you are left with one perfect square less another perfect square. An expression in this form is known as 'the difference between two squares' and is very simple to factorise.

Factorise these expressions, do not forget to look for common factors first:

27. $x^2 - 16$

28. $x^2 - a^2$

29. $x^2 - 81$

30. $4x^2 - 16$

31. $9x^2 - y^2$

32. $2a^2 - 32$

33. $4x^2 - 49$

34. $a^2x^2 - b^2$

35. $3a^2x^2 - 3b^2$

36. $25 - 9x^2$

37. $5 - 80x^2$

38. $100x^2 - 144$

39. $36x^2 - 9y^2$

40. $4 - 25a^2$

41. $x^2 - 121$

42. $16b^2 - a^2$

43. $2 - 8x^2$

44. $16x^4 - 9$

45. $\dfrac{x^2}{4} - 16$

46. $x^2 - \dfrac{1}{9}$

47. $\dfrac{x^2}{9} - 1$

48. $x^2 - \dfrac{1}{25}$

49. $\dfrac{x^2}{36} - 9$

50. $\dfrac{x^2}{36} - 64$

Solving Equations By Factorising

When an expression is factorised the result is a multiple – one number or expression multiplied by another. However consider these : $7 \times 0 = 0$

$$0 \times x = 0$$
$$4x^2 \times 0 = 0$$

any number multiplied by 0 is 0

If we have $\quad xy = 0 \qquad\qquad$ then either $x = 0$ or $y = 0$

and if $\quad (x + 3)(x - 4) = 0 \quad$ then either $(x + 3) = 0 \quad$ or $(x - 4) = 0$

Therefore to solve an equation all the terms have to be grouped on one side and then factorised.

For example: Solve these equations:

$3x^2 - 12x = 0$

$3x(x - 4) = 0$

Either $3x = 0$ or $x - 4 = 0$

$x = 0 \quad$ or $\quad x = 4$

$2x^2 - 5x + 2 \qquad\quad = 0$

$2x^2 - 4x - x + 2 \quad = 0$

$2x(x - 2) - (x - 2) = 0$

$(2x - 1)(x - 2) \qquad = 0$

Either $\quad (2x - 1) = 0 \quad$ or $x - 2 = 0$

$x = \dfrac{1}{2} \quad$ or $\quad x = 2$

Note that when an equation is quadratic (i.e. contains an x^2 term) it has 2 solutions. When the quadratic is a perfect square these two solutions are the same.

Exercise 16G

Solve these equations:

1. $2x^2 - 8x = 0$
2. $x^2 - 4x = 0$
3. $12x^2 - 15x = 0$
4. $x^2 - 16 = 0$
5. $x^2 + 5x + 4 = 0$
6. $x^2 - x - 2 = 0$
7. $x^2 - 6x + 9 = 0$
8. $x^2 - 6x + 5 = 0$
9. $x^2 + 6x - 7 = 0$
10. $4x^2 - 9 = 0$

11. $x^2 + 8x + 16 = 0$
12. $x^2 - 7x + 12 = 0$
13. $2x^2 + 7x + 3 = 0$
14. $3x^2 - x - 2 = 0$
15. $3x^2 - 5x + 2 = 0$
16. $9x^2 - 25 = 0$
17. $4x^2 - x - 3 = 0$
18. $4x^2 - 12x + 9 = 0$
19. $9x^2 - 13x + 4 = 0$
20. $3x^2 - 35x - 12 = 0$

Solve these equations; you may need to rearrange them before you can factorise:

21. $12 = x^2 + 11x$
22. $15x^2 = 24x$
23. $4(3 + x) = x^2$
24. $18 - x^2 = 3 + 2x$
25. $12 = 3 - x^2$
26. $x^2 + 25 = 10x$
27. $2(2x + 5) = 3x^2 - 5$
28. $4 = 20 - 9x^2$

29. $12 = 14x - x^2$
30. $48x - 9 = 4x^2 + 11x$
31. $(3x - 1)^2 = (5x - 1)^2$
32. $x(4x - 1) = 5$
33. $\frac{1}{16} - x^2 = 8x^2$
34. $\frac{x^2}{4} = 9$

Certain problems can be solved by letting an unknown quantity be x. When the resulting equation is quadratic then the equation may be solved by factorising. This may give two answers in which case each needs to be considered, and one may be discarded:

For example:
A rectangle has one side 3cm longer than the other and an area of 40cm^2. How long are the sides?
Let the short side be x

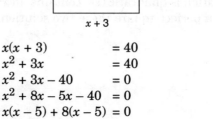

$x + 3$

$$x(x + 3) = 40$$
$$x^2 + 3x = 40$$
$$x^2 + 3x - 40 = 0$$
$$x^2 + 8x - 5x - 40 = 0$$
$$x(x - 5) + 8(x - 5) = 0$$
$$(x + 8)(x - 5) = 0$$
Either $\quad x + 8 = 0 \quad$ or $\quad x - 5 = 0$
$\quad\quad\quad\quad x = -8 \quad$ or $\quad x = 5$
x must be positive and thus the sides are 5cm and 8 cm.

Exercise 16H

1. The sides of a rectangle are $(x + 7)$ and x cm respectively, and the area of the rectangle is 60cm^2. Find the lengths of the sides.

2. A rectangle has one side 5 cm longer than the other. The area of the rectangle is 24 cm^2. What are the lengths of the sides of the rectangle?

3. Two numbers have a difference of 6. Their squares have a difference of 120. What are the two numbers?

5. Two numbers have a sum of 20. Their squares have a difference of 40. What are the two numbers?

6. The sides of a rectangle are $(x + 7)$ and $(x + 3)$ cm respectively, and the area of the rectangle is 45 cm^2. Find the lengths of the sides.

7. Find the lengths of the sides of this rectangle of area 40 cm^2.

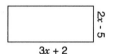

8. Find the lengths of the sides of this rectangle of area 85 cm^2.

9. This square and this rectangle have the same area, find the lengths of the sides of the rectangle:

10. Find the sides of two squares, one of which has sides 4 cm longer than another have a total area of 80cm^2.

11. A square of side $2x$ and a square of side $(x + 6)$ have a difference in area of 60 cm^2. Find the lengths of the sides of the squares.

12. Find the length of the sides in this right angled triangle:

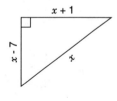

13.   The area of a square picture frame of width 3 cm is 57 cm^2 . How big is the actual picture frame?

14. The area of this right angled triangle is 96 cm^2. Find the length of the three sides.

Extension Exercise 16   *Quadratics and Fractions*

For example: $\dfrac{x+2}{2} = \dfrac{4}{x}$

$$(\times 2x)$$
$$x(x+2) = 8$$
$$(-8)$$
$$x^2 + 2x - 8 = 0$$
$$(x+4)(x-2) = 0$$
$$\text{Either} \quad x + 4 = 0 \quad \text{or} \quad x - 2 = 0$$
$$x = -4 \qquad\qquad x = 2$$

Solve these equations:

1. $\dfrac{x+2}{3} = \dfrac{1}{x}$

2. $\dfrac{x}{2} = \dfrac{8}{x}$

3. $\dfrac{x-8}{3} = \dfrac{3}{x}$

4. $\dfrac{2x-5}{5} = \dfrac{2x-5}{2x}$

5. $\dfrac{x+11}{3} = \dfrac{2x+8}{2x}$

6. $\dfrac{2x+1}{4} = \dfrac{x+3}{3x}$

Simplify the following expressions:

For example: Simplify $\dfrac{x^2 - 4}{2x + 4}$

$$\dfrac{x^2 - 4}{2x + 4} = \dfrac{(x+2)(x-2)}{2(x+2)}$$

$$= \dfrac{x-2}{2}$$

7. $\dfrac{x^2 - 1}{2x - 2}$

8. $\dfrac{4x^2 - 9}{(2x-3)^2}$

9. $\dfrac{(x^2 - 4)^2}{3x^3 - 12x}$

10. $\dfrac{(x-3)^2}{3x^2 - 27}$

11. $\dfrac{x+2}{4} - \dfrac{x-2}{x+2}$

12. $\dfrac{3}{x} + \dfrac{x+7}{x+2}$

Summary Exercise 16

1. Multiply out these brackets and simplify if possible:
   a) $4a(a - 4) - 2(a + 3)$ c) $3x(x + 2) - 3(x + 3)$
   b) $3a(a - 4) + 2b(a + 2)$ d) $5x(x + 3) - 2y(x + 3)$

2. Multiply out these brackets :
   a) $(x + 1)(x + 3)$ c) $(x + 5)(x - 2)$
   b) $(x - 4)(x + 7)$ d) $(x - 5)(x - 6)$

3. Multiply out these brackets :
   a) $(2x + 4)(3x + 3)$ c) $(4x + 1)(3x - 2)$
   b) $(5x - 6)(2x + 5)$ d) $(2x - 7)(3x - 2)$

4. Factorise these expressions:
   a) $x^2 - 3x$ c) $4ax^2 - 12a^2x$
   b) $35x^2yz - 20xy^3z$ d) $39x^2 - 26xy^4 + 13xy$

5. Factorise these expressions:
   a) $x^2 + 5x + 4$ c) $x^2 - 8x + 12$
   b) $x^2 - 5x - 24$ d) $x^2 + 5x - 36$

6. Factorise these expressions:
   a) $2a^2 + ab + 2ab + b^2$ b) $8c^2 + 20c - 10cd - 25d$

7. Factorise these expressions:
   a) $2x^2 + 9x + 9$ b) $3x^2 - 15x + 12$

8. Solve these equations:
   a) $x^2 - 5x - 4 = 0$ d) $x^2 - 7x - 9 = 0$
   b) $x^2 - 8x + 16 = 0$ e) $x^2 - 16 = 0$
   c) $3x^2 - 13x + 8 = 0$ f) $9(x^2 - 2x) = 16$

9. Two numbers are consecutive, but their squares have a difference of 29. What are the two numbers?

10. These two rectangles have the same area. Calculate the dimensions of the two rectangles.

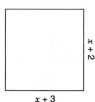

Activity 16 - Exercises in Proof

There are some statements that we make in arithmetic that are assumptions. Now you have the ability to prove some of these using algebra.

Consider the statement that the sum of two consecutive numbers is always an odd number. How could you prove that?

> Let one number be n.
> The next consecutive number is $n+1$
> The sum of two consecutive numbers is $2n + 1$
>
> However as $2n$ is a multiple of 2 it is always even
> Thus $2n + 1$ must always be odd
> And $2n + 1$ is the sum of 2 consecutive numbers
> Therefore the sum of two consecutive numbers must be an odd number.

Try proving these statements by using n as any number:

Consecutive Number Proofs

1. The sum of three consecutive numbers is always a multiple of 3.
2. The sum of five consecutive numbers is a multiple of 5.
3. If m is odd the sum of m consecutive numbers is a multiple of m.
4. The sum of four consecutive numbers is even
5. The sum of 6 consecutive numbers is a multiple of 3.

6. If m is even the sum of m consecutive numbers is a multiple of $\dfrac{m}{2}$

7. The sum of any n numbers from 1 to n, i.e. the nth triangle number, is $\dfrac{n(n+1)}{2}$

Reversed Number Proofs

These proofs need an understanding of the fact that any two digit number such as 93 can be written as 90 + 3, so a two digit number ab can be written as $10a + b$.
The 'reverse' of a number is the number with the reversal of the digits, so the reverse of 93 is 39, the reverse of ab is ba.

Can you prove that the sum of any two digit number plus its reverse is always a multiple of 11?

The two digit number ab can be written as $10a + b$
Its revers is ba and can be written as: $10b + a$
Therefore $ab + ba = 10a + b + 10b + a$
$$= 11a + 11b$$
$$= 11(a + b) \text{ which is a multiple of 11}$$

1. Prove that the difference between any two digit number and its reverse is always a multiple of 9.

2. Put forward a suggestion for the difference between any three digit number and its reverse and prove it.

Use Of The Counter Example

In the above exercise you were asked to **suggest** a result and then prove it. Suggesting a result is also called forming an hypothesis and can be an important part of a longer proof. As in the first set of proof exercises you built up a pattern of answers from which you could make a hypothesis and then prove it. However if you can find a counter example to your hypothesis then it is disproved.

Can you find a counter example to disprove the following:

a) All prime numbers are odd.
b) For any number x then $x < x^2$
c) A year is a leap year if it is a multiple of 4
d) No parallelogram has a line of symmetry
e) If x, y and z are three sides of a right angled triangle then $x^2 = y^2 + z^2$

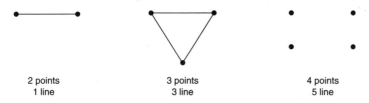

| 2 points | 3 points | 4 points |
| 1 line | 3 line | 5 line |

The last example is typical of how not to investigate a pattern – a hypothesis has been suggested far too early, you do need several results before you can predict and test a pattern.

The example 'If x, y and z are three sides of a right angled triangle then $x^2 = y^2 + z^2$' is also typical of imprecise language that can invalidate a proof. To be acurate this could have read:

'If x, y and z are three sides of a right angled triangle, and x is the hypotenuse, then $x^2 = y^2 + z^2$'

From Pattern To Proof

Dots and Lines
In the dot and line patterns a line must connect each pair of dots, so the correct answer to 4 dots is 6 lines. Continue the pattern, predict and test some results from which you can write a rule for n dots. Can you prove your rule?

Three Twos
a) Take any 3 digit number with 3 different digits (e.g. 471).
b) Write down all the three digit numbers that you can with those three digits (e.g. 417, 147, 174, 714, 741 etc.)
c) Add all your numbers up (2664).
d) Find the digit sum of your original number (12).
e) Divide your answer to part c) by your answer to part d) (222).
f) Try this again with other 3 digit numbers. Do you always get the same answer? Can you prove it?
g) Extend this investigation by looking at 2 and 4 digit numbers. Can you predict for 5 digit numbers? Can you write a rule for n digit numbers?

Chapter 17

Probability

Calculating Probability

The probability of an event can be calculated by considering the possible outcomes of that event, if all outcomes of an event are equally likely.

For example if a normal dice is thrown the possible outcomes are 1, 2, 3, 4, 5 or 6, that is 6 equally possible outcomes. The probability of throwing a 6 is one out of the 6 possible outcomes, this is written:

$$P(6) = \frac{1}{6}$$

In general terms when all the possible outcomes are equally likely the probability of an event

$$P(event) = \frac{\text{the possible no. of times the event occurs}}{\text{the no. of total possible outcomes}}$$

The probability of throwing a number less than 7 when throwing a normal dice is 1 or

say: **P(less than 7) = 1**   **as this is a certainty, and we can**

P(certainty)   = 1
P(impossibility) = 0
P(event not happening) = 1 − P(event)

Example:
A bag contains 12 discs, 5 are blue, 4 are green, 2 are white and the rest black. If one ball is taken out of the bag at random what is the probability that it is a) blue, b) white, c) not green.

P(blue) $= \frac{5}{12}$

P(white) $= \frac{2}{12} = \frac{1}{6}$

P(not green) $= 1 - \frac{4}{12} = \frac{8}{12} = \frac{2}{3}$

Exercise 17A

1. A normal pack of 52 cards is cut and one card is taken at random, what is the probability the card is:
   a) black
   b) a heart
   c) not a royal card.
   d) a king
   e) not a diamond
   f) the Ace of hearts?

2. If a normal dice is rolled what is the probability that the score is:
   a) three
   b) a square number
   c) an even number
   d) less than 6?

3. If a letter is picked at random from the alphabet, what is the probability the letter is:
   a) a vowel
   b) not a vowel
   c) one that appears in the word MATHEMATICS?

4. A bag contains 4 red sweets, 4 green sweets, 2 orange sweets and 1 lemon sweet. If I take one sweet out of the bag at random what is the probability that it is:
   a) red   b) green   c) not orange or lemon?

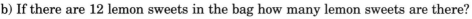

5. Another bag of sweets contains only orange and lemon sweets.
   a) If the probability of picking lemon sweet is what is the probability of picking an orange sweet?
   b) If there are 12 lemon sweets in the bag how many lemon sweets are there?

6. A letter is chosen at random from the letters in the word PROBABILITY, what is the probability that the letter is:
   a) a vowel   b) the letter L?   c) the letter I   d) the letter S?

7. If I have 4 pairs of white socks, 3 pairs of black socks and 5 pairs of grey socks and I take one pair of socks at random what is the probability that I pick a pair of grey socks? If my socks are not in pairs but are lying loose in my sock drawer and I take one sock at random what is the probability that it is a grey sock?

8. I am asked to pick a number between one and 20 (inclusive) at random what is the probability that I pick :
   a) a prime number
   b) a square number
   c) number with more than two factors?
   d) a multiple of 5
   e) a negative number

9. In the school raffle 1000 tickets were sold. If I bought 20 tickets what is the probability of my winning 1st prize? If there were 20 prizes how many tickets would I have to buy to be sure of winning a prize?

10. I buy a pack of containing 20 seeds, the instructions warn that only $\frac{2}{3}$ of the seeds can be expected to germinate, how many seedlings can I expect?

11. There are 320 pupils in the school and 25 of them are in my class. If the headmaster selects one pupil at random what is the probability that he picks a pupil from my class. What assumptions, if any, have you made?

12. The company that makes 'Luckychocs' say that every hundredth sweet they make is a Lucky choc. If I buy a bag of 12 'Luckychocs' what is the probability that I will be lucky? How many bags of 'Luckychocs' should I buy to be sure that I will be lucky?

Combined Probability

The probability of two events can either be dependent on one another or not, for example the probability of picking a king or a ten from a pack of cards are independent events. To calculate this you add the probability of one event to the probability of another:

$$P(\text{king or ten}) = \frac{4}{52} + \frac{4}{52}$$
$$= \frac{8}{52}$$
$$= \frac{2}{13}$$

However if asked for the probability of picking a black card or an ace from a pack of cards then two of the black cards are aces:

$$P(\text{black card or ace}) = \frac{28}{52}$$
$$= \frac{7}{13}$$

The probabilities cannot be added. There is no simple rule to apply here, each situation must be judged on its own merits.

Exercise 17B

1. If a card is drawn at random from a full pack of 52 cards what is the probability that it is:
   a) a two or a three   b) a red card or a knave?
   c) an ace or a king?   d) a red ace or a heart?
   e) a black queen or a red knave?

2. In our class there are 10 boys and 12 girls, 16 of us have pets, the rest do not. 7 of the pet owners are girls. If one of the class is picked at random what is the probability that it is :
   a) a girl   b) a pet owner   c) a boy that owns a pet?

3. In the school as a whole exactly one half the pupils are boys and one half girls. A recent survey shows that $\frac{1}{3}$ of the pupils walk to school, $\frac{1}{4}$ of the pupils come by car and the rest come by public transport. If a pupil is picked at random what is the probability that it is a boy coming to school by public transport, what assumptions, if any, have you made?

4. I have to pick any number from 1 to 20 at random, what is the probability that I pick:
   a) 5   b) a multiple of 5   c) a prime number
   d) a multiple of 5 or a prime number
   e) an odd number or a prime number?

Possibility Space for Combined Events

When two coins are tossed together the result could either be 2 heads, 2 tails or one head and one tail - which looks like 3 events. To be quite clear about what is happening a possibility space can be drawn:

First coin

		H	T
	H	(H,H)	(T,H)
	T	(H,T)	(T,T)

Second coin

From this it is quite clear that there are four possibilities, not three, as one head and one tail can be achieved in two ways.

Exercise 17C

1. Copy and complete this possibility space to show the possible outcomes when throwing two dice:
   When throwing two dice what is the probability of throwing a total score of:
   a) 4
   b) 12
   c) more than 6
   d) 4 or less

First die

		1	2	3	4	5	6
	1	(1,1)	(2,1)	(3,1)	(4,1)		
	2	(1,2)	(2,2)	(3,2)	(4,2)	( )	( )
	3	( )	( )	( )	( )	( )	( )
	4	( )	( )	( )	( )	( )	( )
	5	( )	( )	( )	( )	( )	( )
	6	( )	( )	( )	( )	( )	( )

Second die

2. Draw another possibility space similar to that in question one and use it to find the probability that:
   a) The total score is prime number;
   b) there is a prime number on at least one dice.

3. Draw a possibility space to show all the outcomes when you throw together a normal dice and a dice with its sided numbered 1, 1, 1, 2, 2, 3. Use this probability space to find the probability that:
   a) the total score is 2
   b) the total score is more than 4
   c) a double is thrown
   d) there is a multiple of 3 on each dice.
   e) the total score is a prime number
   f) the total score is 6 or more.

Dependent Events

In the last exercise the outcome on one dice did not effect the outcome of the other - the events were independent. In other situations a second event is dependent on the first. For example if I take a sweet from a bag and do not replace it. In these situations a possibility space cannot be used to help solve the problem:

> For example:
> A bag of sweets contains 6 mint sweets, 4 orange and 2 lemon sweets. if I offer the bag to my little sister what is the probability that she takes an orange sweet?
> $$P(O) = \frac{4}{12} = \frac{1}{3}$$
> In fact my little sister took all the lemon sweets. If I now offer the bag to my brother, what is the probability that he takes an orange sweet?
> $$P(O) = \frac{4}{10} = \frac{2}{5}$$

Exercise 17D

1. A bag contains 8 green sweets, 6 red sweets and 4 yellow sweets.

    a) If the first sweet I take out at random is red what is the probability that the second sweet is (i) red   (ii) yellow?
    b) If the first sweet I take out at random is green what is the probability that the second sweet is (i) green   (ii) yellow?
    c) If the first sweet I take out at random is yellow what is the probability that the second sweet is (i) yellow (ii) red?

2. A mixed bag of snack bars contains 5 caramel bars 4 chocolate bars and 3 orange flavoured bars, I am allowed to choose one bar at random every day for my break time snack.
    a) On Monday what is the probability that the bar I picked was caramel ?
    b) In fact the bar on Monday was an orange flavoured bar, what is the probability that I will choose a caramel bar on Tuesday?
    c) In fact the bar on Tuesday was a chocolate bar, what is the probability that I will choose a caramel bar on Wednesday?
    d) In fact the bar on Wednesday was an orange flavoured bar, how many bars will I have to take out of the bag now to be sure of getting a caramel bar?

3. I am dealt five cards from a pack of cards, these are 3 kings and 2 queens. If no other cards have been taken from the pack what is the probability that the next card will be:
    a) be a royal card   b) will not be a royal card?

4. I am dealt five cards from a pack of cards, these are 3 hearts and 2 diamonds. If no other cards have been taken from the pack what is the probability that the next card will be :
    a) be a heart   b) be a spade?

Using a Probability Tree

Suppose a bag contained 4 red counters and 5 green counters. If a counter is taken out at random the probability of it being red is $\frac{4}{9}$ and the probability of it being green is $\frac{5}{9}$. This can be shown on a diagram:

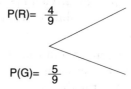

If a red counter was chosen first then there are now 3 red counters and 6 green counters left, but if a green counter was chosen first then there are now 4 red ccounters and 5 green counters left. The probabilities of taking the second counters are different and this can be shown by adding more branches to our tree:

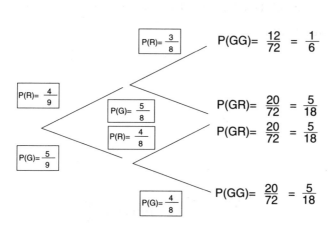

The end of the tree diagram shows the probabilities of the two events. Each is found by multiplying along the stalks,

$$P(RR) = \frac{4}{9} \times \frac{3}{8} = \frac{12}{72} \text{ etc.}$$

As the options can only be RR, RG, GR and GG then it follows that:

$$P(RR) + P(RG) + P(GR) + P(GG) = 1$$

and to check that our calculations are correct we can add up these probabilities:

$$\frac{12}{72} + \frac{20}{72} + \frac{20}{72} + \frac{20}{72} = \frac{72}{72} = 1$$

It is not worth simplifying the fractions until this check has been made. If the total of the probabilities does not add up to one then the previous working needs to be checked.

From the tree diagram we can see that P(RR) = $\frac{1}{6}$ and P(GG) = $\frac{5}{18}$ but the probability

of picking one red and one green = P(RG)+P(GR) = $\frac{5}{18} + \frac{5}{18} = \frac{10}{18} = \frac{5}{9}$.

Exercise 17E

Use Worksheets 17/1 and 17/2 with this exercise.

1. A box contains 5 lead pencils and 7 coloured pencils. Two pencils are taken out of the box at random. Complete the tree diagram on Worksheet 17/1 and use it to find:
    a) the probability that both pencils are lead pencils b) the probability that both are coloured and c) the probability of picking one lead pencil and one coloured pencil.

2. My cat had 5 kittens 2 were ginger and the other 3 were black. They come in through the cat flap in a random order at tea time. Complete the tree diagram on Worksheet 17/1 to find the probability that the first two were:
    a) ginger   b) black   c) one ginger and one black

3. A box contains 4 white balls and 6 red balls. I take two balls out of the box. Draw a tree diagram and use this to show the probability of :
    a) taking 2 red balls   b) taking at least one white ball
    c) the second ball being white.

4. There is a probability of $\frac{2}{5}$ that I will have porridge for breakfast. Copy and complete this diagram:

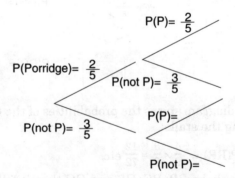

Use the tree diagram to find the probability that I will have porridge for breakfast
    a) twomornings running   b) at least once in two days.

5. I have a bag with 5 orange sweets, 4 lemon sweets and 3 mint sweets in it. I offer these to my little brother who takes 2 of them! Complete the tree diagram on Worksheet 17/2 to find the probability that he took:
    a) 2 lemon sweets   b) 2 mint sweets
    c) 1 orange and 1 lemon sweet
    d) continue some branches of the tree to find the probability of him taking 3 sweets -1 sweet of each flavour.

6. I throw a coin 3 times. Draw a tree diagram to show the possible outcomes of all 3 throws and use the diagram to find the probability of throwing:
a) 3 heads   b) 3 tails   c) 2 heads and one tail
d) If I threw two coins together 20 times how many times would I expect to get
(i) double heads   (ii) one head and one tail?

7. The game of Ludo that we are playing requires that you throw a 6 with a normal dice before you can start to move your playing pieces. Copy and complete this tree diagram showing my first three throws:

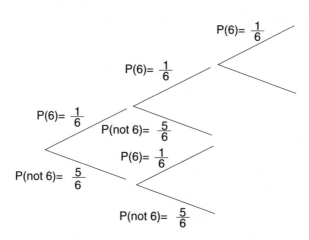

1st throw   2nd throw   3rd throw

Use the tree diagram find the probability that I threw:
a) 3 sixes   b) no sixes   c) one six   d) two sixes
e) Consider an extension of one branch of your tree diagram to find the probability of throwing no 6's in 10 throws.
f) If I threw the dice 30 times how many sixes would I expect to throw?

8. I have a drawer full of socks; 7 are white, 4 are blue and 6 are grey. I take 2 socks out of my drawer at random. Draw a tree diagram to show the possible outcomes and use the diagram to find the probability of my finding a matching pair.

9. Research shows that in May if there is no rain today then the probability of no rain tomorrow is $\frac{4}{5}$, but if it does rain today then the probability of no rain tomorrow is $\frac{2}{5}$.
If today is sunny draw a tree diagram showing the probability of rain or no rain for the next three days. Use the tree diagram to find the probability of:
a) no rain for three days
b) rain on two of the three days
c) rain on every day of the next three days.

10. In a tombola tickets that end in a 5 or 0 win a prize. I buy three tickets. Draw a tree diagram to show the probability of my winning a prize and use it to find:
a) the probability of my not winning any prizes with my three tickets.
b) the probability of my winning at least one prize with my three tickets
c) the probability of winning exactly two prizes with my two tickets.
d) If I bought 20 tickets how many prizes could I expect to win?

Extension Exercises 17 - Harder Probability

1. In a dice game the winner is the first person to throw a 3, if you
    throw a six then you can throw again.
    a) What is the probability of winning on your first throw?
    b) If there are two of you playing what is the probabilty of winning
    on your second go? Do the number of people playing make a difference?

2. I think of a number between one and ten. Each of my friends has to guess my
    number in turn, and I tell them if they are right or wrong. Which number
    guess has the best chance of winning? (Explain your reasoning clearly)

3. On a fruit machine there are three wheels, each has oranges, lemons, cherries
    and plums. The distribution of the fruit on each wheel is as follows:
    1st wheel: 6 oranges 2 lemons, 1 plum, 1 cherry
    2nd wheel: 3 oranges, 3 lemons 2 plums and 1 cherry
    3rd wheel: 2 oranges 5 lemons 2 plums and 1 cherry

    Prizes are given for the following results:
    a) Money back (20p) for a cherry on any wheel
    b) 50p for any 2 cherries in any row
    c) £1 for a row of three oranges
    d) £2 for a row of three lemons
    e) £5 for a row of three plums
    f) £10 for a row of three cherries
    (i) By drawing a tree diagram or using any other method find the probability of
    winning any of the above combinations.
    (ii) If each go is 20p how much money could I expect to win if I put £10 into the
    fruit machine and did not reinvest any winnings?

4. The probability that Alec will solve a certain problem is $\frac{1}{4}$,the probability that
    Bessy will solve it is $\frac{2}{5}$ and the probability that Chung will solve it is $\frac{2}{3}$.
    a) What is the probability that all three will solve the problem?
    b) What is the probability that only one of the three will solve it?
    c) What is the probability that none of them will solve the problem?

5. If I do not pass my Maths exam I will be allowed to resit it. My mother says the

    probability of my passing first time is $\frac{3}{5}$ but if I do not pass first time I will

    work so hard that the probability of my passing the resit will be $\frac{4}{5}$. What is the

    probability that I do not pass my Maths exam at either attempt?

Summary Exercise 17

1. If I cut a normal pack of cards and select one card at random what is the probability that this card will be:
    a) an ace
    b) a diamond
    c) the ten of hearts
    d) either an ace or a king
    e) either a heart or a queen

2. I roll an ordinary dice and a dice numbered 1,2,3,3,5,6. Draw a possibility space and find the probability that I throw:
    a) a double   b) a six on either dice   c) a total greater than 5
    d) a total less than 4.
    e) If I rolled both dice together 30 times how many doubles would I expect?

3. There are eight tins of soup in my cupboard, 3 tomato, two chicken, two beef and one farmhouse vegetable. If I pick one tin at random what is the probability that it is:
    a) tomato   b) suitable for vegetarians   c) not beef?

4. A box contains 3 red balls and 7 white balls. Two balls are taken from the box. Draw a probability tree showing and use it to find the probability of picking:
    a) two red balls   b) two white balls   c) at least one red ball
    d) one ball of each colour.

5. A bowl of fruit contains 4 oranges, 3 apples and 2 bananas. I pass the bowl around my three guests who select one fruit each. Draw a probability tree and find the probability that:
    a) 3 apples were taken
    b) One piece of each fruit was taken.
    c) I was left with any bananas.

6. (i) My maths master Mr Chance is very absent minded. There is a 20% chance that he will forget to set us any maths prep, and a 30% chance that he will forget to ask for it to be given in. However if Mr Chance does remember to ask for it in and we have not done it (regardless of whether it was set or not) then the class gets a detention. What is the probability that:
    a) No homework was set and none was asked for.
    b) Homework was set but was not asked to be given in.
    c) The class got a detention.
    (ii) Actually I am quite absent minded too! There is a 40% chance that I forget to do my homework if it is set. What is the probability that I am given a detention for not handing in prep when it was asked for?
    (iii) If there are 20 nights in a term when I am supposed to have Maths prep how many detentions could I expect to get?

Revision Exercises 3

Give any non-exact answers correct to 3 significant figures unless specified otherwise.

1. a) Write these numbers in standard index form:
    (i) 315 000   (ii) 0.000 000 502   (iii) 2 790 000
    b) If $a = 3.5 \times 10^5$ and $b = 1.5 \times 10^7$ find the value of:

    (i) ab (ii) $\dfrac{a}{b}$ (iii) $a + b$

2. a) Write down the equation of each of these lines:

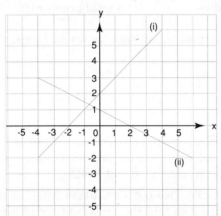
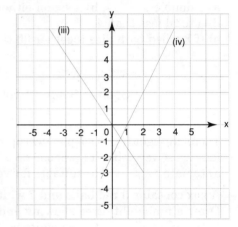

    b) Consider the lines given by these equations:
    $$y = x + 3$$
    $$y = 2x - 3$$
    $$y = 3x + 1$$
    $$y = 2x - 1$$
    $$2y = x + 3$$
    (i) Which two of the lines are parallel?
    (ii) The point (0, 3) lies on which of these lines?

    (iii) Which line is parallel to the line $y - \dfrac{x}{2} = 1$?

3. The angle of elevation from a point P to the top of a tree is 18°. If P is 200m from the base of the tree, on horizontal ground, what is the height of is the tree?

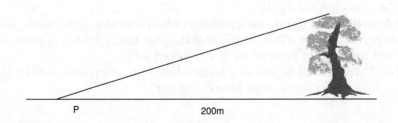

P   200m

4. a) Simplify these expressions:
(i) $5x(x + 2y) - 2y(3 + x)$ (ii) $3x(x - 2) - 2x(x - 5) + 3(3x + 4)$
b) Factorise the following:
(i) $6x^2y - 9xy^2 + 3xy$ (ii) $4x^2 - 24$ (iii) $x^2 - 13x + 36$
c) The base of this triangle is 5cm longer than its height and the area of the whole triangle is 72 cm^2.

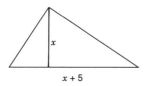

Form an equation in x and solve it to find the base and height of the triangle.

5. Mabel keeps her 5 T-shirts, of which 2 are black, in one drawer and her four pairs of trousers, of which one is black, in another. Mabel takes a T shirt and a pair of trousers out of her drawers at random every morning.Copy and complete this tree diagram :

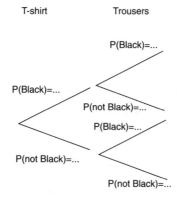

a) What is the probability that Mabel chose a black T shirt and Black trousers?
b) What is the probability that at least one garment was black?
c) What is the probability that neither garment was black?

6. Give your answers to these questions in standard index form to 3 significant figures.
a) How many millimetres are there in 2000 km?
b) An ant colony under investigation started with 100 ants but the population doubled every 40 days. What was the population of the ant colony after 2 years?
c) (i) The Earth is about 150 million kilometres from the sun, Pluto is 40 times further away from the sun. How far is Pluto from the sun?

(ii) If the Earth, The Sun and Pluto were all in line, as in the diagram, how far would the Earth be from Pluto?

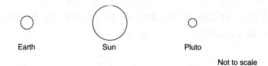

Earth   Sun   Pluto

Not to scale

(iii) The moon is about 387 000 km from the Earth. If the moon lay on a straight line between the Earth and Pluto how much further from the Earth is Pluto than the Moon?

○ ○ Moon   ○
Earth   Pluto

Not to scale

(iv) In the above situation write in the form 1: n the ratio
"Distance of Earth from Sun: Distance of Pluto from Sun".

7. a) The point (2, −4) lies on a line whose gradient is 3. What is the equation of the line?
b) If A is the point (1,3) and B is the point (5, −5) then:
(i) What is the gradient of the line AB?
(ii) What is the equation of the line AB ?

8. A car starting from a stationery position pulls away and accelerates down the road. This table shows the distance s metres it has gone in time t seconds:

t	0	1	2	3	4	5	6	7	8	9	10	20	40
s	0	2	8	18	32	50	72	91	108	162	200	600	1000

a) With t on the horizontal axes with a scale of 1 cm to 2 seconds and s on the vertical axis with a scale of 1cm to 40 metres draw a graph of s against t.
b) At what time did the car stop accelerating and travel at a constant speed?
c) What was this constant speed?
d) At the same time a cyclist was travelling along the same road at a constant speed of 10 ms^{-1}. Draw on the same axes a graph to show the cyclist's journey. How long did it take the car to overtake the cyclist?
e) A pedestrian is standing on the pavement 60 metres in front of the car. When the car starts to move the pedestrian starts walking at 2 ms^{-1} in the same direction as the car. On the same axes draw a graph to show the pedestrian's movement. When does the car overtake the pedestrian? By drawing a suitable line on the graph estimate the speed of the car at this time.

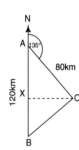

9. An aeroplane travelling from Alpha to Brava has to fly on a bearing of 135° for 80 km to avoid a hill before resuming its course to Brava. Brava lies 120 km due South of Alpha.
a) What is the angle BAC?
b) By considering the line CX find how far East of Alpha the plane flew before it changed course?
c) By considering the line AX find how far South of Alpha the plane flew before it changed course?
d) How much further South has the plane to fly?
e) Calculate the distance that the plane has to fly from point C.
f) Calculate the bearing on which the plane must fly from C to Brava.

10. A 50p coin is in the shape of a heptagon of side 12 mm. Join A to D.
a) Calculate the following angles: (i) ABC (ii) BAD
b) (i) Name the shape ABCD.
  (ii) What is the angle sum of ABCD ?

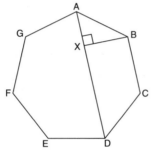

c) BX meets AD at at X and angle BXA is 90°.
  (i) Calculate AX.
  (ii) Calculate AD.
d) Write down the height of the smallest slot in which the coin can be inserted. Give your answer to the nearest 0.5 mm.

11. A jogger travels for 800m at a constant speed of x ms^{-1}, and then slows down by 1 ms^{-1} and continues jogging for 300m before stopping. If the jogger has taken 5 minutes for his 1100m trip form an equation in x and solve it to find his initial speed.

12. Last year I planted 200 nasturtium seeds. 160 of them produced healthy plants that flowered and then produced seeds at the end of the season. I then planted one seed from each of the 160 plants and found that 100 of these produced healthy flowering plants. From the results of this experiment what is the probability that a plant capable of producing reliable seeds will grow from one nasturtium seed?

Chapter 18

Locus

What Is A Locus

Draw a point P in the middle of your page. Using your ruler mark 20 points which are exactly 5cm away from the point A. Your page should look something like this:

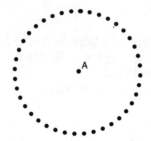

You can see that the points all lie on a circle, centre A and radius 5cm.

Now draw a line AB 7cm long, and draw 20 points exactly 3cm away from the line. You will need a set square to make sure that the points are in the right place:

When you have drawn your points you should have some thing looking like this:

What happens at the ends of the line ? If you continue to plot points you should have a diagram looking like this:

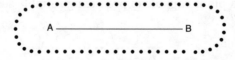

The word LOCUS means a set of points, the first set of points you drew were the locus of a point 5cm from a point A. The second set of points that you drew was the locus of a point 3cm from the line AB, where AB = 7cm.

A locus can be a line or an area. Consider these options:

a) the locus of a point P such that AP = 5cm

b) the locus of a point A such that AP ≤ 5cm

c) The locus of a point A such that AP>5cm.

  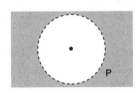

Note that the last two locus are area, and the area in c) is described by a dotted line as the locus of P is described as greater than 5cm, and is not equal to 5cm from A.

A locus can also be a point.
Given two points A and B such that AB = 5cm, draw the locus of P such that AP = 4cm, BP = 3cm and AB = 5cm.
First AB must be drawn and then the locus of all the points 3cm from P and all the points 4cm from A:

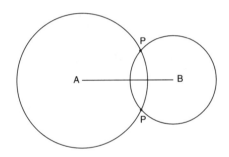

You can see that there are two posible positions for the point P.

Exercise 18A

The locus in this exercise are to be drawn accurately using compasses and ruler. If necessary a rough sketch may help to see what is required. Worksheets 18/1 and 18/2 are to be used with this exercise.

1. Draw the locus of a point P such that AP < 4cm. Describe the locus.

2. Draw the locus of a point P such that BP ≤ 5cm. Describe the locus.

3. Draw the locus of a point P such that P is 2.5cm from a line CD, CD = 6cm. Describe the locus.

4. Draw the locus of a point P such that the area of the triangle ABP = 6cm when AB = 4cm (hint work out the height of the triangle). Describe the locus.

5. Draw the locus of a point P such that P is 4cm from a line CD and PC = 5cm. CD= 6cm. Describe the locus.

6. Given two points A and B such that AB = 8cm, draw the locus of a point P such that AP= 5cm, and BP = 7cm. Describe the locus.

For the next four questions use Worksheet 18/1.

7. A theme park is to be built at a site that is 150km from London and 250km from Liverpool. Draw the possible sites of the theme park.

8. Aeroplanes can be heard in an area up to 50km from their flight paths Show the area where the aeroplane noise from the flights from London to Belfast can be heard.

9. An oil rig is to be built in the sea 300km from Inverness and not less than 125km from the mainland coast. Shade the area where the oil rig can be sited.

10. I am looking for a house that is not more than 150km from Cardiff and not more than 100km from London. The house must be more than 150km from Birmingham. Shade the area where I should look.

11. There are three towns Alpha, Beta and Comma. Alpha lies 120km due South of Beta, and Comma lies 150km due East of Beta. Using a scale of 1cm to 10km draw a plan showing Alpha, Beta and Comma.
    Fred sets off from Beta. He wants to stop for lunch when he has travelled more that 70km, but is still more than 50km from both Alpha and 150km from Comma. Shade the area where Fred could have lunch.

Use Worksheet 18/2 for question 12.

12. The rectangle ABCD in this diagram represents a garden to the South of a house at AB. The garden is drawn to a scale of 1cm to 4m. The garden plan is being considered. On each diagram on the worksheet draw each of these proposals:
    a) Grass is to be planted in an area at least 10m from the house. Shade the area.
    b) Grass is to be planted in an area at least 8m from the tree. Shade the grassed grassed area.
    c) The area where grass is to be grown is represented by the locus of points more than 5m from the garden fence. Shade this area.
    d) The area to be planted with grass is represented by the locus of points more than 10m from each corner of the garden. Shade this area.
    e) The grassed area is the locus of the points not more than 10m from the tree but more than 15m from the house. Shade this area.
    f) The grassed area is to be the locus of the points more than 6m from the tree, more than 8m from the corners C and D of the garden and more than 10m from the house.

Use Worksheet 18/3 for questions 13 and 14.

13. The rectangle in this diagram represents a shed drawn to a scale of 1cm to 1m. A goat is tethered at corner A by a rope 3m long. Draw the locus of the area that the goat can reach.

14. The diagram represents a coast line with radio transmitters at A and B. Radio Audio transmits from A and can be heard in a region up to 25km from the transmitter. Radio Blast transmits from B and can be heard in a region 35km from B. Shade the areas where a yacht at sea can hear:
    a) only Radio Audio
    b) both Radio Audio and Radio Blast.

More Constructions

1. Perpendicular Bisector

The locus of a point that is an equal distance from two points A and B looks like this:

If you measure any point P on the line you can see that AP = BP, if you draw the line AB you can see that the locus divides AB in half and is at right angles to it. This locus is the perpendicular bisector of AB.

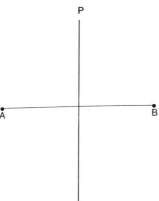

To draw the perpendicular bisector:

With centre A draw two arcs of any length greater than half AB above and below the line AB.

With centre B draw two arcs of the same radius to cross the first two arcs. Join up the two points of intersection.

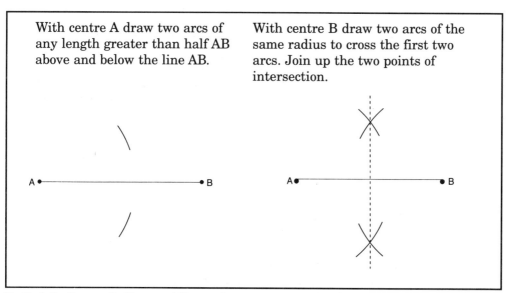

To find the locus of a line equidistant from any two points construct the perpendicular bisector of the line joining the two points. (The actual line joining the points does **NOT** have to be drawn.)

2. The Angle Bisector

The locus of a point equidistant from two intersecting lines looks like this:

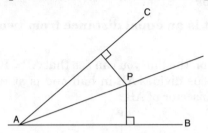

If you measure the angle BAC you can see that the locus bisects the angle, if you measure any point P on the locus you will see that it is equidistant from AB and AC.

To construct the angle bisector:

One of the properties of a rhombus is that the diagonals bisect the angles. If we treat the two intersecting sides as sides of a rhombus and draw the other two sides, then the diagonal will bisect the angle:

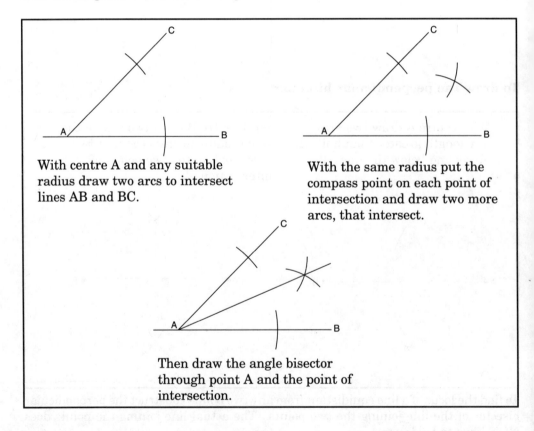

With centre A and any suitable radius draw two arcs to intersect lines AB and BC.

With the same radius put the compass point on each point of intersection and draw two more arcs, that intersect.

Then draw the angle bisector through point A and the point of intersection.

To find the locus of a point P equidistant from two lines AB and BC construct the angle bisector of angle ABC.

Exercise 18B

1. Draw the locus of a point P equidistant from points A and B where AB = 12cm.

2. Draw the locus of a point P which is equidistant from lines XY and YZ. Angle XYZ = 60°.

3. Construct a triangle ABC where AB = 10cm, BC = 8cm and AC = 6cm. By drawing the angle bisector of angle ABC and the perpendicular bisector of AB find the locus of a point P which is equidistant from points A and B, and equidistant from lines AB and AC.

4. Construct a triangle PQR with PQ = 8cm, and RPQ = 50° and angle PQR = 45°. Find the locus of a point P which is equidistant from R and P, and 4cm from point Q. (Are there two possible points?) Describe the locus.

5. On a scale of 1cm to 2km draw two points A and B 15km apart. Construct the locus of a point P, where P is less than 9km from B but closer to A than B. Describe the locus.

6. Near the quay there are two rings, 6m apart. Dog owners tie their dogs to the rings while they visit the chandlery. I tied my dog Fred to a ring with a piece of string 4m long.
   A woman arrived and tied her dog, Butch, to the other ring with a piece of string 3.5m long.
   Fred and Butch took no notice of each other until a cat came along and walked carefully down an imaginary line equidistant between the two rings.
   Draw a diagram to a scale of 2cm to 1m showing the area in which both Fred and Butch could catch the cat.

7. Farmer Jones and Farmer McTavish are in dispute over this field. To settle the dispute the field is divided in two by a fence that is equidistant from A and C. Farmer McTavish keeps a goat in his half tethered to a post at point C by a rope 16 m long. Farmer Mc Tavish grows oats in his half of the field. One day the goat broke through the fence. Make a scale drawing of the and show the area where the goat could eat the oats.

8. A boat set off from a port C on a bearing of 072° and sailed for 5km, to a point A; another boat set off from the same port on a bearing of 127° and sailed for 6km to a point B. At this moment a buoy D is equidistant from A and B, and is also equidistant from the imaginary lines AC and BC. Draw a scale drawing to show the relative positions of A, B, C and D with a scale of 1cm to 500km and use your drawing to find the bearing and distance of the buoy from C.

9. In the diagram, Angle APB = 90° where point P is a point on the circumference of a circle of diameter AB.
a) AB = 10cm and is a diameter of a circle. Draw AB and the circle.

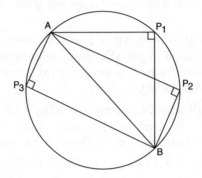

b) A point P lies on the circumference of the circle. Choose any point P and measure angle APB.
c) Draw two other circles of different diameter and mark various points P on the circumference. Measure the angle APB. What can you deduce about an angle APB where P is a point on the circumference of a triangle of diameter AB?

10. AB = 10cm. Draw the locus of a point P such that ∠APB = 90°.

11. AB = 12cm. Draw the locus of a point P such that ∠APB = 90° and the area of triangle APB = 24cm².

12. In the diagram, Angle AP_1B = angle AP_2B where point P is a point on the circumference of a circle with fixed chord AB. A circle of diameter 10cm has a

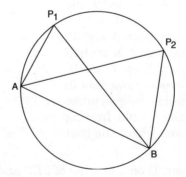

chord AB = 6cm. Draw the circle and the chord AB. A point P lies on the circumference of the circle. Draw various positions of point P and measure angle APB. What do you notice? Draw some other circles and measure similar sets of angles.

13. AB = 10cm. Draw the locus of a point P such that angle APB = 60°. This is quite difficult to do, start by drawing an equilateral triangle APB. The points A, B and P all now lie on the circumference of the circle centre O. Can you now find O given that OA = OB = OC?

Circumcircle And Incircle

(When drawing these constructions draw the construction lines neatly but faintly so that they help you to reach your solution without interfering with the lines needed to answer the question. Do not rub the construction lines out – they are a necessary part of your working.)

Construct two triangles ABC, each with AB = 9cm, BC = 8cm and AC = 7cm. Construct three perpendicular bisectors, to bisect AB, BC and AC. These should all meet at a point:

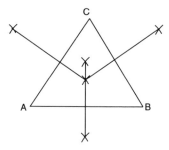

With your compass point at the point of intersection of the three perpendicular bisectors draw a circle that passes through the points A, B and C:

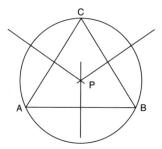
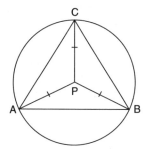

This is the CIRCUMCIRCLE, and its centre, P, is equidistant from the points A, B, and C.

On the second triangle construct the three angle bisectors of angles A, B, and C. These should also meet at a point. This time put the compass point on the point of intersection and draw a circle that just touches the sides AB, BC and AC:

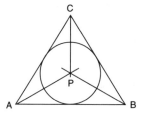
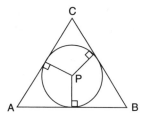

This is the INCIRCLE and its centre is equidistant from the lines AB, BC and AC.

Exercise 18C

Use Worksheets 18/4, 18/5 and 18/6 for this exercise:

1. Draw a triangle ABC with AB = 8cm, BC = 10cm and AC = 11cm. Find the locus of a point P which is equidistant from A, B and C.

2. Draw a triangle ABC with AB = 11cm, BC = 9cm and AC = 10cm. Find the locus of a point P which is equidistant from AB, BC and AC.

3. On worksheet 18/4 there is a plan of a treasure island; it shows the position of three palm trees A, B, and C. Captain Bones has buried his treasure at a point equidistant from the three palm trees, can you find the spot?

4. On worksheet 18/5 there is a plan of a triangular courtyard. The mad baron has buried treasure in the courtyard, his instructions say that the treasure is buried at a point that is equidistant from the three sides of the courtyard. Can you find the spot?

5. On the treasure island on Worksheet 18/4 another pirate, Jolly Roger has dug up Captain Bones' treasure and has carried it off. He tried to make it to Wrecker's Cove but on the way a storm blew up and he has not been seen since.
    All we know of Jolly Roger's track is that he was more than 2km but less than 5km from where he dug up the treasure. He was nearer to B than C but more than 4km from B. On the worksheet mark the possible area where Jolly Roger and the treasure could lie.

6. The mad Baron's courtyard on Worksheet 18/5 is haunted by a mad monk. The mad monk walks under a full moon in an area that is closer to the East side of the courtyard than the North side, yet is nearer to the Red tower than the Black tower, and more than 25m from the White tower. Shade the area on the worksheet where the mad monk walks.

7. On Worksheet 18/6 there is a detail of the map of the Southern Oceans which shows three atolls in a coral reef. Three sailors – Ali, Baba and Chris are shipwrecked on the three atolls marked A, B, and C.
    a) What is the bearing of: (i) C from B   (ii) A from C ?
    b) A helicopter drops a food parcel at a point exactly equidistant from the three atolls. By careful construction find this point of the chart and label it F.
    c) Ali, Baba, and Chris all start to swim towards the food parcel, however they do not know that the area is patrolled by man-eating sharks.
    Shark R patrols the area that is more than 700m from an imaginary line AB.
    Shark S patrols the area that is more than 1km from C but less than 750m from A.
    Shark T patrols up and down the line that is equidistant from the imaginary lines AB and BC.
    d) By careful construction show the area patrolled by the three sharks and find which sailors, if any, can reach the food parcel safely.

Other Locus

The locus in the previous exercises have been constructed using standard compass and ruler techniques. There are other locus that are harder to construct, but can be sketched by drawing possible positions of the point.

For example:
A ladder 3m long is propped up vertically against a wall. The foot of the ladder slides until the ladder lies horizontally on the floor. Sketch the locus of the mid point of the ladder.

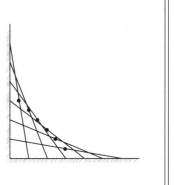

Exercise 18D

Sketch the following locus, then draw them accurately, if possible:

1. A dog is tied by a piece of string 3m long to a point on a tree of diameter 40cm. If the dog walks clockwise round and round the tree sketch the locus of the end of the string.

2. A rectangle ABCD with AB = 3cm and BC = 2cm is rotated about point A. Draw the locus of point B.

3. A square ABCD of side 3cm is rolled along the horizontal. Sketch the locus of the corner A as the square is rolled:

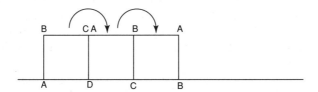

4. Repeat question 2. for (a) a triangle of side 5cm and (b) a hexagon of side 2cm.

5. A chord AB lies on a circle of diameter 10cm . Sketch the locus of the mid-point of the chord.

6. AB = 10cm. A point P is such that AP = 2PB. Sketch the locus of point P.

7. AB = 8cm. A point P is such that AP + PB= 12cm. Sketch the locus of point P. (Drawing pins and string might be useful here.)

Summary Exercise 18

1. Given a point A draw the locus of a point P such that AP = 5cm.

2. Given two points A and B so that AB = 8cm draw the locus of a point P such that AP = BP.

3. Given two points A and B so that AB = 5cm draw the locus of a point P such that P is exactly 3cm from a line AB.

4. Given two points A and B so that AB = 5cm draw the locus of a point P such that Triangle APB has area 12cm^2 .

5. Given that A is a fixed point with B due East of A.Sketch the locus of a point P where ABPC is a rectangle of area 12cm^2.

6. This is the boundary between two countries:

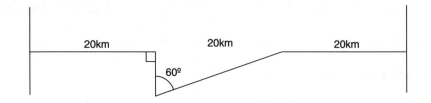

    a) Draw the boundary accurately to a scale of 1cm to 5km.
    b) No Mans land is the area that extends 2.5km each side of the border. Show the boundary of No Man's Land on your scale drawing.

7. In a triangle ABC where AB = 8cm, BC = 7cm and AC =7.5cm construct the locus of a point P such that P is nearer to AB that BC and P is closer to point A than point B. Measure your drawing and calculate the area that P could lie in.

8. Farzam, Gus and Hetty all keep racing pigeons. Farzam lives 125km away from Gus on a bearing of 312°, and Hetty lives 90km away from Farzam on a bearing of 160°. Use a scale of 1cm to 10km and draw the relative positions of Farzam, Gus and Hetty. Use your drawing to find the bearing and distance of Hetty from Gus.
    The three pigeon owners take their prize pigeons to a place that is equidistant from all their houses and let them go. With careful construction find this place on your drawing. Mark it P.
    Farzam's pigeon flies around in an area 30km from where it was released. Gus's pigeon stays more than 80km from home and more than 20km from where it was released and Hetty's pigeon stays in the area which is closer to Gus's home than Hetty's.
    While Gus and Hetty go rushing off to catch their pigeons Farzam stays in one place and catches all three. By careful construction show the possible area where Farzam could have caught the three pigeons.

Activity 18 - Design a Car Park

Is there a staff car park at your school? Is there a small car park near you?

Do a survey with a few of your friends and look at various small car parks. Draw each car park to scale and consider the following questions:
What size are the bays?
How wide are the aisles?
How do you get in and out of them?
How do cars turn?

The last point is very interesting, if you consider the shape of a car's chassis:

A car turns by moving it's front wheels, and then as the car moves forward the rest of the car follows:

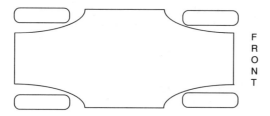

Different cars have different turning circles depending on their design. Look at some cars turning; see how different makes of cars turn in and out of narrow spaces.

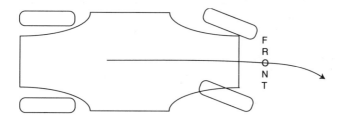

Now design a staff car park for your school. You will have to carry out a survey first:
How many staff drive in daily?
How many staff drive in occasionally?
How many visitors are there ever likely to be?
(Are any of these figures likely to change?)
Where can you site the car park?
How is it going to be organised ? (straight bays, diagonal bays, centre aisle etc.)

Then determine the size of each bay and the amount of space needed to allow each car to turn into the bay, and also to get out of the car park at the end of the day.

Do not forget to think about landscaping with trees and flower beds, and litter bins and interesting paving patterns (tessellating tiles perhaps) .

Keep a careful note of all your calculations and figures so that you can justify your design at a debriefing session!

Chapter 19

Transformations

A point P can be mapped to another point by a transformation. Transformations that you have studied are reflections, rotations, translations and enlargements. The point that P is mapped on to can be by called another letter e.g. Q, or as P', or if it is the first of a series of transformations as P_1, P_2, P_3 etc..

Reflections

A object can be reflected to give a 'mirror image' of itself. The object is reflected in a 'mirror line' or a line of reflection. On a co-ordinate grid this could be a horizontal or a vertical line such as the x axis or the y axis, or a line such as $x = 2$, $y = -3$ etc., or a sloping line such as $y = x$ or $y = -x$ or $y = 3x - 2$, for example.

If a reflection is not on a co-ordinate grid then the image will need to be constructed:

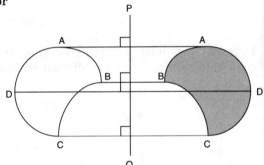

In this reflection of ABCD in the mirror line PQ the point A maps on to A',
  B to B'
  C to C'
  D to D'.

Note that the lines AA', BB'. CC', and DD' are at right angles to PQ and are bisected by PQ.

If you take any other point on the shape ABCD you will see that this is always true.

Also note that AA′, BB′, CC′, DD′ are parallel.

A reflection can be constructed by drawing a line from a point P on the object to meet the mirror line at right angles at X:

A line is then drawn on the opposite side to the image at right angles to the mirror line from X equal in length to PX :

Q' can then be constructed in the same way and the line P'Q' is drawn, the reflection of PQ in the line AB:

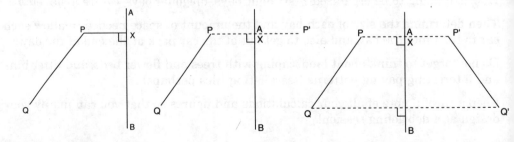

Exercise 19A

You will need Worksheets 19/1 and 19/2 for this exercise.

1. This diagram is also drawn on Worksheet 20/1. Some of these triangles may have a reflected image and some may not. Give the letters of all pairs of objects and image and draw the mirror lines on the Worksheet.

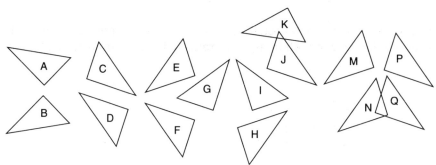

2. On Worksheet 19/1 you will see these object with various mirror lines. Construct the image of the object after a reflection in each mirror line..

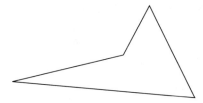

3. On Worksheet 20/1 you will see this object with various mirror lines. Construct the image of the object after a reflection in each mirror line. All the curves are arcs of a circle and you will need a pair of compasses:

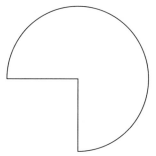

4. On Worksheet 19/1 you will see this object with various mirror lines. Construct the image of the object after a reflection in each mirror line.

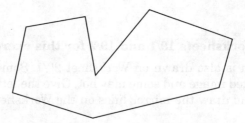

When an object has to be reflected in two lines of symmetry then not only is the object reflected twice but both images are reflected to give an identical fourth image:

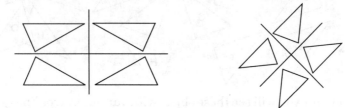

On Worksheet 19/2 you will see these shapes and two mirror lines. Draw the full reflections of the objects in the mirror lines.

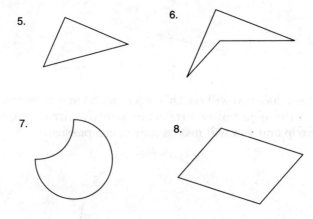

5.

6.

7.

8.

Rotations

A rotation describes the transformation of an object that is rotated about a point. A rotation can be either clockwise (negative) of anticlockwise (positive) and needs to be described not only by the centre of rotation but also by the size of the angle of rotation, and the direction:

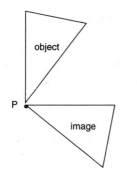

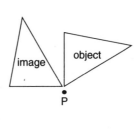

A rotation of 90° clockwise (− 90°) about a point P.

A rotation of 90° anticlockwise (+ 90°) about a point P.

To construct the image of an object after a rotation you need a pair of compasses and a protractor.

For a rotation of 90° clockwise:

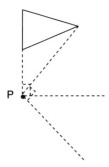

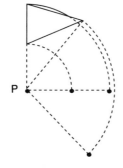

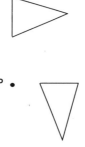

Draw lines from the centre of rotation to each point on the object. Construct lines at 90° to each.

With compasses centre P draw arcs from each point on the object to cross the construction lines.

Draw the image.

Exercise 19B

You will need Worksheets 19/3 and 19/4 for this exercise.

1.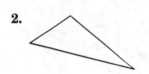
You will see this object on worksheet 19/3.
Draw the image of the object after a rotation of:
a) 90° clockwise about P.
b) 180° about P
c) 270° clockwise about P.

2.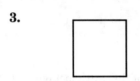
You will see this object on worksheet 19/3.
Draw the image of the object after a rotation of:
a) 60° clockwise about P.
b) 120° clockwise about P
c) 60° anticlockwise about P.

3.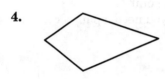
You will see this object on worksheet19/3.
Draw the image of the object after a rotation of:
a) 45° clockwise about P.
b) 135° anticlockwise about P
c) 135° clockwise about P.

4.
You will see this object on worksheet 19/3.
Draw the image of the object after a rotation of:
a) 55° clockwise about P.
b) 160° clockwiseabout P
c) 105° anti-clockwise about P.

Finding The Centre Of Rotation

If you have an object and its image you may need to find the centre of rotation, and from this the angle of rotation. As each point on the object and its corresponding point on the image lie on an arc whose centre is the centre of rotation to find the centre you need to join each point to its image, and find the perpendicular bisector of that line. Where the perpendicular bisectors cross will be the centre of rotation.

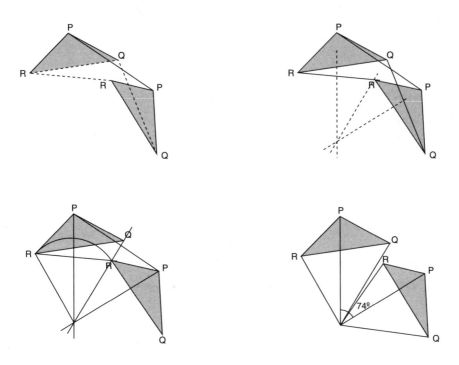

5.-8. On Worksheet 19/4 you find four objects with a corresponding image. For each pair join each pint to its image and construct the perpendicular bisectors to find the centre of rotation and the angle of rotation. However to make sure that each image is a true rotation you must ensure that the perpendicular bisectors ALL cross at a unique point.

Rotational Symmetry

When some objects are rotated about their own centre then some will have images that are identical to the object. These objects have rotational symmetry:

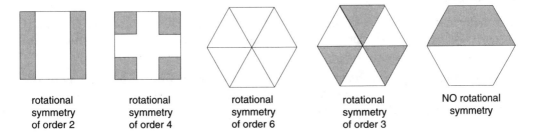

| rotational symmetry of order 2 | rotational symmetry of order 4 | rotational symmetry of order 6 | rotational symmetry of order 3 | NO rotational symmetry |

Exercise 19C

You will need worksheet 19/5 for this exercise.

1.   Write down the rotational symmetry of these shapes:

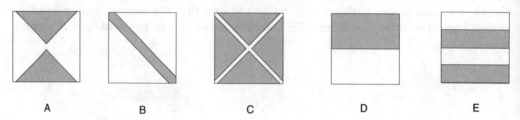

A   B   C   D   E

Now write down the number of lines of symmetry in each shape.

2.   Write down the rotational symmetry of these shapes:

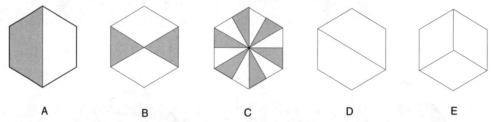

A   B   C   D   E

Now write down the number of lines of symmetry in each shape.

3.   Write down the rotational symmetry of these shapes:

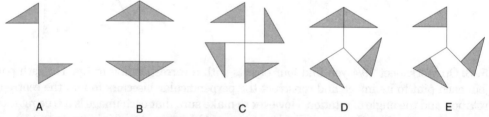

A   B   C   D   E

Now write down the number of lines of symmetry in each shape.

4.– 6. On Worksheet 19/5 you will find various incomplete objects. Complete each object such that it has the number of lines of symmetry and the order of rotational symmetry given.

Translations

A transformation which does not change the shape or orientation of an object but moves it is called a translation. A translation needs to be given in two parts - horizontal and vertical.

As with co-ordinates the horizontal movement is given first, a movement to the right is positive and a movement to the left is negative. A movement up is positive and a movement down is negative.

A translation is given by a vector:

A movement of 5 units right and 2 units up is given by the vector $\begin{pmatrix} 5 \\ 2 \end{pmatrix}$ and is shown on a grid by:

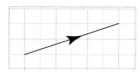

Exercise 19D

You will need Worksheet 19/6 with this exercise.

1. Write down the translations shown by these vectors:

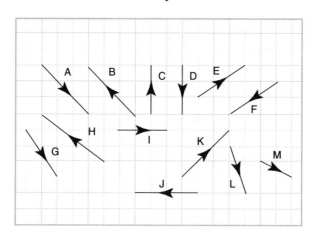

2. On Worksheet 19/6 draw the vectors given by these translations:

a) $\begin{pmatrix} 3 \\ 4 \end{pmatrix}$ b) $\begin{pmatrix} 3 \\ -4 \end{pmatrix}$ c) $\begin{pmatrix} -2 \\ -4 \end{pmatrix}$ d) $\begin{pmatrix} 4 \\ -2 \end{pmatrix}$ e) $\begin{pmatrix} 0 \\ 3 \end{pmatrix}$

f) $\begin{pmatrix} -3 \\ 0 \end{pmatrix}$ g) $\begin{pmatrix} 3 \\ -1 \end{pmatrix}$ h) $\begin{pmatrix} 5 \\ -2 \end{pmatrix}$ i) $\begin{pmatrix} -3 \\ 1 \end{pmatrix}$ j) $\begin{pmatrix} 0 \\ -5 \end{pmatrix}$

When an object is transformed by a translation the whole object moves. This movement can be seen as the result of a horizontal movement followed by a vertical movement, by distances given by the vector. In this diagram the triangle PQR is

mapped on to the triangle P´Q´R´ by a translation given by the vector $\begin{pmatrix} 8 \\ 2 \end{pmatrix}$.

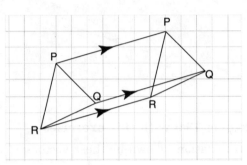

3.   On Worksheet 19/6 translate the following objects:

   a) Translate triangle ABC by the vector $\begin{pmatrix} 3 \\ 5 \end{pmatrix}$

   b) Translate triangle DEF by the vector $\begin{pmatrix} 0 \\ -2 \end{pmatrix}$

   c) Translate PQRS by the vector $\begin{pmatrix} -4 \\ 2 \end{pmatrix}$

   d) Translate WXYZ by the vector $\begin{pmatrix} -3 \\ -1 \end{pmatrix}$

   e) Translate GHIJ by the vector $\begin{pmatrix} 4 \\ 0 \end{pmatrix}$

   f) Translate KLMN by the vector $\begin{pmatrix} -4 \\ 2 \end{pmatrix}$

Translations are often applied to objects on a co-ordinate grid.

4.   a)On worksheet 19/6 plot the following points on the co-ordinate grid.
     A (1, 0)   B (–2, 5)   C (0, –2)   D (3, 2)   E (–2, –4)
     b) Now translate each point by the translation given by the following vectors and write down the co-ordinates of the image:

   A → A´ by the vector $\begin{pmatrix} -3 \\ 0 \end{pmatrix}$ B → B´ by the vector $\begin{pmatrix} 4 \\ -4 \end{pmatrix}$

   C → C´ by the vector $\begin{pmatrix} -1 \\ 3 \end{pmatrix}$ D → D´ by the vector $\begin{pmatrix} -1 \\ -2 \end{pmatrix}$

   E → E´ by the vector $\begin{pmatrix} 0 \\ 4 \end{pmatrix}$

5. Without drawing now write down the co-ordinates of the image of these points after a transformation by the given vector:

a) If A is the point (–1, 3) A → A´ by the vector $\begin{pmatrix} 2 \\ 4 \end{pmatrix}$

b) If B is the point (0, –3) B → B´ by the vector $\begin{pmatrix} -2 \\ 4 \end{pmatrix}$

c) If C is the point (2, 4) C → C´ by the vector $\begin{pmatrix} -3 \\ -5 \end{pmatrix}$

d) If D is the point (–1, –2) D → D´ by the vector $\begin{pmatrix} -2 \\ 5 \end{pmatrix}$

e) If E is the point (–4, 0) E → E´ by the vector $\begin{pmatrix} 6 \\ -5 \end{pmatrix}$

6. On worksheet 19/6 draw the position of the points A to E after a translation by one vector followed by another. In each case write down the co-ordinates of the image:

a) A → A´ by the vector $\begin{pmatrix} 3 \\ 2 \end{pmatrix}$ followed by $\begin{pmatrix} 1 \\ 3 \end{pmatrix}$

b) B → B´ by the vector $\begin{pmatrix} -1 \\ -3 \end{pmatrix}$ followed by $\begin{pmatrix} 1 \\ 3 \end{pmatrix}$

c) C → C´ by the vector $\begin{pmatrix} 3 \\ -2 \end{pmatrix}$ followed by $\begin{pmatrix} -4 \\ -1 \end{pmatrix}$

d) D → D´ by the vector $\begin{pmatrix} -4 \\ 5 \end{pmatrix}$ followed by $\begin{pmatrix} 5 \\ -3 \end{pmatrix}$

e) E → E´ by the vector $\begin{pmatrix} 4 \\ -4 \end{pmatrix}$ followed by $\begin{pmatrix} 2 \\ 5 \end{pmatrix}$

7. Without drawing now write down the co-ordinates of the image of these points after a translation by one vector followed by another:

a) If A is the point (3, 4) A → A´ by the vector $\begin{pmatrix} -1 \\ -2 \end{pmatrix}$ followed by $\begin{pmatrix} 4 \\ -3 \end{pmatrix}$

b) If B is the point (–2, 1) B → B´ by the vector $\begin{pmatrix} -2 \\ 4 \end{pmatrix}$ followed by $\begin{pmatrix} 3 \\ 1 \end{pmatrix}$

c) If C is the point (3, –2) C → C´ by the vector $\begin{pmatrix} 5 \\ -3 \end{pmatrix}$ followed by $\begin{pmatrix} 3 \\ -2 \end{pmatrix}$

d) If D is the point (–1, –4) D → D´ by the vector $\begin{pmatrix} -3 \\ -2 \end{pmatrix}$ followed by $\begin{pmatrix} 1 \\ 0 \end{pmatrix}$

e) If E is the point (4, –5) E → E´ by the vector $\begin{pmatrix} -10 \\ 8 \end{pmatrix}$ followed by $\begin{pmatrix} 9 \\ -6 \end{pmatrix}$

8. Without drawing now write down the co-ordinates of the image of these points after a translation by one vector followed by another:

a) If A is the point (x, y) A $\rightarrow$ A′ by the vector $\begin{pmatrix} 3 \\ 4 \end{pmatrix}$ followed by $\begin{pmatrix} 1 \\ 2 \end{pmatrix}$

b) If B is the point (x, y) B $\rightarrow$ B′ by the vector $\begin{pmatrix} 3 \\ 4 \end{pmatrix}$ followed by $\begin{pmatrix} -1 \\ -2 \end{pmatrix}$

c) If C is the point (x, y) C $\rightarrow$ C′ by the vector $\begin{pmatrix} 2 \\ -3 \end{pmatrix}$ followed by $\begin{pmatrix} -1 \\ -4 \end{pmatrix}$

d) If D is the point (x, y) D $\rightarrow$ D′ by the vector $\begin{pmatrix} -3 \\ -2 \end{pmatrix}$ followed by $\begin{pmatrix} 5 \\ -2 \end{pmatrix}$

e) If E is the point (x, y) E $\rightarrow$ E′ by the vector $\begin{pmatrix} x \\ 2 \end{pmatrix}$ followed by $\begin{pmatrix} -1 \\ y \end{pmatrix}$

f) If F is the point (x, y) F $\rightarrow$ F′ by the vector $\begin{pmatrix} 2x \\ -x \end{pmatrix}$ followed by $\begin{pmatrix} -x \\ -3x \end{pmatrix}$

g) If G is the point (x, y) G $\rightarrow$ G′ by the vector $\begin{pmatrix} -y \\ 3x \end{pmatrix}$ followed by $\begin{pmatrix} 2x \\ -y \end{pmatrix}$

h) If H is the point (x, y) H $\rightarrow$ H′ by the vector $\begin{pmatrix} -3x \\ 2y \end{pmatrix}$ followed by $\begin{pmatrix} x \\ -5y \end{pmatrix}$

i) If I is the point (x, y) I $\rightarrow$ I′ by the vector $\begin{pmatrix} x \\ -2y \end{pmatrix}$ followed by $\begin{pmatrix} -3 \\ 4 \end{pmatrix}$

j) If J is the point (x, y) J $\rightarrow$ J′ by the vector $\begin{pmatrix} 4 \\ -3x \end{pmatrix}$ followed by $\begin{pmatrix} 2y \\ -5 \end{pmatrix}$

k) If K is the point (x, y) K $\rightarrow$ K′ by the vector $\begin{pmatrix} ax \\ by \end{pmatrix}$ followed by $\begin{pmatrix} cx \\ -dy \end{pmatrix}$

l) If L is the point (x, y) L $\rightarrow$ L′ by the vector $\begin{pmatrix} 4ax \\ -2by \end{pmatrix}$ followed by $\begin{pmatrix} -3ax \\ 5by \end{pmatrix}$

Enlargements

A transformation that changes the size of the object, and thus also the position of an object is an enlargement.

The enlargements that you have met before have all had a scale factor that is a positive whole number. However scale factors can be negative, and they can be less than one.
Consider these figures:

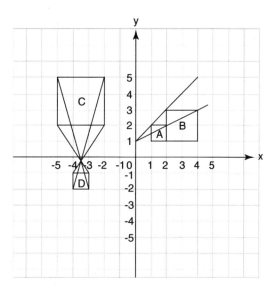

B is the enlargement of A by a scale factor 2 and centre of enlargement (0, 1)

but A is half the size of B and so we can also say:

A is the enlargement of B by a scale factor $\frac{1}{2}$ and centre of enlargement (0, 1

C is three times the size of D however joining the correspomding points of the two figures in the manner shown puts D on the other side of the centre of enlargement than C.

C is the enlargement of D by a scale factor of –3 and centre of enlargement   (–3.5, 0)

D is the enlargement of C by a scale factor of $-\frac{1}{3}$ and centre of enlargement   (–3.5, 0)

A negative scale factor means that the image is drawn on the opposite side of the centre of enlargement to the object, a fractional scale factor means that the lengths of the image are reduced.

Exercise 19E

You will need Worksheet 19/7 and 19/8 for this exercise.

1.-8. On Worksheet 19/7 you will see 8 pairs of quadrilaterals, an object ABCD and its image A´B´C´D´. For each pair join the corresponding vertices and hence find the centre of enlargement and the scale factor.

For nos. 9-18. you will need Worksheet 19/8.
Enlarge each shape in these questions by the given scale factor and with the given centre of enlargement.

Transformations On A Grid

A transformation is a general term for an application that transforms the original object into its image. A transformation can be a rotation, a reflection, a translation or an enlargement. A transformation can be could be more than one of these.

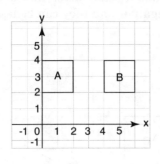

B is the image of A after any one of these:
a reflection in the line $x = 3$
a rotation of 180° about the point (3,3)
a rotation of 90° clockwise about the point (3,1)
a rotation of 270° anticlockwise about the point (3,5)

a translation given by the vector $\begin{pmatrix} 0 \\ 4 \end{pmatrix}$

an enlargement of scale factor – 1 and centre of enlargement (3, 3)

To differentiate between these you may need to add letters:

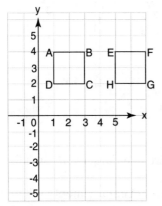

EFGH is the image of ABCD after a translation given by the vector $\begin{pmatrix} 4 \\ 0 \end{pmatrix}$

FEHG is the image of ABCD after a reflection in the line $x = 4$

GHEF is the image of ABCD after a rotation of 180° about the point (4,3) or an enlargement of –1 about (4,3)

FGHE is the image of ABCD after a rotation of 90° clockwise about the point (4,1)

HEFG is the image of ABCD after a rotation of 90° anticlockwise about the point (4,5)

The order of the letters is important, if we compare the last three examples:
In the first rotation A→G, B→H, C→E and D→F
In the second rotation A→F, B→G, C→H and D→E
In the third rotation A→H, B→E, C→F and D→G

Note the description of each transformation, it is important to describe these in full taking care not to miss out any piece of information.

Exercise 19F

You will need Worksheet 19/9 for this exercise.

1. a) Describe the reflection A→C.
   b) Describe the rotation C→D.
   c) Describe the translation A→B
   d) Describe the enlargement E→B.
   e) Describe the enlargement B→E.

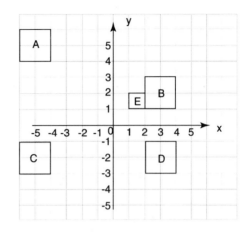

2. Describe as many single transformations as you for each of these:
   a) ΔP → ΔR
   b) ΔQ → ΔP
   c) ΔR → ΔS
   d) ΔP → ΔR
   e) ΔS → ΔT
   f) ΔS → ΔQ

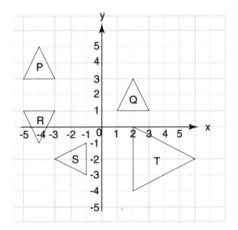

3. Describe the single transformation such that:
   a) ΔC → ΔD
   b) ΔB → ΔD
   c) ΔA → ΔD
   d) ΔB → ΔA
   e) ΔC → ΔF
   f) ΔD → ΔE

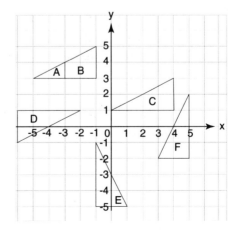

4. Describe the single transformation
    such that:
    a) $\Delta V \to \Delta Y$
    b) $\Delta V \to \Delta W$
    c) $\Delta Y \to \Delta X$
    d) $\Delta Y \to \Delta Z$
    e) $\Delta W \to \Delta Y$

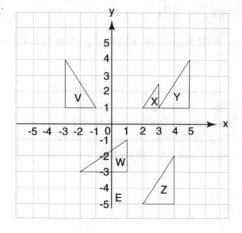

You will need Worksheet 19/9 for the next six questions.

5. Draw a triangle ABC with vertices at (A–5, 1) B(–3, 5) and C(–1, 2)
    a) Draw the image $A_1B_1C_1$, the rotation of ABC 90° clockwise about (–5, 1).
    b) Draw the image $A_2B_2C_2$, the rotation of $A_1B_1C_1$ through 180° about (1, 1).
    c) Describe a single transformation such that ABC $\to A_2B_2C_2$.

6. Draw a triangle XYZ with vertices at X(–3, 2) Y(–2, –4) and Z(–4, –4).
    a) Draw the image $X_1Y_1Z_1$ the enlargement of XYZ by scale factor X 2 and
    centre of enlargement (–6, –4).
    b) Draw the image $X_2Y_2Z_2$, the enlargement of XYZ by scale factor × –2, centre
    of enlargement (–2, –2).
    c) Describe a single transformation such that $X_1Y_1Z_1 \to X_2Y_2Z_2$.

7. Draw the rhombus PQRS with vertices given by P(4, 5) Q(6, 2) R(4, –1) and S(2, 2).
    a) Draw the image $P_1Q_1R_1S_1$, the rotation of PQRS 90° clockwise about (4, –3).
    b) Draw the image $P_2Q_2R_2S_2$, the reflection of $P_1Q_1R_1S_1$ in the line.
    c) Describe a single transformation such that PQRS $\to R_2Q_2P_2S_2$.

8. Draw the kite ABCD, with vertices at A(–5, 2) B(–3, 4) C(1, 2) and D(–3, 0).
    a) Draw the image $A_1B_1C_1D_1$, the reflection of ABCD in the line $y = x - 2$.
    b) Draw the image $A_2B_2C_2D_2$, the rotation of ABCD by 90¡ clockwise about the
    point (–3, 0).
    c) Describe the single transformation such that $A_1B_1C_1D_1$ $A_2D_2C_2B_2$.

9. The square KLMN has vertices at K(3, 3) L(4, 2) M(3, 1) and N(2, 2). Draw KLMN.
    a) Draw the image $K_1L_1M_1N_1$, the enlargement of KLMN by scale factor –2 and
    centre of enlargement (1, 2).

    b) Draw the image $K_2L_2M_2N_2$, the translation of $K_1L_1M_1N_1$ by the vector $\begin{pmatrix} 7 \\ -2 \end{pmatrix}$.

    c) Describe the single transformation such that $K_2L_2M_2N_2 \to$ KLMN.

10. Draw the triangle XYZ with vertices at X(–2, 0) Y(–1, 2) and Z(1, 0).

a) Draw the image $X_1Y_1Z_1$, the enlargement of XYZ by scale factor 3 and centre of enlargement (–1, 1).

b) Draw the image $X_2Y_2Z_2$, the translation of XYZ by the vector $\begin{pmatrix} 0 \\ -4 \end{pmatrix}$.

c) Describe the single transformation such that XYZ→$X_2Y_2Z_2$.

Extension Exercise 19A

One transformation followed by another. Use Worksheet 19/10 with this exercise.

Consider the triangle A with vertices at (5,2) (2,3) and (4,5).

R is a reflection in the y axis and **S** is a rotation of 90° clockwise about the origin.

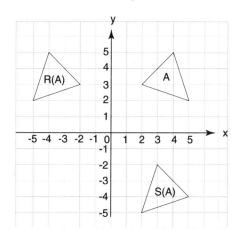
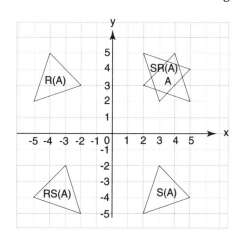

A can be transformed by a combination of transformation, either **RS** or **SR**. (Note that for a combined transformation the transformation nearest to the object is performed first)

R is a reflection in the y axis

S is a rotation of 90° clockwise about the origin

T is a reflection in the line $y = -x$

U is an reflection in the line $x = 2$

V is an enlargement of scale factor 2 and centre of enlargement (0, 0)

1. On worksheet 20/10 draw the following transformations:

a) **R(A)**   b) **S(A)**   c) **RS(A)**

d) **RS(A)**   e) **T(A)**   f) **ST(A)**

2. On worksheet 20/10 draw the following transformations:

a) **V(B)**   b) **RV(B)**   c) **UV(B)**

d) **U(B)**   e) **SU(B)**   f) **VU(B)**

3. **S** followed by another transformation **S** is **S** × **S** or **S²**.

Copy the co-ordinate grid and triangle A in the example and draw the following transformations: a) **S(A)**   b) **S²(A)**   c) **S³(A)**   d) **S⁴(A)**

Explain your results.

Extension Exercise 19B

Finding a general rule for a transformation.

When looking at vectors it became apparent that there was a simple rule to find the image of a point P (x, y) after a translation by a vector .
The image will be the point P' $(x + a, y + b)$

To find a rule for the following transformations use another copy Worksheet 20/10. There are two co-ordinate grids on the worksheet, with a triangle **A** with vertices at (4,5) (5,1) and (1,2) on the first and triangle **B** with vertices at (–5, 4) (–5, 1) and (–2, 2) on the second.

Draw the image of each triangle after the following transformations and then consider the co-ordinates of the image. Thus write down the co-ordinates of P', the image of P (x, y) after each transformation.

1. A reflection in the x axis.

2. A reflection in the y axis.

3. A reflection in the line $y = x$.

4. A reflection in the line $y = -x$.

5. A rotation of 90° clockwise about the origin.

6. A rotation of 180° about the origin.

7. A rotation of 270° clockwise about the origin.

8. A rotation of 90° anticlockwise about the origin.

9. An enlargement of scale factor 2 and centre of enlargement (0, 0)

10. An enlargement of scale factor 2 and centre of enlargement (0, 0)

11. Now investigate some further transformations and see if you can find any other rules, here are some you might consider:
    a) A reflection in the line $x = 3$
    b) A reflection in the line $y = 2x + 1$
    c) A rotation of 90° clockwise about (1,1)
    d) A rotation of 180° about (2,1)
    e) An enlargement of scale factor –1and centre of enlargement (0, 0)
    e) An enlargement of scale factor 2and centre of enlargement (1, –1)

Summary Exercise 19

Use Worksheet 19/11 with this exercise.

1. On worksheet 19/11 you will see this object with various mirror lines. Construct the image of the object after a reflection in each mirror line.

2. You will see this object on Worksheet 19/11.
Draw the image of the object after a rotation of:
a) 60° clockwise about P.
b) 120° clockwise about P.
c) 60° anticlockwise about P.

3 (i) Write down the order of rotational symmetry of these shapes:

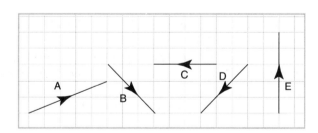

A   B   C   D   E

(ii) Write down the number of lines of symmetry in each shape.
(iii) Draw a sixth octagon with rotational symmetry of order 2 but no lines of symmetry.

4. Write down the translations shown by these vectors:

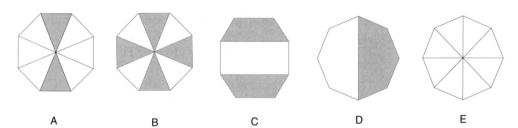

5. On Worksheet 19/11 draw these vectors:

a) $\mathbf{A} = \begin{pmatrix} 4 \\ 1 \end{pmatrix}$ b) $\mathbf{B} = \begin{pmatrix} 4 \\ -1 \end{pmatrix}$ c) $\mathbf{C} = \begin{pmatrix} -4 \\ 0 \end{pmatrix}$ d) $\mathbf{D} = \begin{pmatrix} 0 \\ -2 \end{pmatrix}$ e) $\mathbf{E} = \begin{pmatrix} -1 \\ -5 \end{pmatrix}$

6.   Without drawing a diagram write down the co-ordinates of the image:

a) If A is the point (–4, 1) A→A´ by a translation given by the vector $\begin{pmatrix} 2 \\ -3 \end{pmatrix}$

b) If B is the point (x, y) B→B´ by a translation given by the vector $\begin{pmatrix} -2x \\ y \end{pmatrix}$

7.   Without drawing a diagram write down the co-ordinates of the image A´:

a) If A is the point (1, –4) A→A´ by a translation given by the vector $\begin{pmatrix} 3 \\ -2 \end{pmatrix}$

followed by the vector $\begin{pmatrix} -2 \\ -5 \end{pmatrix}$.

b) If B is the point (x, y) B→B´ by a translation given by the vector $\begin{pmatrix} 3x \\ -2y \end{pmatrix}$

followed by the vector $\begin{pmatrix} x+3 \\ 1-y \end{pmatrix}$.

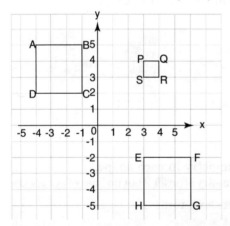

8. Describe the transformation that maps:
a) ABCD onto EFGH
b) ABCD onto GFEH
c) ABCD onto GHEF
d) ABCD onto RSPQ

9.   Draw x and y axes with values of x and y from –5 to 5. Draw the kite ABCD, which has vertices A(1, 3) B(3, 4) C(4, 3) and D(3, 2).
a) Draw the image $A_1B_1C_1D_1$, the reflection of ABCD in the line $y = -x$.
b) Draw the image $A_2B_2C_2D_2$, the rotation of ABCD by 90¡ clockwise about the point (0, 2).
c) Describe the single transformation such that $A_1B_1C_1D_1 \to A_2D_2C_2B_2$.

Activity 19 - Probability Experiments

Using the Random Number Key

On your calculator you should find a button marked RAN (usually a second function). Press this button and you should be presented with a three figure number preceded by a decimal point.

Ignore the decimal point and record the number, do this again and again until you have recorded twenty numbers, or 60 single digits.

If these numbers are produced in a truly random fashion how many of each digit from 0 to 9 would you expect to find in your 60 digits? How many of each digit have you actually recorded? Is this a good way of generating random numbers (if your results looked like they were not truly random try repeating this experiment until you have 120 digits and see if this looks any better).

Look also at the first digit of each of your three digit numbers, with twenty numbers you should get about 2 examples of each digit. Do you?

You have probably not, it is likely that you will have more of some digits than others. This is not a mistake, it is because that is what happens to random events in real life - they bunch together. (Accidents happen in threes, pairs of consecutive numbers appear in three lottery draws in a row). This is an important fact when considering planning using random events

A random event happens at random, time does NOT divide itself into equal intervals such that each time interval is equal to:

$$\frac{\textbf{time under consideration}}{\textbf{number of probable occurrences}}$$

Using statistics from past history, disasters such as floods and severe rain storms are classified under the probability of them occurring:

> a once in every fifty year storm, or a once a century flood.

However you could get two 'once every fifty year rainfalls' in ten years and then no more for another eighty years.

Statisticians use random numbers to help them model real probability problems. Let us look at some simple modelling.

Picking a pupil at a random

There are five years in my school, with approximately the same number of pupils in each year. I can therefore allocate random numbers as follows:

0–1	1st Year	2–3	2nd Year	4–5	3rd Year
6–7	4th Year	8–9	5th Year		

The headmaster picks a child in the school at random each day to bring him the day's notices. Use your random number button to see which years the five pupils chosen this week come from. Repeat this several times. How many weeks run before the year groups are fairly represented?

Model A Queue

A theme park has turnstiles which allow one person through every ten seconds, that is six people in a minute. To decide how many turnstiles are needed for a new attraction the architects need to look at how people arrive during peak times. A survey was done of the time between people arriving at the turnstile in peak time (note the time is the gap between people not the time after the survey started):

Times in secs:

5	9	1	7	3	15	1	25	4	1
12	2	25	8	4	18	2	55	2	1
4	26	29	32	4	23	12	15	19	5
17	19	7	27	12	5	8	12	56	11
56	21	8	21	78	2	5	3	5	17

a) You may notice that the low numbers tend to happen in clumps. Why is this?

b) Rewrite the times in order of size, and in groups of 5. This starts like this:

   1, 1, 1, 1, 2,
   2, 2, 2, 3, 3,
   4, 4, 4, 4, 5,
   5, 5, 5, ...

c) Take the average of each row. This will start like this:

   1, 1, 1, 1, 2,   1.2
   2, 2, 2, 3, 3,   2.4
   4, 4, 4, 4, 5,   4.2
   5, 5, 5, ...

d) Allocate a random number to each average time:
   $0 - 1.2$ $1 - 2.4$ $2 - 4.2$ $3 - 5.8$

e) Prepare a chart like this:

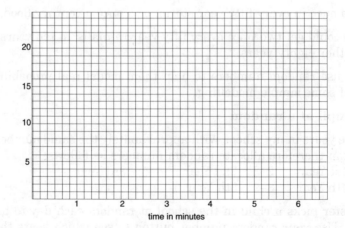

f)   You can now start the modelling. If visitor one arrives at time 0, then you can put one visitor in the 10 second box. From now on use the random number button and choose the first digit of the three figure number. Suppose your numbers in succession were : 1, 3, 0, 2. Using the times allocated above you could say that the 2nd visitor arrived 1.2 seconds after the 1st, the 3rd 5.8 seconds after the 2nd, the 4th 1.2 a seconds after the 3rd, and the 5th 4.2 seconds after the 4th. At the end of the 10 seconds, 4 people are waiting. On the chart this looks like this:

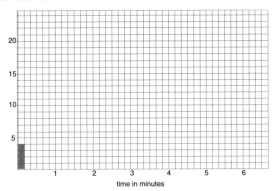

Before the fifth person arrives 1 person is allowed in. For the 10 – 20 second bar you already start off with a queue of 3 people. This is represented by the black bar, as more people arrive in this band of ten seconds then they will be added to in grey. The 5th person arrives at 12.4 secs.

If the next two random numbers were 2, 3, (5.8 secs, 4.2 secs) then the 6th person arrives at 18.2 secs, at the end of 20 secs two more people are waiting making a total of 7:

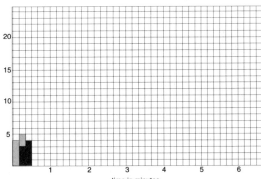

Notice that for 20-30 seconds there are already 6 people waiting (or one of the 7 has gone through the gate).

g)   Try this yourself for a few more numbers and then start with a new chart andstart your own model. What is the longest queue? Does it keep getting longer? What happens if you use two turnstiles, or even three at once?

h)   Now you are ready to do a real simulation of your own. Survey either the queue at a drinking fountain or the lunch queue, or any other queue that you can think of. You might like to design the chart differently so that you know how long each person waits, or any other appropriate variation to your survey.

Chapter 20

More Graphs

Everyday Graphs

A table of figures may give accurate numerical information which can be quite hard to analyse. A graph gives a pictorial representation of the relationship between two variables, and this can be easier to understand. Consider these two graphs of the monthly sales totals for two companies:

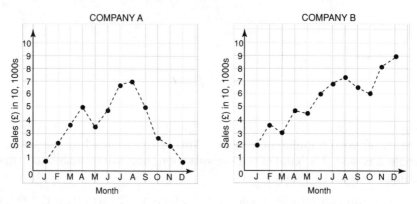

These graphs show 'trends'; that is the general pattern of rise and fall of the total sales. At first glance it would seem that the prospects for Company B look a lot more healthy than for Company A. But what else do the graphs tell us?

These graphs consist of a point for each monthly total joined by a dotted line, the line is dotted because there is no absolute value for the sales in between each dot. Although Company A's sales have declined rapidly in the winter months they climbed from a low position at the start of the year to peak around June, July and August. This does suggest that the business is seasonal and possibly depends on good weather in the summer.

Company B has a steady escalation in sales. Although there was a slight depreciation during August and September this has not effected the overall growth in Sales, and probably reflects the lack of purchasers during and immediately after holiday months.

Exercise 20A

1. a) Suggest possible businesses that Company A and Company B could be.
    b) How would you explain the rise in Company A's sales in April?

2. Consider the possible pattern of sales for a company that makes umbrellas and draw a monthly sales graph for an umbrella manufacturer. Explain any trends in your graph.

3. Here are four sales graphs for companies selling ski-clothes, swim-wear, bicycles and computer software. Write about the trends for each graph and say which you think goes with which company and why:

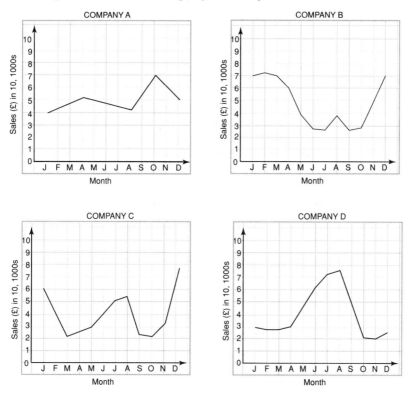

4. Here is a graph showing school attendance as a percentage of the total number of pupils over a school day in January:

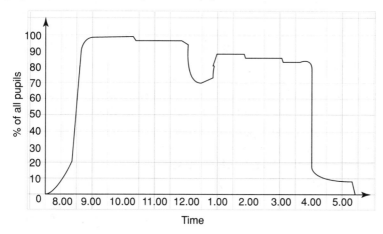

a) What time does the school day start and end?

b) What do you think happens between 12.00 and 1.00 p.m. ?

c) What is the percentage decrease in pupils over the school day ? Do you consider this to be normal? If this is not normal what do you think may be happening?

5.   Here are four distance/ time graphs:

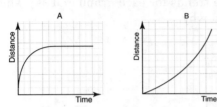 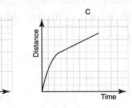 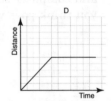

Which one best represents the following situations:
a) The car accelerated steadily for the first five minutes and then travelled at a steady speed.
b) The car travelled at a steady speed for twenty minutes and then stopped.
c) The car decelerated steadily for twenty minutes and then travelled at a steady speed.
d) The car decelerated for twenty minutes and then stopped.

6.   Which of these graphs best fits each of these statements:

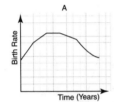 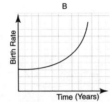 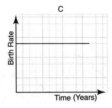 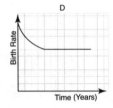

a) The birth rate remained constant.
b) The birth rate was falling but is now constant.
c) The birth rate is now rising much more rapidly than before.
d) The birth rate was rising but is now falling.

7.   Draw four sketch graphs of population against time to demonstrate these statements:
a) The Black Death wiped out 25% of the population.
b) With better medicine the population started to increase rapidly at the end of the 19th century.
c) In the first half of the 18th Century the population remained fairly constant, but began to rise steadily in the second half of the century.
d) The entire dinosaur population was wiped out in the Ice Age.

8.   Here is a graph showing the population against time of two species which were introduced to a controlled environment at the same time. Describe the trends of each specie and explain what is happening:

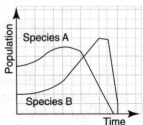

From Function To Graph

A function in mathematics is when two variables are related such that each value of one variable gives a corresponding value in the other. A function of x can be written as $f(x)$ such that either:

$$f(x): x \rightarrow x + 3 \qquad \text{or} \qquad f(x) = x + 3$$

More commonly we appoint another variable, such as y, to represent the function of x and write this as an equation :

$$y = x + 3$$

The three variations above all represent a function whose variables vary directly with one another, their graph will be a straight line.

Consider these functions: $\qquad y = 3x^2 - 2 \qquad f(x) = \dfrac{5}{x} \qquad f(x): x \rightarrow 7 - 3x^3$

These functions contain at least one variable to a power that is not 1: x^2, x^{-1}, x^3
What will be the shape of the graphs of these functions?

Graphs Of Quadratic Functions

Exercise 20B

1. Copy and complete this table of values for x and y for : $y = x^2$

x	−3	−2.5	−2	−1.5	−1	−0.5	0	0.5	1	1.5	2	2.5	3
y	9				1						4		

Use a scale of 2cm to 1 unit on the x-axis and 1cm to 1 unit on the y-axis and draw the graph of $y = x^2$.

2. Copy and complete this table of values for x and y for : $y = 5 - x^2$

x	−3	−2.5	−2	−1.5	−1	−0.5	0	0.5	1	1.5	2	2.5	3
y	−4				4						1		

Use a scale of 2cm to 1 unit on the x-axis and 1cm to 1 unit on the y-axis and draw the graph of $y = x^2 + 2$.

3. Copy and complete this table of values for x and y for $y = 2x^2$ and then draw a graph :

x	−3	−2.5	−2	−1.5	−1	−0.5	0	0.5	1	1.5	2	2.5	3
y	18				2						8		

Your graphs should be symmetrical curves which flatten out as they cross the line of symmetry. Any graph of a function in the form $f = ax^2 + bx + c$ has this distinctive curve known as a **parabola**.

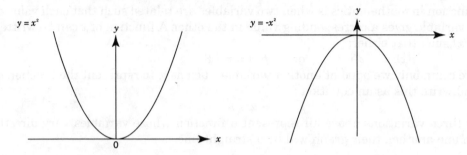

Answer the following questions to see the effect of the additional terms to the position of the graph:

4.   Using a scale of 2cm to 1 unit on the x - axis for values of x in the range $-2 \leq x < 4$, and 2cm to 5 unit on the y-axis for values of y in the range $-10 \leq y < 25$, draw graphs of the following on the same pair of axes :

   a) $y = x^2 - 5$ b) $y = x^2 + 2x$ c) $y = x^2 + 2x - 5$

5.   Using a scale of 2cm to 1 unit on the x - axis for values of x in the range $-2 \leq x < 4$, and 2cm to 5 unit on the y-axis for values of y in the range $-20 \leq y < 10$, draw graphs of the following on the same pair of axes :

   a) $y = -x^2$ b) $y = 7 - x^2$ c) $y = 7 - 3x - x^2$

6.   Using a scale of 2cm to 1 unit on the x- axis for values of x in the range $-2 \leq x < 4$, and 2cm to 5 unit on the y-axis for values of y in the range $-20 \leq y < 10$, draw graphs of the following on the same pair of axes :

   a) $y = 2x^2 + 3$ b) $y = 2x^2 - x$ c) $y = 2x^2 - x + 3$

The addition of a number term in the function translates the parabola vertically.

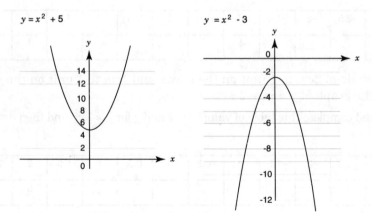

The addition of a term with a single power of x to give an equation of the form $y = ax^2 + bx$ translates the parabola diagonally so that the curve cuts the x axis when $x = 0$ and $x = -b$:

$y = x^2 + 2x$

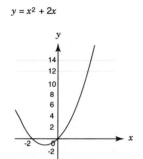

$y = x^2 - 2x$

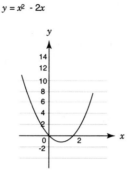

$y = x^2 + 4x$

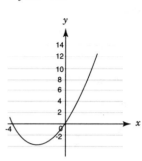

To find where a graph cuts the x-axis, or the line $y = 0$, let the function equal 0, and then solve the resulting equation in x.

To find where a graph cuts the y-axis, or the line $x = 0$, substitute the value $x = 0$ into the function to find the corresponding value of y:

The graph of $y = 2x^2 - 4x$ will cut the x - axis when $y = 0$

$$2x^2 - 4x = 0$$
$$2x(x - 2) = 0$$

Either $\qquad 2x = 0 \qquad$ or $\quad x - 2 = 0$
$\qquad\qquad\qquad x = 0 \qquad$ or $\qquad x = 2$

The graph will cut the y axis when $y = 2 \times 0^2 - 4 \times 0 = 0$.
The graph cuts the x axis when $x = 0$ or 2
and the graph cuts the y axis when $y = 0$.

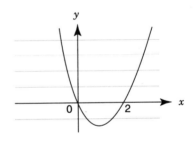

The graph of $y = x^2 - 2x - 3$ will cut the x - axis when $y = 0$
$$x^2 - 2x - 3 = 0$$
i.e. $\qquad\qquad (x - 3)(x + 1) = 0$

Either $\qquad x - 3 = 0 \qquad$ or $\qquad x + 1 = 0$
i.e. $\qquad\qquad x = 3 \qquad$ or $\qquad\quad x = -1$

The graph cuts the x axis when
$x = 3$ or -1 and the graph cuts the y axis
when $x = 0$ or $y = -3$.

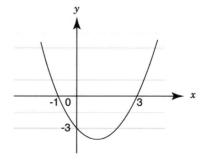

The solution to the equation f(x) = 0 can be found graphically by the points where the graph crosses the x axis.
e.g. the function $y = x^2 - 2x - 3$ crosses the x axis at $x = -1$ and 3
The solutions to the equation $x^2 - 2x - 3 = 0$ are $x = -1$ and 3.

It is possible to have a function, for example or which does not cross the x–axis. If the function does not cross the x axis then the equation has no real solution.

Exercise 20C

1.   a) Match these functions to the correct graph:

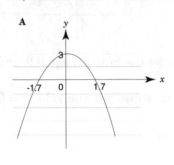 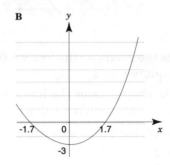 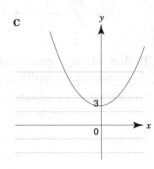

   b) Hence deduce the approximate solutions, if any, to these equations:
      (i) $x^2 + 3 = 0$ (ii) $3 - x^2 = 0$ (iii) $x^2 - 3 = 0$

2.   a) Match these functions to the correct graph:

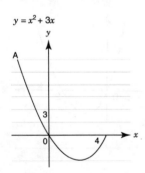 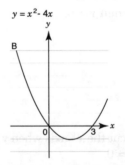 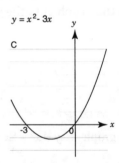

   b) Hence deduce the approximate solutions, if any, to these equations:
   (i) $x^2 + 3x = 0$ (ii) $x^2 - 4x = 0$ (iii) $x^2 - 3x = 0$

3. Match these functions to the correct graph:
a) $y = 3x - x^2$
b) $y = x^2 - 3x + 4$
c) $y = 3x^2 + 3x$
d) $y = x^2 + 2x - 3$
e) $y = x^2 + 3x + 2$
f) $y = 3x - 3x^2$

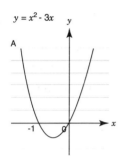

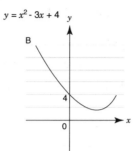

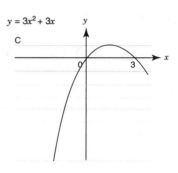

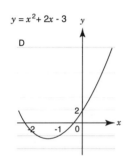

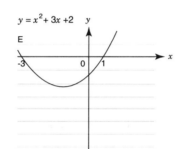

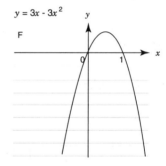

4. Sketch the graphs of these equations, show clearly where each crosses the y – axis, and the x – axis, if possible:
a) $y = x^2 + 4$
b) $y = 4x - 4x^2$
c) $y = 6 - x - x^2$
d) $y = 2 - x^2$
e) $y = x^2 + x$
f) $y = x^2 - 4x + 4$
g) $y = 2x^2 - 4x$
h) $y = x^2 + 2x + 8$
i) $y = -4 - x^2$

The Reciprocal Curve

Exercise 20D

1. Copy and complete this table of values for $y = \dfrac{1}{x}$:

x	−5	−3	−1	−0.5	−0.25	0	0.25	0.5	1	3	5
y											

The value of y for $x = 0$ has been blocked out, try this on your calculator and see what you get.
Try calculating values of y for smaller and smaller values of x. What do you notice?
You should notice that as x gets smaller the value of y gets closer to 0 but never actually reaches it.

Using a scale of 2cm to 1 unit on the x - axis for values of x in the range $-5 \le x \le$ 5, and 2cm to 5 unit on the y–axis for values of y in the range $-25 \le y \le 25$, draw a graphs of $y = \dfrac{1}{x}$. Your graph should approach the axes, but not touch them. The axes in this case are known as **asymptotes**, that is lines that the curve approaches but does not touch. The shape of the reciprocal curve is called a **hyperbola**.

2. Draw graphs of the following equations; write down the equations of the lines that are the asymptotes to each one:

a) $y = \dfrac{4}{x}$

b) $y = \dfrac{1}{x-4}$

c) $y = \dfrac{1}{x^2}$

d) $y = \dfrac{1}{2x}$

e) $y = \dfrac{1}{2-x}$

f) $y = -\dfrac{1}{x^2}$

Other Curves

Exercise 20E

1. Copy and complete this table of values for x and y for $y = x$, $y = x^3$ and $y = x^5$.

x	-3	-2.5	-2	-1.5	-1	-0.5	0	0.5	1	1.5	2	2.5	3
x^3	-27				-1						8		
x^5	-243				-1						32		

Use a scale of 2cm to 1 unit on the x-axis and 1cm to 10 units on the y-axis and on the same pair of axes draw the graphs of $y = x$, $y = x^3$ and $y = x^5$.

2. Copy and complete this table of values for x and y and for $y = x^2$ and $y = x^4$.

x	-3	-2.5	-2	-1.5	-1	-0.5	0	0.5	1	1.5	2	2.5	3
x^2	9				1						4		
x^4	81				1						16		

Use a scale of 2cm to 1 unit on the x-axis and 1cm to 10 units on the y-axis and on the same pair of axes draw the graphs of $y = x^2$ and $y = x^4$.

3. Can you make any general statements about the graph of an equation in the form $y = x^a$?

4. Find the values of y for $y = 4 + 2x - x^3$ for values of x such that $-2 \le x \le 4$. Choose a suitable scale for each axis and draw the graph of $y = 4 + 2x - x^3$ From the graph find the value of x when y=0 and hence the solution of the equation $4 + 2x - x^3 = 0$.

5. A rectangle has a perimeter of 20cm and a length of x *cm*:

a) Show that the area A of the rectangle can be given by the formula
$$A = 10x - x^2$$

b) Take values of x from 0 to 10 and calculate the corresponding values of y.

c) Draw a graph with x along the horizontal axis and y on the vertical axis, choose a suitable scale for each axis.

d) From your graph find the maximum possible area and the corresponding length and width of the rectangle.

6. A cuboid has a square base and a total surface area of 100cm^2.

a) If the base has a side of x cm show that the height of the cuboid can be given

by the expression $\dfrac{50 - x^2}{2x}$.

b) Show that the volume V of the cuboid is given by the formula
$$V = \frac{50x - x^3}{2}$$

c) By calculating V for suitable values of x draw a graph of x against V and find the maximum and minimum possible values for the volume of the cuboid.

7. The net of an open topped box is cut from a square 20 cm by 20 cm.

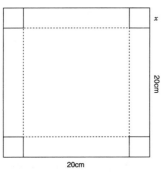

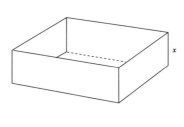

a) If the height of the box is x cm show that the square base of the box has sides of length $20 - 2x$.

b) Find an expression for the volume of the box in cm^3.

c) Draw a graph of x against the volume. From your graph find the value of x that gives a maximum value of the volume.

8. Repeat question 7 for nets cut from squares of 10 cm by 10 cm, 30 cm by 30 cm and 50 cm by 50 cm. Can you find a general rule? (You may like to set up a spreadsheet programme for this and use the computer to draw the graphs.)

Extension Exercise 20A

Using graphs to Solve equations
Use Worksheets 20/1 and 20/2 with questions 2 and 3 of this exercise.

Consider this graph of the function $y = x^2 - 7x - 3$.

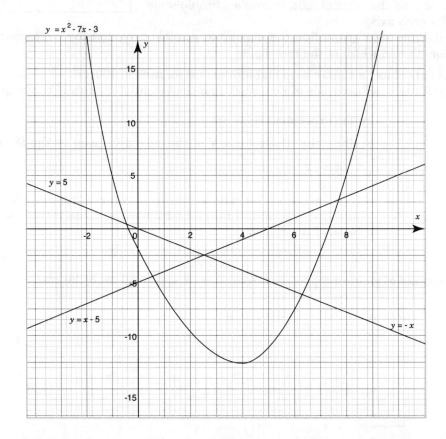

The graph of the function $y = x^2 - 7x - 3$ crosses the x axis at the points $x = -0.4$ and 7.4 approximately.

As the x axis is also the line $y = 0$ then the pair of simultaneous equations $y = x^2 - 7x - 3$ and $y = 0$ can be solved graphically to give a pair of solutions:

$$x = -0.4, y = 0 \text{ and } x = 7.4, y = 0.$$

Another way of looking at this is to think of these points as being the points on the curve $y = x^2 - 7x - 3$ where $y = 0$, and thus the solutions to the equation

$$x^2 - 7x - 3 = 0$$

From the graph the solutions to the equation $x^2 - 7x - 3 = 0$ are $x = -0.4$ and $x = 7.4$ approximately.

Similarly the approximate solution to the pair of simultaneous equations $y = x^2 - 7x - 3$ and $y = 5$, can be found graphically at the points of intersection of the graphs of the functions i.e. at $(-1, 5)$ and $(8, 5)$.

The approximate solution to the equation $x^2 - 7x - 3 = 5$ is found in exactly the same way - the points of intersection of the graphs of the functions $y = x^2 - 7x - 3$ and $y = 5$ i.e. $x = -5$ and $x = 8$

The equation $x^2 - 7x - 3 = 5$ would more commonly be written $x^2 - 7x - 8 = 0$. It is worth noting that equations can be rewritten so that their approximate solutions can be read off the graph.

For example:
1. Show that the equation $x^2 - 6x - 3 = 0$ can be written as $x^2 - 7x - 3 = -x$ and hence find the approximate solutions to the equation $x^2 - 6x - 3 = 0$.

$$x^2 - 6x - 3 = 0$$
$$(-x)$$
$$x^2 - 7x - 3 = -x$$

The approximate solutions are at the points of intersection of the graphs of the functions $y = x^2 - 7x - 3$ and $y = -x$.

$$x = -0.5 \text{ and } x = 6.5$$

2. Show that the equation $x^2 - 8x + 2 = 0$ can be written as $x^2 - 7x - 3 = x - 5$ and hence find the approximate solutions to the equation.

$$x^2 - 8x + 2 = 0$$
$$(+x)$$
$$x^2 - 7x + 2 = x$$
$$(-5)$$
$$x^2 - 7x - 3 = x - 5$$

The approximate solutions are at the points of intersection of the graphs of the functions $y = x^2 - 7x - 3$ and $y = x - 5$.
$$x = 0.3 \text{ and } x = 7.7$$

When drawing the graphs remember the following 5 point rule:
1. Use a pencil with a point **sharp** enough to hurt you.
2. Label the **axes** and the origin.
3. Plot **points** with a small but clear + sign.
4. Draw curves smoothly and **label** your graphs.
5. Read off your graph by drawing dotted **lines** onto the axes.

Extension Exercise 20A

Use Worksheets 20/1 and 20/2 with questions 2 and 3 of this exercise.

1. Consider this graph of the function $y = x^2 + 3x - 5$:

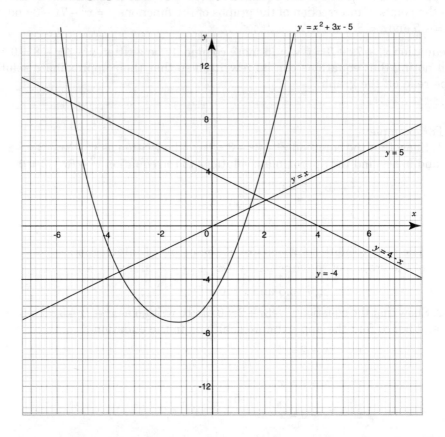

a) Use the graph to find the approximate solutions to the equation $x^2 + 3x - 5 = 0$.

b) Use the graph to find the approximate solutions to the equation $x^2 + 3x - 5 = 5$.

c) Show that the equation $x^2 + 3x - 1 = 0$ can be written as $x^2 + 3x - 5 = -4$ and hence find the solution to the equation.

d) Show that the equation $x^2 + 2x - 5 = 0$ can be written as $x^2 + 3x - 5 = x$ and hence find the solution to the equation.

e) Show that the equation $x^2 + 4x - 9 = 0$ can be written as $x^2 + 3x - 5 = 4 - x$ and hence find the solution to the equation.

2. On Worksheet 20/1 is a graph of the function $y = 2x^2 - 2x - 3$. First work out what lines you will need to draw to solve the following equations, then use the graph to find the approximate solutions:
   a) $2x^2 - 2x - 3 = 0$
   b) $2x^2 - 2x - 10 = 0$
   c) $2x^2 - 2x = 0$
   d) $2x(x - 1) = 5$
   e) $2x^2 - 3x - 3 = 0$
   f) $2x^2 - x - 3 = 0$

3. On Worksheet 20/2 is a graph of the function $y = 6 - 4x - x^2$ and the graph of the function $y = \dfrac{1}{x}$. First work out what lines you will need to draw to solve the following equations, then use the graph to find the approximate solutions:

   a) $6 - 4x - x^2 = 0$

   b) $x(x + 4) = 0$

   c) $\dfrac{1}{x} = 5$

   d) $\dfrac{1}{x} = -x$

   e) $6 - 4x - x^2 = \dfrac{1}{x}$

4. a) Draw the graph of $y = 2x^2 + 3x - 2$ for $-4 \le x \le 2$. Take 2cm to 1 unit for x on the horizontal axis and 2cm to 2 units for values of y on the vertical axis.
   b) Use your graph, and the graphs of any other functions that you may need to draw, to find approximate solutions to the equations:
      (i) $2x^2 + 3x - 2 = 0$.
      (ii) $2x^2 + 3x - 4 = 0$.
      (iii) $2x^2 + 4x - 2 = 0$.
      (iv) $2x^2 + 3x = 0$
      (v) $2x^2 + 2x - 2 = 0$.

5. Draw the graph of $y = 2x^2 - 3x$ for $-2 \le x \le 3$. Draw suitable straight lines to find approximate solutions to:
   a) $2x^2 - 3x - 3 = 0$
   b) $2x^2 - 4x - 2 = 0$

Extension Exercise 20B

Using the Reciprocal Curve

1. a) Draw the graph of $y = \dfrac{x^2}{2} - 7$ for $-5 \le x \le 5$.

    b) Draw suitable straight lines to find approximate solutions to:

    (i) $\dfrac{x^2}{2} - 7 = 0$ (ii) $\dfrac{x^2}{2} - 7 = -4$

    c) Show by rearranging the equations that your answers give approximate solutions to $\sqrt{14}$ and $\sqrt{6}$. Check this with your calculator.

    d) Use your graph to find an approximate value for $\sqrt{6}$.

2. a) Show that the equation $x^3 - 2x^2 - 3x - 1 = 0$ can be written as

    $$x^2 - 2x - 3 = \dfrac{1}{x}$$

    b) Draw the graphs of $y = x^2 - 2x - 3$ and $y = \dfrac{1}{x}$ for $-4 \le x \le 2$. Take 2cm to 1 unit for x on the horizontal axis and 2cm to 2 units for values of y on the vertical axis.

    c) Use your graph to find approximate solutions to the equation.

3. a) Draw the graph of $y = \dfrac{12}{x}$ for $-6 \le x \le 6$.

    b) (i) Draw a suitable straight line to find approximate solutions to:
    $$\dfrac{12}{x} = x$$
    (ii) Show that your answer gives approximate solutions to $\sqrt{12}$

    c) Draw suitable straight lines to find approximate solutions to:

    (i) $\dfrac{12}{x} = -x$ (ii) $\dfrac{12}{x} + x = 4$ (iii) $\dfrac{12}{x} + x = 7$

    Explain your answers.

4. a) Draw the graph of $y = 2^x$ for $-4 \le x \le 4$.
    b) Draw suitable straight lines to find approximate solutions to:

    (i) $2^x = 5$ (ii) $2^x = \dfrac{1}{5}$ (iii) $2^x = x$ (iv) $2^x = 3 - x$

Summary Exercise 20

1. Which of these graphs of a car journey best fits each of these statements:
   a) The car accelerated and then decelerated.
   b) The car stayed in the garage.
   c) The car decelerated and then travelled at a constant speed.
   d) The car accelerated slowly and then stopped.

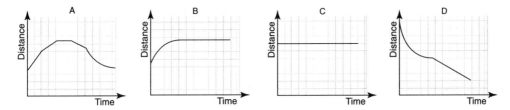

2. a) Copy and complete this table of values for and for $y = 5 - 2x - 2x^2$.

x	−3	−2.5	−2	−1.5	−1	−0.5	0	0.5	1	1.5	2	2.5	3
y	−10			2							−3		

   b) Use a scale of 2cm to 1 unit on the x-axis and 1cm to 1 unit on the y-axis and draw the graph of $y = 5 - 2x - 2x^2$.
   c) Use your graph to find the approximate solutions to the equation $5 - 2x - 2x^2 = 0$

3. Match these functions to the correct graph:

   $y = x^2 + 3x$ $y = x^2 + 6x + 9$ $y = 3 - x^2$

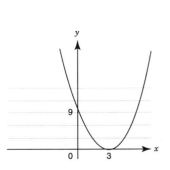 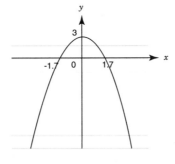 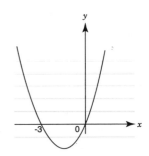

4. Sketch the graphs of these equations, showing clearly where each crosses the y – axis, and the x – axis, if possible:
   a) $y = x^2 + 5$ c) $y = 5 - x^2$ e) $y = x^2 - 5x$
   b) $y = 6 - 5x - x^2$ d) $y = x^2 + 7x + 6$ f) $y = 2x^2 - 7x + 6$

Activity 20 - Graphs from a Spreadsheet

Load the spreadsheet programme on your computer.

These instructions work for the spreadsheet function on Clarisworks, but most programmes are fairly similar and should work in much the same way.

1. We are going to make a series of numbers .
In the cell A2 type –5 then RETURN to insert 1 in the first cell.
The active cell should be A3.
Type =A2 + 1 and then RETURN. Cell A3 should read —4. The = sign tells the programme that we are writing a calculation.

	A	B	C
1			
2	–5		
3	–4		
4			
5			
6			

Now highlight cells A3 to A17 and from the calculate menu select 'Fill down' or use keyboard short cut Command – D. The selected cells should go in sequence from –5 to 10.

	A	B	C
1			
2	–5		
3	–4		
4	–3		
5	–2		
6	–1		

2.   Now we are going to write a formula. Think of the values in the A column as x and the values in the B column as y. Click in A1 and type x.
Let the formula by $y = x^2$
Click in B1 and type y=x^2 (the ^ sign is usually SHIFT plus 6 and means to the power of). This cell does not do anything but is purely to remind us which formula is in the column.

Now click in cell B2 and type = A2^2 and then RETURN.
Cell B2 should read 25. Now highlight cells B2 – B17 and select "Fill Down" from the Calculate menu or use Command – D.

Your column in B should now contain a sequence of square numbers down from 25 to 0 and then back up to 100.

	A	B	C
1			
2	−5	25	
3	−4	16	
4	−3	9	
5	−2	4	
6	−1	1	

3. Now highlight all cells from A1 to B17. Select Make chart from the Options menu. From the menu that you are offered choose x-y line. You will then see a graph like this on the screen:

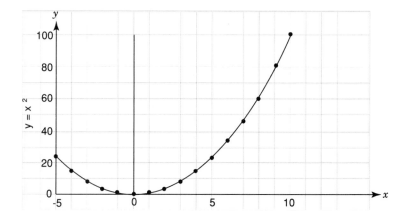

You can see that this is a parabola going through the point (0, 0).

4. Adjust your formula in first B1 to y=x^2 – 20 and then B2 to =A2^2 – 20 and fill down. Your graph will transform to this:

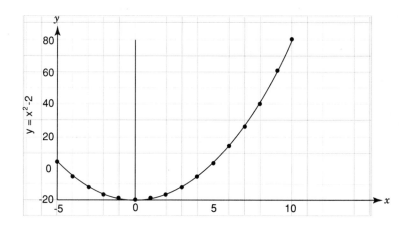

5.   Work through the exercises in drawing graphs in the last chapter and use the spreadsheet to check your answers.

6.   Try and see if you can produce graphs with similar shapes to these:

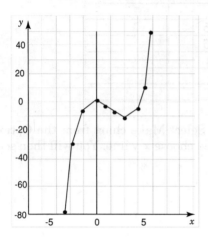
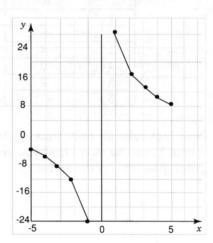

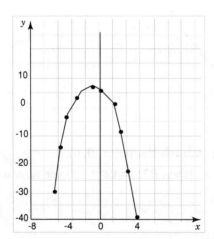
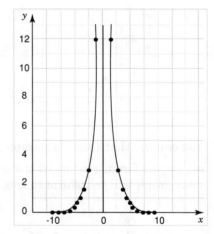

Chapter 21

Ratio And Proportion

When we looked at enlargement in Chapter 19 we considered the effect of the scale factor on the enlarged shape, now we are going to look more closely at what happens to the area and volume of enlargements.

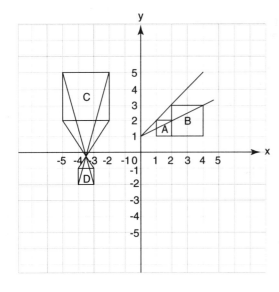

Comparing Area And Volume

Look at the original enlargements:
B is the enlargement of A by a scale factor 2
and centre of enlargement (0, 1)

A has an area of 1 square unit and B has an area of 4 square units.

C is the enlargement of D by a scale factor 3
and centre of enlargement (−3.5, 0)

D has an area of 1 square unit and C has an area of 9 square units.
The area of the image is increased by the square of the scale factor of the enlargement.

This is true for any enlargement:

Here is a scale drawing of my bedroom on a scale of 1:100:

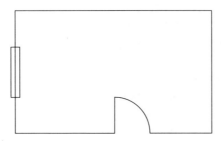

The drawing measures 5cm by 3cm and so has am area of 15cm^2.
The bedroom is actually 5m by 3m, or 500cm by 300cm and has area 15m^2, or 150 000cm^2.

The lengths are enlarged by a scale factor of 100, but the area is enlarged by a scale factor of 10 000.

Consider this cube, and the enlargement of the cube by a scale factor 3:

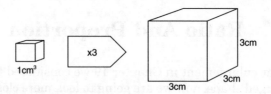

The sides of the enlarged cube will all be 3cm.
The area of each face of the enlargement will be 9cm^2.
The volume of the enlargement will be 27cm^3.

In general terms we can say that if an object is enlarged by a scale factor k

The lengths of the image is enlarged by scale factor k
The area of the image is enlarged by scale factor k^2
The volume of the image are enlarged by scale factor k^3

For example:
1. What is the area of a square of side 4cm after an enlargement of scale factor 5?

Scale factor k = 5
Area Scale factor k^2 = 25
Area of Image = 25 × Area of object
$\qquad\qquad\quad$ = 25 × 16
$\qquad\qquad\quad$ = 400cm^2

Example 2: A model house is made to a scale of 1/20th of the original.
If the height of the model is 12cm what is the height of the original?
If the volume of the original is 30m^3 what is the volume of the model?

Scale factor k $\qquad$ = 20   Volume scale factor = k^3 = 8000
Height of original   = 20 × height of model
$\qquad\qquad\qquad\quad$ = 20 × 12
$\qquad\qquad\qquad\quad$ = 240cm = 2.4m

Volume of original = 30m^3 = 30 000 000cm^3
Volume of original = k^3 × Volume of model
$\qquad$ 30 000 000 = 8 000 × volume of model

$\qquad$ Volume of model = $\dfrac{30\ 000\ 000}{8000}$

$\qquad\qquad\qquad\qquad$ = 3750cm^3.

Exercise 21A

1. A square of side 3cm is enlarged by scale factor 4. What is the area of the enlargement?

2. A triangle of base 8cm and height 5cm is enlarged by a scale factor of 3. What is the area of the enlargement?

3. This kite is enlarged by scale factor 6. What is the area of the enlargement?

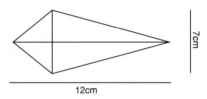

4. This kite is enlarged by scale factor 3. What is the area of the enlargement?

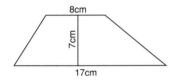

5. A cube of volume 4cm^3 is enlarged by scale factor 3. What is the volume of the enlarged cube?

6. A cube has been enlarged by scale factor 4. The enlarged cube has a volume of 192 cm^3, what is the volume of the original cube?

7. Look at Worksheet 21/4. On it is a plan of a study bedroom drawn to a scale of 1:25.
   a) Fill in the scale details at the top of the sheet.
   b) Write down the correct measurements of
      (i)   length and width of the desk
      (ii) length and width of the bed
      (iii) length of the radiator.
   c) Calculate the correct floor area of
   (i) the desk   (ii) the bed   (iii) the wardrobe
   d) Carpet costs £15 per square metre. Calculate the cost of carpeting the room, including the wash room.
   e) I have been given a rug 1.5m by 2m. Draw the rug on the floor of the bedroom.
   f) The bookcase is 1m high. Calculate the true volume of the bookcase.
   g) The volume of the room is 45m^3. Calculate the height of the room.

8. Here is a family of jugs. Each is an exact enlargement of the smallest jug:
   If the smallest jug contains 0.25 litres what volume of fluid will each of the other jugs contain?

Height =   20cm   17.5cm   15cm   12.5cm   10cm

9. I am making a model of a water tower. The actual water tower is in the shape of a cylinder of 10m diameter and contains 200m³ of water. My model is being made to a scale of 1cm to 1m.
    a) How tall is the real water tower?
    b) How tall is my model?
    c) What will be the volume of my model?
    d) What is the curved surface area of the real water tower?
    e) What is the curved surface area of the model?

10. 'Super Clean' Fluid comes in two sizes, a small container for domestic use and a large drum for commercial use. The large drum is identical to the small drum, but enlarged by a scale factor of 10.

    a) If the label on the large drum is has area 2400cm², what is the area of the label on the small drum?
    b) If the height of the small drum is 12cm what is the height of the large drum?
    c) If the large drum contains 1.5m³, how many litres does the small drum contain?

Similarity And Proportion

In the examples that we have looked at one object has been an enlargement of the other, that is to say the two objects are SIMILAR. They are the same shape but of different size:
Triangles ABC and DEF are the same shape but not the same size, they are similar.

$$\angle A = \angle D, \quad \angle B = \angle E, \quad \angle C = \angle F$$

If two objects are SIMILAR then their corrresponding lengths are in proportion, or in the same ratio.:

AB:DE=AC:DF=BC:EF

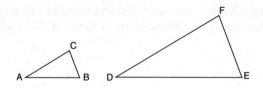

Triangles - Similar Or Congruent?

When you learnt to draw triangles accurately you knew that you had to be given three facts about a triangle to be able to draw the exact triangle:

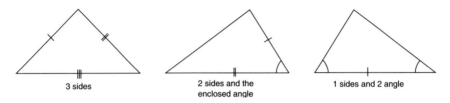

| 3 sides | 2 sides and the enclosed angle | 1 sides and 2 angle |

But no two sides and any other angle which could give two different triangles (unles the angle is a right angle):

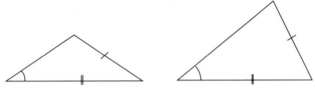

and not three angles and no sides as you would not know what size to draw this triangle.

Triangles that are identical in size and shape are CONGRUENT.
Two triangles are congruent if they contain the information that would allow you to always draw that identical triangle:
   (SSS) 3 sides
   (SAS) 2 sides and the enclosed angle
   (ASA) 1 side and two angles

Two sides and a non-enclosed angle is NOT aceptable as a case for congruency except for the special case:
   (RHS) Right angle, Hypotenuse and a side.

If a pair of triangles all have the same shape then all the angles are the same, but they are not the same size. The triangles are similar (AAA).

For example: Are the triangles ABC and DEF congruent, similar or

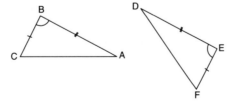

neither of these?
   Triangle ABC and triangle DEF are congruent (ASA)

Exercise 21B

1.– 6. State whether these pairs of triangles are congruent, similar or neither. If the triangles are congruent give your reason (SSS, SAS, ASA, RHS)

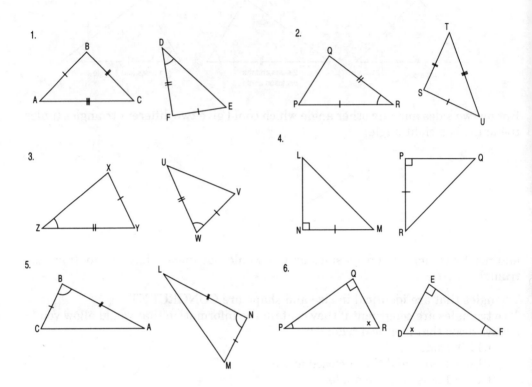

7. State whether triangles ABC and ADE are congruent, similar or neither. If the triangles are congruent give your reason.

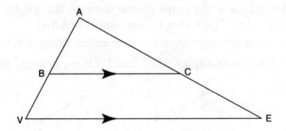

8. State whether triangles ABD and CDB are congruent, similar or neither. If the triangles are congruent give your reason.

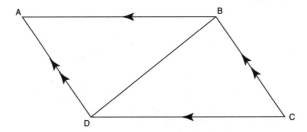

9. O is the centre of a circle and A, B, C, and D are points on the circumference. Find as many pairs of congruent triangles as you can, and give the reason for their congruence.

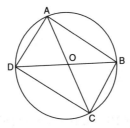

10. State whether triangles ABE and DBC are congruent, similar or neither. If the triangles are congruent give your reason.

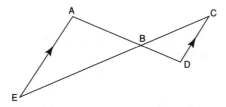

Finding Missing Lengths

Exercise 21C

1. Triangle DEF is an enlargement of triangle ABC by scale factor 2. Copy the diagram and fill in all the missing dimensions:

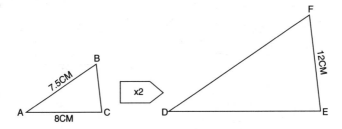

2. Triangle XYZ is an enlargement of triangle PQR by scale factor 3. Copy the diagram and fill in all the missing lengths, including PQ and XY, and find the area of triangle PQR:

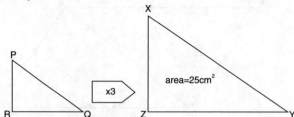

3. XYZ is an enlargement of ABC. Find the scale factor of the enlargement and hence the lengths AB and YZ.

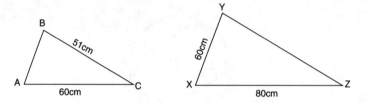

4. Photograph A is 15 cm by 10 cm. It is enlarged to a rectangle of height 15 cm. What is the width of the enlargement?

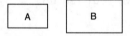

5. In this enlargement the area of the object is given, this should help you to find the missing dimensions:

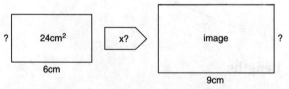

What is the ratio of the area of the object to the area of the image ?

6. Find the missing dimensions in this enlargement:

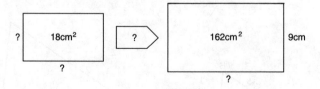

7. Find the missing dimensions in this enlargement:

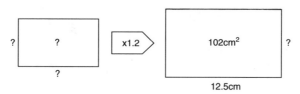

8. Rectangle B is an enlargement of Rectangle A by scale factor of $\frac{2}{3}$. Fill in the missing dimensions and calculate area B.

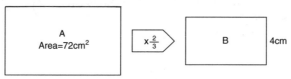

When the scale factor of an enlargement is not a whole number it can be useful to use a ratio method to calculate missing values:

For example:

In $\triangle ABC$ AC = 10cm, in $\triangle ADE$ AD = 20cm and DE = 30cm.

AB is parallel to DE and B divides AD in the ratio 2 :3.

a) Calculate AB, BC, and AE,

b) Give the ratio of the Area of $\triangle ABC$: Area of $\triangle ADE$

$\angle ABC = \angle ADE$ (corresponding angles)

$\angle ACB = \angle AED$ (corresponding angles)

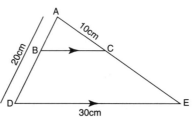

$\triangle ABC$ is similar to $\triangle ADE$

If   AC : CE = 2 : 3

Then AC : AE = 2 : 5

$$\frac{AB}{AD} = \frac{AC}{AE} = \frac{BC}{DE} = \frac{2}{5}$$

$$\frac{AB}{20} = \frac{10}{AE} = \frac{BC}{30} = \frac{2}{5}$$

AB = 8cm

AE = 25cm

BC = 12cm

Area of $\triangle ABC$: Area of $\triangle ADE$ = $2^2:3^2$:

                            = 4 : 9

9. In ΔABC AC = 3cm, in ΔADE AD = 6cm and
    DE = 7.5cm.
    AB is parallel to DE and B divides AD in the
    ratio 1:2.
    a) Calculate AB, BC, and AE,
    b) Give the ratio of the Area of
    ΔABC:Area of ΔADE

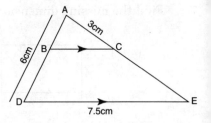

10. In ΔPQR PQ = 9cm and QR = 6cm, in ΔPST   PT = 15cm
    QR is parallel to ST and Q divides PS in the ratio 3 : 2.
    a) Calculate ST, PS, and PR.
    b) Give the ratio of the Area of ΔPQR : Area of ΔPST

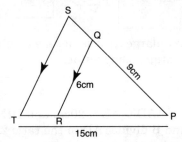

11. In ΔJKL JL = 4m and KL = 3.5m, in ΔJMN KM = 1.5m
    KL is parallel to MN and L divides JN in the ratio 5 : 3.
    a) Calculate JK, MN, LN, and JN.
    b)Give the ratio of the Area of ΔJKL : Area of ΔJMN

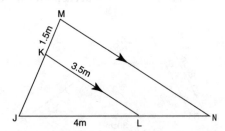

12. In ΔABC, MN is parallel to AB. AB = 18cm, CM = NB = MN = 12cm. Calculate
    CN and AM and find the ratio of the area of ΔCMN : area of ΔCAB.

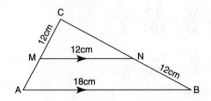

13. In ΔPST QR is parallel to ST. T divides PS
    such that PQ = 40cm and QS =1m. PR = 30cm
    and ST = 1.4m.
    a) Find the ratio of PQ:PS and calculate RT
    and RQ.
    b) What's the ratio of Area PQR: Area RQST ?

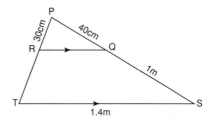

14. BG, CF and DE are parallel. AG = 5cm, BC = 2cm, BG =3cm, CF = 4.5cm and
    DE = 6cm. Angle ADE = 90°.
    a) Calculate the ratio BG: CF: DE and hence AB: BC: CD
    b) Calculate AB, CD, GF and FE
    c) Calculate Area ΔABG, ΔACF and ΔADE and hence calculate the ratio of the
    areas ABG: BCFG: CDEF

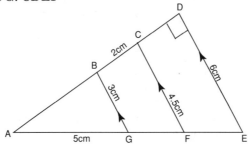

More Ratio Problems

Treating the ratio 2:5 as a fraction $\dfrac{2}{5}$ can be the simplest way of solving ratio problems.

Some problems about quantities that are in the same proportion do not immediately
present themselves as ratio problems but can also be solved like this .

Exercise 21D

Give non exact answers correct to 2 decimal places

For example: 1kg is equivalent to 2.2 lb..
How many kg are equivalent to 5 lb.?

Let x be the no. of kg equivalent to 5 lb.

$$\frac{1}{2.2} = \frac{x}{5}$$

$$\frac{5 \times 1}{2.2} = x$$

$$x = 2.2727...$$
$$= 2.27 \text{ (to 2 d.p.)}$$

---

1. I can buy 15 packets of crisps for £1.20. How many packets can I buy for £1.68?

2. Four of my hand spans make 60cm. How many hand spans will I need to make 2m?

3. 13 feet are equal to 4 metres. How many feet are there in 7 metres?

4. I sell 4 dozen cakes for a total of £6.00. How much should I sell a pack of 5 cakes for?

5. To cook rice you add two cups of rice to seven cups of water. How many cups of water will I need for five cups of rice?

6. If 77 000 people form 88% of the local electorate, how many people make u p the remaining 12% ?

7. 3 crates of oranges weigh 720kg, how much do 8 crates of oranges weigh?

8. My bicycle is geared in the ratio 1:3. One turn of the pedals turns the wheel round three times. The circumference of the wheel is 90cm.
    a) How far does the bicycle go in 10 turns of the pedals?
    b) How many turns of the pedal do I need to go 1km?

9. A metal alloy is made up of tin and copper in the ratio 2:7. If I have 14g of tin how many grams of the alloy will I make?

10. Three children are left some money in their grandfather's will. The money is left in the ratio of their ages. Alf receives £495, Bertha £315 and Little Charlie £270. Charlie is 12 years old, how old are Bertha and Alf ?

£315   £270   £495

Direct Proportion

In all the examples that we have looked at the quantities have been in **direct proportion**. This means that one quantity goes up at the same rate as the other. This is true of many quantities.

For example: If a car travels at a constant speed then the distance travelled is in direct proportion to the time spent.

If petrol costs £1.40 a litre then the price that you pay is in direct proportion to the number of litres bought.

The mass of a solid object is proportional to its volume.

To show that quantities are proportional the symbol ∝ is used.

If we let mass be m and the volume be V then we can say:

$$m \propto V$$

The sign can always be replaced by a scale factor or constant; this constant is usually written as **k**, and thus we can write:

$$m = \boldsymbol{k} V$$

If two quantities are in direct proportion then the graph connecting them is a straight line passing through the origin:

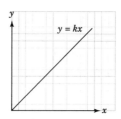

For example:
If x is directly proportional to y and $x = 6$ when $y = 9$
Find a) x when $y = 5$ and b) y when $x = 10$

Since	$x \propto y$
Let	$x = ky$
Then	$6 = k \, 9$

$$k = \frac{6}{9} = \frac{2}{3}$$

a) When $y = 5$ $x = \frac{2}{3} \times 5$ b) When $x = 10$ $10 = \frac{2}{3} \times y$

$$= 3\frac{1}{3}$$ $$y = 15$$

Exercise 21E

1. If x is directly proportional to y and $x = 4$ when $y = 8$
    Find a) x when $y = 6$ and b) y when $x = 12$

2. If a varies as b and $a = 12$ when $b = 3$
    Find a) a when $b = 4$ and b) b when $a = 20$

3. If m varies directly with and $m = 10$ when $n = 2$
    Find a) m when $n = 5$ and b) n when $m = 17$

4. If s is directly proportional to t and $s = 6$ when $t = 8$
    Find a) s when $t = 10$ and b) t when $s = 120$

5. Hooke's Law states that the extension x of a spring is proportional to the force N applied to it.
    An object extends by 5cm when a force of 12 N is applied to it.
    a) Find the extension when a force of (i) 24N (ii) 30N is applied
    b) Find the force needed to produce an extension of (i) 15cm and (ii) 12cm.

6. The exchange rate is now 74 French Francs (FF) to £10.
    At this rate of exchange find :
    a) the amount of French Francs that are worth (i) £150 and (ii) £25
    b) The value of pounds sterling (£) that are worth (i) FF200 and (ii) FF50

Some quantities are proportional to the square of another, for example the area of a circle is proportional to the square of its radius. This can be written:

$$A \propto r^2$$
$$A = \pi\, r^2 \qquad \text{(we know that in this case } k = \pi)$$

For example: If x is proportional to y^2 and $x = 6$ when $y = 2$
Find a) x when $y = 3$ and b) y when $x = 24$

$$x \propto y^2$$
$$x = ky^2$$
$$6 = k\, 2^2$$

$$k = \frac{6}{4} = \frac{3}{2}$$

a) When $y = 3$ $x = \frac{3}{2} \times 9$ b) When $x = 24$ $24 = \frac{3}{2} \times y^2$

$$= 13\frac{1}{2}$$ $$y^2 = 16$$

$$y = \pm\, 4$$

---

7.   If x is proportional to y^2 and $x = 18$ when $y = 3$
     find a) x when $y = 5$ and b) y when $x = 8$

8.   If a is proportional to b^2 and $a = 12$ when $b = 2$
     find a) a when $b = 4$ and b) b when $a = 27$

9.   If s is proportional to t^2 and $s = 10$ when $t = 5$
     find a) s when $t = 25$ and b) t when $s = 40$

10. If x is proportional to y^2 and $x = 2$ when $y = 6$
     find a) x when $y = 17$ and b) y when $x = 27$

11. The distance that a stone falls from rest is proportional to the square of the time taken. If the stone falls 50 metres in 5 seconds find:
     a) how far the stone fell in (i) 2 seconds   (ii) 10 seconds
     b) the time taken for the stone to fall (i) 32m and (ii) 98m.

12. A snack bar works out the prices on its menu in direct proportion to the square of the cost price of the items. The cost price of a bowl of salad is 50pence and the snack bar charges £1.50.
     a) How much will the snack bar charge for:
         (i) a plate of chips of cost price 40p ?
         (ii) a pork chop of cost price 80p?
     b) What was the cost price of
         (i) a glass of Cola sold for 45p ?
         (ii) A meat pie sold for £2.16?

13. Given that $x \propto y$ copy and complete this table:

x	2	4		16
y	3		18	

14. Given that $x \propto y^2$ copy and complete this table:

x	3	27	48	
y	2			10

15. Here is a table of results from an experiment showing extention (x) in cm against load (y) in grams:

x	0.6	1.2	2.4	3.6	4.2
y	100	200	400	600	700

a) Draw a graph of the extention against load, taking load as the horizontal axis.
b) State whether the extension and load are directly proportional or not.
c) Write a formula connecting x and y.

16. Here is a table of results from an experiment showing distance (s) incm against time (t) in seconds:

s	9.8	40	88	245	625
t	1	2	3	5	8

a) Draw a graph of distance against time taking time as the horizontal axis.
b) State whether the distance and time are directly proportional or not.
c) If not calculate the values of t2 and draw a graph of s against t^2 .
c) Write a formula connecting s to t.

Indirect Proportion

The above examples all consider variables that both increase or both decrease. Sometimes two variables are such that as one increases the other decreases. For example as the average speed of a car increases the journey time decreases.

In an electrical circuit if the resistance increases the current decreases.
In a regular polygon the exterior angle decreases as the number of sides increases.
Variables that are related in this way are **indirectly proportional** to one another.

If x is inversely proportional to y then we say $x \propto \dfrac{1}{y}$

$$x = \frac{k}{y}$$

If two quantities are in indirect proportion then the graph connecting them is a hyperbola - that is the same shape as the reciprocal curve:

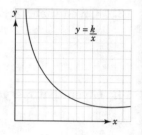

For example: x is inversely proportional to y, and $x = 3$ when $y = 2$.
Find a) x when $y = 4$ and b) y when $x = 5$

Since $\qquad x \propto \dfrac{1}{y}$

Let $\qquad x = \dfrac{k}{y}$

Then $\qquad 3 = \dfrac{k}{2}$

$\qquad\qquad k = 6$

a) x when $y = 4$ $\quad x = \dfrac{6}{4}$ $\qquad\qquad$ b) y when $x = 5$ $\quad 5 = \dfrac{6}{y}$

$\qquad\qquad\qquad\qquad x = 1.5$ $\qquad\qquad\qquad\qquad\qquad\qquad y = 1.2$

Exercise 21F

1. x is inversely proportional to y, and $x = 3$ when $y = 0.5$.
   Find a) x when $y = 2$ and b) y when $x = 6$.

2. a is inversely proportional to b, and $a = 4$ when $b = 5$.
   Find a) a when $b = 10$ and b) b when $a = 40$.

3. m is inversely proportional to n, and $m = 0.4$ when $n = 5$.
   Find a) m when $n = 1.6$ and b) n when $m = 0.5$.

4. A is inversely proportional to t, and $A = 10$ when $t = 0.3$.
   Find a) A when $t = 5$ and b) t when $A = 60$.
   c) Draw a graph to show the relationship between s and t .

5. x is inversely proportional to y^2, and $x = 4$ when $y = 0.5$.
   Find a) x when $y = 6$ and b) y when $x = 24$.

6. a is inversely proportional to b^2, and $a = \dfrac{1}{3}$ when $b = 1.5$.

   Find a) a when $b = 5$ and b) b when $a = 20$.
   c) Draw a graph to show the relationship between a and b .

7. When 8 men dig a hole it takes them 4 hours. How long would it take one man to dig the same hole?

8. The Volume V of a gas V varies inversely with the pressure P. When the Volume is 0.5m^3 the pressure is 1800N/m^2.
    a) Find the volume when the pressure is 500 N/m^2
    b) Find the pressure when the Volume is 4m^3.
    c) Draw a graph to show the relationship between P and V.

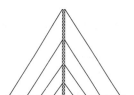

9. The wavelength, l , of a radio wave varies inversely with its frequency, f. When the frequency is 200kHz the wavelength is 1350m.
    a) Find the frequency when the wavelength is 600m.
    b) Find the wavelength when the frequency is 450kHz.

10. If x is inversely proportional to y, and $x = 8$ when $y = 0.25$.
    a) Find an equation connecting x and y . In how many different ways can you write the equation?
    b) If x is also directly proportional to z and $x = 4$ when $z = 5$, find an equation connecting x and z.
    c) Write a single equation connecting x, y and z.

11. a varies directly with b but indirectly with the square of c.
    $a = 6$ when $b = 3$ and $c = 0.5$.
    Write a single equation in a, b and c.
    Find c when $a = 16$ and $b = 10$.

12. If x is directly proportional to y^2.
    a) What will happen to x if y is doubled?
    b) What can you say about y if x is doubled?
    c) What will you have to do to y to double x?

13. If x is inversely proportional to y^2.
    a) What will happen to x if y is doubled?
    b) What can you say about y if x is doubled?
    c) What will you have to do to y to double x?

14. If a is inversely proportional to b^2.
    a) What will happen to a if b is doubled?
    b) What can you say about b if a is divided by 16 ?
    c) What will you have to do to b to halve a ?

Extension Exercise 21

Further Variation

Some variables are connected by a formula but are neither in
direct or indirect proportion. For example a hire firm charges
a flat fee of £10 plus £5 per day for bicycle hire . If the total
cost of hire is C and the number of days is d then the Cost can
be given by the formula:

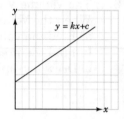

$$C = 10 + 5d$$

The graph for this type of relationship looks like this:
k is the gradient of the line and c is the intercept on the y-axis.
Problems with this type of relationship may need to be solved using simultaneous
equations.

1. x and y are variables with the relationship in the form $y = a + bx$.
     When $x = 20$, $y = 300$ and when $x = 50$ $y = 900$.
     Calculate a and b and then write an equation connecting x and y .

2.   A straight line passes through the points (2, 9) and (7, 3) .
     Find the equation of the line.

3.   A car hire firm hires out its cars for a flat fee per
     day plus a charge per mile. I hire a car from the
     firm for two days during which time I travel 150
     miles. This cost me £55. The following week I hired
     a car from the same firm for three days and drove
     it for 220 miles. This cost me £82.
     a) Calculate the daily rate and the mileage rate
     that the company is charging.
     b) How much would it cost to hire a car for 7 days to do a return trip of 150
     miles each way?

4.   If v and t are variables given in the formula:
     $$v = u + at$$
     When $t = 2$ $v = 30$ and when $t = 5$ $v = 75$.
     Calculate u and a and hence calculate v when $t = 10$.

5.   If v and t are variables given in the formula:
     $$v = u + at$$
     When $t = 2$, $s = 40$ and when $t = 5$, $s = 70$.
     a) Calculate u and a and hence calculate v when $t = 7$.
     b) What will be the value of t when $v = 0$?

More Area and Volume Problems

6. Which of these shapes will always be similar regardless of their dimensions: a pair of cones, a pair of cylinders, a pair of spheres, a pair of square based pyramids, a pair of regular tetrahedra ?

7. A large metal sphere is melted down and used to make several smaller spheres of radius $\frac{1}{5}$ the length of the radius of the original sphere. How many little spheres can be made?

8. A sphere **T** has a volume of $V \text{cm}^3$, surface area S and radius r.

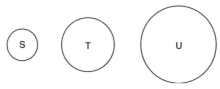

a) What is the surface area and volume of sphere **U** with radius 2r?

b) What is the surface area and volume of sphere **S** with radius $\frac{2}{3}$r?

c) (i) Give the ratio Surface Area of **S**: Surface area of **U**.
   (ii) Give the ratio Volume **S**: Volume **U**.

9. A cone is divided into 3 parts of equal height.
a) If the area of the base of the top cone 1 is A what is the area of the base of the whole cone?
b) What is the ratio of the Area of the Base of Cone 1: Area of Base of whole cone?
c) Parts 1 and 2 together make a middle-sized cone. What is the area of the base of this cone? What is the ratio of Area of base 1: Area Base 2: Area of Base 3?

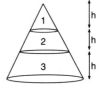

d) If the Volume of the top cone 1 is V find the volumes of the middle-sized cone and the whole cone.
e) What is the ratio of Volume 1: Volume 1 + 2: Volume 1 + 2 + 3?
f) What is the ratio of Volume 1: Volume 2: Volume 3 ?

10. The formula for the volume of a square based pyramid of side x and height h is $V = \frac{1}{3}x^2h.$

a) Calculate the volume of a pyramid with a square base of side 4cm and height 6cm.
b) Write down the volume of a similar pyramid
i) 12cm high   ii) 36cm high

Summary Exercise 21

1. A square of side 5cm is enlarged by scale factor 3. What is the area of the enlargement?

2. A cube has been enlarged by scale factor 5. The enlarged cube has a volume of 750 cm³, what is the volume of the original cube?

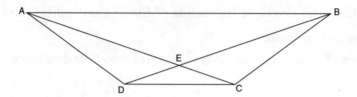

3. ABCD is an isosceles trapezium.
   State whether the following pairs of triangles are congruent, similar or neither. Give reasons for each statement that you make.
   a) Δ ACB and Δ BDA
   b) Δ AEB and Δ CED
   c) Δ AED and Δ BEC

4. Find the value of k and hence find x, y , and z. in this enlargement:

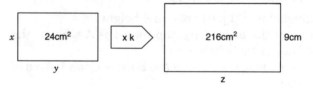

5. In ΔABC, MN is parallel to AB. AB = 18cm, MN = 12cm, CM = 8cm, and NB = 4.5cm. Calculate CN and AM and find the ratio of the area of ΔCMN : area of ΔCAB.

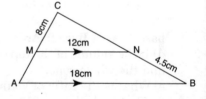

6. If x is proportional to y^2 and x= 28 when y = 4 Find a) x when y = 2 and b) y when x = 252

7. If a is inversely proportional to b and a= 8 when b = 3 Find a) a when b = 6 and b) b when a = 48

8. A cone has a smaller cone cut off its tip. The small cone has height one quarter the height of the whole cone.
   a) If the small cone has height h what is the height of the remaining piece, in terms of h?
   b) If the small cone has a curved surface area of A what is the surface area, in terms of A, of the remaining piece?
   c) Find the ratio of the volume of the small cone to the volume of the original cone and hence the ratio of the small cone to the volume of the remaining piece.

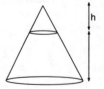

Activity 21 - Data Collection

When preparing a report it is necessary to collect and analyse data. The next chapter deals with analysing data, but first it must be collected.

Data to be collected comes in 3 forms:

1. Measured Data

This is collected from an experiment and consists of measurements of whatever variable or physical condition that is being measured. This could be, for example, temperature, height, distance, time.

2. Absolute Data

This is data which is a fact, for example your age is an absolute value and is not measured. but calculated. The number of people living in an area at a fixed time is also an exact value and not a measurement.

3. Opinion

This is the hardest type of data to collect. If you are asked questions about how you feel about something then there are several variables that could effect your reply. For example: how you feel that day, what information you last heard, whether you like the person asking the question, and so on.

Your Favourite Subject

Here are several versions of a question that you might ask to find out a favourite subject:
> *Is Maths your favourite subject?*
> *What is your favourite subject?*
> *What is your least favourite subject?*
> *List the subjects that you take in order of preference with 1 for your favourite etc.*

Which of these questions do you think would give you the most reliable answer? Which question do you think would get the least helpful answer?

Your Political Preferences

Here are three versions of the same question:
> *Will you vote Labour at the next election?*
> Who will you vote for at the *next election*?
> Will you vote for the government at the *next election*?

Which of these questions do you think would give you the most reliable answer? Which question do you think would get the least helpful answer?

Your Own Questionnaire

Compile a brief questionnaire to canvas opinions on a subject that interests you. This could be local issues, environmental issues or something to do with your school. Work with a friend, each compile a questionnaire on the same subject but with questions phrased in different ways.

Collect your answers from the same group of people and then compare your answers. Do you both the same results?

Chapter 22

Looking at Data

Charts And Diagrams

Data can be collected in many forms, but it is hard to interpret when in a purely numerical format. It helps to be able to "see" the distribution of data using a graph, chart or diagram. Comparing sets of data is made easier by considering an average, which could be the mean, median or mode.

Pie Charts

A pie chart, so called because it shows slices in a pie, is used to show the proportion of various amounts that add up to a whole.

My computer has a total memory of 150 mB. This is currently allocated as follows:
    System :   36mB   Applications: 53mB   Games: 27mB
    Documents: 13mB   The remainder is unused.
This can be shown on a pie diagram.

As 150mB is a full circle i.e. 360°, then 1mB will be represented by $\frac{360}{150}^{\circ}$.

The angles at the centre of the circle are thus :

$$\text{System} = \frac{360}{150} \times 36 = 86.4 \approx 86°$$

$$\text{Applications} = \frac{360}{150} \times 53 = 127.2 \approx 127°$$

$$\text{Games} = \frac{360}{150} \times 27 = 64.8 \approx 65°$$

$$\text{Documents} = \frac{360}{150} \times 13 = 31.2 \approx 31°$$

$$\text{Unused} = \frac{360}{150} \times 21 = 50.4 \approx 50°$$

$$\text{Check : } 86 + 127 + 65 + 31 + 50 = 359$$

The check is important. As the angles have been rounded up or down the total may not be exactly 360°. In this case the total comes to 359°.

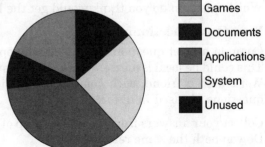

I am going to round the angles off to the nearest half degree and they become:
System 86.5°, Applications 127°, Games 65°, Documents 31° and Unused 50.5°.
Total = 360°.

The pie chart is labelled with only the subject headings. You do not need to label the actual values or the degrees.

Bar Chart

The same information could have been shown on a bar chart, but bar charts are more usually shown to compare numbers, or frequencies of occurrences. A bar chart often needs a tally table, or frequency table to be drawn first.

Here is a set of raw data. The numbers represents the battery life of a number of torch batteries of the same brand that we tested in the laboratory. The times are in hours:

24	18	22	19	30	11	23	25	29	10
17	21	27	31	14	26	25	22	18	29
22	32	17	26	31	23	27	14	24	26

These results are recorded in a frequency table:

Time in hours	Tally	Frequency
6 -10	I	1
11 - 15	III	3
16 - 20	⊬Ⅲ	5
21 - 25	⊬Ⅲ ⊬Ⅲ	10
26 - 30	⊬Ⅲ III	8
31 - 36	III	3

Note the divisions of the hours into bands of the same length. This information is used to draw the bar chart:

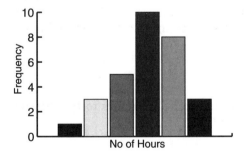

Remember always to label the bar chart and that for bars rising vertically frequency is **always** on the vertical axis. Bar charts are occasionally drawn with horizontal bars.

Scatter Graphs

Scatter graphs plot one variable against another and can be used to see if there is any relationship between two variables, for example height against shoe size. When all the points have been plotted it is sometimes possible to draw a line of best fit.

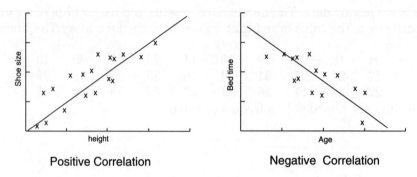

A line of best fit should have the same number of points plotted above it as below it:

Shoe size increases with height   Bedtime is earlier as adults get older

A line of best fit can be drawn by inspection, but it is quite hard to get it exactly right. Another way of drawing the line of best fit is to draw the narrowest possible rectangle that encloses all the points, and then draw a line through the middle of that rectangle with the same number of points on each side of it.

Mean, Median and Mode

When considering data it is useful to look at the average. The average can be considered as either a mean average, the middle value known as the median or the value or group of values that occurs most, which is known as the mode or modal group.

Range

The range for a set of numerical data refers to the difference between the largest value less the smallest value.

Mean

To find the mean of a set of values add up all the elements and divide by the number of elements:

To find the mean of 1, 3, 7, 5, 8, 4, 3, :

$$\text{Mean} = \frac{1+3+7+5+8+4+3}{7}$$

$$= \frac{31}{7}$$

$$= 4\frac{3}{7}$$

Note that the answer will not always be a whole number and some thought may be given as to how to treat the remainder. The answer above is given as a mixed number but could have been given as 4 (to the nearest whole number) or 4.4 (to 1 d.p.) Care should be given to read the question as it is possible that the degree of accuracy required is given, but in general 1 d.p. will be acceptable.

Median

A different way of looking at the average of the marks is to look at the **median** or actual "middle" mark. If there is no actual "middle" term the median is taken as the average of the two "middle" values.

To find the median of 3, 6, 2, 5, 7, 9, 4, 6, 8, 3, 7
        2, 3, 3, 4, 5, 6, 6, 7, 7, 8, 9   : 11 numbers
      Median will be the 6th number (the middle) = 6.

To find the median of 3, 9, 8, 5, 1, 5, 7, 6:
        1, 3, 5, 5, 6, 7, 8, 9   : 8 numbers

$$\text{Median is average of 4th and 5th} = \frac{5+6}{2} = 5.5$$

Mode

The **mode** is another way of looking at the average of a sample of the data, and refers to the value that occurs most frequently or most often. The group of items with value equal to the mode is called the **modal group.** The number of times each value appears is called the **frequency**. In the two examples above the mode would have been 5 in the first and 3, 6 and 7 in the second. The mode is particularly useful when analysing measurements such as shoe size, when there is no value between one size and the next (i.e. there is no size 36.2).

For example:

The daily rainfall in the month of April was recorded and the results, correct to the nearest 0.1 cm, are shown below in cm. Give the range of values and calculate the mean, median and mode. Group the data in appropriate bands and illustrate the distribution with a bar chart. Write a brief summary of your findings.

1.20	0	0.8	2.4	1.8	0	0	0.4	0.2
0 0	1.5	1.2	2.1	2.6	3.1	1.8	0.5	0.2
0 2.1	1.8	0	1.5	1.7	2.5	2.4	0	0.7

Maximum value = 3.1
Minimum value = 0
Range = 3.1

Rainfall in cms	Tally	Frequency
0 - 0.4	︙ ︙ ‖	12
0.5 - 0.9	‖	2
1.0 - 1.4	‖‖	3
1.5 - 1.9	︙ ‖	6
2.0 - 2.4	‖‖‖	4
2.5 - 2.9	‖	2
3.0 - 3.4	‖	1
		30

Mean= (1.2 + 0.8 + 2.4 + 1.8 + 0.4 + 0.2 + 1.5 + 1.2 + 2.1 + 2.6 + 3.1 +
       1.8 + 0.5 + 0.2 + 2.1 + 1.8 + 1.5 + 1.7 + 2.5 + 2.4 + 0.7) / 30

$$= \frac{32.5}{30}$$

$$= 1.0833..$$

$$= 1.08 \text{ (to 3 s.f..)}$$

Mode = 0

Median: There are 30 items and so when these are arranged in order of size there is no middle term and so the median is taken to be the mean of the 15th and 16th values:

$$9 \times 0, 0.2, 0.2, 0.4, 0.5, 0.7, 0.8, ...$$

$$\text{Median} = \frac{(0.7 + 0.8)}{2} = 0.75$$

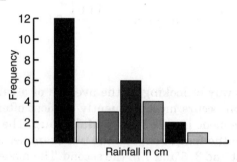

Rainfall in cm

The month was mostly dry with periods of no rain at all but when it did rain it rained hard. The distribution is therefore skewed towards zero, which is also the mode, and the mean is 1.08 which reflects the heavy rainfall when it did occur, but the median of 0.75 reflects the overall dryness of the month.

The above example is unusual as it shows a very uneven distribution with quite different values of mean, median and mode. The fact that these are different is interesting but the distribution is not really clear until the bar chart is considered.

Note the horizontal scale on the bar chart. This does not immediately reflect the groups of the frequency table. However the groups could have been written :

$$0 \leq x < 0.5, \quad 0.5 \leq x < 1.0, \quad 1.0 \leq x < 1.5 \quad \text{and so on where } x \text{ is the rainfall.}$$

Had the data been recorded more accurately, to one tenth of a millimetre perhaps, then this method of grouping the data would have been the most appropriate. This is reflected by the scale on the bar chart.

Finding The Total

If the mean of a set of data is known that the total can be calculated:
"There are 22 classes in the school, with an mean average of 19.5 pupils per class."

$$\text{This means} = \frac{\text{total number of pupils}}{\text{no. of classes}} = 19.5$$

$$\text{total no. of pupils} = 19.5 \times 22$$
$$= 429$$

Note that averages (mean and median) can quite often look impossible e.g. 19.5 pupils, but this is acceptable given the nature of the calculation.

Exercise 22A

Give any non exact answers correct to one decimal place.

1. Give the range, mean, mode and median of these sets of data:
   a) 1, 3, 4, 5, 2, 5, 2, 6, 7, 2, 1, 2
   b) 1.3, 2.3, 1.4, 1.2, 1.5, 1.2, 2.6, 1.7, 1.5, 2.1,
   c) 75, 32, 53, 25, 65, 72, 78, 91, 56, 67, 70, 62, 83, 95, 43
   d) 34, 38, 39.5, 37.5, 36, 37.5, 42, 40, 39, 40.5, 41,

2. Suggest what measurements each set of data in question one might represent.

3. My brother is 10 years old and my sister is 21. The mean of our three ages is 15. How old am I?

4. 40 boys have a mean height of 1.48m. 60 girls have a mean height of 1.52 m. What is the mean height of all 100 children?

5. The daily rainfall in the month of September was recorded and the results, correct to the nearest 0.1 cm, are shown below in cm.

1.2	0	1.5	0.8	2.4	1.6	1.6	1.1	0.4	2.6
1.1	1.2	1.5	1.2	2.1	2.6	3.1	1.8	2.8	0.2
1.5	2.1	1.8	0	1.5	1.7	2.5	2.4	0	0.7

   a) Give the range of values and calculate the mean, median and mode.
   b) Group the data in appropriate bands and illustrate the distribution with a bar chart.
   c) Write a brief summary of your findings.
   d) Compare the rainfall this month with the rainfall in the month of April in the example.

6. In science we collected a number of seed pods and counted the number of seeds in each pod. These were our results:

2	4	6	3	5	3	5	3	4	5
3	5	6	4	7	4	4	5	3	5
5	4	2	5	3	6	4	5	4	4
4	5	5	3	6	4	5	5	5	3
6	7	3	5	4	4	6	7	5	3

   a) Draw up a frequency table to find the frequency of the number of seeds in each pod.
   b) This information is to be shown in a pie chart. Use the information in the frequency table to calculate each angle.

c) Draw the pie chart.

d) Comment on the results of this experiment.

7.   Here is a pie chart showing the results of a similar sample of seed pods, but these were gathered in a wetter environment.

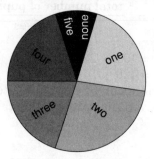

What can you say about the comparative results of these two surveys? (Compare all the information you have, including the range, mean, median and mode and the general distribution).

8.   a) A supermarket is selling 2.5 kg of nectarines in a net. The exact number of nectarines in each net varies. A survey of 40 nets contains these numbers of nectarines:

```
20  18    22    19    23    18    20    21    22    19
20  23    21    20    21    21    19    22    21    21
23  22    20    21    20    21    19    21    20    22
20  21    21    18    21    19    22    21    21    20
```

Draw a frequency table to record this information and use this to draw a bar chart to show the distribution. Calculate the mean, median and mode of the sample.

b) A sample of another 60 nets found that the mode and the median of this sample were both 20 and the mean was 20.6 nectarines per net. Which, if any, of the mean, median and mode can you work out for the whole sample of 100 nectarines?

9. Here are the results of a survey that I carried out looking at the different numbers of people number of people living in each house. in our street .

No. in house	Tally	Frequency	Total people
2	II	......	2 x 2=4
3		4	3 x 4=12
4		......	....
5	₩₩	7	5 x 7 =35
6	III	......	6 x 3 =18
7	I	1	....
	total	......	108

Mean = $\dfrac{108}{......}$ = 4.32

Mode = 4
Median = ...

Unfortunately I opened a can of drink when I had finished and sprayed my page with Fizz. Some of the numbers and tallies have been washed away. Can you copy out my results and fill in all the missing data ?

10. Here is the result of a similar survey:

No. in House	2	3	4	5
Frequency	4	x	9	5

a) What is the mode and median of this set of data if x is (i) 8 (ii) 9 or (iii) 10 ?
b) In fact the mean, to two decimal place, is 3.60. What is x, the mode and the median?

11. A supermarket chain surveyed its total sales from its meat counters in two supermarkets in different locations. Here are the results:

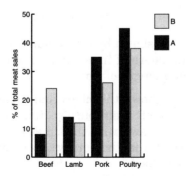

What can you say about the results of the supermarket's survey?

12. If the above survey had been comparing the sales of two different months, A and B, in the **same** store what could you say about the results of the survey?

13. The manager of the supermarket chain wants to find out more about the customers that shop in each store. Draw up a list of ten questions that could be asked to shoppers that would give the manager more information to help him to draw conclusions from the results of his survey.

14. Before the January exams we were all asked how much revision we had done in total over the holidays. This information is recorded below with our final position in the examinations.

No. of hrs. :	18	24	13	11	10	14	20	10	18	8	10	20	24	20	19	21	9	18	21	16
Exam positn.	6	2	14	9	1	11	8	18	15	20	16	5	13	3	7	19	17	10	4	12

a) Compare this information on a scatter graph. Draw a line of best fit and state whether these results show positive or negative correlation.

b) What quantities could have been compared that would have given the opposite correlation?

c) Some candidates have a result which does not fit the general pattern of the other results. Suggest as many reasons as you can for these.

15. Pupils in my school took part in a survey to find out how long their journey to school took them in the morning. The headmaster produced the results of this survey in the form of this bar chart:

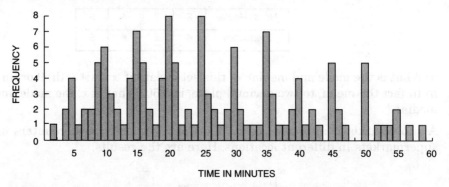

a) What was the mode as shown by the Headmaster's bar chart?

b) What was the mean length of time taken to come to school?

c) What was the median length of time?

The Head of Maths was shown this chart and commented that it showed that most people had rounded off their journey time to the nearest 5 minutes and suggested that it was re drawn with the times in groups of 5 minutes.

d) Draw up a frequency table with the journey times in groups $0-5, 6-10, 11-15$ etc.

e) Draw the revised bar chart.

f) How many pupils took part in the survey?

g) What was the modal group in the survey?

Working With Grouped Data

Data is often presented in grouped form. When data is collected in whole numbers, e.g. when considering numbers of people this is known as discrete data. When data is collected as a measurement then this is known as continuous data.

Drawing Bar Charts

With discrete data the groups can be written within absolute limits :

    1 – 10, 11 – 20, 21 – 30 ....

When considering the horizontal scale on a bar chart this could lead to a gap:

To avoid this the limit between the two bars on the chart is written as 10.5, 20.5 etc.:

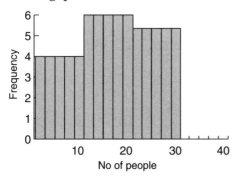 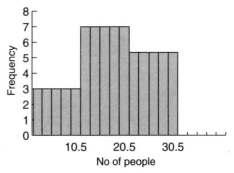

When considering continuous data the groups have boundaries that cannot be written to a single whole number, or even to one decimal place and thus is best written in the form:
$0 \le x < 10$, $10 \le x < 20$, $20 \le x < 30$, $30 \le x < 40$, and the boundary limit on the bar chart will be 10, 20, 30 and so on.

Frequency Polygon

To compare data on a bar chart sometimes a frequency polygon may be drawn. The mid point on the top of each bar is marked with an x, and the x's are joined to form a polygon:

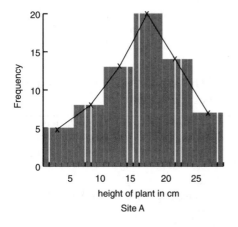

Site A

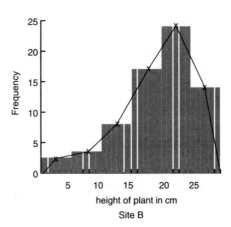

Site B

Estimating The Mean

When information is presented as grouped data the mean cannot be calculated as an exactly accurate number. However the mean may be estimated by considering the mean of the range of the grouped data. An estimate of the total of each group can then be calculated and the mean estimated:

For example:
The ages of people travelling on the local Bus Service are recorded below. Use this information to give the modal group, and estimate the mean average age.

Age Range	0≤x<10	10≤x<20	20≤x<30	30≤x<40	40≤x<50	50≤x<60	60≤x<70	70≤x<80
Frequency	8	16	25	12	8	12	18	4

Mean age ≈

$$\frac{(8 \times 5) + (16 \times 15) + (25 \times 25) + (12 \times 35) + (12 \times 55) + (18 \times 65) + (4 \times 75)}{103}$$

$$= \frac{4325}{103}$$

$$= 41.99... = 42.0 \text{ (to 1 d.p.)}$$

Modal Group $= 20 \leq x < 30$

Exercise 22B

Give non - exact answers correct to one decimal place.

1. Here are the results of a survey that was taken of the ages of passengers taking the Eurostar train to Paris on a weekday:

Age Range	0≤x<10	10≤x<20	20≤x<30	30≤x<40	40≤x<50	50≤x<60	60≤x<70	70≤x<80
Frequency	5	3	55	42	25	18	50	22

a) Draw a bar chart to show the distribution.
b) Why do you think there were so few young passengers on the train?
c) Why do you think there are so many over 60 year old passengers?
d) Estimate the mean age of the passengers.
e) What is the median age of the passengers?

2. Here are the results of another survey of the ages of passengers taking the Eurostar train to Paris. This one was done at a weekend:

Age Range	0≤x<10	10≤x<20	20≤x<30	30≤x<40	40≤x<50	50≤x<60	60≤x<70	70≤x<80
Frequency	25	34	27	51	35	12	32	4

a) Draw a bar chart to show the distribution.
b) What is the difference in the ages of the passengers at a weekend?
c) Estimate the mean age of the passengers.
d) What is the median age of the passengers?

3. Draw a pair of frequency polygons to compare the data in the two surveys above.

4. As you know teachers get quite long holidays. We asked the staff in our school how many days they had spend abroad last year. Here are the results of our survey.

No of Days	0	1 - 7	8 - 14	15 - 21	22 - 28	29 - 40	41 - 100
Frequency	4	3	15	8	6	5	1

a) Why do you think that we grouped the data in the way we did?
b) What kind of teacher do you think might have spent between 41 to 100 days abroad last year?
c) Estimate the mean number of days that the teachers spent abroad last year.
d) Only one teacher is in the last group of data. If this one teacher had spent 41 days abroad what would you estimate the mean to be?
e) If this teacher had spent 100 days abroad what would you estimate the mean to be?

5. Last year 120 children in the school took part in a Readathon to raise money for charity. This frequency table shows how many children raised how much money:

Amount in £	$0 \leq x < 10$	$10 \leq x < 20$	$20 \leq x < 30$	$30 \leq x < 40$	$40 \leq x < 50$
Frequency	8	22	47	34	9

a) Draw a bar chart to show the distribution.
b) How much money did the school raise in total?
c) What was the approximate mean amount raised per pupil?

6. Here are a pair of frequency polygons showing the heights of plant samples taken from two different sites:

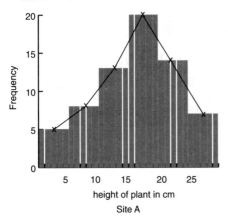

Site A

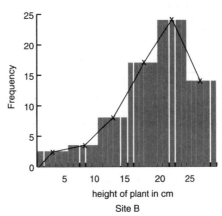

Site B

a) Calculate the number of plants sampled from each site.
b) Estimate the mean height of the plants in each site.
c) Compare the mean height to the modal group in each site.
d) What can you say about your findings?

Chapter 22:Looking At Data

7. The school doctor measured all 120 pupils in our year and has organised the data into 5 cm ranges. Unfortunately he spilt some water over his results and washed out the results in the last two sections. However he had worked out that the mean height of the 100 pupils surveyed was 154.55. Can you complete his survey results.

Height Range	$140 \leq x < 145$	$145 \leq x < 150$	$150 \leq x < 155$	$155 \leq x < 160$	$160 \leq x < 165$	$165 \leq x < 170$
Frequency	5	17	29	33		

Cumulative Frequency

In the frequency tables that we have looked at so far the frequency of each event or group of events was considered, however it is often useful to consider a running total, or cumulative frequency, in order to see how many events are above or below a certain value.

Consider again the table of the ages of people travelling on a local Bus Service :

Age Range	$0 \leq x < 10$	$10 \leq x < 20$	$20 \leq x < 30$	$30 \leq x < 40$	$40 \leq x < 50$	$50 \leq x < 60$	$60 \leq x < 70$	$70 \leq x < 80$
Frequency	8	16	25	12	8	12	18	4

To consider the cumulative frequency the table must be re drawn:

Age Range	Frequency	Cumulative Frequency	Limit
$0 \leq x < 10$	8	8	< 10
$10 \leq x < 20$	16	8 + 16 = 24	< 20
$20 \leq x < 30$	25	24 + 25 = 49	< 30
$30 \leq x < 40$	12	49 + 12 = 61	< 40
$40 \leq x < 50$	8	61 + 8 = 69	< 50
$50 \leq x < 60$	12	69 + 12 = 81	< 60
$60 \leq x < 70$	15	81 + 15 = 96	< 70
$70 \leq x < 80$	4	96 + 4 = 100	< 80

The cumulative frequency column is calculated by adding the frequency of all the values up to the limit. Therefore the number of passengers that are under 30 is found by adding 8, 16 and 25 to make 49.

Exercise 22C

1. My class carried out a survey of the amount of money that each pupil visiting the tuck shop spent. Here is a frequency table showing our results:

Amount in pence	$0 \le x < 20$	$20 \le x < 40$	$40 \le x < 60$	$60 \le x < 80$	$80 \le x < 100$	$100 \le x < 120$
Frequency	5	28	43	27	15	2

   a) Draw a cumulative frequency table to show this information.
   b) How many pupils visited the tuck shop on the day of the survey?
   c) How many pupils spent less that 60 pence at the tuck shop?

2. At the end of each term a class teacher has to add up the number of half days each pupil has been absent, this table shows the absence records for our class:

No of half days	0	1-2	3-4	5-6	7-8	9-10	11-20	21-30	31-50
Frequency	4	3	5	7	5	4	2	2	1

   a) Draw a cumulative frequency table to show this information.
   b) How many pupils are in the class?
   c) How many pupils were absent for 10 half days or less?

3. The whole year sat the same Mathematics exam last term. Here is a frequency table showing the results:

Percentage	0-30	31-40	41-50	51-60	61-70	71-80	81-90	91-100
Frequency	1	5	12	25	23	19	11	4

   a) Draw a cumulative frequency table to show this information.
   b) How many pupils are in the year?
   c) How many pupils scored 60% or less?

4. In a survey for a Biology project we had to measure the lengths of leaves that had fallen from a tree. Here are the results of my survey:

Age Range	$0 < x \le 5$	$5 < x \le 6$	$6 < x \le 7$	$7 < x \le 8$	$8 < x \le 9$	$9 < x \le 10$	$10 < x \le 11$	$11 < x \le 12$
Frequency	4	12	21	32	24	14	10	3

   a) Draw a cumulative frequency table to show this information.
   b) How many leaves did I include in my survey?
   c) How many leaves were 8 cm or less in length?

5. The school doctor is weighing and measuring all the pupils. Here are the results of the survey of the masses in kilograms of the 90 boys in my year:
Here are the results of our survey:

Mass in Kilos	$40 \leq x < 45$	$45 \leq x < 50$	$50 \leq x < 55$	$55 \leq x < 60$	$60 \leq x < 65$	$65 \leq x < 70$
Frequency	2	4	7	11	15	19

Mass in Kilos	$70 \leq x < 75$	$75 \leq x < 80$	$80 \leq x < 85$	$85 \leq x < 90$	$90 \leq x < 95$	$95 \leq x < 100$
Frequency	5	28	43	27	15	2

a) Draw a cumulative frequency table to show this information.
b) How many boys have a mass of 60 kg or less?
c) How many boys have a mass greater than 80 kg?

6. In science we carried out a survey of the number of daisies on a field. First we divided an area into 100 squares each 20cm × 20cm, and then we counted the number of daisies in each square. Here are the results of the survey:

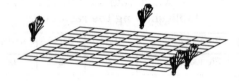

No of Daisies	0	1	2	3	4	5	6	7	8
Frequency	5	11	15	23	18	13	9	4	2

a) Draw a cumulative frequency table to show this information.
b) What is the total number of daisies in the survey?
c) What is the mean number of daisies in a 20 cm by 20 cm square?
d) The field is 44.2 m by 65.8 m. If the square surveyed is typical of the field estimate the number of daises on the field.

Cumulative Frequency Curves

Although the frequency tables in the last exercise show us something about the way in which the data is distributed the most efficient way to consider data is in a diagram. To show cumulative frequency we need to draw a Cumulative Frequency Curve on graph paper. The limit of the set of data is plotted against the horizontal axis and the cumulative frequency, either as a frequency or as a percentage of the total number of items in the survey is plotted against the vertical axis.

Look at the results of the survey of the money spent in the tuck shop in question 1:

Cum. Frequency	Limit
5	<20
33	<40
76	<60
103	<80
118	<100
120	<120

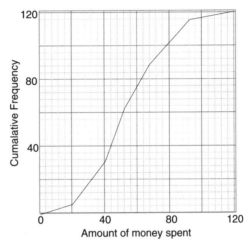

If the points are connected with straight lines you have a Cumulative Frequency Polygon. However the lines do show that the points can be joined by a distinctive curve, and this is probably the best way to represent this set of data.

This curve shows a steep increase in the middle of the distribution. To analyse this further we divide the frequency into **quartiles**. That is we mark each 25% of the distribution. For this curve we need to mark at 30, 60, and 90 :

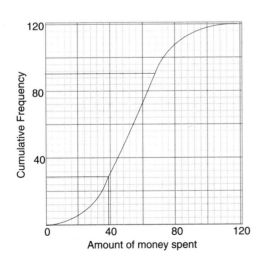

The line at 30 marks the LOWER QUARTILE and the line at 90 marks the UPPER QUARTILE.

The difference between these two values is known as the INTERQUARTILE RANGE.

The line at 60 marks the middle or the MEDIAN value.

For this distribution:

The interquartile range = 68 − 38
$$= 30$$
The Median = 52

Exercise 22D

1.   Here is a Cumulative frequency curve showing the results of the recent Mathematics exam for Year 9:

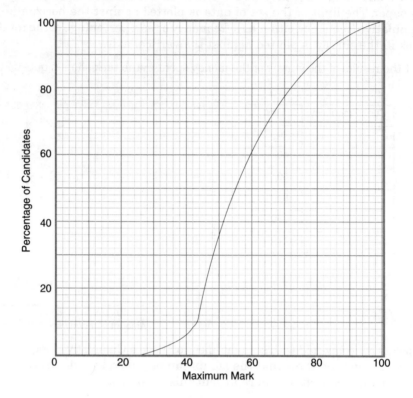

a) What was the median mark?
b) What is the interquartile range?
c) What was the lowest mark?
d)What percentage of candidates scored over 90%?
e) What percentage of candidates scored less than 50%?
f) What percentage of candidates scored at least 70%?
g) If the pass mark was 50% what percentage of the candidates passed the exam?
h) If 15 % of the candidates were awarded a grade A what was the lowest percentage score that was awarded a grade A?

2.   a) From your cumulative frequency table for Question 2 in the previous exercise draw a cumulative frequency curve showing the distribution of the number of half day absences.
b) From your graph give an estimate of the median mark?
c) What was the interquartile range?
d) What percentage of pupils were absent for at least that 10 half days?
e) What percentage of pupils were absent for a maximum of 5 half days?

3. a) From your cumulative frequency table for Question 3 in the previous exercise draw a cumulative frequency curve showing the distribution of the marks for the Mathematics exam.
b) From your graph give an estimate of the median mark?
c) What was the interquartile range?
d) If 70% of pupils passed the exam what was the pass mark?
e) What percentage of pupils scored at least 70%?
f) What percentage of pupils scored less than 55%?

4. a) From your cumulative frequency table for Question 4 in the previous exercise draw a cumulative frequency curve showing the distribution of the lengths of the leaves in the biology survey. Make the vertical axis the percentage of leaves not the actual number.
b) From your graph give an estimate of the median mark?
c) What was the interquartile range?
d) At least 60% of the leaves fell into what range of lengths?
The survey was repeated for the lengths of leaves that had fallen from another tree of the same species and the same age but in a different habitat. Here are the results of the second survey:

Length in cm	0<x≤5	5<x≤6	6<x≤7	7<x≤8	8<x≤9	9<x≤10	10<x≤11	11<x≤12
Frequency	9	15	29	20	7	5	3	2

e) Draw a cumulative frequency curve of the second survey on the same axis as the first survey.
f) From your graph give an estimate of the median mark?
g) What was the interquartile range?
h) At least 60% of the leaves fell into what range of lengths?
i) What conclusions can you draw from the results of the two surveys?

5. a) From your cumulative frequency table for Question 5 in the previous exercise draw a cumulative frequency curve showing the distribution of the masses in kilograms of the boys in my year. Make the vertical axis the percentage of boys not the actual number.
The school doctor then weighed all the girls. Here are the results of the survey of the masses in kilograms of the 80 girls in my year:

Mass in Kilos	40≤x<45	45≤x<50	50≤x<55	55≤x<60	60≤x<65	65≤x<70
Frequency	5	8	9	12	19	11

Mass in Kilos	70≤x<75	75≤x<80	80≤x<85	85≤x<90	90≤x<95	95≤x<100
Frequency	8	5	2	1	0	0

b) Draw a cumulative frequency table to show this information and then draw a cumulative frequency curve of the masses of the girls on the same pair of axes as the curve showing the masses of the boys.
c) What comparisons can you make between the two samples?

Summary Exercise 22

1. Find the range and the mean, median and mode of these sets of data:
    a) 1, 3, 4, 1, 2, 3, 2, 1, 4, 5,
    b) 3.4, 5.1, 1.2, 4.2, 1.8, 4. 2, 5.1, 3.1, 4.7, 4.2, 2.9, 5.8
    c) $2\frac{1}{2}, 3\frac{1}{4}, 1\frac{3}{4}, 2\frac{1}{4}, 3\frac{1}{2}$

2. In a manufacturing company 18 employees earn £14 000 per annum, 15 employees earn £22 000 per annum 3 employees earn £32 000 per annum and the chairman earns £75 000 per annum. Calculate the mean, median and modal earnings of the company. Which measure of the average would you use if:
    a) You wished to negotiate a pay rise ?
    b) You were the company secretary and were writing the annual report?
    c) You wished to recruit more workers to the company?

3. My team are practising for the relay race on sports day. Our times have been:
    12m 40s, 11m 55s, 12m 25s, 11m 50s, 12 35s and 11m 47s.
    a) What is our mean time?
    b) On the day we did not beat our best time but our mean time was improved by 2 seconds. In what time did we run our race?

4. My class have been growing bean plants from seeds. After a month we had to measure their height correct to the nearest cm. These are the heights that we recorded:
48	22	34	26	0	41	25	34	37	25
37	16	23	42	0	0	35	46	24	36
27	0	20	31	37	29	19	0	33	18

    a) Draw a frequency table to record this information. (You will need to group the data in suitable bands.) Use this to draw a bar chart to show the distribution. Calculate the mean, median and modal group of the sample.
    b) What can you say about your survey?
    c) 5 plants did not grow at all. If you leave these 5 out of your calculations what difference does this make to the mean, median and modal group?
    d) Do you think that you should or should not leave these 5 plants in your results?

5. For the summer exams we had two maths papers. The Head of Maths has drawn up this distribution table to show the results of the two papers:
    Paper One

Percentage	0-30	31-40	41-50	51-60	61-70	71-80	81-90	91-100
Frequency	1	3	9	15	21	17	10	4

   Paper Two

Percentage	0-30	31-40	41-50	51-60	61-70	71-80	81-90	91-100
Frequency	2	9	11	24	22	8	3	1

   a) Draw two cumulative frequency tables and from these draw a cumulative frequency curve for each exam on the same pair of axes.
   b) For each paper find (i) the median mark (ii) the interquartile range.
   c) What percentage of the pupils scored at least 50 % on each paper?
   d) Anna scored 75% on paper one but missed the second exam. What mark would you expect her to obtain?

Revision Exercises 4

1. Copy each of these shapes on to squared paper.
Draw any lines of symmetry on each shape.

  A   B   C   D   E

State the order of rotational symmetry of each shape.

2. a) Mark a point A on your page. Draw the locus of a point P such that AP≤5 cm.
b) Here is a side elevation of a cube with all sides equal to 3 cm:

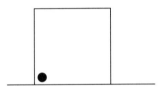

The cube rolls along the ground as shown below. Draw accurately the locus of
the tip of the corner marked with the black dot:

4. Copy this shape accurately on to graph paper, with x and y axes drawn with
values from 0 to 10.:

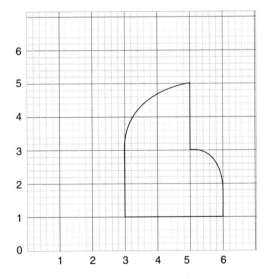

Draw the image of the object after an enlargement of scale factor $1\frac{1}{2}$ and centre $(5, 2)$.

5. For the school play we need a rostrum in the shape of the frustum of a cone:

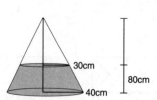

The frustrum has a height of 80 cm, a top radius of 30 cm and a base radius of 40 cm

a) Calculate the height of the whole cone.

b) If the volume of a cone is given by the formula

$$V = \frac{1}{3}hr^2$$

Calculate the volume of the frustrum.

6. Consider these graphs. The label is missing from the vertical axis, but the horizontal axis on all the graphs represents "Time in years".

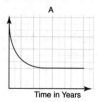

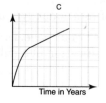
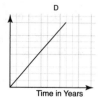

Which of these graphs is most likely to have a vertical axis labelled:

a) Distance travelled by the Earth

b) Height of tree.

c) Amount in deposit account invested for 20 years at fixed interest rate.

d) Value of Average family car.

7. a) On graph paper draw a pair of axes with values of x from -3 to 10, and values of y from -5 to 5 on a scale of 2 cm to 1 unit.

b) Copy and complete this table and use it to draw a graph of $y = x^2 + 3x - 4$

c) Use your graph to give the solutions to the following equations:

  (i) $x^2 + 3x - 4 = 0$

  (ii) $x^2 + 3x - 6 = 0$

x	-5	-4	-3	-2	-1	0	1	2	3	4	5
x^2	25				1						8
$3x - 4$	-19				-5						
y	6				-4						

d) On the same pair of axes draw the graph of $y = x + 3$. Use this graph to find the solution to the equation $x^2 + 3x - 6 = x + 3$.

8. The mileage of the 30 cars for sale at the car auction was noted, and recorded in the following table:

Mileage (in 1000's)	Frequency
0≤x<30	1
30≤x<50	2
50≤x<100	6
100≤x<150	7
150≤x<200	10
200≤x<300	1

a) Estimate the mean mileage of the 30 cars.
b) In which range does the median mileage lie?
c) Which range is the modal group?
d) Draw a frequency polygon to show this distribution of mileage.

9. Three Radio masts stand in the middle of the Australian outback, Mast B lies 200 km from mast A on a bearing of 120°. Mast C lies 250 km from mast A on a bearing of 235°.

a) Using a scale of 5 cm to 100 km construct a scale drawing showing the relative positions of the three radio masts.
b) A county boundary runs between radio mast B and C and is equidistant from both masts. Show accurately the county boundary on your plan. County X lies to the West and County Y to the East.
c) Radio A has a transmission range of 150 km, Radio B has a transmisssion range of 175 km and Radio C has a transmission range of 160 km. Show accurately the area in County X that can receive signals from Mast A and B but not C.

10. a) If s is directly proportional to t and $s= 6$ when $t = 8$
Find (i) s when $t= 3.2$ and (ii) t when $s = 9$
b) m is inversely proportional to n, and $m = 12$ when $n = 5$.
Find a) m when $n = 4.5$ and b) n when $m = 66$

c) A cuboid is a model of an apartment block build to a scale of $\frac{1}{20}$ th of the original block.
(i) If the appartment block is 25 metres tall how tall is the model?
(ii) If the appartment block has 100 windows how many windows has the model?
(iii) The model has a floor plan of 3 m². What is the floor area of the actual appartment block?
(iv) What is the volume of the model?

11. In this diagram Angles ADC, DAB and
DBC = 90° and ∠BDC = 50°
a) State whether Triangles ABD and DBC
are similar or congruent or neither. Give
reasons for your statements.
b) If AD = 40 cm and AB = 30 cm state the
length of BD.
c) Calculate the length of BC.

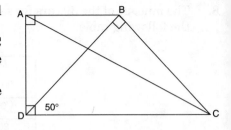

12. Without drawing write down the co-ordinates of the image of these points after
a translation by one vector followed by another:

a) If A is the point $(2, -3)$ A $\rightarrow$ A´ by the vector $\begin{pmatrix} -3 \\ -2 \end{pmatrix}$ followed by $\begin{pmatrix} 4 \\ -3 \end{pmatrix}$

b) If B is the point $(-1, 4)$ B $\rightarrow$ B´ by the vector $\begin{pmatrix} -2 \\ 4 \end{pmatrix}$ followed by $\begin{pmatrix} 5 \\ 1 \end{pmatrix}$

c) If C is the point (x, y) C $\rightarrow$ C´ by the vector $\begin{pmatrix} 2 \\ -2x \end{pmatrix}$ followed by $\begin{pmatrix} -y \\ -3 \end{pmatrix}$

13. a) On graph paper draw a pair of axes with values of x and y from -8 to 8.
b) Draw a quadrilateral **A** with vertices at $(-2, 4)$ $(-4, 3)$ $(-4, 1)$ and $(-2, 0)$.
c) Draw a reflection of **A** in the line $x = 2$. Label the image **B**.
d) Draw the image of **A** after a rotation of 90° anticlockwise about the
point $(-1, -2)$. Label the image **C**.
e) Draw the image of **A** after a translation of $\begin{pmatrix} 7 \\ -6 \end{pmatrix}$. Label the image **D**.
f) Draw the image of **A** after an enlargement of scale factor -2 and centre of
Enlargement $(0, 1)$.

14. To assess each households council tax bill the value of each house in our district
has been assessed by the local Estate Agents. Here is the result of their surveys:

Value (in 1000's)	Percentage
0≤x<30	8
30≤x<70	12
70≤x<120	23
120≤x<200	35
200≤x<300	17
300≤x<450	5

a) Draw a cumulative frequency curve to show this distribution.
b) From the curve estimate the median value of a property in this area.
c) From the curve give the interquartile range of the distribution.